Italian Foreign Policy, 1918–1945
A Guide to Research and Research Materials

Guides to European Diplomatic History
Research and Research Materials

Series Editor
Christoph M. Kimmich
Brooklyn College
The City University of New York

British Foreign Policy, 1918-1945
Revised Edition
By Sidney Aster
ISBN: 0-8420-2310-0

European International Economic Relations, 1918-1945
By Harold James and Diane B. Kunz
ISBN: 0-8420-2370-4

French Foreign Policy, 1918-1945
Revised Edition
By Robert J. Young
ISBN: 0-8420-2308-9

German Foreign Policy, 1918-1945
Revised Edition
By Christoph M. Kimmich
ISBN: 0-8420-2311-9

International Organizations, 1918-1945
Revised Edition
By George W. Baer
ISBN: 0-8420-2309-7

Italian Foreign Policy, 1918-1945
Revised Edition
By Alan Cassels
ISBN: 0-8420-2307-0

Soviet Foreign Policy, 1918-1945
By Robert H. Johnston
ISBN: 0-8420-2312-7

Available from Scholarly Resources Inc.
Wilmington, Delaware

Italian Foreign Policy 1918–1945

A Guide to Research and Research Materials

*Compiled and Edited
by
Alan Cassels*

Revised Edition

Wilmington, Delaware

The paper used in this publication meets the minimum requirements of the American National Standard for permanence of paper for printed library materials, Z39.48, 1984.

©1991 by Scholarly Resources Inc.
All rights reserved
First edition published 1981
Revised edition published 1991
Printed and bound in the United States of America

Scholarly Resources Inc.
104 Greenhill Avenue
Wilmington, DE 19805-1897

Library of Congress Cataloging-in-Publication Data

Cassels, Alan, 1929–
    Italian foreign policy, 1918–1945: a guide to research and research materials / compiled and edited by Alan Cassels. — Rev. ed.
        p.   cm. — (Guides to European diplomatic history research and research materials)
    Includes bibliographical references and index.
    ISBN 0-8420-2307-0
    1. Italy—Foreign relations—1914–1945—Archival resources. 2. Italy—Foreign relations—1914–1945—Library resources. 3. Italy—Foreign relations—1914–1945—Bibliography. I. Title. II. Series.
Z6465.I8C37 1990
[DG498]
327.45—dc20
                                                  90-31288
                                                      CIP

ABOUT THE EDITOR

Alan Cassels was born in Liverpool, England; he took his B.A. at Oxford University and Ph.D. at the University of Michigan. He has taught at Trinity College, Hartford, Connecticut, and the University of Pennsylvania, Philadelphia, and is now professor of history at McMaster University in Hamilton, Ontario. The author of *Mussolini's Early Diplomacy* and other books and articles on fascism and twentieth-century diplomatic history, he is now preparing a study of ideology in international relations in the modern world.

INTRODUCTION TO THE SERIES

The reception accorded this series when it first appeared confirmed the editors in their belief that these research guides would meet a genuine need. It seems appropriate, therefore, since new material, published and unpublished, has become available over the last decade, that the series be brought up to date. A second edition is also an opportunity to add further volumes to the series. The series now consists of revised volumes on France, Germany, Great Britain, Italy, and International Organizations, and new volumes on the Soviet Union and on International Economic Relations.

The series is intended for scholars doing research for seminar papers, dissertations, and books dealing with European diplomatic history between 1918 and 1945. It provides information to assist them in their researches and to guide them on their visits to libraries and archives. It will enable them to find their way quickly and efficiently through the voluminous research and research materials that have become available in recent years and will point them toward solutions to the problems they will encounter in the course of their work.

The individual handbooks in this series are organized to serve the researcher's needs. Each has its own distinctive features, for the archival holdings and the research based on these holdings vary considerably. They are, however, meant to be complementary. They focus on materials relevant to different subject areas and, within the limits set by the history of international relations, avoid unnecessary repetition. They are organized along similar lines, and researchers who need to consult several volumes will have no trouble finding their way.

The first chapter will help the reader understand the nature and significance of the sources and allow him to determine where to concentrate his research, how to allot research time, and, not least, how best to approach the materials in the archives. It describes how foreign policy was made - how the foreign ministry was organized and how it functioned, how it affected the conduct of foreign affairs and diplomacy, and how it was influenced by bureaucratic politics, domestic developments, and public opinion.

The second chapter brings together the most current information on public and private archives, libraries, research institutes, and newspaper collections. It indicates what work can be undertaken on this side of the Atlantic and what has to be left for a visit to Europe, and further, what repository will be most useful and rewarding.

The remainder of the volume is bibliography. Sections on general and bibliographical reference works are followed by a survey of the literature in the field, ranging from documentary series to memoirs to significant secondary sources. Arranged topically within a broadly chronological framework, largely annotated, this bibliography permits ready reference to specific books and articles, historical personalities, and diplomatic events. Together with the archival information, the bibliography will suggest areas for further research or reassessment.

Each volume is edited by an authority in the field. Each reflects experience gained on the spot in archives and libraries as well as knowledge shared by colleagues, archivists, and librarians. The volumes therefore are as current and reliable as possible. They will be valuable companions to all who are interested in international affairs and diplomacy.

Christoph M. Kimmich
Series Editor

CONTENTS

I.	Introduction to the Revised Edition	1
II.	Italy's Foreign Ministry and Foreign Policy	
	A. The Old Consulta	5
	B. The Structure of the Foreign Ministry	6
	C. The Foreign Ministry, Italian Nationalism, and Mussolini, 1922-1936	10
	D. The Fascist Foreign Ministry, 1936-1943	13
	E. Two Foreign Ministries, 1943-1945	17
	F. Appendix	
	1. Italian Diplomats, 1918-1945	19
	2. Foreign Diplomats in Italy, 1918-1945	27
	3. The Vatican and Major Power Diplomatic Representation, 1918-1945	30
III.	Archives, Libraries, Newspapers	
	A. Italian Archives and Archival Material	33
	1. Archivio Storico del Ministero degli Affari Esteri (ASME)	34
	2. Ministero della Difesa	39
	3. Archivio Segreto del Vaticano	40
	4. Archivio Centrale dello Stato (ACS)	40
	5. Economic Archives	44
	6. Private Papers	46

		7.	Aids to Italian Archival Research	52
	B.	Non-Italian Archival Sources		
		1.	United States	58
		2.	Great Britain	61
		3.	France	64
		4.	Germany	67
		5.	Russia	70
		6.	League of Nations	71
	C.	Libraries and Research Institutes	
		1.	Italian	72
		2.	Other Nations	74
	D.	Newspapers	
		1.	Italy's Newspapers, 1918-1945	80
		2.	Newspaper Collections	84
IV.	Bibliography		
	A.	General	
		1.	Bibliographical Aids	87
		2.	Works of Reference	100
		3.	Scholarly Journals	106
	B.	Documentary and Official Publications	
		1.	Italian Documents	113
		2.	Non-Italian Documents	127
	C.	Diaries and Memoirs	
		1.	Diaries	141
		2.	Italian Memorialists	147
		3.	Non-Italian Memorialists	159

D. Secondary Literature
   1. European International Affairs, 1918-1945 . . . 173
   2. History of Italy, 1918-1945 . . . 179
   3. Italy in International Affairs, 1918-1945 . . . 186
   4. The Foreign Policy of Liberal Italy, 1918-1922 . . . 190
   5. Fascist Foreign Policy . . . 195
   6. The Second World War . . . 219
   7. Colonial Questions . . . 231
   8. Military Matters . . . 235
   9. Vatican Foreign Policy . . . 240

V. Index . . . 245

I. INTRODUCTION TO THE REVISED EDITION

It is an unfortunate truism that every bibliography is out of date the moment it is completed. Perhaps, then, a revised bibliographical edition needs no justification. On the other hand, it is now a half-century since the outbreak of the Second World War, and the further we move from events, the less fresh evidence and revelation must be expected. It seems reasonable, therefore, at the start to give some idea of what and how much new material has appeared since the first edition of this guide was published.

The bibliographical content of this volume, like that of its companions in the series, falls into two categories: first, archival source material, and second, printed titles. Probably, the chief merit of these research guides to European diplomatic history is the provision of background, provenance, nature, and location of unpublished material. In this matter of basic sources, Italy has always lagged behind, say, the United States, Great Britain or Germany - with respect to both archival accessibility and organization. Hence, it is of the utmost importance for researchers into Italian foreign policy that the Archivio Storico del Ministero degli Affari Esteri in Rome has embarked on the microfilming (with attendant compilation of inventories) of the records of the gabinetto del ministro for the two decades 1923-43. These files provide the most comprehensive and authentic account of the formulation of Italian foreign policy, especially in the crucial years 1936-43 when decision-making was forcibly centralized in the gabinetto. As described in chapter IIIA, filming has begun with those sensitive files hidden from the Germans in 1943 in the basement of the Palazzo Lancellotti. The gabinetto del ministro project constitutes beyond question the most significant archival development in the field of Italian foreign policy in the last ten years. At the same time, more private papers have come to light or become more readily available. Here, one would mention above all the deposit in Italy's Foreign Ministry archives of a mass of papers left by Carlo Sforza and an equally large collection by Dino Grandi, both sets of papers formerly held in private hands.

As for secondary literature, this has proliferated even more in the 1980's. In part, this is merely witness to the never-ending publication explosion. More important, however, the greater accessibility of primary sources, particularly in the Foreign Ministry's historical archive, has spawned a quantity of recent authoritative studies in both monograph and article form. In order to accommodate these latest research results without expanding this volume to inordinate length, I have omitted certain secondary titles that appeared in the first edition. The omissions are mostly dated works, written more than twenty-five or thirty years ago, although many d'un certain age retain their place as classics or because no subsequent scholar has reworked their subject matter. In addition, I have excluded articles whose author has later integrated the research and conclusions into a book-length study - a common academic practice the world over. As in the first edition of this guide, in view of its probable audience, almost all the material presented is in one of the major western languages - English, Italian, French or German.

Every generation, it seems, claims to write a "new" international history, although as often as not there is more rhetoric than substance in the boast. The irreducible core of diplomatic history remains the relationship among nation states expressed through interchange between governments and foreign ministries. This traditional interpretation informs the choice of the bulk of the items in this guide. There is, of course, another side to the study of international politics, namely the question of how a nation's foreign policy comes to be made. This is always susceptible to re-evaluation and fresh approaches. It is almost thirty years since Fritz Fischer published his Griff nach der Weltmacht (Düsseldorf, 1961), which reinterpreted Germany's war aims and foreign policy, 1914-18, in terms of that country's internal social and political character. Arguably, this work more than any other has forced diplomatic historians to relinquish the shibboleth of the Primat der aussen Politik and to take note of domestic factors behind national foreign policies. Bibliographically speaking, this has opened up great vistas, and multiplied enormously the task of establishing clear limits to what is and what is not relevant material in the sphere of international relations. This consideration explains why a number of entries in this guide pertain to Italy's internal situation between 1918 and 1945.

For instance, no account of diplomacy in our present century of mass politics can ignore the role of public opinion, even when a Mussolinian dictatorship held sway. The attempt to inculcate a spirit of integral nationalism in the Italian people went hand in hand with the development of an aggressive foreign policy, a genuine symbiotic relationship. In the Italian case, too, it is impossible to overlook the influence of emigration on external policy-making. How far Italy's interwar assertiveness on the world stage can be traced to closure of her traditional emigration outlets is a debatable but certainly credible conjecture, and a vainglorious Fascist regime was not one to resist the lure of appealing to the patriotic sentiments of millions of Italians around the globe. But perhaps the most fruitful of recent inquiries into the domestic springs of foreign policy concerns the role of business interests. Several past international problems have been greatly illuminated by reference to the archives of industrial and financial concerns able to exert influence on national policy. For this reason I have added to this edition a section on Italy's economic archives. Not a few Italian firms self-servingly endorsed an expansionist foreign policy, and their records have only lately been opened to researchers.

One other newly fashionable facet of diplomatic history warrants mention. What is now regularly dubbed the "missing dimension" refers to the impact of intelligence reports on policy calculations. Unfortunately, in Italy, as nearly everywhere, officialdom is loath to release its espionage and counterespionage source material. Copies of intelligence reports are routinely weeded out of departmental files before these are opened to scholars, although it is sometimes incompletely done and the researcher may stumble on evidence of cloak-and-dagger operations in, say, foreign or service ministry archives. Nevertheless, research in this area remains problematical, which, however, has not deterred a host of writers, serious and otherwise, from commentating at length on the spy business. For reference to the intelligence factor in this guide, then, it is not

INTRODUCTION

possible to designate any depository of primary source material, but the bibliographical section of printed titles contains a number of relevant items.

I have seen fit to retain from the first edition citations of the principal primary sources in Italian military and colonial history, 1918-45, as well as secondary works in these fields that bear upon international affairs. Military and colonial matters exist on the fringe of diplomatic history, yet patently shaped Italy's foreign policy decisions, particularly as the Fascist regime grew more bellicose and imperialistic with the passage of time. Also carried over from the first edition is the treatment of Vatican diplomacy. In one sense the Papacy and the Italian government negotiated with each other as sovereign bodies, a situation formalized by the Lateran Treaties of 1929. But Roman Catholicism's intimate place in Italian society makes this relationship less a diplomatic one than an inextricable part of Italian domestic politics, which is why Italo-Vatican relations are not covered in this guide. On the other hand, the Papacy's geographical location guaranteed that its dealings with other states, although pursued independently, could not be divorced utterly from the foreign policy of secular Italy. Certainly, the world's chancelleries considered the Vatican a useful listening post in Italy and occasionally a means of influencing Italian policy. It is therefore the Vatican's non-Italian diplomacy that receives attention in this guide. It should be emphasized, however, that no claim is made here to provide a complete bibliography of Italy's military and colonial policies, nor of Papal diplomacy at large.

For whatever reason, foreign policy studies of the interwar years appear to center on one great problem in each country: in the U.S., isolationism; in Great Britain, appeasement; in France, naturally, the debacle of 1940. But the closest analogue to the Italian case is the crystallization of debate in German historical scholarship around the continuity, or lack of continuity, between Germany's nationalist tradition and Nazi ambitions in the east. Italian diplomatic historiography has come to revolve around the same kind of question. To what extent was the foreign policy of Fascism, in aims and methods, an extension of that of liberal Italy? Put another way, was Fascism, which at the outset owed so much to the pre-1922 Nationalist movement, destined by its nature ultimately to embrace aggressive imperialism and violent international revisionism? These questions are but the tip of a larger iceberg of controversy launched many years ago when Benedetto Croce characterized Fascism as an anomalous "parenthesis" in Italian history. Often the issue is to be glimpsed between the lines, rather than stated explicitly, in diplomatic studies that have no particular axe to grind. None the less, it serves to give shape to the historiography of Italian foreign policy in the era bounded by the two world wars.

No bibliographer, however hard-working, can sustain his or her endeavors without the aid of fellow scholars. In revising this guide I have incurred my fair share of intellectual indebtedness, which I am delighted to acknowledge. First and foremost, I want to thank Professor Enrico Serra, superintendent of the Archivio Storico del Ministero degli Affari Esteri, both for his unfailing courtesy and for the latest information about the exciting developments within his jurisdiction; next Dr. Jens Petersen of the Istituto Storico Germanico in Rome, whose bibliographical expertise is unparalleled; and finally in Italy's capital, Dr. Egmont Lee, director of the Canadian Academic Centre in Italy, whose office helped smooth my path into appropriate archives and libraries. Other scholars to whom I owe particular gratitude include Dr. W. Simon of the United Nations Library in Geneva, Dr. Brian R. Sullivan, Dr. H.J. Burgwyn, and also my fellow authors in this series. The omissions and errors to which all bibliographies are heir, need it be said, are the fault of the present writer alone.

Finally, to return to the point with which this introduction began, every bibliographical compiler anticipates with foreboding the appearance of a crucial work at the very moment his own book is going to press. The present author is not surprised therefore to find himself in this quandary. And given what has been written above and in chapter IIIA(1) about the significance of the recently launched microfilming project within the Italian Foreign Ministry's archival service, bearing particularly on the Lancellotti files, it seems worthwhile to alert the reader at this last moment to a very relevant guide: <u>Carte del Gabinetto del Ministro e del Segreteria Generale dal 1923 al 1943</u>, printed in 1990 by the Istituto Poligrafico dello Stato, Rome. Intended primarily for use in the diplomatic archives themselves, its availability in the public domain remains to be seen. On the other hand, a valuable introduction to the index, written by Pietro Pastorelli, was previously published in <u>Storia delle Relazioni Internazionali</u>, 5 (1989): 313-48. In addition, an important monograph, which has appeared too late for inclusion in chapter IVD(6), is Jonathan Steinberg's <u>All or Nothing: The Axis and the Holocaust, 1941-1943</u> (London, 1990), a closely researched examination of Fascist Italy's refusal to comply with Hitler's plans for the Holocaust.

II. ITALY'S FOREIGN MINISTRY AND FOREIGN POLICY

A. THE OLD CONSULTA[1]

Throughout Europe the practice of diplomacy at the outbreak of World War I, in spite of the advances of democracy over the previous half century, rested still in the hands of an upper-class coterie. This was nowhere more true than in Italy. The Italian Foreign Ministry (Ministero degli Affari Esteri) mirrored faithfully that conservative oligarchy that had taken charge of the nation's destinies after unification. Since 1870 it had been housed in the Palazzo della Consulta, hard by the royal palace, the Quirinale - a reminder that under the constitution the king retained a certain prerogative in foreign policy that was sometimes exercised. The Consulta, as it was familiarly known, was subject to other powerful forces; entrance into and promotion within the diplomatic service often depended on clientalism, that is to say, on the patronage of some giant of politics or high society. The Italian diplomat to come through this system was likely to belong to one of two aristocracies. The Piedmontese nobility was well represented, which was perhaps natural given its part in risorgimento and unification. More surprising was the influx in the years immediately before 1914 of young Bourbon aristocrats from the south who, being of a generation far enough removed from the event to accept unification as a fait accompli, flocked into the state bureaucracy and in the Foreign Ministry threatened to become a preponderant influence. Among both northerners and southerners titles of nobility were common, while a private income was de rigueur in diplomatic and consular services alike. Almost without exception the education of an Italian diplomat was that of a nineteenth-century gentleman - a schooling in the classics to the exclusion of science and commercial subjects.

Even though the Consulta was wedded to the past in most respects, there was one feature of the modern world that Italy's diplomats embraced wholeheartedly. This was the current of nationalism and imperialism that swept most of Europe at the turn of the century, and that in Italy found vent in colonial ambitions in Africa as well as the aspiration to play a major role in the European balance of power. This search for grandezza and international stature received strong backing in the Foreign Ministry, without much regard for whether the dreams abroad could be sustained by Italy's domestic infrastructure.

The salient characteristics of the Consulta, then, were a deeply rooted conservatism born of its members' social background and an assertive and sometimes unthinking nationalism. These traits were not without their consequence for they would later find an echo in Mussolini's program of antisocialism at home and national aggrandizement abroad. And indeed, in the event Italian foreign ministry officials showed little reluctance to serve the Fascist regime, at least in its early stages.

The First World War had relatively little effect on the Consulta. A degree of continuity was assured since none of its young attachés perished in the trenches. The Foreign Ministry also escaped any serious repercussions arising from Italy's mode of entry into the war in May 1915. Although Foreign Minister Sidney Sonnino had collaborated fully with Antonio Salandra, the premier, and King Victor Emmanuel III in reaching the decision to intervene, the subsequent contentious legal endorsement by parliament fixed attention on the pressure exerted by the royal household and nationalist street mobs. The Foreign Ministry's role in these crucial events was thus obscured, but no doubt the perception of the Consulta as little more than a routine bureaucratic body served to protect it from the postwar campaign for "open diplomacy" to be conducted under democratic parliamentary control. Why expend reformist energy on an institution marginal to the decision-making process? Moreover, the spokesman of open diplomacy was the American president, Woodrow Wilson, whose refusal to countenance Italian claims on the eastern shore of the Adriatic affronted many of Italy's political public. In 1919 any Wilsonian message was likely to fall on deaf ears in Italy. Of course, the foreign ministry had always been technically answerable to the Italian parliament, and since 1913 parliament had been elected on the basis of universal manhood suffrage. But Italian parliaments were notoriously malleable, while democracy in Italy was a new and fragile plant. All in all, therefore, the Consulta looked forward with some confidence in the postwar era to the perpetuation of its orderly and self-contained existence, its exclusive social composition, and its traditional habits of mind unshaken by Armageddon.

B. THE STRUCTURE OF THE FOREIGN MINISTRY[2]

The organization of Italy's Foreign Ministry may conveniently be broken down into four major components: first, the foreign minister himself and the undersecretary of state for foreign affairs; next, the secretary general and his office; third, the principal departments and their dependent bureaus; and finally, the nation's accredited representatives abroad.

The foreign minister and undersecretary provided the bridge between the parliamentary regime and the bureaucracy of foreign affairs. Indeed, it was quite common for foreign ministers in their careers to span both realms, serving in ambassadorial or other high-ranking positions before and after holding the ministerial portfolio. Between 1918 and 1945 Salandra, Sforza, Tomasi della Torretta, Scialoja, Guariglia, and the Fascist Grandi, all wore two hats. While in office, however, the foreign minister was a political figure. Both he and his undersecretary sat in either the elected Chamber of Deputies or the appointed Senate, and both participated in discussions of international affairs in either house. In the Fascist era this activity was to be much diminished even before parliament was abrogated in 1938; attendance at Fascism's own kind of representative assemblies was more important. Within the Consulta the foreign minister was furnished with a secretariat that functioned under the direction of a career diplomat with the title of capo di gabinetto. The private secretary of the minister was usually a Consulta official, thus affording further liaison between politico and gabinetto. The relationship between minister and undersecretary was variable. Italian foreign ministers usually liked to dominate their subordinates, and at times the undersecretaryship was reckoned of very little account, even going unfilled for years on end. On the other hand, Grandi, Suvich, and Bastianini all made an impact on policy while serving as undersecretary.[3]

While the foreign minister was its titular head, the Consulta also possessed a sort of internal chief, the secretary general. First and foremost, this secretary general was in charge of the day-to-day running of the Foreign Ministry. Several offices came under his direct jurisdiction - for example, at the outset of the interwar period, the accounts and press offices, and also the offices of ciphers and correspondence, which distributed documentation and papers throughout the Foreign Ministry. The secretary general's activity, however, was not confined to administrative matters. In practice, he oversaw all questions and was accustomed to share in substantive policy decisions. A career official like the British permanent undersecretary for foreign affairs whom he much resembled, the secretary general could claim to be the authentic voice of the professional diplomats and even to constitute a focal point of loyalty within the Consulta. More than one foreign minister in the past had shown resentment of his secretary general's presumption to speak for the ministry as well as of his expertise in the manifold details of Italian diplomacy. In their efforts to curb the secretary generalship, ministers had appointed nonentities or their clients to the position, and twice Crispi had abolished it altogether. Nevertheless, at the close of World War I the post was still extant and vital to the Consulta's operation. Almost inevitably, the history of tension between foreign minister and secretary general would be repeated under Fascism.

The great part of the routine work of Italian diplomacy was conducted in the <u>direzioni generali</u>, or general departments of the Foreign Ministry. Between 1918 and 1945 these fluctuated considerably in quantity and in title. Indeed, in this period there was perennial change in the central organs of the ministry, increasingly by executive rather than legal fiat. Offices were shuttled back and forth between departments; some new offices were created and some old ones disappeared, although the total number rose markedly. In the main, these structural shifts were not politically motivated, merely a never-ending race to adjust to changing world conditions. None the less, a sense of instability was unavoidable. The Foreign Ministry underwent three major reorganizations between the wars - in 1920, 1932, and 1936. The issue at the core of each change concerned the basic mode of demarcation among the ministry's general departments. By tradition, the Consulta had divided up its business along topical lines, but after 1918 an alternative school of administrative thought argued for a geographical alignment. One may perceive the ebb and flow of this debate in the interwar vicissitudes of those crucial departments charged with handling political matters.

In 1918 there existed a single General Department of Political Affairs. Two years later this was split into two geographical divisions, each of which now embraced both political and commercial affairs: the General Department of Political, Commercial and Private Affairs of Europe and the Levant, and the General Department of Political, Commercial and Private Affairs of Africa, America, Asia and Australia. Notwithstanding the replacement of one political department by two, the 1920 reorganization actually streamlined the Foreign Ministry, reducing the overall number of general departments from nine to four. Largely the work of Carlo Sforza, it was greatly admired at the time and its geographical approach conditioned the ministry's structure for the next decade. Some changes did occur sooner. In 1929 African business was transferred from one political department to the other, and at the same time two new departments with political overtones appeared - one for League of Nations affairs, the other necessitated by the Lateran Accords to transact business with the Vatican. But not until the start of Mussolini's second term as foreign minister in 1932 was a further radical reorganization assayed. At this point a return was made to a topical structure. The old unitary General Department of Political Affairs reappeared, shorn of its concern for commercial and economic business, which was confided to a fresh and separate department. League of Nations affairs no longer occupied a whole department, being consigned again to a subordinate office (that is, until 1937 when Italy withdrew from the League). The Vatican was still deemed worthy of the attention of a general department, the only one of five provided in the 1932 dispensation with anything resembling a regional basis. Yet, a scant four years later, when Galeazzo Ciano became foreign minister, the pendulum swung in the opposite direction. Of the six general departments in the 1936 reorganization two corresponded exactly to Sforza's earlier geographical division, although with different nomenclature: the General Department for European and Mediterranean Affairs and the General Department for Transoceanic Affairs. They were clearly designed for political business alone since the General Department for Economic and Commercial Affairs remained intact, and the distinctive department for Vatican polity disappeared. Finally, the disruption attendant on the fall of Fascism in 1943 produced another and conclusive reversal. The first post-Fascist foreign ministry, denuded of resources and personnel, could not afford the luxury of multiple large departments. Of necessity, in 1944 a single General Department of Political Affairs was created, and it has been maintained by choice until today.

The departments of political affairs have always been the engines, so to speak, of the Italian Foreign Ministry. Although not entrusted with all confidential material, they customarily received papers from other parts of the ministry, including the gabinetto del ministro. The director general, especially of the European and Mediterranean department, traditionally ranked in influence behind only the secretary general and capo di gabinetto among the career officials. Every political department was subdivided into offices that handled questions relating to one country or area, and the views of a capo ufficio would carry some weight in his field of competence.

Of the other general departments note has already been taken of that for economic affairs, although it was out of existence between 1920 and 1932. Matters concerning recruitment, postings, and technical services were the province of the Department of General Affairs; it lapsed in 1930 to be succeeded by a Department of Personnel and Administration, then reappeared in 1936 after which the two departments existed side by side. On the other hand, one general department never absent from the Foreign Ministry between 1918 and 1945, although predictably its name varied, was that overseeing Italian emigrants abroad, their schools, working conditions, and so on.

Needless to say, the idiosyncracies of Fascist policy compelled some modifications in the internal structure of the Foreign Ministry. In general terms, Fascism oversaw the elevation of the gabinetto del ministro at the expense of the direzioni generali. One symptom of this was the creation of ad hoc offices within the gabinetto to deal with issues germane to a specifically Fascist diplomacy - the Spanish Civil War, 1936-39, relations with Nazi Germany between May and August 1940, the armistice with France, 1940-42. But if the Fascist regime added some offices, it could also deprive the Foreign Ministry of others, and one in particular deserves mention. The ufficio stampa had long been a fixture in the Foreign Ministry, although something of a neglected backwater as the aristocrats of the old diplomacy looked askance at the cultivation of press and public opinion. However, it mattered to the Fascist regime, which specialized in the fabrication of mass images at home and abroad. In 1935 the press office was taken out of the Foreign Ministry and integrated into a new Ministry of Propaganda. The Foreign Ministry did not lose all touch with the press for diplomats were regularly seconded to the propaganda ministry or, as it was more famously rechristened in 1937, the Ministry of Popular Culture. Yet, the episode was a setback for the Foreign Ministry and a sign of its growing susceptibility at this time to political pressure.

Italy's diplomatic representation abroad increased steadily after 1918, from 51 to 67 foreign countries with accredited Italian representatives, before the outbreak of World War II enforced an interim curtailment of diplomatic activity. The key posts, of course, were those of ambassadorial rank, whose location reflected a combination of major power realities and Italy's special interests. At the end of the First World War Italian embassies were to be found in the capitals of Brazil (not a great power but a center of Italian emigration), France, Germany, Great Britain, Japan, Spain (the Madrid embassy being something of a courtesy to an erstwhile major power, though also justifiable on the grounds of Italy's vital interests in the Mediterranean), and the United States of America. The status of the former Italian embassies to Turkey and Russia was bedeviled by postwar uncertainties in those nations, but in 1920 and 1924, respectively, embassies were reopened there. During the interwar period Italian representation was raised to ambassadorial level in the other Latin American states with sizable Italian populations - Argentina and Chile; in the other large Far Eastern nation - China; and on the European continent in Belgium as the result of a royal marriage, and for no discernible reason in Poland. In addition, the Conciliation of 1929 made necessary the appointment of an Italian ambassador to the Vatican. Much prestige accrued to the holders of these fifteen embassies, but it should not be assumed automatically that they held much sway over policy. Italy's ambassadorial tradition was a mixed one. To be sure, some individual ambassadors during the nineteenth century had wielded marked influence, and other ambassadors in isolated episodes between 1918 and 1945 would do so again. However, by and large, Italy lacked any equivalent to the British, or even French, tradition of the independent proconsul. On the contrary, it was not unknown for an Italian foreign minister studiously to ignore all advice proffered by his ambassadors and to regard them merely as conduits for his own opinion. Furthermore, the profusion of public figures serving temporarily in top diplomatic posts put a distance between the ambassadors and the general run of career diplomats. Certainly, the ambassadors were not accustomed to pose as spokesmen of Italy's diplomatic corps as a whole. If the latter were to evince any sense of camaraderie and independence of mind, precedent suggested that these qualities would be found within the Foreign Ministry itself rather than in Italy's embassies.

C. THE FOREIGN MINISTRY, ITALIAN NATIONALISM, AND MUSSOLINI, 1922-1936

The turmoil that racked Italy between 1918 and 1922 could not fail to affect the conduct of foreign policy. The rapid turnover of governments and other cabinet reshuffles produced six foreign ministers in the space of four years. Sonnino, the wartime foreign minister, having endured the anguish of trying to establish Italian claims at the Paris Peace Conference, left office in June 1919, to be followed by Tittoni, Scialoja, Sforza, Tomasi della Torretta, and Schanzer. Of Sonnino's successors only Sforza made any impact. The ineffectuality of foreign ministers was thrown into high relief by D'Annunzio's illegal regency at Fiume maintained over fifteen months "in the name of the Italian people." Even Sforza's subsequent reconciliation with Yugoslavia proved ephemeral. The impotence of foreign ministers should not be ascribed solely to the personalities involved; it was symptomatic of that general paralysis of the whole liberal system of government that lent credence to the Fascist argument that Italy required a strong, not to say dictatorial, hand at the helm. At the same time, the shortcomings of the politicians in foreign policy automatically thrust more responsibility on to the shoulders of the professionals in the Consulta. It was no coincidence that the postwar era saw the emergence of one of the most celebrated and vigorous of all secretaries general.

On the final day of 1919 Salvatore Contarini took over the office from Giacomo de Martino, who had been a political appointee and a restrained secretary general. Contarini had entered Italy's foreign service in 1891, one of the numerous southerners to be recruited around the turn of the century. Except for two brief postings abroad, he spent his entire diplomatic career within the walls of the Foreign Ministry, perhaps an apt apprenticeship for one who was later to dominate that institution. As a personality he was not without his quirks - feigned rages at underlings, appointments and meetings set deliberately at mealtimes. Yet behind the eccentric façade there lurked a sharp political acumen, which was readily acknowledged by many foreign diplomats. Among the Italian diplomatic community he enjoyed the deepest respect. It has been said that when Fascism was on its way to power, Italy's intellectuals looked to Benedetto Croce as a bellwether; in 1922 when Mussolini was invited to form a government, the professional diplomats took their cue from Contarini.[4]

The secretary general recognized certain advantages to reside in the new Fascist government. By 1922 Fascism had established its right-wing credentials and was counted on to preserve the interests of the propertied classes. But more important than Contarini's conservatism was his nationalism. He subscribed to the widespread Italian belief that the nation's military victory of 1918 had been "mutilated" in the ensuing peace settlement. Disregarding the favorable frontier delimitation at the Brenner, this discontent fixed on the failure to realize more substantial gains, hinted at if not spelled out in the Treaty of London and other pieces of wartime diplomacy, on the eastern shore of the Adriatic (where Fiume served as a touchstone), in the Mediterranean ("mare nostrum" to Italian nationalists), and not least in the colonial field. To reverse this alleged disparagement of Italy, particularly by Britain and France, it was considered necessary for Italians to cease their civil disputes and to present a united front to the world - precisely the promise held out by Mussolini. Furthermore, the Fascist leader was an unknown quantity whose bluster had already caused ripples of alarm in international circles. The

FOREIGN MINISTRY AND FOREIGN POLICY

Consulta's intention was to trade on foreign apprehension in order to win concessions for Italy, while all the time keeping Mussolini securely under control. Contarini with mordant humor compared the Duce to the blood of San Gennaro in Naples, to be exhibited once a year and at a distance. It was with this reasoning, then, that almost all the Foreign Ministry personnel stayed at their posts on Fascism's assumption of power. There were a few resignations in the lower echelons but only two at a senior level. The Giolittian Alfredo Frassati quietly relinquished the ambassadorship to Weimar Germany. In contrast, Sforza, disappointed at not being invited by Mussolini to resume the foreign affairs portfolio, made a public statement on leaving the Paris embassy; naturally, this stressed his doubts about the new nationalistic government's capacity to maintain his own détente with the Slavs to the east.

In October 1922 Mussolini became not only premier (officially president of the Council of Ministers) but also foreign minister pro tem; not until June 1924 did he waive the interim label. His undersecretary was Ernesto Vassallo, a member of the Catholic Popular party; he retired when his party left Mussolini's coalition in April 1923, whereupon the undersecretaryship was left vacant. From the start the Duce's relations with the professional diplomats was ambivalent. He upset them by promptly moving the Foreign Ministry from the hallowed and tranquil Palazzo della Consulta to the Palazzo Chigi on the corner of the Via del Corso and the Piazza Colonna, one of the busiest street corners in Rome. The purpose behind the change remains obscure. It made the Foreign Ministry the neighbor of, but no more subject to, the Italian parliament. At the time it was suspected that Mussolini planned to harangue the passing Roman crowds from the Palazzo Chigi but, in fact, he found other balconies for this pastime. Probably the move was no more than a gesture to convey the impression that Fascism portended innovation generally. At any rate, the indignation of the professionals was mitigated by Mussolini's willingness to undergo lessons in diplomatic protocol and by his choice as capo di gabinetto of Giacomo Paulucci de' Calboli, a youthful but otherwise safe career diplomat. The truth of the matter was that Mussolini had come to power with the aid of Italy's conventional power structure, of which the Foreign Ministry was a part, and until he had consolidated his political base, he had no choice but to respect the institutions and representatives of the old order on which he still relied.

This situation changed markedly with the Duce's notorious speech of 3 January 1925 that heralded the one-party dictatorship. Indeed, by May of the same year Mussolini seemed bent on bringing the Foreign Ministry to heel through the appointment of Dino Grandi as undersecretary. Grandi, the former squadristi leader in Bologna, was to "fascisticize" the Palazzo Chigi, so it was widely believed. That this did not happen was partly due to the fact that Grandi was not temperamentally suited to the job. In truth, Contarini had already judged him malleable and, hearing of the intention to place a prominent Fascist in the Foreign Ministry, had suggested Grandi's name to Mussolini. The secretary general's judgment was vindicated; Grandi proved eager to assume the attitudes and habits of the career officials. Always sycophantic to the Duce, he nevertheless soon ceased to pose any threat to refashion the Foreign Ministry. The uneasy alliance between the professionals and their Fascist chief was sustained a while longer.

Moreover, it would be kept up so long as ends mattered more than means. As the Palazzo Chigi officials had calculated, they found themselves in sympathy with most of Mussolini's diplomatic objectives - Italian possession of Fiume gained in 1924, tutelage over Albania secured in 1926-27, subjugation of

Ethiopia always on the horizon. All were long-term nationalist, not peculiarly Fascist, goals. The abortive and violent attempt to seize Corfu in 1923 did shock the professionals, but against that could be set their success two years later in persuading a reluctant Duce to sign the Locarno Pacts. The nagging worry of the Palazzo Chigi centered, rather, on some of the more unorthodox diplomatic methods employed by Mussolini. It was disconcerting, to say the least, to learn that private emissaries abroad were operating behind the back of Italy's official representatives. In addition, through these messengers Mussolini entered into contact with the malcontents of Europe - German right-wingers (including the Nazis) and Croation separatists, for instance. This activity smacked of interference in the domestic affairs of foreign countries, as did the encouragement of Fascist tendencies among Italians living overseas. Equally disturbing was the Duce's overall lack of judgment and his simplistic, all-or-nothing attitude. To the Palazzo Chigi, Italian rivalry with Yugoslavia in Albania or with France in the colonial field did not preclude equable relations with those states; to Mussolini it did. Similarly, he viewed all social democratic governments with hostility, regardless of their actual policies. Often these rigid stands were voiced publicly. Thus, having some empathy with the defeated powers of 1918, he announced ringingly in 1928 his support for revisionism, not just selectively but in principle. Even before this, however, the violence of the Duce's public utterances had provoked a minor crisis in the Foreign Ministry.

It was in the new year of 1926 that Mussolini threatened openly to cross the Brenner in defence of Italy's hold on the Alto Adige. This hyperbole was the prelude to the resignation of Alessandro De Bosdari, Italian ambassador in Berlin, and also, momentously, of Secretary General Contarini. The Brenner speech, though, was merely the occasion of Contarini's withdrawal. The deeper cause seems to have been the hurt done to professional *amour propre* by Mussolini's growing preference for the advice of his nationalist cronies over that of the secretary general. Contarini's place was taken by another career official, Antonio Chiaramonte Bordonaro, who, however, had been promised an ambassadorial post. On his transfer to the London embassy in February 1927, the secretary generalship remained vacant. The position was formally abrogated in the 1932 reorganization of the Foreign Ministry, and it was never resurrected in the Fascist era.

The old guard who in 1922 had undertaken to keep Mussolini in leading strings were gradually leaving the stage. Ominously, a regulation issued in 1927 lowered the qualifications for entry into Italy's foreign service, a measure avowedly designed to bring young Fascist party members into the Palazzo Chigi. Yet, in the event, the "ventottisti," as the next year's Fascist recruits were dubbed, were neutralized, virtually all being absorbed in the consular service. The moderating influence of Grandi, a surrogate for that of Contarini, was at work behind the scenes. Surprisingly, Mussolini, who had appeared ready to launch a full-scale campaign to fascisticize the Foreign Ministry, stayed his hand, and even tacitly endorsed Grandi's adoption of conventional diplomatic mores by elevating him to foreign minister in 1929.[5]

Grandi's principal diplomatic activity over the next three years revolved around disarmament, particularly the London Naval Conference of 1930 and the ongoing efforts at the League of Nations to achieve general disarmament. But disarmament was an unusual preoccupation for a supposedly vigorous Fascist foreign minister and, in 1932, the volatile Duce showed his displeasure by taking over the Foreign Ministry himself once more. Italy's seat at the Geneva disarmament conference was filled incongruously by the Fascist air minister, Italo Balbo. Grandi, who had become an Anglophile as well as insufficiently belligerent, was banished, as it were, to the post of ambassador to the Court of St. James's. With Grandi's departure from Rome, the modus vivendi between the Palazzo Chigi and Fascism appeared again in jeopardy. Indeed, Grandi's transfer was only part of a broad reshuffling of positions in the foreign service, one feature of which was the dispatch of some high-ranking staff with long service inside the Foreign Ministry to embassies abroad. Notably, Raffaele Guariglia, director general of the Department of Political Affairs for Europe, the Levant and Africa, was sent to Madrid, and Augusto Rosso, director general of the Department of League of Nations Affairs, found himself in Washington.

In retrospect, this so-called massacre of the innocents can be made out to represent a Mussolinian clearing of the decks in Rome of potential dissenters to the great enterprise on which Fascist Italy was about to embark - the seizure of Ethiopia. Also in 1932, the Duce decreed that African affairs should be handled, not in the Palazzo Chigi, but in the Ministry of Colonies. On the other hand, there were no signs of overt disagreement among the career diplomats with the decision to move on Ethiopia, which, after all, had been an Italian nationalist goal for over half a century. At most, there were qualms about tactics and timing, but these were suppressed as the professionals cooperated willingly enough in planning the Ethiopian campaign, insofar as the Foreign Ministry was privy to such preparations. Mussolini's new capo di gabinetto, Pompeo Aloisi, came from the mainstream of the Palazzo Chigi and, on being appointed head of the Italian delegation to the League of Nations, labored conscientiously to defend the Duce's actions in East Africa. Later, in 1935, Guariglia returned to the Palazzo Chigi expressly to coordinate the ministry's activity in the Ethiopian affair. The professionals took some comfort from the presence near Mussolini of Fulvio Suvich, who had been made undersecretary for foreign affairs in 1932. Suvich, a nationalist from Trieste and a Fascist deputy since 1921, was deemed a moderate, at least in African matters. All in all, the Duce's way of proceeding commended itself to his cautious officials. Military planning was balanced by diplomatic approaches to other powers with vested interests in Ethiopia, namely, France and Britain. It was all comfortingly reminiscent of the Italian acquisition of Libya before the First World War.

What was totally unforeseen was that the Italo-Ethiopian conflict, planned as an old-fashioned colonial enterprise, would escalate into a major international incident affecting the European balance of power. For, trapped in an unexpected world crisis, Fascism responded by changing not simply the style of Italian foreign policy but its substance too. This was something that the career diplomats had not counted on, and it altered entirely their relationship with Mussolini. On the Duce's part, a new foreign policy required a new sort of foreign ministry, and hence the Italo-Ethiopian war of 1935-36 came to mark a clear watershed in the history of the Palazzo Chigi.[6]

D. THE FASCIST FOREIGN MINISTRY, 1936-1943

One cannot deny a certain inconsistency in the attitude of the permanent Foreign Ministry officials. On the one hand, they wanted the assertion of Italian rights, territorial gains, and a place for Italy among the great powers. On the other, their diplomatic prescription to achieve these nationalistic aims did not depart from the cautious tenets of traditional Italian foreign policy. In other words, they desired the fruits of an assertive policy without being prepared to pay the price. Specifically, they clung to the precept that Italy should, if only for reasons of naval strategy, keep on good terms with Britain, but for the rest remain uncommitted in the international balance of power. Then, behind the shield of British friendship, Italy should use her liberty of action to bargain for concessions from stronger powers. Not a heroic posture nor one calculated to increase the national esteem, to be sure, but not a foolish one either for the "sixth wheel of European diplomacy." Certainly, departure from it in 1915 had not brought Italy much joy. Up to 1935 the Fascist regime had basked in the favor of British Conservative governments, and had for the most part retained a position of equidistance among the international power blocs. The Ethiopian crisis, however, shattered the Anglo-Italian entente and propelled Mussolini into the arms of Nazi Germany. This was a veritable revolution in Italian foreign policy the like of which the Palazzo Chigi officials had never contemplated.

There was nothing inevitable about the consequences of the Italo-Ethiopian affair. British support for League of Nations sanctions was half-hearted - and French even more so - and did not prevent the proclamation of the Italian empire in Ethiopia by May 1936. At which juncture, in theory, no obstacle stood in the way of a resumption of the British tie and a continuation of Italy's freedom of action. It was Mussolini's whim alone that determined otherwise. Obsessed by a simple-minded, Social Darwinian vision of world politics that divided nations into effete democracies in decline and virile, authoritarian states on the rise, he perceived the waning British Empire not only as a bar to Italian imperial grandezza but as a future prize. Mutatis mutandis, he sought to move closer to Berlin, offering Nazi Germany a virtual free hand in Austria well before the close of the Italo-Ethiopian war. The Rome-Berlin Axis was invented and proclaimed in the fall of 1936 by Mussolini, not Hitler. In the meantime, the Spanish Civil War had erupted to pit the Fascist and Nazi interventionists against both the forces of the left backed by the Soviet Union and the noninterventionist democracies, thus reinforcing Mussolini's predilection to see things in bipolar, ideological terms. One of the might-have-beens of interwar diplomacy turns on whether Mussolini would have followed the course he did if the Spanish Civil War had not begun so hard on the heels of the Ethiopian crisis. Yet the Duce had made it very plain, in advance of the outbreak of war in Spain, that he was set on a new direction in foreign policy. An unmistakable token of this was a drastic transformation of the Palazzo Chigi.

On 11 June 1936 Mussolini relinquished the Foreign Ministry for the second time, entrusting it to his minister of propaganda, Count Ciano.[7] Of impeccable Fascist background - his father one of the first Fascists, his father-in-law Mussolini himself - Ciano was advanced in order to accomplish what Grandi had promised but not delivered a decade earlier: the subjection of the Foreign Ministry to the party. His undersecretary appeared a suitable assistant for this task; Giuseppe Bastianini had previously run the central party office for Fascist groups abroad (fasci all'estero). By October 1937 Ciano would boast that the Foreign Ministry had been made into the most Fascist of all the ministries. But this was quite untrue in the sense that all foreign service personnel were party members. In fact, the old guard were for the most part left undisturbed in their posts. It was simply that they were deprived of any meaningful role; this is what Ciano meant by the fascistization of his Foreign Ministry. The trick was achieved by a grotesque concentration of business in the hands of the new foreign minister and his gabinetto. Ever since the demise

FOREIGN MINISTRY AND FOREIGN POLICY

of the secretary generalship the gabinetto del ministro had been gaining in stature. As early as 1927 it had acquired an ufficio di coordinamento - initially short-lived but a portent of the centralization to come - and from the beginning of the thirties decade political business found its way increasingly into the gabinetto. This process was accelerated enormously after 1936, the net result being that the gabinetto became the undisputed paramount office within the Palazzo Chigi. Furthermore, this was the one sector of the Foreign Ministry that was now infiltrated by Fascist party members, especially by Ciano's friends from Roman café society. Two such youthful philofascist diplomats, Filippo Anfuso and Blasco Lanza d'Ajeta, were to serve successively as his capo di gabinetto. It was here, then, that a truly Fascist diplomacy would be hatched. More and more, as time passed, important papers were channeled into the gabinetto and, once lodged in the ufficio di coordinamento that was revitalized by Ciano, did not reappear for circulation among the appropriate direzioni generali. The resulting ignorance of detailed policy extended beyond the majority of officials in the Palazzo Chigi to Italy's representatives abroad. Italian ambassadors were not unaccustomed to being kept in the dark by Mussolini, but in the late 1930's the condition grew pandemic.

It was paradoxical, although perhaps not accidental, that the so-called diplomatic experts should have been excluded from the inner circles of power at precisely the moment that foreign policy became the overriding passion of the Fascist regime. Early Fascism had held out the prospect of a radical reform of Italian society and its economic system. This hope had proved vain in the Great Depression and, for a compensatory raison d'être, Mussolini's government turned to militarism and imperialism under the slogan of the Third Rome. Henceforth, Italian Fascism would stand or fall on its performance in the international sphere.

In reality, however, Fascist Italian foreign policy soon ceased to have any identity of its own. The ultimate price exacted by the Germans for the Axis was the Anschluss of March 1938 and, once Nazi troops in Austria were camped on the Brenner, Mussolini lost any real freedom of maneuver. Galled by dependence on Germany, although it was of his own making, the Duce cast about for ways in which Italy might redeem itself. One gesture was the annexation of Albania in April 1939, a coup exalted by bestowing on the freshly appointed foreign undersecretary, Zenone Benini, the title of undersecretary for Albanian affairs. Nevertheless, the very practices of the Palazzo Chigi provided further damning evidence of Italy's subservience to Berlin. The Pact of Steel of 22 May 1939, an offensive as well as defensive accord, was hardly negotiated at all; no Italian terms were proffered, and Mussolini simply accepted the German draft. In like vein, Mussolini's meetings with Hitler and Ribbentrop sometimes took place without any Italian record being compiled; the Palazzo Chigi would make a translation of the German procès-verbal that reached Rome some weeks after the interview.

Italy's career diplomats at this point were described by one observer as "shadows," insubstantial figures going through the motions of running the Foreign Ministry.[8] They had a fleeting success when Italy declined to honor her signature on the Pact of Steel in August 1939, although Mussolini was persuaded to this repetition of 1914 not so much by his diplomats' counsel of prudent neutrality but by military testimony of the country's unpreparedness for war. Still, it was a Palazzo Chigi official who sealed the decision for nonbelligerency. Ambassador Bernardo Attolico in Berlin, being instructed to submit a list of war matériel that Italy needed from Germany in order to make war, added on his own initiative the proviso that these supplies be delivered before Italy declared war - clearly an impossible demand for Berlin to meet. Not surprisingly, the Germans urged that the Italian ambassador be recalled and, also predictably, Mussolini yielded in due course. After deciding in March 1940 to enter the war at the earliest opportunity, he replaced Attolico with the former Fascist minister of popular culture, Dino Alfieri. Another Italian diplomat to take a stand against the German alliance was Rosso who, from the Moscow embassy, sent Mussolini dire warnings first of the coming Nazi-Soviet nonaggression pact and later of the planned Nazi attack on the Soviets. But the outspokenness of Attolico and Rosso was the exception amid the general passivity of Palazzo Chigi officials and, in any case, no criticism by the professionals deflected Mussolini one whit from his fatalistic trust in Nazi Germany.

After Fascist Italy's entry into the Second World War on 10 June 1940, Italian policy came to be decided more than ever in Berlin rather than Rome. Above all, the unmitigated disaster in October of Italy's invasion of Greece - Mussolini's "parallel war" - resulted in the German usurpation of Italian interests in the Balkans, the Mediterranean, and North Africa. The succession of international setbacks and humiliations sparked unrest among the Fascist hierarchs. Indeed, in the waning years of the Fascist era it was from this quarter, not from the career officials, that opposition to Mussolini's foreign policy and particularly the Axis came. Ciano himself had conceived a deep distrust of the Nazis after his conversations with Ribbentrop at Salzburg on the eve of the war. But although his Germanophobe sentiments increased and were well known, the foreign minister with typical irresponsibility never argued the anti-German case forcefully with the Duce; his real thoughts were kept for his diary.[9] Bastianini was another Fascist who grew disillusioned with Mussolinian foreign policy long before the end. In 1939 he had been sent to the London embassy and, like his predecessor there, Grandi, had tried in vain during the next year to convince Mussolini not to underestimate the British. He returned to the central diplomatic stage in February 1943 when Mussolini, in the wake of Axis defeats on the battlefields of Russia and North Africa, sought scapegoats for his own folly by dismissing his entire cabinet. In this new massacre of the innocents Ciano was packed off as ambassador to the Vatican, and Mussolini for the third time assumed direction of the Foreign Ministry. He appointed Bastianini his undersecretary (the position of undersecretary for Albanian affairs having vanished along with other Italian illusions in 1941). The new undersecretary made the last unavailing attempts to free Italy from the German stranglehold; he floated anew a notion that had earlier intrigued Mussolini for an Italian-led league of neutral Balkan states, and he proposed an overture to the Allies for a separate peace. Mussolini, however, was too deep in Hitler's spell. He would freely promise to stand up to the German Führer at their next meeting and to urge on him a separate peace with Russia, but he never did. Events, therefore, moved inexorably to their dénouement at the Fascist Grand Council meeting of 24 July 1943. This body's vote of no confidence in Mussolini's stewardship was provoked by the recent Allied landings in Sicily; but in effect, it was an indictment of Fascist Italy's foreign policy in general.

In some ways the traditional Foreign Ministry benefited by its exclusion from decision-making after 1936. For one thing, its membership had not been purged or torn apart by factionalism. Its very powerlessness had acted as a kind of protection. And left to itself, it had managed to preserve something of its esprit de corps. Moreover, the career diplomats evaded much of the opprobrium incurred by Fascist foreign policy in the Ciano years. Historically, of course, they cannot evade responsibility for some fourteen years of willing, even eager, cooperation with Fascism. But politically speaking, the professionals were enabled to emerge in 1943 with reputations reasonably intact and to resume their old place in government and society after Mussolini's fall.

E. TWO FOREIGN MINISTRIES, 1943-1945[10]

When King Victor Emmanuel III, taking his cue from the Grand Council of Fascism, dismissed Mussolini on 25 July 1943, he hoped to return to the status quo of 1922. Understandably, he turned to the professional diplomats as symbols of that vanished age. In Italy's first post-Fascist government under Marshal Badoglio, the post of foreign minister was accorded to Guariglia, the veteran career official and onetime ambassador in Madrid, Paris, and Ankara, and in many ways the embodiment of the old Consulta style. As further evidence of the return to tradition in the Foreign Ministry, the office of secretary general was quickly revived and entrusted to Rosso, former ambassador to the U.S.A. and the U.S.S.R., and also a long-serving career diplomat.

The new foreign minister's most immediate task, indeed his only one, was to arrange Italy's exit from the war while the Germans were looking over his shoulder. The first approaches to the Allies, made variously in Lisbon, Tangier, and Switzerland, were entrusted to emissaries of some diplomatic experience. Ciano's protegé, Lanza d'Ajeta, Alberto Berio, a career diplomat then serving in the Palazzo Chigi, Alberto Pirelli, the industrialist once involved in international economic negotiations, and even the ubiquitous Grandi, were so employed. They all failed, however, to win a political settlement from the Allies who insisted flatly on Italy's unconditional surrender. Constrained to meet this demand, the royal government now entrusted negotiations to General Giuseppe Castellano, who signed the armistice at Cassibile in Sicily. The Allied announcement of this armistice on 8 September 1943 caught the Italian authorities in Rome unprepared. The Foreign Ministry was concerned to sequester its most sensitive records before the Germans arrived. Guariglia sent some papers abroad for safekeeping, and others were hurriedly transferred to a hiding place in Rome (see chap. III, A1). Then the royal government decamped south to Brindisi. Many Foreign Ministry personnel were trapped in Nazi-occupied Italy and, by the end of October, only a handful were able to reach Brindisi. Because Guariglia did not manage to escape from Rome, Badoglio took over the Foreign Ministry - except that there was no foreign ministry, nor for that matter any other apparatus of government, to take over. The reconstruction of administrative machinery thus proceeded pari passu with the reformulation of a foreign policy.

Meanwhile, in the north the Germans had restored a Mussolinian government, which located its headquarters in Salò on the shores of Lake Garda. This Repubblica Sociale Italiana, like its counterpart in the south, lacked a proper foreign ministry, although for completely different reasons.[11] The vast majority of Italy's career diplomats refused to serve the ex-Duce; even those who fell into the hands of the Nazis and Japanese and were threatened with imprisonment or worse declined almost to a man. The solitary senior diplomat to join Mussolini was Anfuso, Ciano's friend. (This was ironic since Ciano, who had created many enemies in the pro-German wing of the Fascist party, was shortly to be tried and shot at Verona.) Anfuso was dispatched to Berlin where the only real business of the Italian Social Republic would be conducted. With Anfuso thus occupied, Mussolini was unable to call on any other figure of sufficient stature to assume the Foreign Ministry, and reluctantly he kept the portfolio in his own hands.

In reality, however, it proved impossible for the neofascist regime to mount any foreign policy at all. It could win no diplomatic recognition among the neutral nations, while relations with Nazi Germany were not such as characterize two sovereign states. The Germans exercised a veto over everything that Mussolini ventured in northern Italy and, to all intents, annexed those Habsburg territories gained by Italy at the end of the First World War. The essence of this infamous "brutal friendship" was disclosed in the spring of 1945 when the downfall of the Third Reich became visibly imminent. German overtures for surrender to the Allies were made behind Mussolini's back. Anfuso, who had now returned to Salò to serve as foreign undersecretary, and Alberto Mellini Ponce de Leon, Mussolini's capo di gabinetto, spent much of their time tracking down these clandestine Nazi negotiations. For its own part, the Italian Social Republic tried to establish contact with the Allies and the partisans through Cardinal Schuster of Milan, who was also the Germans' go-between. But the Allies were not interested in a separate peace with the neofascist republic. It was the Germans who mattered, and it was with them and not the Italians that an armistice was signed at Caserta on 29 April 1945. By then Mussolini had taken flight for Switzerland. When captured by partisans he was attempting disguise by wearing a German greatcoat; it was an apt symbol of his concluding role as German puppet. His summary execution on the 28th was purportedly in reprisal for Nazi atrocities; to the end he was dogged by the folly of his German connection.

In contrast to the sorry diplomatic record in the north, the Italian Foreign Ministry in the liberated south went from strength to strength. Its internal rehabilitation was largely the work of Renato Prunas, a career diplomat who returned to Italy from his post abroad to become secretary general in November 1943. In this task he was aided by the bulk of Italy's foreign service personnel who rallied to the royal government. After this regime's peregrinations to Brindisi and Salerno, the Foreign Ministry was able to return to the Palazzo Chigi in Rome on the capital's liberation by the Allies in June 1944. Administration then resumed its old order and flow. At the same time more ties with the Fascist past were severed. The Badoglio ministry, after all, was composed of erstwhile collaborators with Fascism, and the king came under pressure from the Allies, who in turn were under pressure from the Italian resistance behind German lines, to appoint a more democratic provisional government. As a result, there was constructed a new cabinet headed by the onetime socialist and pre-Fascist premier, Ivanoe Bonomi, who also served as foreign minister. In December 1944 the Christian Democrat Alcide de Gasperi became foreign minister and continued in the post until the end of the war. Another moving spirit in Italian foreign affairs between 1943 and 1945 was the pre-Fascist foreign minister, Sforza, officially minister without portfolio in the Badoglio and Bonomi ministries; the esteem that he had cultivated during his years of exile from Fascism abroad, especially in the U.S.A., was deployed in helping to restore Italy to the comity of nations.

As the Salò regime in the north was constantly aware of the German presence, so the royal government in the south had to consider first and foremost the Anglo-American occupation authorities. The Foreign Ministry, in particular, succeeded in establishing excellent diplomatic relations with the Allied <u>Consiglio Consultivo per l'Italia</u>, which, in consequence, permitted a wide range of Italian diplomatic activity to unfold. This latitude was used to restore normal diplomatic ties with as many states as possible. Ironically, the first success in this field in March 1944 saw the resumption of diplomatic relations with the U.S.S.R., much to the annoyance of the Anglo-Americans. This contretemps once surmounted, however, a fully accredited Italian political representative was received in London in November 1944, and the following February the Italian embassy in Washington was reopened. Meanwhile, to prepare the ground for future Franco-Italian relations, conversations were held with General De Gaulle and other spokesmen of the Free French movement. Less fruitful were the Italian efforts to persuade the Allies to amend the armistice agreement of 1943. The object was to win for Italy some kind of cobelligerent status in anticipation of the postwar peace negotiations, but no such concession, at least of a formal nature, was forthcoming. Nevertheless, in a scant two years the Italian foreign service had accomplished a great deal in the way of Italy's international rehabilitation. By 1945, in fact, the diplomatic future could be faced, if not with total confidence, then at least with a degree of equanimity.[12]

F. APPENDIX

1. Italian Diplomats, 1918-1945

This list includes Italy's more prominent diplomats who filled positions within the Foreign Ministry and abroad who afforded some possibility of influencing foreign policy.

Aldrovandi Marescotti, Luigi. <u>Capo di gabinetto</u>, 1918-19; secretary general, Italian delegation, Paris Peace Conference, 1919; chargé d'affaires, embassy, Berlin, 1920; minister, Sofia, 1920-23; minister, Cairo, 1923-24; ambassador, Buenos Aires, 1924-26; ambassador, Berlin, 1926-29; member, arbitral commission, Wal Wal incident, 1935; delegate, League of Nations, 1935-36. Papers (Foreign Ministry). Diary.

Alfieri, Dino. Fascist deputy; delegate, League of Nations, 1927-29; minister of press and propaganda, then of popular culture, 1936-39; ambassador, Vatican, 1939-40; ambassador, Berlin, 1940-43. Papers (Archivio Centrale dello Stato). Memoirs.

Aloisi, Pompeo. Press chief, Italian delegation, Paris Peace Conference, 1919; minister, Copenhagen, 1920-23; League of Nations commissioner, Memel, 1923; minister, Bucharest, 1923-25; minister, Durazzo, 1926-27; ambassador, Tokyo, 1928-29; ambassador, Ankara, 1929-32; <u>capo di gabinetto</u>, Foreign Ministry, and head of Italian delegation, League of Nations, 1932-36; delegate, Stresa Conference, 1935. Journal (private, Rome). Diary.

Anfuso, Filippo. Vice consul, Munich, 1927-28; legation, Budapest, 1928-29; embassy, Berlin, 1929-31; first secretary and chargé d'affaires, legation, Peking, 1931-34; first secretary, legation, Athens, 1935-36; <u>capo di gabinetto</u>, Foreign Ministry, 1938-41; minister, Budapest, 1941-43; Salò

Republic's ambassador, Berlin, 1943-45; undersecretary for foreign affairs (Salò), 1945. Memoirs.

Arlotta, Mario. Counselor, embassy, Constantinople, 1920-22; secretary general, Italian delegation, Lausanne Conference, 1922-23; director general, Dept. of Affairs of Europe and the Levant, 1923-26; minister, Athens, 1926-29; minister, Budapest, 1929-32; ambassador, Buenos Aires, 1932-36.

Arone, Pietro. Director general, Dept. of African, American, Asian and Australian Affairs, 1927-29; minister, Lisbon, 1929-32; director general, Dept. of Personnel, 1932-36; ambassador, Moscow and Warsaw, 1936-37.

Attolico, Bernardo. Technical delegate, Paris Peace Conference, 1919; League of Nations secretariat, 1920-27, commissioner, Danzig, 1920-21, vice-secretary general, 1922-27; ambassador, Rio de Janeiro, 1927-29; ambassador, Moscow, 1930-34; ambassador, Berlin, 1935-40; ambassador, Vatican, 1940-42.

Auriti, Giacinto. First secretary, legation, Bucharest, 1913-19; first secretary and counselor, legation, Vienna, 1921-26, then minister, 1926-32; ambassador, Tokyo, 1933-40.

Barzilai, Salvatore. Journalist and nationalist deputy; delegate, Paris Peace Conference, 1919. Papers (Archivio Centrale dello Stato). Memoirs.

Bastianini, Giuseppe. Fascist deputy, 1924-27; secretary, fasci all'estero, 1925-26; minister, Tangier, 1927-28; minister, Lisbon, 1928-29; minister, Athens, 1929-32; ambassador, Warsaw, 1932-36; undersecretary for foreign affairs, 1936-39; ambassador, London, 1939-40; governor, Dalmatia, 1941-43; undersecretary for foreign affairs, 1943. Papers (private, Milan). Memoirs.

Berio, Alberto. Attaché, then first secretary, legation, Sofia, 1925-29; first secretary, legation, Prague, 1932-34; League of Nations secretariat, 1934-37; counselor, embassy, Ankara, 1938-42; consul general, Tangier, 1943 (special mission for armistice); minister, Bern, 1944-47. Memoirs.

Bodrero, Alessandro. General; Mussolini's personal emissary to King Alexander of Yugoslavia, 1923-24; minister, Belgrade, 1924-28.

Bonin Longare, Lelio. Ambassador, Paris, 1917-22; head of Italian delegation, League of Nations, 1920, 1923, delegate, 1923-30. Papers (private, Vicenza).

Boscarelli, Raffaele. Counselor, embassy, Rio de Janeiro, 1925-26; counselor, embassy, Paris, 1927-30; minister, Haiti and Dominica, 1930-33, and Havana, 1931-33; minister, Peking, 1933-34; minister, Athens, 1935-39; ambassador, Santiago, 1939-40; ambassador, Buenos Aires, 1940-42.

Bova Scoppa, Renato. Legation, Belgrade, 1920-23; legation, Addis Ababa, 1923-24; embassy, Moscow, 1925-27; first secretary, embassy, Ankara, 1927-32; first secretary, legation, Bern, 1932-40; assistant secretary general, Italian delegation, League of Nations, 1933-35; minister, Lisbon, 1940-41; minister, Bucharest, 1941-43. Memoirs.

Buti, Gino. Embassy, Washington, 1918-19; delegate, conferences at Cannes, Genoa, The Hague, 1922; member, Young committee, 1929; League of Nations secretariat, 1929, delegate, 1930-31; delegate, naval conference, London, 1930, disarmament conference, Geneva, 1932, Danubian conference, London, 1932, Lausanne Conference, 1932, Stresa Conference, 1935; director general, Dept. of Political Affairs, 1932-36; director general, Dept. of European and Mediterranean Affairs, 1936-42; ambassador, Paris (Nazi occupation), 1942-44.

Caetani, Gelasio. Italian nationalist; delegate, Paris Peace Conference, 1919; ambassador, Washington, 1922-25. Papers (Fondazione Caetani, Rome; Hoover Institution, Palo Alto, CA).

Cantalupo, Roberto. Nationalist deputy; undersecretary for colonial affairs, 1924-26; minister, Cairo, 1930-32; ambassador, Rio de Janeiro, 1933-37; ambassador (to Franco), Burgos, 1937. Memoirs.

Cerruti, Vittorio. Delegate, Paris Peace Conference, 1919; high commissioner, Budapest, 1919-20; chargé d'affaires, then minister, Peking, 1921-26; ambassador, Moscow, 1927-30; ambassador, Rio de Janeiro, 1930-32; ambassador, Berlin, 1932-35; ambassador, Paris, 1935-37.

Chiaramonte Bordonaro, Antonio. Embassy, Madrid, 1918-19; minister, Prague, 1920-24; minister, Vienna, 1924-26; delegate, League of Nations, 1925, Locarno Conference, 1925; secretary general, Foreign Ministry, 1926-27; ambassador, London, 1927-32; delegate, naval conference, London, 1930.

Ciano, Galeazzo. Embassy, Rio de Janeiro, 1925-26; embassy, Buenos Aires, 1926-27; secretary, legation, Peking, 1927-28; consul general, Shanghai, 1929-31; chargé d'affaires, then minister, Peking, 1931-33; minister of press and propaganda, 1933-36; foreign minister, 1936-43; ambassador, Vatican, 1943. Papers (published, microfilm). Diary.

Colli di Fellizano, Giuseppe. Minister, Addis Ababa, 1908-20; minister, Stockholm, 1920-21; minister, Buenos Aires, 1922-23; minister, Addis Ababa, 1924-26.

Colonna, Ascanio. Delegate, Conference of Ambassadors, 1920-21; minister, Stockholm, 1926-32; minister, Budapest, 1932-36; ambassador, Buenos Aires, 1936-38; ambassador, Washington, 1939-41.

Contarini, Salvatore. In charge of Dept. of General Affairs and of overseas economic affairs, 1914-19; secretary general, Foreign Ministry, 1920-26. Papers (Foreign Ministry).

Cora, Giuliano. First secretary, legation, Addis Ababa, 1918; counselor, embassy, Tokyo, 1918-20; counselor, embassy, London, 1921; delegate, Washington Conference, 1921-22; minister, Addis Ababa, 1922-23; minister, Teheran, 1923; consul general, Munich, 1923-25; minister, Durazzo, 1925-26; minister, Addis Ababa, 1926-30; minister, Sofia, 1931-34; ambassador, Chungking, 1937-38. Memoirs.

Crespi, Silvio. Minister of supply, 1918-19; delegate, Paris Peace Conference, 1919. Diary.

De Bosdari, Alessandro. Minister, Athens, 1912-18; ambassador, Rio de Janeiro, 1918-21; governor, Rhodes, 1921-22; ambassador, Berlin, 1922-26. Papers (Archivio di Stato, Bologna).

De Facendis, Domenico. Counselor, legation, Athens, 1924-26; minister, Teheran, 1926-28; minister, Tangier, 1928-32; minister, Prague, 1935-38.

De Martino, Giacomo. Secretary general, Foreign Ministry, 1913-19; delegate, Paris Peace Conference, 1919; ambassador, Berlin, 1920; ambassador, London, 1920-22; ambassador, Tokyo, 1922-25; ambassador, Washington, 1925-32.

De Peppo, Ottavio. First secretary, embassy, Buenos Aires, 1924-25; counselor, embassy, Santiago, 1925-26; counselor, embassy, Madrid, 1927-32; minister, Jeddah, 1932-33; delegate, League of Nations, 1933; capo di gabinetto, Foreign Ministry, 1936-38; ambassador, Ankara, 1938-43.

Diana, Pasquale. Secretary, embassy, Constantinople, 1919-21; secretary, legation, Vienna, 1922-24; first secretary, legation, Budapest, 1924-27;

counselor, embassy, Washington, 1932-33; counselor, embassy, Berlin, 1933-34; minister, Luxemburg, 1934-36; minister, The Hague, 1938-40; minister, Copenhagen, 1942-43.

Di Nola, Carlo. Commercial attaché, embassy, Madrid, 1920-21; commercial attaché, legations, Budapest, 1921-38, Vienna, 1923-38. Memoirs.

Durazzo, Carlo. Chargé d'affaires, then minister, Peking, 1919-21; minister, Tirana, 1922-25; minister, Bucharest, 1925-27; ambassador, Brussels, 1928-30.

Durini di Monza, Ercole. First secretary, embassy, London, 1918-19; minister, Teheran, 1922-23; consul general, Munich, 1923; minister, Budapest, 1924-29; ambassador, Santiago, 1929-31; ambassador, Madrid, 1931-32.

Fransoni, Francesco. Counselor, embassy, Paris, 1932-35; minister, Lithuania, 1935-38; minister, Prague, 1938; minister, Stockholm, 1939-41; minister, Lisbon, 1941-43.

Frassati, Alfredo. Founder and director of La Stampa; ambassador, Berlin, 1921-22. Papers (published).

Galli, Carlo. Delegate, Paris Peace Conference, 1919, Conference of Ambassadors, 1920-22, reparations conferences, London, Paris, Boulogne, Spa, San Remo, 1920; minister, Teheran, 1924-26; minister, Lisbon, 1926-28; minister, Belgrade, 1928-34; ambassador, Ankara, 1934-38. Papers (private, Venice). Diary.

Gambara, Gastone. General; head of military mission, then ambassador, Madrid, 1939-40.

Garroni, Camillo. Ambassador, Constantinople, 1920-23; head of Italian delegation, Lausanne Conference, 1922-23.

Ghigi, Pellegrino. Secretary, Italian delegation, Locarno Conference, 1925; delegate, League of Nations, 1926-27; capo di gabinetto, Foreign Ministry, 1929-32; delegate, naval conference, London, 1930, disarmament conference, Geneva, 1932; minister, Tangier, 1932-35; minister, Cairo, 1935-37; minister, Vienna, 1937-38; minister, Bucharest, 1938-41.

Giannini, Amadeo. Delegate, Paris Peace Conference, 1919; secretariat, Genoa Conference, 1922; delegate, conference of Austrian successor states, Rome, 1924, League of Nations, 1930-31; director general, Dept. of Commercial Affairs, 1936-43. Papers (Archivio Centrale dello Stato). Memoirs.

Grandi, Dino. Fascist ras of Bologna and deputy; undersecretary of interior, 1924-25; undersecretary for foreign affairs, 1925-29; delegate, Locarno Conference, 1925; member, Italian war debt commissions, Washington, London, 1925-26; delegate, League of Nations, 1925-27, 1936, head of Italian delegation, 1929-32; foreign minister, 1929-32; delegate, naval conference, London, 1930, four-power conference, London, 1932, Lausanne Conference, 1932, disarmament conference, Geneva, 1932-33; ambassador, London, 1932-39; delegate, naval conference, London, 1935-36, Spanish Civil War nonintervention committee, London, 1936-39; minister of justice, 1939-43. Papers (Foreign Ministry; microfilm, Georgetown University, Washington). Memoirs.

Grazzi, Emanuele. Consul general, New York, 1932; minister, Honduras and Nicaragua, 1933-35; minister, El Salvador and Guatemala, 1935-37; director general, Dept. of Overseas Affairs, 1937-39; minister, Athens, 1939-40. Memoirs.

Guariglia, Raffaele. Embassy, Paris, 1915-19; first secretary, embassy, Brussels, 1919; delegate, Lausanne Conference, 1922-23; Dept. of Affairs of Europe and the Levant, 1919-32, head of Mediterranean and colonial section, 1923-26, director general, 1926-32; ambassador, Madrid, 1932-35; coordinator, Ethiopian policy, Foreign Ministry, 1935-36; ambassador, Buenos Aires, 1936-38; ambassador, Paris, 1938-40; ambassador, Vatican, 1942-43; ambassador, Ankara, 1943; foreign minister, 1943. Papers (Foreign Ministry). Memoirs.

Imperiali di Francavilla, Guglielmo. Ambassador, London, 1910-20; delegate, Paris Peace Conference, 1919; head of Italian delegation, League of Nations, 1920-22.

Indelli, Mario. Delegate, Allied High Commission, Constantinople, 1919; secretary general, Italian delegation, Lausanne Conference, 1922-23; minister, Tirana, 1934-36; minister, Belgrade, 1936-40; ambassador, Tokyo, 1940-43.

Jacomini di San Sevino, Francesco. Delegate, Genoa Conference, 1922; legation, Bucharest, 1923-24; delegate, Locarno Conference, 1925; member, war debts commission, Washington, 1925; secretary, legation, Durazzo, 1926-27; secretary general, Italian delegation, League of Nations, 1932; delegate, disarmament conference, Geneva, 1932-33; attached to Italian delegation, Stresa Conference, 1935; minister, Tirana, 1936-39; lieutenant governor, Albania, 1939-43. Memoirs.

Jannelli, Pasquale. Embassy, London, 1930-33; first secretary, legation, Sofia, 1933-34; first secretary, legation, Athens, 1937-38; first secretary, embassy, Ankara, 1938-39; first secretary, embassy, Berlin, 1940-41; counselor, embassy, Tokyo, 1941-43. Memoirs.

Lago, Mario. Consul general, Tangier, 1916-19; chargé d'affaires, legation, Prague, 1919-20; director general, Dept. of Affairs of Europe and the Levant, 1920-23; delegate, Lausanne Conference, 1922-23; governor, Dodecanese, 1924-36.

Lanza d'Ajeta, Blasco. Delegate, League of Nations, 1932-34; capo di gabinetto, Foreign Ministry, 1941-43; counselor, legation, Lisbon, 1943 (special mission for armistice). Documentary memoirs.

Lequio, Francesco. Embassy, Berlin, 1920-26; first secretary, legation, Bucharest, 1926-30; first secretary, legation, Cairo, 1930-32; counselor, embassy, Rio de Janeiro, 1932-35; director general, Dept. of Personnel, 1935-40; ambassador, Madrid, 1940-43.

Lojacono, Vincenzo. Director general, Dept. of General Affairs, 1924-27; director general, Dept. of Italians Abroad, and in charge of Albanian Affairs, Foreign Ministry, 1927-32; ambassador, Ankara, 1932-34; ambassador, Peking, 1934-37; ambassador, Rio de Janeiro, 1937-38; ambassador, Brussels, 1938-40.

Macchi di Cellere, Vincenzo. Ambassador, Washington, 1913-1919. Diary.

Magistrati, Massimo. Legation, Peking, 1925-27; secretary and chargé d'affaires, embassy, Rio de Janeiro, 1928-29; delegate, League of Nations, 1931; consul general, Algiers, 1933-34; first secretary, then counselor, embassy, Berlin, 1934-40; minister, Sofia, 1940-43; minister, Bern, 1943-44. Memoirs.

Majoni, Giovanni. Consul general, Munich, 1920-22; minister, Helsinki, 1923; minister, Warsaw, 1924-29; ambassador, Tokyo, 1930-33.

Mameli, Francesco-Giorgio. Capo di gabinetto, Foreign Ministry, 1927-29; counselor, embassy, London, 1929-33; minister, Riga, 1933-36; minister, Lisbon, 1936-40; minister, Belgrade, 1940-41; minister, Sofia, 1943.

Manzoni, Gaetano. Director general, Dept. of Political Affairs, 1913-20; minister, Belgrade, 1920-22; ambassador, Moscow, 1924-27; ambassador, Paris, 1927-32.

Martin Franklin, Alberto. Minister, Mexico, 1917-19; minister, Bucharest, 1919-23; minister, Stockholm, 1923-24; ambassador, Santiago, 1924-26; ambassador, Buenos Aires, 1926-29; ambassador, Warsaw, 1929-31; ambassador, Brussels, 1931-32.

Mazzolini, Serafino. Consul general, Sao Paolo, 1928-32; minister, Montevideo, 1932-38; minister, Cairo, 1938-40; undersecretary for foreign affairs (Salò), 1943-44.

Mellini Ponce de Leon, Alberto. Delegate, League of Nations, 1932-33; legation, Cairo, 1934-36; vice consul, Munich, 1937-41; first secretary, embassy, Ankara, 1941; in charge of Arab affairs, 1942; capo di gabinetto (Foreign Ministry, Salò), 1943-45. Memoirs.

Mondini, Luigi. Military attaché, legation, Vienna, 1937-38; military attaché, legation, Athens, 1938-40. Memoirs.

Montagna, Giulio. Technical delegate, Paris Peace Conference, 1919; minister, Athens, 1919-24; delegate, Lausanne Conference, 1922-23; ambassador, Constantinople, 1924-25; ambassador, Rio de Janeiro, 1925-27.

Negrotto Cambiaso, Lazzaro. Minister, Cairo, 1917-22; minister, Belgrade, 1922-24; ambassador, Brussels, 1926-28.

Orsini Baroni, Luca. Chief of press bureau, 1914-19; minister, Stockholm, 1919-20; minister, Bern, 1920-21; minister, Vienna, 1921-24; ambassador, Brussels, 1924-25; ambassador, Constantinople, 1925-29; ambassador, Berlin, 1929-32.

Pantaleoni, Maffeo. Economist and nationalist; president, League of Nations committee for Austrian reconstruction, 1922-23. Papers (Archivio Centrale dello Stato).

Paternò di Manchi, Gaetano. Delegate, Paris Peace Conference, 1919; minister, Kabul, 1922-23; head of economic delegation, Moscow, 1923-24; minister, Helsinki, 1924-26; minister, Cairo, 1926-30; minister, Addis Ababa, 1930-32; minister, Stockholm, 1932-35.

Paulucci de'Calboli, Giacomo (Barone Russo). Legation, Bern, 1918-19; delegate, Paris Peace Conference, 1919; secretary, embassy, Tokyo, 1920; capo di gabinetto, Foreign Ministry, 1922-27; undersecretary general, League of Nations, 1927-32; ambassador, Brussels, 1940; ambassador, Madrid, 1943-44.

Paulucci de'Calboli, Raniero. Minister, Bern, 1912-19; ambassador, Tokyo, 1919-21; ambassador, Madrid, 1923-27.

Pedrazzi, Orazio. Minister, Prague, 1929-32; ambassador, Santiago, 1932-34; ambassador, Madrid, 1934-36.

Pietromarchi, Luca. Head, Ufficio Spagna, 1936-39, head, Ufficio Armistizio-Pace, Foreign Ministry, 1940-42. Memoirs.

Pignatti Morano, Bonifacio. Counselor, legation, Bern, 1919-23; minister, Luxemburg, 1923; minister, Prague, 1924-26; minister, Bern, 1926-29; ambassador, Buenos Aires, 1930-32; ambassador, Paris, 1932-35; ambassador, Vatican, 1935-39.

Pilotti, Massimo. Jurist; delegate, Paris Peace Conference, 1919, reparations conferences, Spa, Brussels, 1920, The Hague, 1929-30, Locarno Conference, 1925, naval conference, London, 1930, disarmament conference, Geneva, 1932-33; delegate, League of Nations, 1924-32, adjunct secretary general, 1932-37.

FOREIGN MINISTRY AND FOREIGN POLICY

Pirelli, Alberto. Industrialist and economic expert; delegate, Paris Peace Conference, 1919; member, Italian war debt commissions, Washington, London, 1925-26. Diaries.

Preziosi, Gabriele. Embassy, London, 1916-25, first secretary, 1919-22, counselor and chargé d'affaires, 1922-25; delegate, League of Nations, 1922; minister, Luxemburg, 1925-26; minister, Prague, 1926-28; minister, Bucharest, 1928-32; minister, Vienna, 1932-36; ambassador, Brussels, 1936-38; ambassador, Buenos Aires, 1938-40.

Prunas, Renato. Embassy, London, 1927-34, first secretary, 1933-34; counselor and chargé d'affaires, embassy, Paris, 1937-38; director general, Dept. of Overseas Affairs, 1939-43; minister, Lisbon, 1943; secretary general, Foreign Ministry, 1943-46.

Quaroni, Pietro. Embassy, Ankara, 1920-23; embassy, Buenos Aires, 1924-25; first secretary, embassy, Moscow, 1925-28; first secretary, legation, Durazzo, 1928-31; attached to Italian delegation, Stresa Conference, 1935; consul general, Salonika, 1935; minister, Kabul, 1936-43; diplomatic envoy, then ambassador, Moscow, 1944-46. Memoirs.

Renzetti, Giuseppe. Mussolini's personal emissary in Germany; consul, Leipzig, 1926; consul general, Berlin, 1936-41; minister, Stockholm, 1941-44.

Rocco, Guido. Secretary, Italian delegation, Cannes Conference, 1922; in charge of Fiume, Dalmation affairs, Foreign Ministry, 1923; secretary general, Italian delegation, Nettuno Conference, Venice, 1924-25; first secretary, embassy, Paris, 1925-28; delegate, League of Nations, 1925, 1928, 1930-31, secretary general, Italian delegation, 1935; counselor, embassy, Berlin, 1928-29; delegate, naval conference, London, 1930, disarmament conference, Geneva, 1932-33, Lausanne Conference, 1932; minister, Prague, 1932-35; ambassador, Ankara, 1944-45.

Rolandi Ricci, Vittorio. Ambassador, Washington, 1920-22.

Romano Avezzana, Camillo. Minister, Athens, 1918-19; ambassador, Washington, 1919-20; delegate, Portorose conference, 1921; ambassador, Paris, 1922-27.

Rosso, Augusto. Secretary, legation, Oslo, 1916-19; first secretary, legation, Athens, 1919-22; first secretary, embassy, Washington, 1922-25; counselor and chargé d'affaires, embassy, London, 1925-26; delegate, League of Nations, 1927-32, secretary general, Italian delegation, 1931; director general, Dept. of League of Nations Affairs, 1929-32; delegate, naval conference, London, 1930, disarmament conference, Geneva, 1932-33; ambassador, Washington, 1932-36; ambassador, Moscow, 1936-41; secretary general, Foreign Ministry, 1943. Memoirs.

Salandra, Antonio. Premier, 1914-16; delegate, Paris Peace Conference, 1919; head of Italian delegation, League of Nations, 1923-24. Papers (Archivio "Bonghi," Lucera; some published). Memoirs.

Salata, Francesco. Senator; minister, Vienna, 1936-37. Papers (Foreign Ministry).

Schanzer, Carlo. Delegate, League of Nations, 1920-21, 1924; foreign minister, 1922. Papers (Archivio Centrale dello Stato).

Scialoja, Vittorio. Jurist; delegate, Paris Peace Conference, 1919; foreign minister, 1919-20; delegate, League of Nations, 1921-32, head of Italian delegation, 1925-29; delegate, Locarno Conference, 1925.

Sforza, Carlo. Minister, Belgrade, 1916-19; high commissioner, Constantinople, 1919; undersecretary for foreign affairs, 1919-20; foreign minister, 1920-21, 1946-52; ambassador, Paris, 1922; delegate, Lausanne Conference, 1922-23; minister without portfolio, 1944-45. Papers (Foreign Ministry; Archivio Centrale dello Stato). Diary, memoirs.

Sola, Ugo. First secretary and chargé d'affaires, legation, Belgrade, 1923-25; first secretary, embassy, London, 1925-26; minister, Durazzo, 1927-30; minister, Bucharest, 1933-38; ambassador, Rio de Janeiro, 1939-42. Papers (Foreign Ministry).

Suvich, Fulvio. Nationalist and Fascist deputy; delegate, League of Nations, 1925-29, 1931-32, reparations conference, The Hague, 1929-30; undersecretary for foreign affairs, 1932-36; delegate, Stresa Conference, 1935; ambassador, Washington, 1936-38. Papers (private, Trieste; Foreign Ministry). Memoirs.

Talamo Atenolfi, Giuseppe. Legation, Budapest, 1921-24; secretary, legation, Vienna, 1924-25; first secretary, then counselor, embassy, Vatican, 1930-35; counselor, embassy, Paris, 1935-36; minister, Lima, 1936-37; minister, Sofia, 1937-40; minister, Budapest, 1940-41.

Taliani de Marchio, Francesco. First secretary, embassy, London, 1922-23; counselor, embassy, Constantinople, 1924-26; minister, The Hague, 1932-38; ambassador, Chungking, 1938-45. Papers (Foreign Ministry).

Tarchiani, Alberto. Minister of public works, 1944-45; ambassador, Washington, 1945-54. Memoirs.

Tittoni, Tommasco. Foreign minister, 1919; head of Italian delegation, Paris Peace Conference, 1919; head of Italian delegation, League of Nations, 1920. Papers (Foreign Ministry).

Tomasi della Torretta, Pietro. Minister, Vienna, 1919-21; foreign minister, 1921-22; president, conference on Burgenland, Venice, 1921; ambassador, London, 1922-27. Papers (Archivio Centrale dello Stato). Memoirs.

Umiltà, Carlo. Consul general, Split, 1921-24; minister, Panama and Costa Rica, 1927-30; consul general, Zagreb, 1930-37; minister, Bangkok, 1937-39; administrator, Kossovo province, Yugoslavia, 1941-43. Memoirs.

Vannutelli Rey, Luigi. Delegate, Paris Peace Conference, 1919, Conference of Ambassadors, 1920-21, reparations conference, London, 1922; counselor and chargé d'affaires, embassy, Paris, 1923-24; minister, Tangier, 1925-27; minister, Belgrade, 1927; minister, Prague, 1928-29; ambassador, Warsaw, 1931-32; ambassador, Brussels, 1932-36.

Varè, Daniele. First secretary, legation, Peking, 1918-20; delegate, reparations conferences, London, San Remo, 1920; League of Nations secretariat, 1920-23, delegate, 1924; minister, Luxemburg, 1926-27; minister, Peking, 1927-31; minister, Copenhagen, 1931-32; delegate, Spanish Civil War nonintervention committee, London, 1937-39. Memoirs.

Vinci Gigliucci, Luigi-Orazio. Delegate, Paris Peace Conference, 1919, Conference of Ambassadors, 1920, reparations conference, Spa, 1920; first secretary, legation, Budapest, 1921-24; secretary general, Italian delegation, League of Nations, 1926-29; minister, Addis Ababa, 1932-35; minister, Budapest, 1936-40; ambassador, Buenos Aires, 1940.

Viola di Campano, Guido. Delegate, League of Nations, 1922-24, secretary general, Italian delegation, 1925; secretary general, Russo-Italian conference for commercial treaty, 1923-24; minister, Copenhagen, 1927-31; minister, Teheran, 1931-32; minister, Belgrade, 1934-36; ambassador (to Franco), San Sebastian, 1937-39.

Vitetti, Leonardo. Embassy, Washington, 1925-29; delegate, League of Nations, 1931, secretary general, Italian delegation, 1932; delegate, disarmament conference, Geneva, 1932-33, naval conference, London, 1936; director general, Dept. of General Affairs, 1936-42; counselor, embassy, London, 1932-36; director general, Dept. of European and Mediterranean Affairs, 1942-43. Papers (Foreign Ministry). Diary.

Volpi di Misurata, Giuseppe. Financier; governor of Tripoli, 1922-25; minister of finance, 1925-28; head of Italian war debt commissions, Washington, London, 1925-26; president, Italo-Croatian economic commision, 1941-43. Papers (private, Venice and Rome; Archivio Centrale dello Stato; Foreign Ministry).

2. Foreign Diplomats in Italy, 1918-1945

Limited to representatives of those states that had significant dealings with Italy. Heads of diplomatic missions unless stated otherwise.

Albania
    Libohova, Ekrem, 1919, 1924-25.
    Mborja, Tewfik (chargé d'affaires), 1920-24.
    Djemil, Dino, 1926-32.
    Kodheli, Mark (chargé d'affaires), 1933-36.
    Djafer, Villa, 1936-38.
    Beratti, Demetrio, 1938-39.

Austria
    Kwiatkowski, Rémi, 1921-23.
    Egger-Möllwald, Lothar, 1923-33.
    Rintelen, Anton, 1933-34. Memoirs.
    Vollgruber, Alois, 1934-36.
    Berger-Waldenegg, Egon, 1936-38.

Belgium
    Van den Steen de Jehay, Werner, 1911-25.
    Della Faille de Leverghem, George, 1925-31.
    De Ligne, Albert, 1932-37.
    Kerchove de Denterghem, André, 1938-40.

Bulgaria
    Hadji-Michev, Pantcho, 1920-21.
    Radev, Gyorgy, 1922-29.
    Volkoff, Ivan, 1929-34.
    Pomeanov, Svetoslav, 1934-40.
    Karadjov, Detchko, 1940-44.

Czechoslovakia
    Kybal, Vlastimil, 1920-25. Memoirs.
    Mastný, Vojtech, 1925-32.
    Chvalkovský, Franz, 1932-38.

Ethiopia
    Mangascia, Wubié, 1929-32.
    Ghevre Yesus, Afawork (chargé d'affaires), 1932-35.

France
  Barrére, Camille, 1898-1924. Memoirs.
  Charles-Roux, François (counselor), 1921-24. Memoirs.
  Besnard, René, 1924-27.
  Dampierre, Robert de (first secretary), 1925-35. Memoirs.
  Beaumarchais, Maurice Caron de, 1928-32.
  Jouvenel, Henri de, 1932-33.
  Lagardelle, Hubert (special emissary), 1933-37. Memoirs.
  Chambrun, Louis Charles de, 1933-35. Memoirs.
  Cerruti, Vittorio, 1935-37.
  Blondel, Jules (chargé d'affaires), 1936-38.
  François-Poncet, André, 1938-40. Memoirs

Germany
  Berenberg-Gossler, Johann von, 1920-21.
  Prittwitz und Gaffron, Friedrich von (counselor), 1921-27. Memoirs.
  Neurath, Konstantin von, 1922-30.
  Schubert, Carl von, 1930-32.
  Hassell, Ulrich von, 1932-38. Diary.
  Mackensen, Georg von, 1938-43.
  Rintelen, Enno von (military attaché), 1937-43. Memoirs.
  Moellhausen, Eitel (counselor and chargé d'affaires) 1943. Then in diplomatic mission to Salò, 1943-45. Memoirs.
  Rahn, Rudolf (at Salò), 1943-45. Memoirs.

Great Britain
  Rennel Rodd, James, 1908-19. Memoirs.
  Buchanan, George, 1919-20.
  Mallet, Louis, 1920.
  Graham, Ronald, 1921-33.
  Drummond, Eric (Earl of Perth), 1933-39.
  Loraine, Percy, 1939-40.

Greece
  Coromilas, Lambros, 1913-20.
  Metaxas, Demetrio, 1920-22.
  Calergis, Demetrio, 1923-24.
  Carapanos, Alexandros, 1924-25.
  Mavroudis, Nicolas, 1925-30.
  Metaxas, Petros, 1931-39.
  Politis, Jean, 1940.

Hungary
  Nemes de Hidweg, Albert, 1921-26.
  De Hory, Andras, 1926-34.
  Villani, Frédéric de, 1934-41.
  Mariássy, Zoltan, 1941-44.

Japan
  Ijuin, Hidokichi, 1916-19.
  Otchiai, Kentaro, 1920-26.
  Nagai, Natsuzo, 1926.

FOREIGN MINISTRY AND FOREIGN POLICY

Matsuda, Michikazu, 1926-31.
Yoshida, Shigeru, 1931-32.
Matsushima, Hajime, 1932-34.
Sugimura, Yotaro, 1934-37.
Masaaki, Hotta, 1937-38.
Shiratori, Toshio, 1939.
Amau, Eiji, 1939-40.
Horikiri, Zenbei, 1940-42.
Hikada, Shinrakura, 1942-45

Poland
Skirmunt, Konstantin, 1919-21.
Zaleski, August, 1922-26.
Knoll, Roman, 1927-28.
Przezdziecki, Stefan, 1928-33.
Wysocki, Alfred, 1933-38.
Dlugoszowski, Boleslas, 1938-39.

Portugal
Leão, Eusebio, 1912-26.
Coelho, Henrique, 1927-28.
D'Oliveira, Alberto, 1929-31.
Castro, Augusto de, 1931-35.
Lobo d'Avila Lima, José, 1935-45.

Rumania
Lahovary, Alexandro, 1917-28.
Ghika, Demetriu, 1928-31.
Lugosianu, Ion, 1932-37.
Zamfirescu, Alexandro, 1938-39.
Bossy, Raoul, 1939-40.
Vojen, Victor, 1940-41.
Grigorcea, Basil, 1941-43.

Russia (Soviet Union)
Vorovskii, Vatslav (plenipotentiary), 1920-23.
Yurenev, Constantine, 1924-25.
Kerzhkentsev, Platone, 1925-26.
Kamenev, Leo, 1926-27.
Kurskii, Dimitri, 1928-32.
Potemkin, Vladimir, 1932-35.
Stein, Boris, 1935-39.
Gorelkin, Nicolas, 1939-41.

Spain
Villa Urrutia, Wenceslas, 1916-23.
Reynoso, Francisco de, 1923-24.
Muñoz y Menzano, Cipriano, 1924-31.
Alomar Villalonga, Gabriel, 1931-34.
Gomez Ocerin, Justo, 1934-36.
Garcia Conde, Pedro, 1937-41.

Groizard, E. (chargé d'affaires), 1941-42.
Cuesta Merello, Fernandez, 1942-45.

Switzerland
　Wagnière, Georges, 1918-36. Memoirs.
　Ruegger, Paul, 1936-42.
　Vieli, Pietro, 1942-45.

Turkey
　Suad Davaz, Mehmed, 1923-32.
　Vassif, Hussein, 1932-34.
　Ragip Baydur, Hussein, 1934-43.

United States
　Page, Thomas N., 1913-19.
　Jay, Peter A. (chargé d'affaires), 1920.
　Johnson, Robert U., 1920-21.
　Child, Richard W., 1921-24. Memoirs.
　Fletcher, Henry P., 1924-29.
　Garrett, John W., 1929-33.
　Long, Breckinridge, 1933-36.
　Phillips, William, 1936-41. Memoirs.

Yugoslavia
　Ristić, Mikhail, 1909-19.
　Antonievič, Voislav, 1919-26.
　Balugić, Jivoyin, 1926-27.
　Rakić, Milan, 1927-33.
　Ducić, Jovan, 1933-35.
　Antić, Milan, 1935-36.
　Christić, Bosko, 1937-41.

3. The Vatican and Major Power Diplomatic Representation, 1918-1945

(i) Papal Nuncios to the Major Powers

France
　Ceretti, Bonaventure, 1921-26.
　Maglione, Luigi, 1926-36.
　Valeri, Valerio, 1936-44.

Germany
　Pacelli, Eugenio, 1920-29.
　Orsenigo, Cesare, 1930-45.

Great Britain
　Godfrey, William (apostolic delegate), 1938-45.

Italy
　Borgongini Duca, Francesco, 1929-43.

FOREIGN MINISTRY AND FOREIGN POLICY

(ii) Diplomats at the Vatican

France
    Jonnart, Célestin, 1921-23.
    Doulcet, Augustin-Jean, 1923-28.
    Fontenay, Joseph de, 1928-32.
    Charles-Roux, François, 1932-40. Memoirs.
    Bérard, Léon, 1940-44.

Germany
    Bergen, Diego von, 1920-43.
    Weizsäcker, Ernst von, 1943-45. Papers (published). Memoirs.

Great Britain
    Salis, John-F-C. de, 1916-23.
    Russell, Odo, 1923-28.
    Randall, Alec (secretary), 1925-30. Memoirs.
    Chilton, Henry G., 1928-30.
    Forbes, George Ogilvie (chargé d'affaires), 1930-32.
    Kirkpatrick, Ivone (chargé d'affaires), 1932-33. Memoirs.
    Clive, Robert, 1933-34.
    Wingfield, Charles, 1934-35.
    Osborne, Francis d'Arcy, 1936-47.

Italy
    De Vecchi, Cesare, 1929-35.
    Pignatti Morano, Bonifacio, 1935-39.
    Alfieri, Dino, 1939-40. Memoirs.
    Attolico, Bernardo, 1940-42.
    Guariglia, Raffaele, 1942-43. Papers (Foreign Ministry). Memoirs.
    Ciano, Galeazzo, 1943. Papers (published, microfilm). Diary.

END NOTES

[1] A detailed and valuable exposition of Italy's Foreign Ministry on the eve of the First World War is the chapter "The Consulta: The Bureaucrats of Foreign Policy" in R.J.B. Bosworth, Italy: The Least of the Great Powers (London, 1979).

[2] For a factual account of the Italian Foreign Ministry's changing internal structure, see Luigi V. Ferraris, L'Amministrazione Centrale del Ministero degli esteri italiano nel suo sviluppo storico, 1848-1954 (#612). See also E. Serra, La diplomazia in Italia (#96).

[3] For the actual incumbents of Italian Foreign Ministry positions between 1918 and 1945, one may consult the following publications of the Ministero degli Affari Esteri: I documenti diplomatici italiani, series 6-9, appendices 1, 2 (#148), and intermittent issues of Annuario diplomatico and Elenchi del personale (#87). For lists of ministers and top officials going back to 1861, see Il Ministero degli Affari Esteri al servizio del popolo italiano (#93). The best

general biographical guides to diplomats in the twentieth century are the Almanach de Gotha (#81) and the Dictionnaire diplomatique, vol. 5 (#72).

⁴Roberto Cantalupo [Legatus], Vita diplomatica di Salvatore Contarini (#607).

⁵The compromise between Fascism and the Palazzo Chigi, and Grandi's role therein, are the themes of H. Stuart Hughes, "The Early Diplomacy of Italian Fascism," in The Diplomats (#521).

⁶F. Gilbert, "Ciano and His Ambassadors," ibid.

⁷The standard biographies of Ciano are Giordano B. Guerri, Galeazzo Ciano: Una vita 1903-1944, and Diulio Susmel, Vita sbagliata di Galeazzo Ciano (#614).

⁸This well-known epithet was coined by Roberto Cantalupo, Fu la Spagna: Ambasciata presso Franco (#355).

⁹Galeazzo Ciano, Diario, 1937-1943 (#287).

¹⁰On the rehabilitation of Italy's Foreign Ministry as part of the royal government, 1943-45, consult the official publication, Il Ministero degli Affari Esteri al servizio del popolo italiano, 1943-1949 (#93). For a case study, see Enrico Serra, La diplomazia italiana e la ripresa dei rapporti con la Francia, 1943-1945 (#881).

¹¹An authoritative account of the diplomacy of the Repubblica Sociale Italiana is F. William Deakin, The Six Hundred Days of Mussolini (#891).

¹²Information on the Italian Foreign Ministry is, of course, scattered throughout myriad publications. Most of the titles in the foregoing notes dwell expressly on the internal condition of the ministry and the status of the career diplomats. In the final analysis, however, the position of Italy's foreign service between 1918 and 1945 emerges most clearly from the memoirs of the diplomats themselves, even if they are sometimes chatty or tendentious. Recommended particularly: Raffaele Guariglia, Ricordi, 1922-1946 (#336); Dino Grandi, Il mio paese: Ricordi autobiografici and 25 luglio: Quarant'anni dopo (#334); Mario Donosti [Luciolli], Mussolini e l'Europa: La politica estera fascista and Palazzo Chigi: anni roventi. Ricordi di vita diplomatica italiana dal 1933 al 1948 (#330); Pietro Quaroni, Ricordi di un ambasciatore and Valigia diplomatica (#343); Daniele Varè, Laughing Diplomat and The Two Imposters (#348).

III. ARCHIVES, LIBRARIES, NEWSPAPERS

A. ITALIAN ARCHIVES AND ARCHIVAL MATERIAL

A few words, to begin with, on some general characteristics of Italian archives and libraries. On the whole, Italian scholarly repositories are not so well ordered as those in North America and the United Kingdom. Although individual archivists and librarians in Italy are as helpful as their counterparts the world over, they are often hedged by bureaucratic restrictions in the assistance they can render the researcher. Archival access should never be taken for granted. Therefore, it is always wise to write to the appropriate institution(s) well in advance of any research trip to Italy, and to bring any reply received on making the first visit to an archive. It is also useful to carry a letter of accreditation from university or embassy. The deposit of a piece of identification is usually required for physical entry into an Italian archive or library, and the foreign scholar should not be surprised, or alarmed, if asked to leave his or her passport at the entrance lobby. Desk and working space is at a premium in many research locations. The delivery of requested research material, especially of manuscript and unpublished sources, may seem leisurely. The norm in Italian archives is to order records one day and to receive them the next. In sum, the researcher entering the world of Italian archives for the first time is advised to allow ample time to circumvent roadblocks.

The preceding chapter has indicated that Italian foreign policy between 1918 and 1945 was often made and executed in unorthodox fashion. For much of the period the Foreign Ministry functioned under the pressure of Fascism, and for the last two years policy was determined as much by the British, Americans, and Germans as by the Italians themselves. It follows, therefore, that the trail to the sources of modern Italian foreign policy sometimes leads beyond conventional diplomatic documents, and even outside Italy. Yet, in the last resort, that policy was normally conducted through, if not always created within, the Italian Foreign Ministry, and the records of that harried body still constitute by far the most valuable source for Italy's international role from the end of one world war to the end of the next.

Selections from the Foreign Ministry files have been published in the series, I documenti diplomatici italiani (#148). But at present they provide irregular coverage of the years 1918-1945 and afford an inadequate substitute for research in the archives themselves.

ITALIAN FOREIGN POLICY, 1918-1945

1. Archivio Storico del Ministero degli Affari Esteri (ASME)

Piazzale della Farnesina
Roma 00194.

The historical archives of the Foreign Ministry are open from Monday to Friday between 9:30 AM and 3:00 PM, except for an annual summer closing of some six weeks beginning about the third week of July. They are housed in the ministry itself, which is situated about three miles northwest of the center of Rome, adjacent to a pretentious sports complex begun by Mussolini and still boasting some Fascist statuary. A white, rectangular, multistoried building of modern design, the post-World War II Foreign Ministry is architecturally as well as topographically some distance from both the Palazzo della Consulta and the Palazzo Chigi. Although ASME was founded in 1887 and its autonomy outside the state archival system recognized in 1902, the Italian Foreign Ministry lagged behind the other major European chancelleries in opening its records to scholars at large. But over the last decade and under the archive's most recent director, Professor Enrico Serra, the problem of accessibility has decreased tremendously and gratifyingly. Technically, fifty years must pass before official papers are made available and, in the case of material of a personal or private nature, seventy years. In practice, though, the serious scholar may reasonably expect to gain access to most documentation up to 1945. On the other hand, the researcher should be aware that access to ASME is not automatic. He or she should always write for permission in advance to Il Sovrintendente del Servizio Storico e Documentazione, specifying the topics to be investigated.

There exists no overall guide to ASME, although there are good general descriptions in the handbooks by Enrico Serra (#96). In addition, Professor Serra has published brief articles on ASME holdings in certain areas:

> "Les archives diplomatiques italiennes: Qu'y trouve-t-on sur les relations de l'Italie avec la France." Revue d'Histoire Diplomatique, 98 (1984): 166-79.

> "I fondi archivistici sulla Romania esistenti presso il Ministero degli esteri." Storia Contemporanea, 11 (1980): 305-17.

In the same genre see also

> Scheuch, Hanno. "Materialien zur österreichischen Geschichte 1919-30 im Archivio Storico Diplomatico (Rom)." Sterreichisches Staatsarchiv Mitteilungen, 39 (1986): 372-86.

By and large, however, the scholar must rely on several printed inventories to particular series of records held in ASME. Not readily available in libraries at large, they are normally consulted in the Foreign Ministry itself. These are indicated where appropriate in the following description of those collections pertaining to the period 1918-1945.

Archivio di Gabinetto (del Ministro degli Esteri)

The most important and confidential Ministero degli Esteri files selected for the scrutiny of the foreign minister and the secretary general, divided into two sections - ordinary and secret. Although some files go back to the liberal era, the archivio di gabinetto is most celebrated for its documentary record of Fascist diplomacy in the thirties. Particularly after 1936 when Ciano, in the absence of any secretary general since 1927, took the running of foreign affairs into his own hands, the gabinetto became the nerve center of the Foreign Ministry. It usurped the functions of other ministry departments, and its archivio became the depository, sometimes sole depository, of every significant document. For this reason it was the gabinetto files that Foreign Ministry Guariglia sought to keep out of Nazi German hands in September 1943. Some were dispatched to the Italian legation in Lisbon. In 1946 the American government compelled Italy to surrender these documents, which were microfilmed and are now available as follows:

Lisbon Papers. Microcopy T-816, 3 reels. U.S. National Archives, Washington.
Microfilm and photocopy, Foreign Office Library, Cornwall House, London.

The Lisbon papers span Ciano's tenure of the Foreign Ministry, 1936-43. In fact, they comprise for the most part papers that he had assembled for his own personal use (cf. Ciano papers - Rose Garden, p. 47). The leitmotiv of the Lisbon Papers is the Rome-Berlin Axis. They include Ciano's conversations with foreign statesmen and diplomats, and exchanges between Mussolini and Hitler. Many of the Lisbon documents have been published in the various editions of Ciano's Diplomatic Papers (#183), and in Hitler: Mussolini, lettere e documenti (#188). The originals of the Lisbon papers were returned after microfilming to Italy where they have been reintegrated into the gabinetto files in ASME.

A much larger selection of gabinetto papers from the 1930's, 275 boxes, was hidden from the Germans in the basement of the Palazzo dei Principi Lancellotti in Rome. They were recovered and deposited in ASME on the implementation of the Italian peace treaty in 1948. However, it was then discovered that many of these so-called Lancellotti papers had been badly damaged by damp. They were placed for safekeeping in "black boxes" (cassette nere), but the original documents, although rehabilitated, remain unfit for scholarly use and may be consulted only in special cases. They are, however, in the process of being microfilmed (see below).

Of the gabinetto records that in 1943 remained in the Palazzo Chigi the Germans abstracted some that have since vanished. Other gabinetto papers found their way into other Foreign Ministry collections such as the series affari politici described later.

From the above diverse sources the staff of the Foreign Ministry's historical archive has sought to reconstitute the entire archivio di gabinetto from 1923 to 1943, and within the past two years has begun to put the gabinetto records on microfilm. No date can be set for the completion of this ambitious but immensely valuable microfilm project. In ASME's sala di studi one may find "Documentazione su microfilm: Inventario," which will be updated as microfilming proceeds.

In view of the fragility and importance of the Lancellotti files, their microfilming has received some priority. Already filmed and inventoried are:

(1) "Lancellotti - Colloqui." 4 reels. Papers of premier, foreign minister, undersecretary, capo di gabinetto. Minutes of top-level talks held by Italian

politicians and diplomats with their foreign counterparts; personal memoranda and telegrams. One collection of files covers 1930-36, another 1936-43. Subdivided under the names of Mussolini, Grandi, Suvich, Aloisi, Ciano, Bastianini, De Peppo.

(2) "Carte Lancellotti - Ufficio di Coordinamento." 10 reels. Often called "le carte del Libro Verde" after the color of their index with which the filmed collection begins (a title bearing no connotation to parliamentary libri verdi, #147). These comprise the archivio segreto of the key agency in the fascisticized Foreign Ministry. Documentation mostly from 1936-43 and arranged by nation (Germany, Spain, Yugoslavia, Japan, Great Britain, Turkey, Albania, Austria and Hungary, France); some important files simply labelled "varie." Some material, e.g. regarding Germany 1943, illegible.

(3) Segreteria Generale files, 1920-27. 2 reels.

(4) Ufficio Trattati e Società delle Nazioni, 1920-27. 30 reels. Records of an office under the secretary general's jurisdiction deal with post-World War I reparations and war debts.

Some Lancellotti papers have been inventoried in preparation for filming. These include records of special offices created within the gabinetto after 1936, namely:

(5) Ufficio Spagna, 1936-39. 251 buste.

(6) Ufficio Armistizio e Territori Occupati (Armistizio-Pace), 1940-42. 20 buste.

Lancellotti files still to be organized and cataloged:

(7) Records of the archivio ordinario di gabinetto. Political papers organized under 23 countries, followed by a miscellaneous file of letters to Mussolini.

(8) Papers of the undersecretary's secretariat. Much material from the tenures of Suvich and Benini, though of limited value.

(9) Documentation with an I classification originating in Section I (Informazioni), a bureau established inside the gabinetto in 1935. Little if any of this intelligence material is likely to be made accessible to scholars in the near future.

Serie Affari Politici

The basic Foreign Ministry files of the General Department(s) for Political Affairs, the entire series comprehended in two guides: "Indice Archivio 'Affari Politici,' 1919-1930," and "Inventario della Serie Affari Politici, 1931-1945." Organization is primarily by country (including the Vatican and League of Nations in that category); material for each country is arranged chronologically with each year's holdings further subdivided according to topic. A few files deal not with one nation but with a specific question: for example, reparations, the Kellogg Pact, the Lateran Accords, the Dodecanese. Also worth mention are two sets of papers labelled "Etiopia - Fondo di Guerra" and "Spagna - Fondo di Guerra." There are some gaps in the serie politiche created by the German seizure in 1943 of certain political departmental files, which subsequently disappeared.

Serie Rappresentanze Diplomatiche

Files of Italian embassies. Inventories: "Londra, 1861-1950"; "Francia e Russia, 1861-1950"; "Berlino, 1867-1943, e Vienna, 1862-1938." The

ARCHIVES, LIBRARIES, NEWSPAPERS

Second World War wreaked havoc with some embassy files, notably those in Paris and Berlin; the latter were totally destroyed and copies in Rome do not go beyond 1936. Files of other embassies, not inventoried, are accessible to researchers. Arrangement of material chronological with broad topical subdivisions within each year.

Archivio Riservata della Segreteria Generale, 1943-1947

Key documentation for the rehabilitation of Italian diplomacy after Fascism's collapse. Inventory indicates material arranged both topically and by country.

Archivio della Cifra

Telegrams both sent and received. In two series - "gabinetto" or "segreti," and "ordinari" - the former much the more important. Organized according to country, then chronologically within each national category.

Archivio Conferenze

A range of subjects; useful for disarmament conferences.

Archivio della Conferenza della Pace

Full documentation regarding Italian delegation at the Paris Peace Conference, 1919.

Archivio Società delle Nazioni

On political issues involving the League of Nations, consult also serie politiche above.

Archivio Repubblica Sociale Italiana

Four reels of microfilm and inventory. For more substantive documentation of Salò regime, 1943-45, see Archivio Centrale dello Stato (p. 42).

Fondo archivistico "Serie Z - Contensioso"
Fondo "Commissione Centrale Arbitale per l'Emigrazione"

Inventories compiled to both collections of emigration records covering 1908-29. Both inventories published in the series Fonti per la Storia dell'Emigrazione, vols. II, VI (Rome, 1987).

"Serie D" (Direzione dell'Archivio Storico)

Published inventory (Rome, 1988) to material on development and functioning of ASME itself.

Archivi Storici del Soppresso Ministero dell'Africa Italiana

Italian colonial affairs were handled through the Foreign Ministry until 1912 when a separate Ministry of Colonies was created. In 1937 it was renamed the Ministry of Italian Africa. With the loss of empire during and after World War II, this ministry was abolished in 1953 and its archives lodged with ASME in 1959. These records are naturally of tangential relevance to the story of Italy's foreign policy. Libya figures prominently, and for a while planning for the Ethiopian conquest was conducted in the Colonial Ministry - although significantly lacking are the files on the Wal Wal incident of 1934 taken by the British at the close of World War II. A number of records on Ethiopia have been microfilmed (10 reels). ASME has a total of four inventories to this African material. A partial inventory is a published work:

Giglio, Carlo, ed. <u>Gli archivi storici del soppresso Ministero dell'Africa Italiana e del Ministero degli Affari Esteri dalle origini al 1922</u>. Leiden, 1971.

Other Ministry of Italian Africa records are in the Archivio Centrale dello Stato (p. 43).

Ministero della Cultura Popolare

About a thousand miscellaneous dossiers (some microfilmed on 2 reels) containing notes on foreign diplomats in Rome, foreign statesmen, anti-Fascist exiles, the propagation of Italy's viewpoint in the world press. Given the political reasons for which these files were assembled, they should be used with caution. Other Minculpop records are in the Archivio Centrale dello Stato (p. 43).

Fondi privati

The Italian Foreign Ministry does not possess extensive deposits of private papers. Such collections as it does own should not be taken to constitute an individual's entire private archive. Sometimes the contents are little more than copies of documents available in official files. The absence of inventories makes it difficult to gauge the value of this material.

For the organizational purposes of this guide all private papers relevant to Italian diplomacy, 1918-1945, are collected and cited in alphabetical order on pp. 47–52. There one may find specific Foreign Ministry holdings under the names of:

Aldrovandi Marescotti, Luigi
Contarini, Salvatore
Grandi, Dino
Guariglia, Raffaele
Salata, Francesco
Sforza, Carlo
Sola, Ugo
Sonnino, Sidney
Suvich, Fulvio
Taliani, Francesco

ARCHIVES, LIBRARIES, NEWSPAPERS

Tittoni, Tommaso
Vitetti, Leonardo
Volpi di Misurata, Giuseppe

2. Ministero della Difesa

Ufficio Storico dello Stato Maggiore dell'Esercito
Via Lepanto, 5
Roma 00192.

Ufficio Storico dello Stato Maggiore della Marina Militare
Via Romeo Romei, 5
Roma 00136.

Ufficio dello Stato Maggiore dell'Aeronautica
Piazza dell'Aeronautica
Roma 00185.

Like the Foreign Ministry, Italy's Ministry of Defence possesses its own distinct archives - three of them, in fact, for the army, navy, and air force, each at a different location in Rome. And like the files of the Ministry of Italian Africa, those of the armed forces may be regarded as peripheral to Italian diplomacy. But, of course, they can throw fascinating light on the making of foreign policy in crucial episodes - for instance, in the Corfu crisis, disarmament negotiations, the Ethiopian affair, and, above all, the adoption and then rejection of nonbelligerency in 1939-40. Moreover, some information about Italy's intelligence activities can be gleaned from the service ministry files. Although as state archives the three military historical offices operate formally according to the fifty- and seventy-year rules of access, the researcher may encounter obstacles. A partial inventory of material in the service archives with exclusive reference to North Africa is

Giglio, Carlo, ed. <u>Gli archivi storici del Ministero della Difesa (Esercito, Marina, Aeronautica) dalle origini al 1922.</u> Leiden, 1972.

Some Italian military records, however, are to be found outside the <u>uffici storici</u> of the services. Before the transformation of the Ministero della Guerra into the Ministero della Difesa, a number of armed forces papers were deposited in the Archivio Centrale dello Stato (p. 43).

Most readily accessible of all, though, is a vast collection of microfilm:

Italian Armed Forces Records. Microcopy T-821, 490 reels. U.S. National Archives, Washington.
Cabinet Office, Hepburn House, London; Imperial War Museum, Lambeth, London. Small selection of films divided between two venues.

Between 1943 and 1945 the Germans sequestered a large quantity of Italian military records, mostly dealing with the World War II period, at their <u>Aktensammelstelle Süd</u> near Munich where they were captured by the Americans in 1945. Together with other military documents seized inside Italy, they were taken to the U.S. where some 60 percent of the total haul was microfilmed. The originals were returned to Italy and now reside in the uffici storici of the Ministry of Defence. An index to the microfilm is U.S. National Records and Archives Service, Guide to the Records of the Italian Armed Forces, 3 parts (Washington, 1967), also available as Microcopy T-94, 1 reel.

3. Archivio Segreto del Vaticano

Città del Vaticano
Holy See S.C.V. 00120.

Before leaving the subject of ministerial archives, a word is in order about the Vatican's diplomatic records. These are now open to scholars up to 1922, the end of Benedict XV's pontificate. The files of the Segreteria di Stato are equipped with two finding aids:
 (1) The Protocolli itemize every document despatched and received by the Papacy's diplomatic office. The listing is in strict chronological order; vols. 414-74 of Protocolli run from Nov. 1918 to Dec. 1922.
 (2) The Rubricelle classify the same documentation but by topic in alphabetical order for each year. In this category is a special index, "Guerra Mondiale," which cites material up to 1921.
 There is also a general index to private papers held in the Archivio Segreto Vaticano, although none appear pertinent to interwar diplomacy.
 It might be observed here that the Vatican has seen fit to publish some of its records dealing with the Second World War (#208). In addition, one occasionally gleans something of Vatican diplomacy from the appropriate files in ASME.
 For a general account of Vatican archives, see Maria L. Ambrosini, The Secret Archives of the Vatican (Boston, 1969), Ital. trans. L'archivio segreto del Vaticano (Milan, 1972).

4. Archivio Centrale dello Stato (ACS)

Piazzale degli Archivi
EUR, Roma 00144.

Among institutions ACS is, after ASME, the most fruitful source of archival material for Italian foreign policy. As the national depository for state papers, ACS is Italy's counterpart of the U.S. National Archives and British Public Record Office, and yet it is less than these in some ways. For one thing, the National Archives and P.R.O. house all that part of their national records open to the public, whereas ACS is deprived of a substantial segment of Italy's official documentation. It has been observed that the foreign and service ministries possess their own archives, as does the Italian parliament. Furthermore, ACS is younger than its Anglo-American peers and lacks the stature that time alone can confer. In fact, its very name and autonomy date only from 1953. On the other hand, ACS has gradually been growing in repute. The legal framework within which ACS, and indeed all Italy's state archives, operate was set in 1962-63 (Legge di delega, 17 Dec. 1962, no. 1409; Decreto del Presidente della Repubblica, 30 Sept. 1963, no. 1863). This legislation aimed at raising the general standards of the archives and, in particular, at extending archival jurisdiction into the realm of private papers. And indeed, over the last three decades ACS has accelerated markedly its acquisition of both public and private records. It has become a lively center of scholarly enquiry to the point that concern is beginning to be expressed at the wear and tear of the more popular items of original material.

The Archivio Centrale dello Stato is located in a modern building in EUR, the new "city" on the southern outskirts of Rome inaugurated by Mussolini and completed after the Second World War. It is open Monday to Friday, 9:00 AM - 5:30 PM, Saturday, 9:00 AM - 1:30 PM, and is closed during August. Applications to consult documentation in ACS should be made to Il Sovrintendente, Dirigente Generale, and permission is granted jointly by the Ministry of the Interior and the Archivio Centrale. Restrictions on documents are applied flexibly. While by law records are accessible only after fifty years, in reality the cut-off date is 1945.

ACS will send on request its pamphlet in the series, Itinerari Archivisti Italiani, which describes its nature, function and, in broad terms, its holdings. This may be supplemented by Costanzo Casucci, "Saggio per una bibliografia dell'Archivio centrale dello Stato," Rassegna degli Archivi di Stato, 31 (1971): 335-91, which lists 337 titles based on research in ACS and gives actual sources used. See also Renato Grispo's brief "L'Archivio centrale dello Stato," L'Urbe, 44 (1979): 34-39.

Holdings in ACS of relevance to Italian foreign policy, 1918-1945, are as follows:

Real Casa: Ufficio del Primo Aiutante di Campo

Only a small part of a large royal archive, most of the remainder being in the hands of the descendants of Italy's royal family (see under Vittorio Emanuele III, p. 52). This selection concerns mostly routine and formal business, but with occasional political and diplomatic references.

Presidenza del Consiglio dei Ministri: Atti

Papers of the premier's office are divided into three groups: those of the gabinetto of the president of the Council of Ministers; those from individual ministries represented on the council, including the Foreign Ministry; and a general collection with sections devoted to various foreign states among its list of alphabetically arranged topics. Since the foreign and service ministries have abstracted the meatiest material for their own archives, not much on foreign policy, either in quantity or quality, is to be unearthed in these files. On the other hand, all other ministries deposit their records with ACS, and the researcher into the domestic roots of Italian diplomacy will discover here a basic documentation of Italy's internal policies.

Verbali del Consiglio dei Ministri

Fifty-nine volumes span the years 1859-1951. A self-evidently valuable source, although it should be remembered that under Fascism discussion of national policy was conducted as much in the Grand Council of Fascism (for verbali see Segreteria Particolare del Duce, below) as in the Council of

Ministers itself. (Minutes of the Council of Ministers meetings from 1938 onwards are deposited in the Presidenza del Consiglio: Atti, above.)

Segreteria Particolare del Duce, 1922-1943

Unquestionably, for the purposes of this research guide, the most important collection in ACS. On its significance and scope, consult

> De Felice, Loretta. "Un fondo bibliografico, d'interesse documentario, conservato nell'Archivio Centrale dello Stato." Storia Contemporanea, 14 (1983): 473-517.
>
> See also Gaetano Contini, "Current State of Fascist Materials in the Archivio Centrale dello Stato," Italian Quarterly, no. 93 (1983): 65-71.

Mussolini's private secretariat contains material on a wide variety of topics. Much of it pertains to individuals, and the names of foreign statesmen, notably Hitler, are frequently encountered. The emphasis on foreign affairs in Fascism's second decade is inevitably reflected in the Duce's most confidential files. They are in two parts. The carteggio ordinario runs to almost 2,500 containers, the subject of each duly noted in an extensive filing-card index. But the heart of the collection resides in the carteggio riservato in 134 containers, of which six hold verbali of the Fascist Grand Council. Consultation of the carteggio riservato is facilitated by a printed inventory kept in the sala di studio of ACS. Mussolini's confidential files for 1943-45 are found under Repubblica Sociale Italiana, as follows.

Repubblica Sociale Italiana, 1943-1945

In a sense the continuation of the Segreteria Particolare del Duce, above, the bulk of this material in 136 containers is listed as carteggio riservato e ordinario. Naturally, the relationship between the neo-Fascist republic and the German occupation authorities in northern Italy is featured. There are seven containers of Ministry of Popular Culture records, 1944-45, but perhaps symptomatic of the Salò regime's impossible diplomatic situation, only one under the heading of Ministry of Foreign Affairs, 1944-45.

At this point it should be noted that there exists an important microfilm collection whose nucleus consists of the material in ACS just discussed:

> Personal Papers of Benito Mussolini. Together with Some Official Records of the Italian Foreign Office and the Ministry of Culture, 1922-44, Received by the Department of State. Microcopy T-586, 318 reels. U.S. National Archives, Washington.
> Microfilm and photocopy designated "Italian Documents," Foreign Office Library, Cornwall House, London; St. Antony's College, Oxford.

This microfilm is the result of an Anglo-American project undertaken at the close of World War II to film as much as practically possible of the Segreteria Particolare del Duce, both from the Fascist era, 1922-43, and from the two-year span of the Italian Social Republic. When in September 1943 Mussolini set up his neofascist republic in northern Italy, he took away from Rome the carteggio riservato and a little of the carteggio ordinario, and housed these segments of his private secretariat in the Villa Feltrinelli, the seat of his new administration on Lake Garda. In 1945 the Allies seized those documents left behind in Villa Feltrinelli, recovered some that Mussolini had with him when captured by partisans (the so-called handbag files), and picked up sundry other records in northern Italy. All were filmed before being released to the Italians in 1948.

As the microcopy title indicates, the contents represent an eclectic assortment, for many ministry documents were deposited in Mussolini's personal papers. The collection includes 139 reels of material from the Segreteria particolare, virtually the entire carteggio riservato. Among the remaining reels are 24 of Italian Foreign Ministry records; these contain some valuable material - for example, some of the secret reports on 62 foreign countries drawn up annually in the 1930's in the Palazzo Chigi, and Anfuso's reports from Berlin, 1943-45. In addition, there are 8 reels of documentation from the Italian Armistice Commission in France, 6 from the Ministry of Italian Africa, 10 from the Ministry of Popular Culture, and 18 from the Japanese embassy in Rome (absent from the St. Antony's College collection). Although there is a concentration of documents from the years 1943-44, such is the size of the collection that there yet remains much material from the earlier Fascist era.

Both American and British microfilm sets have indices attached, but these do not correspond to the inventories with the original material in ACS.

Ministero della Cultura Popolare

Germane to Italian foreign policy, given Fascism's propensity for mixing propaganda and diplomacy, are these 482 boxes with an inventory attached. Although the Ministry of Popular Culture was not formally created until 1937, its files go much further back in time. Minculpop records are also located in ASME and the Personal Papers of Benito Mussolini (pp. 38, 42).

Ministero dell'Africa Italiana

Twenty-six containers of records from the Ministry's General Department of Political Affairs, 1927-43. The rest of the Ministry of Italian Africa files are housed in ASME (p. 38). Some also appear in Mussolini's personal papers (p. 42).

Ministero della Difesa

Before the establishment of the Ministry of Defence, the armed forces deposited with ACS the files of both the naval ministry's gabinetto, 1934-50, and the air ministry's gabinetto, 1926-54, as well as some minor documents from the Ministero della Guerra. Scholars wishing to view this material may expect to have their request vetted by the defence ministry.

Carteggio di Personalità

It has already been remarked that the archival law of 1963 did not confine itself to the subject of governmental and official documents but also took account of private papers. Specifically, it enabled archival authorities to designate collections in private hands "of noteworthy historical interest," which obligated owners to abide by reasonable archival practices, and in extreme cases private archives could be compulsorily transferred to the state. In fact, the objective was to persuade owners of private papers to place them in public archives. Without accomplishing all that its framers intended, the 1963 legislation none the less fostered a climate of opinion in which Italy's archives might grow in size and importance. ACS, above all, has benefited from this atmosphere to build up its holdings of private papers, the majority of which are inventoried.

However, in order to avoid too much cross-referencing, all private papers relevant to Italy's foreign policy, 1918-1945, are cited together alphabetically in a later section of this guide. ACS collections are there listed under the names of:

Alfieri, Dino
Badoglio, Pietro
Barzilai, Salvatore
D'Annunzio, Gabriele
De Bono, Emilio
Giannini, Amadeo
Giolitti, Giovanni
Grandi, Dino
Graziani, Rodolfo
Mussolini, Benito
Nitti, Francesco Saverio
Orlando, Vittorio Emanuele
Pantaleoni, Maffeo
Schanzer, Carlo
Sforza, Carlo
Sonnino, Sidney
Tomasi della Torretta, Pietro
Volpi di Misurata, Giuseppe

5. Economic Archives

Over the past twenty years something of a new dimension has been added to diplomatic history by the exploration of the archives of industrial and financial concerns. It is a truism that economic interests can and do shape international politics. Italy has been no exception to this rule, as explained by Enrico Serra, "Financial and Economic Factors in Foreign Policy: The Italian Example," Journal of European Economic History, 16 (1987): 607-20, although most of his instances are drawn from the pre-World War I years. In the interwar period it is well known that certain economic interests encouraged Italian Nationalist and Fascist expansionism. They calculated that they stood to gain from the extension of Italian influence along the Dalmatian coastline, in Asia Minor, in the Mediterranean at large, and in parts of Africa, as well as from participation in programs of rearmament and national economic mobilization. It is in this context that economic archives may be expected to throw light on the formulation of both liberal and Fascist foreign policy.

Over the years Italian business houses have been reluctant to open their records to scholars because, it has been suggested, they feared the resultant studies linking capitalism and Fascism. Of late, however, distinct signs of change have appeared. In part, this is the result of mounting scholarly interest. See for example, Franco Bonelli, "Per la conservazione degli archivi delle imprese: Prime osservazioni e proposte," Rassegna degli Archivi di Stato, 33 (1973): 10-18; Michele Lungonelli, "Gli archivi d'impresa," Passato e Presente, (Jan.-June 1983): 173-78. In addition, an entire issue of the Rassegna degli Archivio di Stato, 44 (May-Dec. 1984), ed. Paola Carucci, was given over to "Gli archivi di impresa." Herein were printed papers delivered at an Ansaldo-sponsored conference in Genoa, 1982, on the state of business archives in various countries; Renato Grispo presented "Gli archivi economici in Italia," pp. 466-79. Briefer contributions were also made on specific Italian economic archives, some of which are quoted below. This issue of the Rassegna closes with appendices listing "Archivi di impresa conservati negli archivi di stato italiani," and "Archivi di impresa dichiarati di notevole interesse storico."

Furthermore, first tentative steps have been taken toward a national inventory of Italian economic archives. See Consiglio Nationale delle Ricerche e Soprintendenza Archivistica per la Toscana, Archivi di imprese industriali in Toscana (Florence, 1982); Soprintendenza Archivistica per il Lazio, Guida degli archivi economici a Roma e nel Lazio, ed. Maria Guercio, Quaderni della Rassegna degli Archivi di Stato, no. 54 (Rome, 1987).

Italy's business community, for its part, has responded to all this scholarly activity by liberalizing its archival practices markedly, in some cases to the extent of disseminating brief archival descriptions. Following is a list of industrial concerns with an interest in foreign policy whose archives are known to be accessible, with such guides as exist:

Archivio Alfa Romeo, Milan. D. Bigazzi, "L'archivio della Direzione generale dell'Alfa Romeo, 1933-1945," Società e Storia, 2/4 (1979): 215-21.

Archivio Storico Ansaldo, Genoa. Direzione Relazioni Esterne Ansaldo, Ansaldo Archivio Storico (Genoa, 1985); Franco Bonelli, "L'archvio storico Ansaldo," Rassegna degli Archivi di Stato, 44 (1984): 631-46.

Centro Storico FIAT, Turin.

Archivio IRI (Istituto per la Ricostruzione Industriale), Rome.

Archivio Storico ITALSIDER, Genoa. Luciano Segreto, Archivio storico nuova italsider (Genoa, 1985).

Archivio Storico Pirelli, Milan. D. Bigazzi, "L'archivio storico delle industrie Pirelli," in Quaderni di Documentazione Regionale della Regione Lombardia, no. 9 (Milan 1980), pp. 144-50.

Archives of financial institutions relevant to foreign policy-making:

Archivio Banca Commerciale Italiana, Rome. Bernardo Crippa, "Archivio storico della Banca Commerciale Italiana," Rassegna degli Archivi di Stato, 44 (1984): 703.

Sezione Storica della Banca d'Italia, Rome. Sergio Manzano and Benedetto Valente, "La sezione storica della Banca d'Italia," Rassegna degli Archivi di Stato, 44 (1984): 671-76. Also holds Archivio di Alberto De Stefani (see next section).

Finally, mention should be made of the Fondazione Luigi Einaudi in Turin, which has amassed a considerable quantity of economic records, including the papers of F.S. Nitti and Paolo Thaon Di Revel (see below).

6. Private Papers

Fundamentally, there are two categories of collections of private papers - those in the public domain and those held in private hands.

Of the former located in archives and libraries, the majority are to be found in either the Foreign Ministry (its <u>archivio storico</u> or the Commissione per la Pubblicazione dei Documenti Diplomatici Italiani also lodged in the Ministero degli Esteri) or the Archivio Centrale dello Stato. For observations on private papers in these two sources, see pp. 38, 43.

Privately held papers pose something of a problem. It is a time-honored Italian practice for a statesman or senior public servant to take with him on leaving office a quantity of papers, both personal and official, sometimes to assist in the composition of memoirs. These collections often remain in his family's possession indefinitely, and not infrequently vanish altogether. The archival law of 1963 sought to curb these practices, and not without some effect. Nevertheless, old traditions die hard, particularly in Italy's conservative diplomatic community. The deposit of private papers in a public institution, at least after the original owner's death - a common enough practice elsewhere in the west - is still not the norm in Italy. Thus, one can be sure that a considerable number of Italian records continue in private hands. The difficulty is to ascertain their scattered whereabouts, for regrettably there is no Italian equivalent of the U.S. <u>National Union Catalog of Manuscript Collections</u> or the British Historical Manuscripts Commission's National Register of Archives wherein information might be collated. The next task is to gain access to those family papers of which scholars are aware, and here it must be said that Italian owners of private collections are not famous for their sympathy with the scholar's right to see and know. For these reasons some of the entries in the list of personal papers that follows must remain tantalizingly imprecise. On the other hand, it should not be concluded that Italian private archives are axiomatically closed to researchers. Some are open to all bona fide researchers; others have been made available to individual scholars on request.

Yet, the truth of the matter is that Italian private archives, more than those of most western nations, invite scholarly detective work - not only to gain entry to those <u>fondi</u> to which the scholarly community is already alert but also to uncover sources hitherto unknown. There are more than a few personalities of twentieth-century Italian diplomacy whose presumptive personal papers have not yet come to light. One thinks, for instance, of two A's - Attolico and Anfuso - both of whom played key if contrasting roles in the Rome-Berlin Axis, and who ostensibly left behind no private records. Archival source material for Italian foreign policy is not exactly in short supply, but it is to be anticipated that the future will disclose still more.

Papers of the following personages are known to exist. For details of holders of diplomatic posts, consult chapter II, appendix I.

ARCHIVES, LIBRARIES, NEWSPAPERS

Aldrovandi Marescotti, Luigi. (1) ASME: papers used in I Documenti diplomatici italiani, 1929-30.

(2) Hoover Institution on War, Revolution and Peace, Palo Alto, CA: one folder of diary and memoirs, published (#281).

Alfieri, Dino. ACS, 13 files (1915-60).

Aloisi, Pompeo. Papers in family hands, Rome, include diary re Albanian affairs in the 1920's and the Ethiopian issue in the 1930's; portion for 1932-36 published (#282).

Badoglio, Pietro. ACS, 24 files, 10 boxes (1925-46): extensive archive of marshal whose career spanned two world wars. As chief of general staff, 1925-40, prominent when military calculations taken into account, e.g. Ethiopian crisis, World War II; head of royal government, 1943-44.

Bastianini, Giuseppe. In absence of any Bastianini papers in any public archive, those held by descendants in Milan could be of some scholarly significance.

Bonin Longare, Lelio. The family archive near Vicenza goes back for several centuries and probably contains papers relevant to post-World War I diplomacy.

Bonomi, Ivanoe. Papers of premier before and after Fascism in Archivio di Stato, Mantua; inventory in ACS.

Caetani, Gelasio. (1) Fondazione Caetani, Palazzo delle Botteghe Oscure, Rome: family papers with regrettably little on diplomatic activity. See Francesco Gabrieli, "Le ultimi Caetani," Nuova Antologia, 506 (May-Aug. 1969): 48-57.

(2) Hoover Institution on War, Revolution and Peace, Palo Alto, CA: 3 boxes of miscellaneous papers (1906-34).

Ciano, Galeazzo. (1) Hoover Institution on War, Revolution and Peace, Palo Alto, CA: typescript (not original) of diary, 1937-43. See Ciano's published Diario (#287).

(2) Rose Garden Papers. Microcopy T-120, reel 4597. U.S. National Archives, Washington.
Photostats, Foreign Office Library, Cornwall House, London.

Anticipating publication of his diary, Ciano assembled certain vital papers as supporting evidence. These passed into German hands but vanished at the end of the Second World War. However, a German translation, together with a few sheets of the Italian originals, was unearthed in a German rose garden. They were integrated into the Allied microfilm of captured German Foreign Ministry records (Microcopy T-120, p. 67). These 223 Rose Garden papers, which illuminate Italo-German relations primarily, are almost identical to those Palazzo Chigi records sent to Lisbon to avoid capture by the Nazis in 1943 (p. 35). Many have also been published in Ciano's Diplomatic Papers (#183), and Hitler: Mussolini, lettere e documenti (#188).

Colosimo, Gaspare. Archivio di Stato, Catanzaro: 12 files of diary and documentary material of Italy's minister of colonies, 1916-19, throw light on colonial questions at the Paris Peace Conference. Consult Carlo Gasbarri, "La politica africana dell'Italia nelle carte di Colosimo," Africa, 28 (1973): 439-60; Pietro Pastorelli, "Le carte Colosimo," Storia e Politica, 15 (1976): 363-76. Some of this material has been published: see Colosimo, Opera (#359); Colapietra (#163).

Contarini, Salvatore. ASME: small package of papers, mostly duplicates of official documents.

D'Annunzio, Gabriele. (1) Archivio della Fondazione del Vittoriale, Gardone.

(2) ACS, 8 buste (1919-37).

Selections from both the large archive at Gardone and the ACS holdings have been published in Carteggio D'Annunzio-Mussolini (#188). D'Annunzio was spokesman for the sort of nationalism that informed much Italian diplomacy under Fascism; also architect of post-World War I Fiume crisis.

De Bono, Emilio. ACS, 2 boxes (1915-44): papers of the Fascist general charged with launching Ethiopian campaign contain an interesting diary for 1935, a version of which has been published (#159).

De Bosdari, Alessandro. Archivio di Stato, Bologna: unpublished memoir on Germany, 1922-26, quoted in I documenti diplomatici italiani.

De Marinis, Alberto. ACS, 1 file (1920-37); Italian general on League of Nations commission supervising Upper Silesian plebiscite in 1920.

De Stefani, Alberto. Archivio in Sezione Storica della Banca d'Italia: papers of Mussolini's first finance minister, 1922-25, for reparations, war debt questions.

Federzoni, Luigi. Papers of Mussolini's first colonial minister, in family's possession in Rome, reputedly do not contribute much on foreign affairs.

Frassati, Alfredo. Papers in hands of daughter in Turin; most now published (#185).

Galli, Carlo. Archivio dell'ambasciatore Carlo Galli, Venice: Galli kept a diary at least for his years of service in Yugoslavia. Excerpts published (#292).

Gasparini, Jacopo. Papers in care of Professor Renzo De Felice, Città Universitaria, Rome. Open to serious researchers who give De Felice advance notice, 6 folders of records of colonial administrator and governor of Eritrea after the First World War; material on Anglo-Italian relations in the Middle East.

Giannini, Amadeo. ACS, 16 boxes (1890-1960): long service and advantageous position within Italian Foreign Ministry make this an important collection.

Giolitti, Giovanni. ACS, 17 files, 55 boxes (1858-1928): papers of oft-times premier whose final term was in 1920-21. Many have been published (#186).

Grandi, Dino. (1) ASME: large and important archive that bears comparison with papers left behind by Mussolini and Ciano. Renzo De Felice provides an evaluation and description in "I diari, le memorie e le carte di Dino Grandi," <u>Rassegna degli Archivi di Stato</u>, 43 (1983): 371-79; also published with Eng. trans., <u>Italian Quarterly</u>, no. 93 (1983): 49-64.

A few years before his death Grandi placed 173 folders and 207 dossiers of his papers at the disposal of Professor Renzo De Felice to assist the latter in composing his monumental biography of Mussolini (#558), on the understanding that the entire archive ultimately be deposited in ASME. Virtually all, and certainly all important diplomatic, documents have now been transferred to the Foreign Ministry's historical archive.

On fleeing Italy in 1943, Grandi hid three sets of papers, of which two survived to comprise this collection. The archive is in six sections; most of the material concerning Grandi's diplomatic activities, 1925-39, is in the second section. Pride of place goes to a diary Grandi kept conscientiously while undersecretary and foreign minister. Later, after 1932, entries become intermittent (mostly 1937-40), but instead Grandi assembled copious documentation from his London embassy. An unusual enclosure is a "Summary of Adrian Dingli's Action" written by a London barrister who served as unofficial but important liaison between the Italian embassy and Prime Minister Chamberlain (see Quartararo, #814).

A selection of the Grandi papers on negative film is accessible to North American scholars at Georgetown University Library, Washington. These concentrate on matters affecting the United States but include the diary for 1929-32 and the Dingli memorial. For printed extract from Grandi diary, see #293.

(2) ACS, 1 <u>busta</u> (1925-43): mainly diplomatic material but dwarfed in size and significance by ASME collection above.

Graziani, Rodolfo. ACS, 93 files, 5 packets (1923-48): mostly military records of marshal whose exploits lay in colonial field, including Ethiopia, 1936-41. Some of Graziani's papers from 1943-45, when he rallied to Mussolini at Salò, are elsewhere in ACS under <u>Repubblica Sociale Italiana</u> (p. 42).

Guariglia, Raffaele. Ministero degli Affari Esteri, Commissione per la Pubblicazione dei Documenti Diplomatici Italiani: two containers of papers, including some copies of files from the Paris embassy, 1938-40.

Mussolini, Benito. ACS, 48 buste (1922-45).

Of special interest are a small set of letters in Mussolini's own hand and some originals of the "carte della valigia" (handbag files), that is, such documents from two briefcases the Duce carried with him on his last odyssey, April 1945, as have been recovered. Some of these papers were published after World War II in mysterious circumstances in Hitler: Mussolini, lettere e documenti (#188). Also in this collection are papers from the Segreteria Particolare del Duce (p. 42).

Nitti, Francesco Saverio. (1) ACS, 50 boxes (1894-1926): papers of post-World War I premier faced with D'Annunzian Fiume crisis; later, opponent of Fascist hypernationalism.

(2) Fondazione Luigi Einaudi, Turin: some 7,000 documents of Nitti's activities, 1917-23. See St. Marinotti Dorigo, ed., "L'Archivio Francesco Saverio Nitti," Annali della Fondazione Luigi Einaudi, 8 (1974): 375-437.

Orlando, Vittorio Emanuele. ACS, 111 files (1901-50): papers of premier during First World War and Paris Peace Conference.

Pantaleoni, Maffeo. ACS, 1 busta (1877-1924): papers of well-known Italian economist in service of League of Nations in its early days.

Pariani, Alberto. Civiche Raccolta Storiche, Milan: 46 quaderni (1934-39) of General Pariani, successively deputy chief and chief of staff of Italy's army, and then undersecretary for war, contain much political material, including communications with Mussolini and Ciano.

Petacci, Clara. ACS, 18 boxes (1932-45): papers of Mussolini's mistress include diaries, correspondence with the Duce.

Salandra, Antonio. Archivio di Communale "Ruggero Bonghi," Lucera; see especially collection "Vertenza italo-greca" on Salandra's role at League of Nations in Corfu crisis, 1923. Note that Salandra's papers in ACS have nothing after 1917.

Salata, Francesco. ASME: papers of rumored architect of Austro-German Gentleman's Agreement of July 1936.

Schanzer, Carlo. ACS, 35 files, 1 box, 18 volumes (1912-50): papers of last pre-Fascist foreign minister and League of Nations delegate.

Sforza, Carlo. (1) ASME: large and principal collection of Sforza papers deposited in Foreign Ministry's archives by Sforza family. In process of organization, classification.

(2) ACS, 10 boxes (1913-52).

Sola, Ugo. Ministero degli Affari Esteri, Commissione per la Pubblicazione dei Documenti Diplomatici Italiani: papers on Albanian affairs in the 1920's quoted in I documenti diplomatici italiani, though mostly official files.

ARCHIVES, LIBRARIES, NEWSPAPERS

Sonnino, Sidney. (1) Archivio Sonnino, Montespertoli, Florence.

Vast archive of some quarter of a million pieces covering Sonnino's entire term as foreign minister, 1914-19, and including a diary that runs to 1922. Typical of the fate that can overtake private papers in Italy, these were lost in a family home after Sonnino's death. Rediscovered behind a cupboard only in 1967 through the efforts of Professors Giorgio Spini and Benjamim F. Brown, the vital nucleus of the collection is now available on microfilm:

Sonnino Papers. 54 reels. University Microfilms, Ann Arbor, MI, 1968.

About 100,000 documents have been filmed. Most deal with the World War I years. Only 2 of 27 reels of "telegrammi in arrivo" are from the Italian delegation to the Paris Peace Conference, and only 1 of 19 reels of "telegrammi in partenza" is to Paris. Besides these Consulta records, there are papers from Sonnino's personal files that deal particularly with problems of national self-determination in eastern Europe. A valuable index is Benjamin F. Brown, ed., The Sonnino Papers: A Guide to the Microfilm Series (Ann Arbor, MI, 1969); Ital. trans. Opera omnia di Sidney Sonnino (Bari, 1972).

(2) ASME: selection of key documents removed from Sonnino's general papers on his death. A printed inventory compiled within the Foreign Ministry is Le scritture del "Gabinetto Crispi" e le carte Sonnino, ed. Francesco Bacini (1952).

(3) ACS, 1 busta (1914-19).

Excerpts drawn from all three Sonnino collections have been published in his Carteggio (#190) and Diario (#303).

Suvich, Fulvio. (1) Papers in Trieste reported to include candid photographs from 1930's but to be otherwise sparse.

(2) ASME: records from the undersecretary's office, routine rather than private papers.

Taliani, Francesco. ASME: small collection, mostly on post-1945 career.

Thaon Di Revel, Paolo. Fondazione Luigi Einaudi, Turin: some 11,000 documents of Mussolini's finance minister, 1935-43, throw light on Fascist Italy's rearmament program, Italo-German economic relations. See Marina Storaci and St. Marinotti Dorigo, eds., "L'Archivio Paolo Thaon di Revel," Annali della Fondazione Luigi Einaudi, 2 (1968): 333-615; 6 (1972): 219-75.

Tittoni, Tommaso. ASME: mainly official papers on post-World War settlement.

Tomasi della Torretta, Pietro. ACS: 1 box (1922-27); papers on Anglo-Italian relations.

Vitetti, Leonardo. ASME: useful collection of private papers, including diary, 1939-41, some of which has been published in Nuova Antologia (#304).

Vittorio Emanuele III, King. Papers with family in Lausanne, Switzerland.

The status of the huge quantity of papers taken by Italy's royal family into exile in Cascais, Portugal, remains murky. Probably many have been lost or destroyed, but a great number are in possession of Crown Prince Umberto's daughter, presently resident in Switzerland. Access may be possible on request, although the records are believed to be in such disarray as to be unusable without much expense of time and effort. Negotiations may be under way for their return to Italy. Possibly some royal records are under lock and key in the presidential Quirinale.

By constitutional right and personal inclination, all Italian kings played an active role in foreign policy-making. King Victor Emmanuel III (1900-46) was no exception - witness his part in keeping Italy out of war, 1939, and in changing sides in mid-conflict, 1943. Hence, the royal archives might one day prove quite revelatory.

Volpi di Misurata, Giuseppe. (1) Archivio Giuseppe Volpi, Palazzo San Beneto, Venice.

(2) Archivio Giuseppe Volpi, Via Quattro Fontane, Rome.

(3) ACS, 16 buste (1925-29).

(4) ASME: overlaps material in ACS.

As Mussolini's minister of finance, Volpi negotiated Italy's war debt settlements with U.S. and Britain, 1925-26; also a participant in German reparation negotiations. Later, in World War II, presided over Italian economic penetration of Croatia.

7. Aids to Italian Archival Research

Already mentioned in passing above are those inventories normally kept with the archive they serve as well as publications that describe a specific collection. Listed here are works of a more general nature, albeit with special reference to the Italian archival scene. Before citing actual titles, however, it is worth observing that a good deal of archival information may be gleaned from the avvertenza to the relevant volumes of I documenti diplomatici italiani (#148), wherein are set forth the archives from which documentation has been drawn; the changing significance between 1918 and 1943 of diverse Foreign Ministry files is there nicely encapsulated.

International Guides

Annuaire international des archives/International Directory of Archives. Paris, 1975.

Contains a section on Italy drawn from Archivum, 22-23 (1972-73), "International Directory of Archives." Introductory matter in French, English, Spanish, German.

Centre National de la Recherche Scientifique. Répertoire des bibliothèques, collections, dépots de manuscrits et archives dans le monde/The International Directory of Manuscript Collections, Libraries, Private Collections, Repositories and Archives. Vol. 1, Europe. Paris, 1979- .

Ambitious but stalled project; published so far, part 1 of first volume merely lists names, locations of repositories. Parts 2 and 3 intended to specify collections and contents.

Cook, Christopher P., et al., eds. Sources in European Political History. Vol. 2, Diplomacy and International Affairs. London, 1989.

Potentially valuable undertaking executed rather inconsistently. Guide to personal papers of 1,000 individuals active 1870-1945; included are statesmen, diplomats from all European countries save Britain (covered in separate guide by same editor, see p. 64). Presented by name in alphabetical order with short annotations. Vol. 1 in the series dealt with the European Left; vol. 3 to come will consist of figures under the rubric "War and Resistance."

Thomas, Daniel H., and Case, Lynn M., eds. The New Guide to the Diplomatic Archives of Western Europe. Philadelphia, 1975.

Chapters on Italy and the Vatican, but sketchy account of twentieth-century archival material.

U.S. Department of State, Historical Office. Public Availability of Diplomatic Archives. Washington, 1976.

Very brief, worldwide survey.

Italian Archival Guides

See also Serra (#96).

Carucci, Paola. Le fonte archivistiche: Ordinamento e conservazione. Rome, 1983.

Mostly on state repositories; some attention to business archives. See also the same author's Il documento contemporaneo (Rome, 1987), an essay on problems of contemporary historical research in Italy.

Council for European Studies, Columbia University. Guide to Italian Archives and Libraries, comp. Rudolf J. Lewanski, ed. Richard C. Lewanski. New York, 1979.

Comprehensive coverage of all Italian archives, libraries, and institutes. Only brief profiles of holdings, but useful practical information - addresses, dates and times of opening, types of catalog available, photocopying services, etc.

Della Peruta, Franco. Biblioteche e archivi: Guida alla consultazione. Milan, 1984.

Great Britain, Imperial War Museum, Foreign Documents Centre. Provisional Reports. No. 3, Repositories in Italy. London, 1967.

Mostly on ACS, but also information on uffici storici of service ministries. Also relevant, first report of series lists thirteen depositories in Britain holding unpublished World War II enemy records.

Italy, Ministero per i Beni Culturali e Ambientali. Guida generale degli archivi di Stato italiani, 5 vols. Rome, 1982- .

Publication yet to be completed of most authoritative guide to Italian archives. Extensive inventory, lengthy descriptions of archival contents. With particular reference to research into twentieth-century Italian history, see the same ministry's publication of 1984 conference proceedings: Gli archivi per la storia contempranea: Organizzazione e fruizione (Rome, 1986).

Pavone, Claudio. "Gli archivi italiani: Uno sguardo d'assieme." Italian Quarterly, nos. 75-76 (1976): 97-112.

Petersen, Jens. "Die zeitgeschichtlich wichtigen Archive in Italien: Ein überblick." Quellen und Forschungen aus italienischen Archiven und Bibliotheken, 69 (1989): 312-78.

Wide-ranging enterprise both in terms of repositories covered and types of historical material, e.g. sections on diplomatic, military, industrial and financial archives.

Italy's Archival Legislation

Italy, Ministero dell'Interno, Direzione Generale degli Archivi di Stato. La legge sugli archivi. Rome, 1963.

Texts of legislation, especially the 1963 law, and commentary; updated by the ministry's Aggorniamenti, 1965-1986 (Rome, 1987). See also Archivum, 19 (1969), "Archival Legislation": Section 1, "Europe"; Part 2, "Italie-Yougoslavie."

Lodolini, Elio. Organizzazione e legislazione archivistica italiana. Bologna, 1980.

Italian Archival Access

A debate over the accessibility of Italian records in the wake of the 1963 law was conducted in the Rassegna degli Archivi di Stato:

Carucci, Paola. "Alcune osservazioni sulla consultabilità dei documenti." 33 (1973): 282-91.

D'Angiolini, Piero. "La consultabilità dei documenti d'archivio." 35 (1975): 198-249.

Olla Repeto, Gabriella. "In tema di consultabilità dei documenti amministrativi dello Stato." 30 (1970): 9-57.

Saladino, Antonio. "Il problema degli archivi privati e il primo triennio di applicazione della legga del 1963." 28 (1968): 316-28. Reprinted in A. Saladino, Gli archivi privati (Rome, 1970).

Studies of Italy's Archives, 1943-1945

The vicissitudes of Italian archives, official and private, in the turbulent final years of the Second World War have understandably spawned some interesting literature on their fate.

Contini, Gaetano. La valigia di Mussolini: I documenti segreti dell'ultima fuga del duce. Milan, 1982.

Gencarelli, Elvira. Gli archivi italiani durante la seconda guerra mondiale. Rome, 1979.

Smyth, Howard McGaw. Secrets of the Fascist Era: How Uncle Sam Obtained Some of the Top-Level Documents of Mussolini's Period. Carbondale, IL, 1975.

Establishes provenance and authenticity of Italian documentary collections now available on microfilm, principally the Lisbon and Rose Garden papers, military records mainly from Aktensammelstelle Süd, and the files of the Segreteria Particolare del Duce and Ministry of Popular Culture. The nature and contents of the microfilms are rehearsed in detail, which makes this an indispensable reference work, especially for North American researchers.

Smyth also discusses and dismisses the rumor of a Mussolini-Churchill correspondence that has circulated since 1945. Such tenuous evidence as the rumormongers have assembled is set out in Arrigo Petacco, Dear Benito, Caro Winston: Verità e misteri del carteggio Churchill-Mussolini (Milan, 1985).

Toscano, Mario. "Le vicende degli archivi segreti di Palazzo Chigi: I diari di prigionia di Mussolini catturati dai nazisti dopo l'armistizio secondo inediti documenti diplomatici tedeschi." Nuova Antologia, 481 (Jan.-Apr. 1961): 299-326. Reprinted in the same author's Pagine di storia diplomatica contemporanea, 2: 249-81 (#528).

Originals of those Italian Foreign Ministry files and Mussolini's diary for summer 1943 seized by the Nazis have disappeared; contents here recreated in outline from captured German documents. The salvation of other

Foreign Ministry records in the Palazzo Lancellotti has been described in a newspaper article by Enrico Serra: "La scomparsa di Pietro Lancellotti: L'uomo che salvà dai nazisti l'archivio segreto degli Esteri," La Stampa, 12 May 1988.

Serial Guides to Italian Archives

Certain serials help the researcher to keep abreast of archival developments as they happen, carrying news of the discovery or release of new material.

Archivi per la Storia. Florence, 1988- . Biannual.

New venture of Associazione Nazionale Archivistica Italiana to discuss common problems of archivists and librarians.

Archivio Storico Italiano. Florence, 1873- . Quarterly.

The standard journal of Italian archivists; emphasis on premodern archival sources, although occasional references made to twentieth-century records. Articles in Italian, English, French, German.

Rassegna degli Archivi di Stato. Ministero per i Beni Culturali e Ambientali, Rome, 1941- . Triannual.

Useful mixture of latest news on archives and articles, the latter often summarized in several languages, including English. See also the same ministry's occasional publications, Quaderni della Rassegna degli Archivi di Stato and Pubblicazioni degli Archivi di Stato, which mainly give inventories of regional archives.

Newsletters

A number of scholarly organizations issue periodic newsletters that sometimes contain relevant archival information. The location of the following that are recommended is subject to change according to the newsletter's editor:

American Committee on the History of the Second World War, newsletter. Southern Illinois University, Carbondale, IL.

American Historical Association. Perspectives. Washington.

Arbeitsgemeinschaft für die neueste Geschichte Italiens (Gruppo di studio per la storia contemporanea italiana). Distributes Bibliographische Informationen zur italienischen Geschichte im 19. und 20. Jahrhundert and Storia e Critica (#40). Universität Trier, FRG.

Association for the Study of Modern Italy, newsletter. University College, Oxford/Corpus Christi College, Cambridge.

Center for Research Libraries. "Focus on the Center for Research Libraries." Chicago, IL.

ARCHIVES, LIBRARIES, NEWSPAPERS

    Conference Group on Italian Politics and Society. "Italian Politics and Society." McGill University, Montreal.

    Council for European Studies. "European Studies Newsletter." Columbia University, New York.

    Society for Italian Historical Studies, newsletter. Boston College, Chestnut Hill, MA.

B. NON-ITALIAN ARCHIVAL SOURCES

The account of a nation's foreign policy drawn from its own archives should always in principle and as far as possible be confirmed or refined by reference to the archival holdings of its diplomatic trading partners. For reasons already given, this lesson applies particularly to Italy towards the end of the period 1918-1945. Of course, there is only space here to make brief mention of some of the major diplomatic archives of other states, and only those of the great powers and League of Nations at that. To obtain further details of non-Italian primary sources, one can begin in no better way than by consulting the companion volumes in this series of research guides:

Aster, Sidney. British Foreign Policy, 1918-1945, rev. ed.

Baer, George W. International Organizations, 1918-1945, rev. ed.

James, Harold, and Kunz, Diane B. European International Economic Relations, 1918-1945 (forthcoming, 1991).

Johnston, Robert H. Soviet Foreign Policy, 1918-1945 (forthcoming, 1991).

Kimmich, Christoph M. German Foreign Policy, 1918-1945, rev. ed.

Young, Robert J. French Foreign Policy, 1918-1945, rev. ed.

1. United States

An overall guide to U.S. archives is U.S. National Historical Publications and Records Commission, Directory of Archives and Manuscript Depositories in the United States, 2d ed. (Washington, 1988). For current information, consult the regularly updated microfiche, "National Inventory of Documentary Sources in the United States" (Chadwick & Healey); this covers the presidential libraries, the Library of Congress Manuscript Division, and by far the most important source of foreign policy material, the National Archives.

National Archives (Washington, DC)

The holdings of America's national depository of records are set out in

ARCHIVES, LIBRARIES, NEWSPAPERS

U.S. National Archives and Records Service. Guide to the National Archives of the United States. Washington, 1974.

Of most relevance to all diplomatic historians are the records of the U.S. Department of State. Virtually all material over thirty years old is open to scholarly inspection. The mass of U.S. diplomatic archives is to be found in Record Group 59, which contains the Decimal File, established by the State Department in 1910 and divided into chronological blocks: 1910-29, 1930-39, 1940-44, 1945-49. The organization of this vast documentation is described in

U.S. National Archives and Records Service. Recordkeeping in the Department of State, 1789-1956, comp. Stephen Helton. Washington, 1975.

Suffice it to say here that there are two keys. The initial number of a file denotes its general subject area, with political matters covered by numbers 7 (relations between states) and 8 (internal affairs). Then, every country is accorded a numeral, Italy being 65 and the Vatican 66. Hence everything in State Department records on Italian domestic affairs is located in files beginning 865. A number after the decimal point indicates the particular type of internal matter. Italy's relations with another country are filed under 765. followed by the other nation's numeral so long as it is higher than 65. A special file on the Italo-Ethiopian war, for instance, is designated 765.84. If, however, the other nation bears a numeral lower than 65, the procedure is reversed. To take the central example, the United States is represented by the number 11, and so Italo-American relations are filed under 711.65. Once the appropriate files have been identified, research is facilitated by a system of purport lists and cards. These provide a synopsis of every document in the Decimal File as well as cross-references to other papers.

The U.S. government has microfilmed many of its records, which are available from Scholarly Resources, Inc. (unless otherwise specified below). One very valuable filmed collection, as described in a pamphlet issued by the National Archives and Records Service, is

Purport Lists for the Department of State Decimal File, 1910-1944 (1976). Microcopy 973, 654 reels.

Documentary material on microfilm from Record Group 59 dealing specifically with Italian affairs includes:

Records of the Department of State Relating to Political Relations Between the United States and Italy, 1910-1929, and Between Italy and Other States, 1910-1929 (1969). Microcopies 529, 530, 3 and 8 reels.

Records of the Department of State Relating to Internal Affairs of Italy, 1910-1929, 1930-1939 (1968). Microcopies 527, 1423, 60 and 33 reels.

There is equivalent filmed material regarding Vatican relations with the U.S. and other states as well as the internal affairs of the Holy See, 1910-1929. Microcopies 561, 562, 563, 3 reels.

ITALIAN FOREIGN POLICY, 1918-1945

For filmed Decimal File material on Italy during the Second World War, see "Italy: Foreign Affairs, 1940-1944," and "Italy: Internal Affairs, 1940-1944" (University Publications of America, 8 and 44 reels).

Other National Archives record groups containing U.S. diplomatic material pertinent to Italy are:

Record Group 84, "Foreign Service Posts of the Department of State."

Bound volumes of U.S. embassy and consular papers, including those from posts in Italy. For index, see List of Foreign Service Post Records in the National Archives, rev. ed. (Washington, 1967).

Record Group 256, "American Commission to Negotiate Peace, 1918-1931." Also available as Microcopy 820, 563 reels.

Includes minutes of the Conference of Ambassadors, 1920-31. See index, General Records of the American Commission to Negotiate Peace, 1918-1931 (Washington, 1972).

Record Group 43, "U.S. Participation in International Conferences, Commissions, and Expositions."

Material, for example, on the Lausanne Conference, 1922-23, naval and disarmament conferences.

Record Group 165, "Correspondence of the Military Intelligence Division Relating to General, Political, Economic, and Military Conditions in Italy, 1918-1941." Also available as Microcopy 1446, 26 reels.

Material from War Department, General and Special Staffs. See also synopsis of U.S. military intelligence views of Italy during the 1930's in "Military Intelligence Reports: Biweekly Intelligence Summaries, 1928-1938" (University Publications of America, 6 reels).

Material captured from the Axis powers at the close of the Second World War is also held on microfilm in the National Archives, Record Group 242, "World War II Collection of Seized Enemy Records." This documentation is discussed in the sections of this guide devoted to Italian and German archives.

Also from the enemy camp in the Second World War are documents in Record Group 457 known as "Magic - Diplomatic Summary" (University Publications of America, 14 reels). These are intercepts made by U.S. signals of messages passing between Japan's foreign ministry and its diplomats in the field, including those in Rome and the Vatican. Their accuracy is sometimes approximate because of variable radio reception and translation difficulties at the time.

Private Papers

Most significant in this category are the papers of those American statesmen directly involved in Italian affairs as a result of the two world wars. Thus, on the subject of Italy and peacemaking in 1919, one might usefully turn to the

ARCHIVES, LIBRARIES, NEWSPAPERS

papers of Woodrow Wilson, Robert Lansing, and Edward M. House. Concerning Italo-U.S. relations on the eve of and during World War II, the private collections left behind by Franklin D. Roosevelt and Cordell Hull are worth exploring. Papers have also been bequeathed by the successive occupants of the American embassy in Rome after the First World War, namely, Page, Johnson, Child, Fletcher, Garrett, and Long. None of these ambassadors, however, made an outstanding mark as a diplomat, and their papers are of presumptive limited value. Of special interest are the records of William S. Donovan (U.S. Military Institute, Carlisle Barracks, PA); these contain information on Donovan's role as special presidential investigative agent in the Italo-Ethiopian crisis as well as on O.S.S. activity in Italy, 1940-45. The pursuit of personal papers in the U.S. is eased by the

National Union Catalog of Manuscript Collections, 1959- . Hamden, CT, 1962- .

Three vols. published for accessions 1959-62, then succeeding vols. in 1966, 1969, 1974. Now published annually with 5-year cumulative indices beginning 1975. Gives location of private archives, brief outline of contents, cross-references among collections. Some repositories linked in an on-line searching system. A more limited guide is U.S., Library of Congress, Manuscripts on Microfilm, comp. Richard D. Bickel (Washington, 1975).

2. Great Britain

Useful introductions are Janet Foster and Julia Sheppard, eds., British Archives: A Guide to Archive Resources in the United Kingdom (Detroit, 1982); Sydney L. Mayer and William J. Koenig, The Two World Wars: A Guide to Manuscript Collections in the United Kingdom (London, 1976).

Public Record Office (Kew, Richmond, Surrey)

Counterpart of the U.S. National Archives, the Public Record Office is the British national depository of records. For its general scope, see

Great Britain, Public Record Office. Guide to the Contents of the Public Record Office, 2d ed., 3 vols. London, 1963-68.

This standard aid is updated by the Current Guide to the Contents of the Public Record Office, 3 parts (London, 1978-), parts 2 and 3 of which are issued annually. In addition, a great deal of material in the Public Record Office has been put on film, and indeed almost all of the records enumerated below can be found in the P.R.O.'s microfilm catalog on microfiche (latest update, 1986).

Also like the National Archives, the Public Record Office houses its nation's diplomatic papers as they become accessible under a general thirty-year rule. A guide to these diplomatic holdings comprises one in a series of archival handbooks:

ITALIAN FOREIGN POLICY, 1918-1945

Great Britain, Public Record Office. <u>The Records of the Foreign Office, 1782-1939</u>. P.R.O. Handbook no. 13. London, 1969.

This thorough and valuable explication may be complemented by <u>The Second World War: A Guide to Documents in the Public Record Office</u>, P.R.O. Handbook no. 15 (London, 1972), which includes a section on Foreign Office wartime papers.

By far the most significant class of Foreign Office documentation is known as

General Correspondence after 1906: Political (F.O. 371).

These papers are culled from all political departments within the Foreign Office that customarily have been divided along regional lines. In 1920, after the dissolution of a temporary wartime organization, Italian business was consigned to the Central Department until 1933 when it was transferred to the Southern Department (although the Vatican remained within the Central Department's purview). Most political files dealing with Italy, therefore, bear the initial letter C(entral) until 1933 and R (for Southern) afterwards. In addition, as in the U.S. State Department, countries were allocated identifying numerals that, in the Foreign Office, appear at the end of a file denotation. Italy was represented by number 22 (though the Vatican was not given a numeral). These two file indicators can be illustrated by reference to the annual reports of British ambassadors in Rome - which incidentally provide handy summaries of Anglo-Italian relations: that for 1920, the first such in the interwar years, is designated C1746/1746/22; that for 1938, the last report composed before World War II, R2955/2955/22. In practice, the researcher's path through the thickets of the Foreign Office filing system is eased by an invaluable guide to F.O. 371:

Great Britain, Foreign Office. <u>Index to General Correspondence, 1920-</u>. Nendeln, Liechtenstein, 1969- .

Ongoing reprint of the Foreign Office's own catalog. Each annual index appears in four volumes as papers are made available under the 30-year rule; hence the series is complete to 1945. Subject entries diverse, comprehensive, and cross-referenced. Citation is to a numbered file that, to be obtained, must be translated into a folder number by means of a key kept in the P.R.O.

Index includes "green papers," in effect the Confidential Print of records of limited circulation within the F.O.; there are separate green paper indices for 1920-38, 1939, and 1940 to enable the researcher to isolate this material.

Series opens in 1920 because the F.O. began a new filing system in that year. For earlier records, one must use annual card indices, 1906-19, held in the P.R.O. Difficulties attendant on the new filing method resulted in much 1920 correspondence being listed in the card index for 1919.

Other classes of Foreign Office papers containing material relevant to Italy are:

ARCHIVES, LIBRARIES, NEWSPAPERS

> Confidential Print. Italy, 1919-33, 1942-46 (F.O. 425); Italy, 1934-41 (F.O. 434).
>
> Substantial portions of the Confidential Print are scheduled for publication in the immediate future, see #231.
>
> Archives of Conferences. Lausanne Conference, 1922-23 (F.O. 839); Locarno Conference, 1925 (F.O. 840); Conference of Ambassadors, 1920-30 (F.O. 893).
>
> Archives of Commissions. Spain: International Committee for the Application of the Agreement regarding Non-Intervention, 1936-39 (F.O. 849).

Special mention should be made of a rich source of Foreign Office papers drawn from the private offices of foreign secretaries, undersecretaries, career diplomats, and other public servants. Examples of collections holding material on Italian affairs are the correspondence of three foreign secretaries: Lord Curzon, 1919-24 (F.O. 800/149-58), Sir Austen Chamberlain, 1924-29 (F.O. 800/256-63), and Sir Samuel Hoare, 1935 (F.O. 800/295).

Besides Foreign Office records, the Public Record Office also houses the Cabinet papers, some of which bear on international politics generally and Italy in particular. For example:

Cabinet minutes, 1919-39 (CAB 23).

Cabinet memoranda, 1915-39 (CAB 24).

Cabinet Committee of Imperial Defence, minutes, 1902-39 (CAB 2).

International Conferences, 1916-1939 (CAB 29).

Cabinet registered files: Italy and Abyssinia (CAB 21).

Cabinet Foreign Policy Committee, 1936-39 (CAB 27).

War Cabinet minutes, 1939-45 (CAB 65).

War Cabinet memoranda, 1939-45 (CAB 66).

Private Papers

In addition to the holdings in the Public Record Office already mentioned, many papers of British statesmen and diplomats are held in a myriad other archives and private hands. Indeed, an appendix of The Records of the Foreign Office, cited above, supplies a list of such private collections of foreign secretaries. Two provincial archival depositories deserve special mention. (1) Birmingham University Library is custodian of all the Chamberlain papers as well as those of Anthony Eden. In view of the importance both Sir Austen and Neville Chamberlain attached to ties with Italy, and Foreign Secretary Eden's stormy relationship with Mussolini, these represent important sources. (2) The fastest growing aggregation of papers of twentieth-century British public servants is that in the Churchill College Archives, Cambridge. Centerpiece of the archive consists of Churchill's own papers, though access is restricted. Of other holdings the papers of Sir Maurice Hankey, who held among many posts that of cabinet secretary between the wars, are especially interesting. It should also be reported that the papers of some of Britain's ambassadors to Italy are extant in various locations. Regrettably, none of the collections left by Rennell Rodd, Graham, Drummond, and Loraine appears to have much to offer beyond what can be found in governmental files.

To track down these and other collections, there are several useful guides. The standard compendium one may begin with is

> Royal Commission on Historical Manuscripts. <u>Record Repositories in Great Britain: A Geographical Directory</u>, 7th ed. London, 1982.

The same institution maintains and constantly updates a National Register of Archives, organized by depository. Comprehensive but requires finding aids at the commission's offices to utilize.

Adequate and simpler guides are:

> Cook, Christopher P. et al., comps. <u>Sources in British Political History</u>. Vol. 2, <u>A Guide to the Private Papers of Selected Public Servants</u>. London, 1975.

> Hazlehurst, Cameron, and Woodland, Christine. <u>A Guide to the Papers of British Cabinet Ministers, 1900-1951</u>. London, 1974.

3. France

A good English-language general guide has been edited for the Council for European Studies by Erwin K. Welsch, <u>Libraries and Archives in France</u>, rev. ed. (New York, 1979). Absolutely essential, however, for French diplomatic archives is

> Ministère des Relations Extérieures. <u>Les archives du Ministère des Relations Extérieures depuis les origines: Histoire et guide suivis d'une étude des sources de l'histoire des affaires étrangères dans les dépôts parisiens et départementaux</u>, 2 vols. Paris, 1984-85.

Vol. 1 relates the historical development of France's Foreign Ministry archives. Vol. 2 contains essays describing, often in detail, the contents of depositories of diplomatic material throughout France. Some contributions cover the range of source material on a specific topic; for example, "Les documents relatifs à l'Ethiopie," pp. 102-3. Most, but not exclusive, attention is naturally given to the holdings of the Ministère des Relations Extérieures, until recently and from 1918 to 1945 the Ministère des Affaires Etrangères.

ARCHIVES, LIBRARIES, NEWSPAPERS

Les Archives de la Ministère des Relations Extérieures (Quai d'Orsay, Paris)

In the fashion of European continental states, France's diplomatic archives are lodged in the Foreign Ministry itself, which has printed a brief Guide du lecteur (Paris, 1977). A number of inventories are available in the salle de consultation. Here, the archival situation was, and to some extent still is, conditioned by the tremendous destruction and dislocation of diplomatic records wrought by the French defeat in June 1940. In the wake of the Second World War the Ministère des Affaires Etrangères was faced with the same task of reassembling its files as the Ministero degli Esteri in Rome after the events of 1943-45, although the French had the larger problem and therefore proceeded more slowly. Only in 1982 did the principal series of papers, termed the Political and Commercial Correspondence files, become available for the entire interwar period. Even so, there is much more material from diplomats in the field than from the Quai d'Orsay itself. (It should be noted too that no formal record was kept of French Council of Ministers meetings.)

Research into Franco-Italian relations begins, then, with various series of the

Correspondance Politique et Commerciale

Series Z: "Europe, 1918-1940"

Arranged geographically with subseries "Italie, 1918-1929" (224 folders) and "Italie, 1930-1940" (146 folders). These Italian files are further broken down into topical divisions, e.g. "Politique étrangère," "Relations avec la France," "Négociations franco-italiennes, 1930-39," and several groups of files on the Ethiopian affair. Series Z also comprises "Europe, 1944-1949," which has its own subseries of files on Italy useful for the World War II years.

Series Y: "Internationale, 1918-1940"

Here, arrangement of files is by topic, e.g. "Affaires politiques," "Conférence des Ambassadeurs, 1920-31," "Paix, 1920-40." Like Series Z, Series Y contains records under "Europe, 1944-1949" and an Italian subseries with material as far back as the Franco-Italian armistice of 1940.

Among other classifications with information pertinent to Italy are:

Series A: "Paix, 1914-1920" (including subseries "Italie, 1915-20")

Series P: "Tunisie, 1917-1929"

Series: "Société des Nations, 1917-1940"

Series: "Guerre, 1939-1945" (In two subseries: One, "Z-Vichy-Europe," contains 16 folders designated "Italie." The other, "Londres-Alger," has a score of folders devoted to relations with Italy.)

Another important source within the Archives des Relations Extérieures consists of the papers of French statesmen and diplomats. Listed as private papers, they are in truth more official than personal records. They are lodged in two <u>fonds</u> (although not all are listed in the appropriate inventories):

(1) Papiers d'agents

At ministerial level are to be found the papers of Georges Clemenceau, Pierre-Etienne Flandin, Gaston Doumergue, Gabriel Hanotaux, Edouard Herriot, Georges Leygues, Alexandre Millerand, Joseph Paul-Boncour, and André Tardieu. Collections of French diplomats whose service took them to Italy and the Vatican include those of the well-known ambassadors Barrère, Charles-Roux, De Jouvenel, and of the French consul at Trieste, 1914-20, René Dollot. Also of interest are the papers of Paul Mantoux, interpreter for the Council of Four at the Paris Peace Conference, 1919; Philippe Berthelot, secretary general at the Quai d'Orsay, 1920-22, 1925-33; René Massigli, deputy director of political affairs, 1933-37, and member of the League of Nations sanctions committee in the Ethiopian crisis; Joseph Avenol, deputy secretary general, League of Nations, 1923-33, then secretary general, 1933-40.

(2) Fonds 1940: Papiers '40

Particularly valuable for papers of political office-holders of the 1930's and 1940's, notably, Paul Baudouin, Georges Bonnet, Edouard Daladier (photocopies), Pierre Laval, Philippe Pétain, and Paul Reynaud. Functionaries whose papers contain material on Italy include those of Albert Fouques-Duparc, Henri Hoppenot, and Charles Rochat. Also worthy of mention are the papers of Alexis Léger, secretary general of the Foreign Ministry, 1933-40, and the records of the Bureau d'Etudes Chauvel, a study group set up within the ministry after the fall of France in 1940 (see Maurice Vaïsse, "Les bureaux d'études des Affaires Etrangères et l'Italie," <u>Revue d'Histoire Diplomatique</u>, 97 [1983]: 322-40.)

Archives Nationales (Rambuteau)

In the records category Series F, "Administration de la France," a subseries F7, "Police générale," contains files on international relations. Seventeen volumes of such files on Italy, 1925-34, would seem pertinent in view of the diplomatic importance attached to the activities of Italian anti-Fascist <u>fuorusciti</u> in France.

Among collections of personal papers in the Archives Nationales some have diplomatic significance, namely, those of Premiers Paul Painlevé, Paul-Boncour and Reynaud.

Private Papers

In seeking French private papers outside the Quai d'Orsay archives and the Archives Nationales, the researcher faces difficulties not unlike those in Italy. The custom of donating private collections to public institutions is not strongly established. Two major depositories of private papers in Paris are the Bibliothèque Nationale (papers of Flandin, Millerand, Raymond Poincaré), and

ARCHIVES, LIBRARIES, NEWSPAPERS

Fondation Nationale des Sciences Politiques (papers of Léon Blum, Daladier, Herriot). Sometimes private diplomatic papers are found in provincial archives, e.g. those of Célestin Jonnart, France's representative to the Holy See, 1921-33, in the archives départmentales of the Pas de Calais. There is no comprehensive French publication listing private archives, such as exists in the U.S., Britain, and Germany; the closest one can come is

> France, Archives Nationales. <u>Guide des Papiers des Ministres et Secrétaires d'Etat, de 1871 à 1974</u>. Paris, 1978.

4. Germany

For a succinct overview in the English language, see Erwin K. Welsch, ed., <u>Libraries and Archives in Germany</u>, for the Council for European Studies (Pittsburgh, 1975).

Politisches Archiv (Auswärtiges Amt, Bonn)

The bulk of German diplomatic records from both the Second and Third Reich were captured by the Western Allies at the end of World War II. Almost all were returned to Germany in the 1950's and are now accessible to scholars in the Foreign Ministry of West Germany's Federal Republic.

Before their restoration, however, literally hundreds of thousands of documents were microfilmed. Most but not all of the filmed records for the period 1867-1920 are located in the U.S. National Archives, Washington. All for the years 1920-45 are in the National Archives where they constitute Microcopy T-120, 5,206 reels. In Britain the films are accessible in the Public Record Office, Kew, Richmond, Surrey. Estimable guides to this mass of microfilm are:

> American Historical Association, Committee for the Study of War Documents. <u>A Catalogue of Files and Microfilms of the German Foreign Ministry Archives, 1867-1920</u>. Oxford, 1959, reprint 1970.

> Kent, George O., ed. <u>A Catalog of Files and Microfilms of the German Foreign Ministry Archives, 1920-1945</u>, 4 vols. Palo Alto, CA, 1962-73.

> Schwandt, Ernst, comp. <u>Index of Microfilmed Records of the German Foreign Ministry and the Reich's Chancellery covering the Weimar Period Deposited at the National Archives</u>. Washington, 1958.

From these publications one may gather a very good idea of what exists in the Politisches Archiv pertaining to Italy. Kent's guide is the most pertinent for researchers in interwar Italian foreign policy: his first volume lists the more important files, 1920-36; his second, the less important files, 1920-36; his third, files for 1936-45; his fourth, mission and consular files, 1920-45. On the other hand, it should be noted that the originals of the Auswärtiges Amt files for 1920-45 have been rearranged somewhat in Bonn so that the printed guides do not always lead one directly to the actual archival holdings. For the latter the researcher should use inventories in the Politisches Archiv itself.

The most important German Foreign Ministry records are, characteristically, the political files, which in fact make up the great majority of the filmed collections. Until 1920 when the Auswärtiges Amt underwent an administrative overhaul (hence the dividing line between the two sets of microfilm), all political matters were handled in Abteilung I. For filing purposes letters were used to indicate regional subdivisions of political papers. IA denoted political documentation concerning Europe and IAB political documentation concerning non-German states in Europe. Furthermore, each country was accorded a letter; Italy was "e." Thus, the researcher looking for information on Italy in the aftermath of World War I will find it under the code IABe.

The reorganization of 1920 lasted until 1936. Its central feature was the establishment of a Büro des Reichsministers and a Büro des Staatssekretärs into which were channelled the main political papers, including a number of files labelled "Italien" and others on topics of Italian connotation (e.g. "Mussolini Pakt 1933" in the files of the foreign minister's office). More papers relevant to Italy are located among those of the political department for Western Europe, Abteilung IIA, and also in the interdepartmental category of Secret Files (Geheimakten). A further administrative reshuffle in 1936 saw the appearance of a newly coined Büro des Reichsaussenministers, not many of whose records have survived. Consequently the best documentation of the Rome-Berlin Axis is found in the files of the state secretary's office. The political department dealing with Italian affairs between 1936 and 1945 was Abteilung IV, that for Southeastern Europe. Finally, the papers of German missions abroad, whose arrangement was unaffected by the 1936 change, include those from the Rome and Vatican embassies.

The Politisches Archiv holds some private collections, which also appear in Microcopy T-120. Most substantial are the Nachlass Stresemann, which throw some light on the Austrian and Alto Adige questions in the 1920's. More directly relevant to Italian affairs are the papers of German diplomats who served in the Rome embassy: Von Mackensen, Von Schubert, and Von Prittwitz. Unfortunately, Rahn's papers do not cover his time in Italy.

Bundesarchiv (Koblenz)

Housed in the Federal Archives are the Reich Chancellery records, which, like the Foreign Ministry papers, were seized by the Allies in 1945 and are now returned to West Germany. They contain the minutes of those Weimar cabinet meetings at which international affairs were discussed. These records of the so-called Alte Reichskanzlei, 1919-33, have, in addition, been filmed as part of Microcopy T-120. The Bundesarchiv also holds some private papers: for example, of Von Weizsäcker on his Vatican mission, and of Otto Bene, a German diplomat involved in the population transfer from the South Tyrol after 1939. A general guide to the entire archive is

> Granier, Gerhard; Henke, Josef; Oldenhange, Klaus, eds. Das Bundesarchiv und seine Bestände, 3d ed. Boppard, 1977.

Bundesarchiv - Abteilung Militärchiv (Freiburg)

This branch of the Bundesarchiv holds military and naval records. Army files hold copies of some Auswärtiges Amt documents from the World War II period not in the Foreign Ministry's own archive. More relevant to this guide,

ARCHIVES, LIBRARIES, NEWSPAPERS

however, are the naval files that include the Tambach Archives, so-called after the castle where they were seized by the Anglo-Americans in 1945. Before their return to the Federal Republic many Tambach papers were filmed and given the designation U.S. National Archives, Microcopy T-1022. Some files were microfilmed explicitly to illustrate "political" relations between Germany and Italy. Of 188 reels of film 20 refer directly to Italy and consist largely of reports by German naval attachés in Rome, 1932-44. See

> A Catalogue of Selected Files of the German Naval Archives Microfilmed at the Admiralty, London, for the University of Cambridge and the University of Michigan, directed by Frank H. Hinsley and Howard M. Ehrmann. London, 1959-64.

The microfilm is on deposit in the U.K. at the Naval Historical Branch of the Ministry of Defence, London, and Cambridge University, and in the U.S. at the National Archives, Washington, and (in part, though including the Italian material) the University of Michigan, Ann Arbor, MI.

N.S.D.A.P. Party Records

Such was the dominance of the Nazi party in totalitarian Germany, 1933-45, that not even foreign policy was immune from NSDAP intervention. Consequently, a quantity of diplomatic documents found their way into the files of the party chancellery, some of course from the Nazis' own Auslands-Organisation. These records are to be found in the Berlin Document Center administered by the U.S., and scattered among other West German repositories. However, a comprehensive reference work with a multiple indexing system (see especially under "Auswärtige Angelegenheiten") gives their location and contents:

> Heiber, Helmut, ed. Akten der Partei-Kanzlei der NSDAP, 2 vols. plus index. Munich & Vienna, 1983. Also available on microfiche (K.G. Saur).

Nuremberg War Crimes Trials Records

At Nuremberg the accused were charged with "crimes against humanity," and also "crimes against the peace," or planned aggression. On these counts 22 top Nazis were tried before the International Military Tribunal (IMT) from November 1945 to October 1946. Lesser Nazi officials and other Germans appeared before the American Military Tribunal (AMT) between October 1946 and April 1949. The records of both the IMT and AMT contain evidentiary material, some not presented in court, as well as trial proceedings in German, English, French, and Russian. The original records were deposited with the International Court of Justice at The Hague, and copies with the U.S. National Archives (Record Group 238), Washington, the Imperial War Museum in London, and the Archives Nationales in Paris. Other copies, complete or partial, have been purchased by various institutes and libraries in the United States, Britain, and Germany. Probably the most comprehensive index to this mass of material is kept by the Institut für Zeitgeschichte, Munich.

The National Archives has microfilmed many Nuremberg records. Particularly relevant to Nazi foreign policy and Italy are the prosecution documents from the IMT material that include the case against Nazi foreign ministers, Ribbentrop and Von Neurath (Microcopy T-988), and in the AMT series the Weizsäcker case (Microcopy T-897). For printed Nuremberg documentary collections, see International Military Tribunal (#249).

Zentralarchiv (Potsdam)

The official depository of the East German Democratic Republic holds some diplomatic papers of Germany's imperial past, although apparently of limited application to Italy. Access for western scholars is possible but not automatic. Consult

>   Lötzke, Helmut, ed. Übersicht über die Bestände des deutschen Zentralarchivs Potsdam. Berlin, 1957.

Private Papers

Several German diplomats involved in Italian affairs have left behind private papers, although like some Italian collections, their accessibility is variable and even problematical. Under one dispensation, those of Von Mackensen, as already mentioned, are open to all scholars in the Politisches Archiv, Bonn, but under another Von Neurath's are locked away in Potsdam. Other Germans who served in Rome to leave papers are Von Prittwitz, Von Hassell, and Von Weizsäcker. All the above collections are comprehended in an invaluable guide to private papers in both Germanies:

>   Mommsen, Wolfgang A., and Denecke, Ludwig, eds. Verzeichnis der schriftlichen Nachlässe in deutschen Archiven und Bibliotheken, 3 vols. Boppard, 1971-83.

5. Russia

As an unequivocal major power Russia merits at least a passing mention, albeit a negative one. Despite glasnost, the Soviet Union's diplomatic archives for the years after 1917 remain at the moment of writing hermetically sealed to western scholars. In the anticipated event of their opening in the future, they should throw light particularly on Italy's commercial and political relations with the early Bolshevik regime, on rumored confidential relations between Mussolini and Stalin, and on the Soviet role in liberated Italy, 1943-45; see remarks by Sergei Slipchenko, "Veterans Speak of the Diplomatic Service," International Affairs [Moscow] (Oct. 1989): 132. At which point the researcher will turn gratefully to

>   Grimsted, Patricia K., ed. Archives and Manuscript Repositories in the U.S.S.R.: Moscow and Leningrad. Princeton, NJ, 1972.

The same author has also compiled supplementary volumes on regional archives within the Soviet Union.

ARCHIVES, LIBRARIES, NEWSPAPERS

6. League of Nations

United Nations Library (Palais des Nations, Geneva)

Italy was a permanent member of the League of Nations Council from the outset. And given Mussolini's embroilment with the League of Nations over the Corfu and Ethiopian issues, its archives deserve a place in any guide to Italian foreign policy, 1918-1945. Except for some personal papers and documents of nations whose own archives are closed, League records are open to scholars under a forty-year rule. A brief but useful guide is

> United Nations Library. Guide to the Archives of the League of Nations, 1919-1946. Geneva, 1978.

Once in the archives the researcher will find an excellent "Répertoire général," prepared by Yves Pérotin, which lists the entire complement of League files. Another welcome research tool is a short article by Pier Luigi Orsi, "L'archivio della Società delle Nazioni e la politica italiana," Rivista di Storia Contemporanea, 10 (1981): 282-91, which indicates those categories of League records germane to Italian interwar diplomacy.

The main category of files is designated "The Secretariat Archive Group, 1917-1947." The League of Nations Archives also possess some private papers, although none of great relevance to Italy. There is a file of papers of the League's secretary general, 1919-33, Sir Eric Drummond, who as the Earl of Perth later served as British ambassador in Rome; most of his papers were destroyed in 1940. Also one box of papers of Joseph Avenol, secretary general during the Ethiopian crisis; most of Avenol's papers are in the French Foreign Ministry archives (p. 66).

C. LIBRARIES AND RESEARCH INSTITUTES

The institutions considered in this section are notable not so much for their archival treasures, although one or two do possess some original records, as for their strength in published material on Italian foreign policy, 1918-1945. Such strength derives either from comprehensiveness of holdings, as is the case of national libraries, or else from a concentration in specialist libraries on international politics or Italian affairs. International guides to libraries and research institutes are <u>Access Research Guide: An International Directory of Information on War, Peace, and Security</u>, ed. William H. Kincade and Priscilla B. Hayner (Cambridge, MA, 1988), and the annual <u>World of Learning</u>, 39th ed. (London, 1989). See also Richard C. Lewanski, ed., <u>Subject Collections in European Libraries</u>, 2d ed. (New York & London, 1978).

1. Italian

Speaking broadly, Italian libraries, public and institutional, do not measure up to their counterparts in the English-speaking world. In the field of modern history, particularly, both book and periodical holdings tend to be uneven, and non-Italian literature scanty. Moreover, libraries in Italy are burdened with restrictions. Open stacks are not common, and the number of volumes a reader is permitted to order at any one time is often irritatingly small. Identification is normally required. All of which is not to say that one cannot find in Italian libraries valuable material that is hard to come by outside Italy; simply that perseverance is a prerequisite.

National Libraries

Among the various national libraries administered by the Italian state, two enjoy the cachet of national central library, indicating their theoretical right to receive a copy of every title published in Italy. They are:

Biblioteca Nazionale Centrale
Piazza Cavalleggeri, 1
Firenze 50122.

Biblioteca Nazionale Centrale "Vittorio Emanuele II"
Viale Castro Pretorio, 105
Roma 00185.

ARCHIVES, LIBRARIES, NEWSPAPERS

For researchers working in the capital's archives (ASME, ACS) the Rome library is patently the more convenient, and it also houses the central offices for the coordination of bibliographical information amongst Italian libraries. Yet, the National Central library at Florence is the more prestigious institution. It has been a library of deposit since 1870 (Rome only since 1939), and its seniority is evidenced by a superior coverage of most fields and by its monthly publication of Bibliografia Nazionale Italiana, listing copyright titles in Italy (#48). It has, however, frailties in its day-to-day operation; see Desmond Gill, "Le bibliotheche pubbliche fiorentine: Impressioni di uno storico straniero," Passato e Presente (July-Dec. 1982): 147-52.

Specialist Libraries and Institutes

The largest Italian research organization, an umbrella organization for a variety of research groups and projects in all scholarly fields, is

Consiglio Nazionale delle Ricerche (CNR)
Piazzale Aldo Moro, 7
Roma 00185

The principal Italian historical institute, though its work is not particularly geared to diplomatic history, is

Istituto Italiano per gli Studi Storici
Via Benedetto Croce, 12
Napoli 80134

Several scholarly centers in Rome merit attention. Beyond question, the most useful for a study of modern Italy's foreign policy is

Biblioteca di Storia Moderna e Contemporanea
Via Michelangelo Caetani, 32
Roma 00186.

This library is especially strong in relevant Italian journals and contains a good range of recent monographs, including all titles issued by the Istituto Storico Italiano of the University of Rome, whose headquarters are also located in the Biblioteca di Storia Moderna e Contemporanea.

Deutsches Historisches Institut
Via Aurelia Antica, 391
Roma 00165.

The Istituto Storico Germanico, to give it its Italian name, has a library well-stocked with good runs of Italian journals and bibliographical titles; it also holds some ASME inventories. See Jens Petersen, "Arbeit im Bereich der neuesten Geschichte," in Reinhard Elze and Arnold Esch, eds., Das Deutsche Historische Institut in Rom, 1888-1988 (Tübingen, 1989). The Institute publishes Quellen und Forschungen aus italienischen Archiven und Bibliotheken (#137) and excellent bibliographical series (#40).

ITALIAN FOREIGN POLICY, 1918-1945

Like most western countries Italy boasts foreign affairs institutes geared more to contemporary than past diplomacy. Nevertheless, their libraries can be rewarding to historians. The best-known are:

Istituto Affari Internazionali
Viale Mazzini, 88
Roma 00195.

Istituto per gli Studi di Politica Internazionale
Palazzo Clerici, Via Clerici, 5
Milano 20121.

The latter, founded in 1933 as a Fascist exercise in organizing a consensus for its foreign policy (see Montenegro, #671), is now an eminently respectable political scientific organization. It publishes the weekly Relazioni Internazionali (#116).

Some General Guides to Italian Libraries

Besides the catalogs of specific libraries above, a number of guides to Italian libraries at large are in print. Some of these reference works embrace both archives and libraries, and have therefore already been cited apropos the former. In this context the practical guide to both archives and libraries by Lewanski (p. 53) is worth recalling. Additional library aids:

Apolloni, Ettore, ed. Annuario delle biblioteche italiane, new ed., 5 vols. Rome, 1969-81.

Much on buildings, less on contents.

Italy, Centro Nazionale per il Catalogo Unico delle Biblioteche Italiane e delle Informazioni Bibliografiche. Primo catalogo colletivo delle biblioteche italiane. Rome, 1962- .

First attempt at an Italian national catalog, but progress very slow and only includes pre-1957 imprints. See also the same body's Guida alla catalogazione nell'ambito del Servizio Bibliotecario Nazionale, 2 vols. (Rome, 1987).

Unione Internazionale degli Istituti di Archeologia, Storia e Storia dell'Arte in Roma. Catalogo dei periodici esistenti in biblioteche di Roma, 3d ed. Rome, 1985.

Very handy directory for the history scholar working in the Italian capital.

2. Other Nations

United States

(1) General Libraries

ARCHIVES, LIBRARIES, NEWSPAPERS

Library of Congress
Washington, DC.

Preeminent in terms of general coverage of scholarly fields in all languages. Its value to the student of twentieth-century Italian foreign policy lies not just in monographs and memoirs but also in runs of Italian government publications, notably parliamentary debates and papers. The Main Catalog of the Library of Congress covering accessions 1898-1980 has been reproduced on 9,000 microfiche (K.G. Saur). In book form the Library of Congress catalog was for many years and until 1982 folded into the U.S. National Union Catalog; since 1983 the N.U.C. has been issued on microfiche and is updated monthly.

New York Public Library
5th Avenue and 42d Street
New York, NY.

Ranks second in comprehensiveness among U.S. libraries. It, too, holds series of printed Italian parliamentary papers, which are listed in the New York Public Library's Catalog of Government Publications in the Research Libraries, vol. 16 of 40, and supplement (Boston, 1972-76). This publication is updated annually by the Bibliographic Guide to Government Publications - Foreign, (Boston, 1976-), which lists accessions to both the New York Public Library and the Library of Congress. A limited quantity of secondary literature on Italy in the era of the world wars is revealed in New York Public Library, Subject Catalog of the World War I Collection, 4 vols. (Boston, 1961), and Subject Catalog of the World War II Collection, 3 vols. (Boston, 1977).

Widener Library
Harvard University
Cambridge, MA.

The other general library to have published a catalog of its European holdings, though its General European and World History (Cambridge, MA, 1970) is arranged by neither author nor topic but by shelf classification.

(2) Institutes and Special Collections

For a general guide to North American research institutes, see Margaret L. and Harold C. Young, eds., Directory of Special Libraries and Information Centers, 9th ed., 3 vols. (Detroit, 1985); vol. 4 for those in humanities and social sciences.

Center for Research Libraries
6050 South Kenwood Avenue
Chicago, IL.

The most far-reaching of all U.S. research organizations offers a swift interlibrary loan service of a broad selection of primary and published sources, and is particularly strong in serial titles. Although it spans many academic disciplines, history is perhaps the most prominent among its holdings, which are being constantly expanded. Among its Italian material are the microfilm collections of Mussolini's and Sonnino's papers (pp. 42, 51). The researcher, however, should be aware that he or she may only use the Center's services by operating through one of its 150 component institutional members, mostly North American universities. An introductory guide is Center for Research Libraries, Handbook (Chicago, 1987). A catalog of actual holdings is available on microfiche, and the Center also issues a bimonthly newsletter (p. 56).

    Hoover Institution on War, Revolution and Peace
    Stanford University
    Palo Alto, CA.

A research institute with an inclination towards diplomatic history in this century. Its emphasis is more on the Soviets and Eastern Europe than the Mediterranean and Western Europe, but it possesses a modest amount of original Italian material - for instance, photocopies of some gabinetto del ministro documents concerning the Munich and Danzig crises and some private papers (see p. 47ff.). There is a larger quantity of holdings of Italian printed documents - Italian parliamentary debates and papers, records of the Camera dei Fasci e Corporazioni, Atti del Partito Nazionale Fascista, and sundry Fascist publications. The Institute also has Nazi German documentation that reflects on Italy. Consult Guide to the Hoover Institution Archives, comps. Charles D. Palm and Dale Reed, (Palo Alto, CA, 1980); Archival and Manuscript Material at the Hoover Institution: A Checklist of Major Collections (Palo Alto, CA, 1975); Catalog of Western-language Publications, 63 vols. (Boston, 1969), and supplements, 11 vols. (Boston, 1972-77); Western Europe: A Survey of Holdings at the Hoover Institution (Palo Alto, CA, 1975), ed. Agnes F. Peterson.

    Council on Foreign Relations
    58 East 68th Street
    New York, NY.

Founded after World War I to promote public interest in foreign affairs and now influential on the frontier of academe and public service. The Council's principal scholarly endeavors stress current international politics, and its library now concentrates on acquiring material on world affairs in the past decade. The Council publishes the quarterly, Foreign Affairs (#125), and in the past has published valuable bibliographies of twentieth-century diplomatic history (#10).

    Council for European Studies
    Columbia University, New York, NY.

Similarly rather orientated to presentist scholarship. But through its newsletter (p. 57) it serves as a useful clearing house for information of interest to all students of modern and contemporary Europe.

    Casa Italiana
    Columbia University, New York, NY.

An Italian cultural center. It has a small library and sponsors occasional symposia on Italian themes.

ARCHIVES, LIBRARIES, NEWSPAPERS

Great Britain

(1) General Libraries

British Library
London, W1.

The equivalent in world renown of the U.S. Library of Congress. Formerly the Library of the British Museum, whose buildings it will continue to inhabit until its new premises at St. Pancras are ready in a few years. And testimony to the publishing explosion and pressure on shelf space, the British Library has now ceased acquiring every U.K. copyright title. Printed editions of the library's catalog run to several hundred volumes and cover titles received up to 1985; subsequent accessions are kept on an updated microfiche.

Foreign and Commonwealth Office Library
Cornwall House, Stamford Street
London, SE1.

Holds the Foreign Office's collection of World War II enemy records, mostly German (though see Ciano papers, p. 47). The Library has a considerable selection of secondary titles, several catalogs of which have been published.

Imperial War Museum
Lambeth Road
London, SE1.

The Museum's collections concentrate, of course, on military history, but its library contains a number of titles in diplomatic history, as well as some Nuremberg Trials records. A subject guide to the library's holdings is in print.

(2) Institutes and Special Collections

A standard directory is Stephen Roberts et al., comps., <u>Research Libraries and Collections in the United Kingdom</u> (Hamden, CT, 1978).

Royal Institute of International Affairs
Chatham House, 10 St. James's Square
London, SW1.

Familiarly known as Chatham House after its address. The need felt at the close of the First World War to stimulate public knowledge of world events, which produced the Council on Foreign Relations in New York, brought forth this similar institute in London. Now its library, like that of the Council on Foreign Relations, makes acquisitions only in the areas of recent international affairs (the last twenty years). None the less, it is useful for published documents and other titles printed between the world wars, and has some well-charted periodical runs: see Royal Institute of International Affairs, <u>Index to Periodical Articles, 1950-64, 1965-72, 1973-78</u>, 4 vols. (Boston, 1965-79). See also the R.I.I.A. publications, <u>Documents on International Affairs</u> (#217); <u>Survey of International Affairs</u> (#100); <u>International Affairs</u> (#132).

Institute of Contemporary History and Wiener Library
4 Devonshire Street
London, W1.

An organization committed to the study of interwar history, with a prime interest in the sociopolitical aspects of Nazism and Fascism rather than in international politics. But inevitably its library contains many items relevant to diplomatic history.

Institute of Historical Research
University of London
London, WC1.

Probably best-known of historical research institutes located in British universities. The foundation has always been keenly interested in world affairs and, for example, holds the library of the late G.P. Gooch.

Centre for Advanced Study of Italian Society
University of Reading, Berks.

The center hosts seminars on recent and contemporary Italian history whose proceedings are sometimes published, and is responsible for assembling much Italian material in Reading University's library. The emphasis is not on foreign policy, but the library holds a number of valuable out-of-the-way publications, particularly on Italian Fascism.

St. Antony's College
Oxford University, Oxon.

Specializes in the study of modern international relations. Library holds a photocopy of Mussolini's segreteria particolare (p. 42), and has useful monographs and memoirs from the immediate post-1945 period, but is short on recently published titles.

France

For a basic guide, see Erwin K. Welsch, ed. Libraries and Archives in France, rev. ed. (see above, p. 64).

Bibliothèque Nationale
58 rue Richelieu
Paris.

France's central library, for which a new site in Paris's 13th arrondissement is planned. Although holdings are considerable, they do not match either the Library of Congress or British Library in coverage of modern diplomatic history, especially in foreign publications. The Bibliothèque Nationale is a notoriously difficult library to use. Although a printed catalog of several hundred volumes exists, its cataloging system is characteristically complex.

ARCHIVES, LIBRARIES, NEWSPAPERS

>Institut d'Histoire du Temps Présent
>44 rue de l'Amiral Monchez
>Paris.

Interdisciplinary center, successor to the Comité d'Histoire de la Deuxième Guerre Mondiale. Emphasis is on contemporary history since the 1930's, especially World War II.

>Société d'Histoire Générale et d'Histoire Diplomatique
>13 rue Soufflot
>Paris.

Long-established organization for study of diplomacy; publishes Revue d'Histoire Diplomatique (#140).

Germany

An inventory of libraries in both Germanies is found in Erwin K. Welsch, Libraries and Archives in Germany (see above, p. 67). Note that the West German Federal Republic lacks a formal "national" library.

>Bibliothek für Zeitgeschichte - Weltkriegsbücherei
>Konrad Adenauerstrasse, 8
>Stuttgart.

Established during the First World War, this library concentrates on nineteenth- and twentieth-century world history; it has been described as the FRG's Hoover Institution. Its published and updated catalogs are invaluable bibliographical tools for German works (see Jahresbibliographie, #38).

>Institut für Zeitgeschichte
>Leonrodstrasse, 46b
>Munich.

Founded after World War II expressly to promote the study of Germany's recent past, the institute has acquired a deserved reputation for scholarship. It holds much original source material on Nazism; see Werner Röder, "Die archivalischen Sammlungen im Institut für Zeitgeschichte im München," Archivar, 38/4 (1985): 415-24. The library's Alphabetischer Katalog: Sachkatalog: Länderkatalog: Bibliographischer Katalog, 18 vols. (Boston, 1967-73) is a model of cross-referencing. Publishes Vierteljahrshefte für Zeitgeschichte (#142), including Bibliographie zur Zeitgeschichte (#37).

D. NEWSPAPERS

The role of newspapers in the study of diplomatic history has always been hazy. Historians seem to go to newspapers for one of two reasons. The lesser motive is to gain information. One should never underestimate the skill of the foreign correspondent in ferreting out a story; there is little that is later resuscitated or confirmed from documents that did not receive some contemporary journalistic observation, however vague and intermixed with rumor. But unless one can begin with a precise reference, culling information from newspapers is a wearisome task, for only two newspapers in the world - the New York Times and The Times (London) - are indexed for the period 1918-1945. Hence, more often, scholars turn to the press in search of elusive public opinion. Of course, it hardly needs to be said that press and public opinion are not at all the same thing. The most one learns from newspapers in this regard are the views of certain interest groups or of a political regime that may or may not embody the national will.

1. Italy's Newspapers, 1918-1945

In Italy, mass literacy came slowly and late, and even in the aftermath of World War I the traditional newspapers were inclined to address themselves to a fairly narrow political public. However, within this limited spectrum some variety of opinion found expression. And yet, although foreign affairs received their share of publicity during the postwar peace negotiations, it cannot be said that any great debate unfolded in the Italian press. The Wilsonians, or rinunciatari (renouncers of territorial gains), won scant hearing. Rather, there was widespread agreement that Italy had been cheated out of her wartime deserts in the peacemaking, although there was some disputation over the need to reach an understanding with the new state of Yugoslavia. The responsible papers adopted a general nationalistic tone while favoring détente in the Adriatic in principle, thus riding with both hare and hounds.

But with the imposition of the Fascist dictatorship in 1925 all vestige of free opinion vanished. The left-wing press was suppressed, and censorship transformed the middle-of-the-road papers into mouthpieces for the regime. In this capacity the latter were to a great extent put in the shade by the Nationalist and Fascist party press, which now came into its own. At first, these party papers exhibited some nuances within the Fascist and Nationalist outlook on world affairs, but once Mussolini made foreign policy the touchstone of his regime, even this had to cease. The Ministry of Popular Culture was formally created in 1937 to enjoin total press conformity. On Fascist press regulations, see the documentary works by Francesco Flora, Stampa dell'era fascista: le note

ARCHIVES, LIBRARIES, NEWSPAPERS

di servizio (Rome, 1945), and Claudio Matteini, <u>Ordini alla stampa: La politica interna ed estera del regime fascista nelle "disposizioni" emanate ai giornali dal Ministero della Cultura Popolare</u>, (Rome, 1945).

By its very nature Mussolini's "regime of gestures" conducted much of its business in the public eye. Foreign affairs were no exception; on many occasions official or quasi-official thinking on the international situation was deliberately displayed in the media. In this phenomenon, unquestionably, lies the principal value of Italian newspapers between 1918 and 1945.

For a full list of Italian journalistic publications in these years, consult <u>Annuario della Stampa Italiana</u> (Rome, 1916-42). Most of the titles listed below for their reflection of or influence on Italian foreign policy are available in microform for 1918-1945 <u>in toto</u> or in part. To locate, see <u>Newspapers in Microform</u> (p. 84) or <u>Guide to Microforms in Print</u> (#41).

Selected Italian Titles

<u>Avanti!</u>, Milan. Official Socialist party paper, edited by Mussolini before World War I. After 1918 sympathetic to Wilsonianism but sceptical of its realization; critical of postwar settlement from anti-imperialist position. Suppressed 1926.

<u>Il Corriere della Sera</u>, Milan. Authentic voice of Italian liberal oligarchy. Increasingly nationalist in tone during and after World War I, though never stridently so. Because of paper's stature Fascism made a direct attack on the paper's integrity, forcing the celebrated Albertini family to relinquish control in 1925. Glauco Licata, <u>Storia del "Corriere della Sera"</u> (Milan, 1976), is a massive volume based on extensive archival research. Composed for the paper's centenary, it asserts claim of <u>Corriere</u> to be Italy's national daily. See also Denis Mack Smith, <u>Storia di cento anni di vita italiana vista attraverso il "Corriere della Sera"</u> (Milan, 1978), which has useful chapters on the paper's attitude to international events, and Loredana Ricci, "L'immagine dell'Unione Sovietica attraverso il <u>Corriere della Sera</u> nel periodo fascista," <u>Il Politico</u>, 53 (1988): 153-66.

<u>Il Corriere Padano</u>, Ferrara. Paper controlled by Fascist hierarch Italo Balbo, who had a taste for international politics. Generally revisionist, though occasionally critical of Germany.

<u>Il Giornale d'Italia</u>, Rome. Sonnino's paper, which endorsed his expansionist policies. Nationalist bias commended it to Fascism, hence in Mussolini era came into prominence under editorship of chauvinistic Virginio Gayda. Particularly combative towards Yugoslavia. Alberto Bergamini's <u>Storia del "Giornale d'Italia"</u> (Rome, 1975) is a brief synopsis of the period 1901-23 when the author was editor.

<u>L'Italia</u>, Rome. Began as moderate Catholic paper, organ of post-World War I Popular party. Vaguely Wilsonian without renouncing fruits of victory. After 1925 fell into the hands of clerico-fascists.

<u>Il Messaggero</u>, Rome. The capital's main daily. Editorially supported whatever government in power between the wars. See Giuseppe Talamo,

"Il Messaggero" e la sua città: Cento anni di storia, 2 vols. (Florence, 1979-84); vol. II, Un giornale durante il fascismo, 1919-1946.

L'Osservatore Romano, Rome. As official Vatican paper, not strictly an Italian journal, and also exempt from Fascist dictatorial control. At first sympathetic to Mussolini's overseas activity, including Ethiopian venture; later, hostile to Rome-Berlin Axis and racist corollary, openly so until the death of Pius XI in 1938, much more timidly under Pius XII. Francesco Leoni, "L'Osservatore Romano": Origini ed evoluzione (Naples, 1970), is a short survey from 1861 to 1949.

Also for Catholic thinking, consult the influential Jesuit fortnightly, Civiltà Cattolica (Rome); see anthology of Civiltà Cattolica, 1850-1945, 4 vols. (Florence, 1971). A brief sketch useful for the religious press other than Osservatore Romano is Glauco Licata, Giornalismo cattolico italiano, 1861-1943 (Rome, 1964).

Il Popolo d'Italia, Milan. Established by Mussolini in 1914 as interventionist paper; in 1919 became official Fascist organ, remaining so until 1943. Edited by Benito's influential brother, Arnaldo, 1922-31, and afterwards by son, Vittorio, although the Duce always took a keen interest in daily composition. Hence, a key journalistic source; much of Mussolini's Opera omnia (#152) is drawn from Popolo d'Italia.

On the subject of the official Fascist party press, one should not overlook the monthly journal Gerarchia (Milan). Its comments on foreign affairs, however, were usually couched in rhetorical generalizations, reflecting belligerent nationalism but with random reference to specific diplomatic problems.

Il Secolo, Milan. Moderately radical paper, useful for views of rinunciatari after World War I. Ceased independent existence in 1927.

La Stampa, Turin. Another esteemed voice of liberal establishment, Giolittian wing. Indulged in restrained nationalism. Owned by Alfredo Frassati, briefly ambassador to the Weimar Republic; reflected his sympathy with the German position on reparations. Like Corriere della Sera, lost individuality and became the regime's mouthpiece after 1925. See Alfredo Signoretti, "La Stampa" in camicia nera, 1932-1943 (Rome, 1968), reminiscences of the editor during eleven Fascist years.

Il Tevere, Rome. Run 1938-43 by Telesio Interlandi, a racial Fascist; paper hostile to Britain and France, radically revisionist. Mussolini liked to float ideas in Il Tevere.

La Tribuna, Rome. Had embraced uncompromising nationalism before 1914; absorbed well-known Idea Nazionale 1926. Under editorship of Roberto Forges-Davanzati, another journalist crony of Mussolini, preached Anglophobia, anti-Slavism, and generic revisionism, though not automatically support for Germany.

ARCHIVES, LIBRARIES, NEWSPAPERS

L'Unità, Milan. Published by Italy's fledgling Communist party until its suppression in 1926.

Italian Press Excerpts

Del Buono, Oreste, ed. Eia, Eia, Eia, Alalà! La stampa italiana sotto il fascismo, 1919-1943. Milan, 1971.

Popular nationalist propaganda, cartoons, illustrations.

Gaeta, Franco, ed. La stampa nazionalista. Bologna, 1965.

Extracts mostly from 1914-25, on Treaties of Versailles and Rapallo, Corfu crisis, Anschluss.

Maugeri, Francesco, ed. Verso la 2a guerra mondiale: Cronache politiche. "Acta Diurna," 1933-1940. Bari, 1979.

Over a thousand articles, editorials written by Guido Gonella for L'Osservatore Romano. Other journalistic pieces reflecting a Catholic view can be found in Alcide De Gasperi, Scritti di politica internazionale, 1933-1938, 2 vols. (Vatican City, 1981).

Melograni, Piero, ed. "Corriere della Sera," 1919-1943. Bologna, 1965.

Lengthy introductory essay on Corriere followed by extensive selections, mostly from editorials signed and unsigned; sections on Fiume, Axis, World War II.

General Works

Cannistraro, Philip V. La fabbrica del consenso: Fascismo e mass media. Rome-Bari, 1975.

On radio and films as well as press; describes role of Ministry of Popular Culture. See also Lucio Ceva, "Polivalenza e attaulità del Minculpop," Risorgimento [Milan], 34 (1982): 147-58, and Pini (#342).

Castronovo, Valerio. La stampa italiana dall'Unità al fascismo, 2d ed. Bari, 1984.

Best single survey, with a documentary appendix on fascistization of press. Also highly recommended are the essays in series Storia della stampa italiana, ed. V. Castronovo and N. Tranfaglia, 6 vols. (Rome & Bari, 1976-80); vol. 3, La stampa italiana nell'età liberale; vol. 4, La stampa italiana nell'età fascista.

Cesari, Maurizio. La censura nel periodo fascista. Naples, 1978.

Murialdi, Paolo. Stampa del regime fascista. Bari, 1986.

Vigezzi, Brunello, ed. <u>1919-1925: Dopoguerra e fascismo. Politica e stampa in Italia</u>. Bari, 1965.

Analytical essays on <u>Avanti!</u>, <u>Corriere della Sera</u>, <u>Giornale d'Italia</u>, <u>L'Italia</u>, <u>Popolo d'Italia</u>, <u>Il Secolo</u>, <u>La Stampa</u>, <u>La Tribuna</u>, <u>L'Unità</u>.

2. Newspaper Collections

Italy

The useful practice of congregating runs of newspapers, often in microform, in one location is of recent origin, and in Italy is still virtually unknown. There are no Italian newspaper repositories per se.

On the other hand, Italy's premier national library - the Biblioteca Nazionale Centrale, Florence - has made a point of building up its newspaper holdings. Unfortunately, many housed in the library's basement were ruined in the great flood of November 1966. See also Franca Alloatti, Gabriella Fonti, Claudia Romano, eds., <u>Catalogo dei quotidiani nella Biblioteca Nazionale Braidense</u> (Rome, 1987).

A small center to investigate the interplay of public opinion and foreign policy was set up in the 1960's at the University of Milan under the direction of Professor B. Vigezzi. For its own work this body assembled some newspaper runs. On this enterprise, see

Vigezzi, Brunello. "Politica estera e opinione pubblica," <u>Itinerari</u> (1961), nos. 47-55, pp. 53-63, 140-48, 214-22, 270-78, 298-308.

United States

On the whole, the researcher will probably find it easier to locate major Italian newspapers, at least in microform, in the English-speaking world than in Italy itself. Consult Grace D. Parch, ed., <u>Directory of Newspaper Libraries in the U.S. and Canada</u> (New York, 1976). It will be discovered, however, that libraries and institutes normally give German, French, and Spanish press material priority over Italian. In consequence, Italian holdings are sometimes fragmentary.

A general guide to filmed newspaper collections, mainly but not exclusively of U.S. provenance, is

U.S., Library of Congress. <u>Newspapers in Microform</u>. Washington, 1975- . Annual.

There is also a cumulative index to this title covering 1948-83 in 3 vols.; vol. 3 devoted to foreign newspapers.

Besides the Library of Congress, which has Italian newspapers in its own broad collection, some of the other American institutions described in the preceding section possess Italian press material. Preeminent in this field is the Center for Research Libraries, which is constantly adding to its press collection in original print and in microform. Even the Center's microfiche catalog does

ARCHIVES, LIBRARIES, NEWSPAPERS

not list all its more than three thousand newspaper titles, nor does its otherwise useful printed catalog:

    Center for Research Libraries. <u>Newspaper Catalog</u>, 2d ed. Chicago, 1978.

Other libraries with substantial newspaper holdings are the New York Public Library Newspaper Annex (10th Avenue and 43d Street) and the Hoover Institution. Consult

    New York Public Library. <u>Guide to the Research Collections of the New York Public Library</u>, comp. Sam P. Williams. Chicago, 1975.

    Hoover Institution on War, Revolution and Peace. <u>Catalogs of Western-language Serials and Newspaper Collections</u>, 3 vols. Boston, 1969. Vol. 3 for newspapers.

Great Britain

The principal British repository of newspaper material is the British Library's Newspaper Annex in Colindale, London, NW9. This holds western-language newspapers from the eighteenth to twentieth centuries. An extensive index is in print, although it covers accessions only up to 1971:

    The British Library. <u>Catalogue of the Newspaper Library, Colindale</u>, 8 vols. London, 1975.

Vols. 1-4 provide lists of newspapers held by geographical area (vol. 3 for European and Italian titles); vols. 5-8 an alphabetical list of all titles. A list of newspapers microfilmed by the British Library, which includes more recent acquisitions, is available on request. There is access to databases for computer searching.

An index arranged by country to British newspaper collections, exclusive of the Colindale holdings, has been compiled by Rosemary Webber, <u>World List of National Newspapers: A Union List of National Newspapers in Libraries in the British Isles</u> (London, 1976).

Of other British scholarly bodies mentioned earlier in this chapter, the Royal Institute of International Affairs has a distinctive press library of its own. Inaugurated in 1924 to supply information for the Institute's <u>Surveys of International Affairs</u> (#100), it has a large collection of press clippings, domestic and foreign, Italian included. Its newspaper runs go from 1924 to 1939, and are in process of being microfilmed.

IV. BIBLIOGRAPHY

A. GENERAL

1. Bibliographical Aids

Bibliographical titles continue to proliferate. Many of them overlap, which makes it difficult to place them in categories. The divisions that follow are perforce arbitrary. General bibliographies by definition span several historical fields and are useful for preliminary surveys. Under subject bibliographies are to be found titles limited at least to twentieth-century international affairs and with particular reference to Italy. By retrospective bibliographies are meant those published before a certain date, in this case circa 1950, whose chief function is to lead scholars to the publications of the actual period 1918-1945. Current bibliographies are of great practical worth; these are titles issued at more or less regular intervals, which enables the researcher to keep up-to-date with the latest work to appear in print. Finally, bibliographical essays normally published in periodicals are valuable for assessing the historiography of a problem.

The most comprehensive bibliography of bibliographies is Theodore Besterman's A World Bibliography of Bibliographies, 4th ed., 5 vols. (Lausanne, 1965-66), with a two-volume supplement for 1964-1974, ed. Alice F. Toomey (Totowa, NJ, 1977). This is a classified index, arranged alphabetically by subject; it lists bibliographic titles but not bibliographies that form part of a larger work. The Bibliographic Index (New York, 1938-) appears biannually as well as in annual volumes. It includes bibliographies published separately or as parts of books, periodicals, and review essays, and is particularly useful in pursuing smaller topics. More specific and very relevant to this guide is Berenice A. Carroll, Clinton F. Fink, Jane E. Mohraz, eds., Peace and War: A Guide to Bibliographies (Santa Barbara, 1983). International in scope, this specifies 1,398 bibliographies produced between 1785 and 1980. A starting point for inquiries into unpublished doctoral work is Michael M. Reynolds, ed., A Guide to Theses and Dissertations: An International Bibliography of Bibliographies, 2d ed. (Phoenix, AZ, 1985). Finally in the field of English-language publications, a National Registry for the Bibliography of History has been inaugurated at Georgetown University, Washington, D.C., under the aegis of Professor Thomas T. Helde. The aim is to inscribe as many bibliographic projects as possible under way in the U.S. and Canada in all areas of history, and to serve as a clearing house of information. The register is published each year in American History: A Bibliographical Review (Westport, CT, 1985-).

ITALIAN FOREIGN POLICY, 1918-1945

The only Italian publications in this category are sadly dated: La bibliografia italiana, 2d ed., ed. Giannetto Avanzi (Rome, 1946), covers Italian works that appeared between 1921 and 1946; the same editor compiled a brief "Elenco bibliografico delle relazioni estere," in La documentazione in Italia, (Rome, 1952), pp. 155-59. An annual and general bibliography of Italian bibliographies was then launched but ceased publication after a few years: Italia Bibliographica (Florence, 1952-61); cumulative indices for 1952-56, 1956-61 were edited by Giuseppe Sergio Martini and Bona Edlmann.

General Bibliographies

1. American Historical Association. Guide to Historical Literature, ed. George F. Howe. New York, 1961.

   Selective, annotated bibliography of source materials, reference works, and secondary literature; section on Italy compiled by C.E. Boyd. Now dated, but new edition in preparation; Italian section to be compiled under supervision of Emiliana P. Noether.

   Also in the planning stage, a series of bibliographies in European history to be issued under the imprimatur of the Royal Historical Society of Great Britain.

2. Farber, Evan Ira, ed. Combined Retrospective Index to Book Reviews in Scholarly Journals, 1886-1974, 15 vols. Arlington, VA, 1979-82.

   Vols. 1-12 author listing, 13-15 titles. Reference to about a million reviews from nearly 500 journals. Further 150 journals indexed in Combined Retrospective Index to Book Reviews in Humanities Journals, 1802-1974, 10 vols. (Woodbridge, CT, 1982-84). For indices of book reviews beyond 1974, see Book Review Index (#39); Zeller (#53).

3. Harcourt, Freda, and Robinson, Francis, eds. Twentieth Century World History: A Select Bibliography. London & New York, 1979.

   Some 1,500 mostly theoretical works grouped according to world problems; no annotations or indices.

4. International Committee of Historical Sciences. International Bibliography of Historical Sciences in Festschriften and Miscellanies, 2 vols. Paris, 1955-65.

   Listings by country and by topic, with author index to individual essays. See also Internationale Jahresbibliographie der Festschriften (#47).

5. Kuehl, Warren F., ed. Dissertations in History: An Index to Dissertations Completed in History Departments of U.S. and

Canadian Universities, 1873-1970, 2 vols. Lexington, KY, 1965-72. Supplement (1970-80), Santa Barbara, CA, 1985.

More specific though limited and dated is Doris M. Cruger, ed., A List of American Doctoral Dissertations on Africa, 1961/2-1962/5; France, 1933/4-64/5; Italy, 1933/4-1964/5 (Ann Arbor, 1967). For up-to-date information, consult Doctoral Dissertions in History (#33); Dissertation Abstracts International (#103); Historical Abstracts (#104).

6. Roach, John P.C., ed. A Bibliography of Modern History. Cambridge, 1968.

 Selective bibliography of 6,000 items compiled mainly by contributors to the New Cambridge Modern History (#506). Cites printed sources (documentary publications, books, articles); limited commentary.

7. Wile, Annadel N., ed. Combined Retrospective Index Set to Journals in History, 1838-1974, 11 vols. Washington & Inverness, 1977-78.

 Bibliographical information on some 400,000 articles in over 500 English-language journals in history, political science, sociology. Vols. 1-9 list entries by subject, vols. 10-11 by author; vol. 3 for Italy. For articles after 1974, see Humanities Index, etc. (#44).

Subject Bibliographies

8. Bloomberg, Marty, and Weber, Hans H., eds. World War II and Its Origins: A Select Annotated Bibliography of Books in English. Littleton, CO, 1975.

 Competent introductory bibliography of 1,600 titles, including reference materials, to most aspects of the subject. Organized topically with author and title index.

9. Boulding, Elise; Passmore, Robert J.; Gassler, Robert Scott, eds. Bibliography on World Conflict and Peace, 2d ed. Boulder, CO, 1979.

 A peace-studies product. One thousand English-language books and articles published mainly 1945-79; arranged in four sections by subject matter.

10. Council on Foreign Relations. The Foreign Affairs 50-Year Bibliography, ed. Byron V. Dexter. New York, 1972.

 A bibliography of important works published in the half-century after the First World War, reviewed from a later perspective. In a sense a continuation of Foreign Affairs Bibliography: A Selected and Annotated List of Books on International Relations, 1919-32, 1932-

42, 1942-52, 1952-62, 1962-72, 5 vols. (New York, 1935-76), a bibliographical series always strong on Europe, 1918-45.

11. Delzell, Charles F. Italy in the Twentieth Century. American Historical Association pamphlet no. 428. Washington, 1980.

Excellent bibliography with commentary on English- and Italian-language works; updates the same author's bibliographical articles in the Journal of Modern History, 28 (1956): 374-88; 35 (1963): 339-53; 38 (1966): 53-58. Brief but useful is A Select Bibliography of English-Language Books on Modern Italian History, comp. Roland Sarti (Amherst, MA, 1989).

12. Funk, Arthur L., ed. The Second World War: A Select Bibliography of Books in English Published since 1975. Claremont, CA, 1985.

Supplements the same editor's The Second World War: Select List of Publications Appearing since 1968 (Gainesville, FL, 1972). Lists of secondary literature arranged by subject, prepared for American Committee on the History of the Second World War.

13. International Commission for the Teaching of History. The Two World Wars: Les deux guerres mondiales. London & Brussels, 1964.

Brief chapters on origins of 1914 and 1939 wars followed by about 1,800 printed sources - documentary collections, memoirs, secondary works; some annotated. Bibliography for 1919-39 prepared by E. Anchiere, for 1939-45 by H. Michel and J-M. d'Hoop. In both English and French.

14. Italy, Stato Maggiore dell'Esercito: Ufficio Storico. Bibliografia della seconda guerra mondiale, 1945-1975. Rome, 1980.

Slanted understandably towards warfare but not exclusively military history; good range of Italian titles on World War II origins and wartime diplomacy.

Of peripheral interest to diplomatic historians are Italy's official war histories; consult Oreste Bovio, L'Ufficio Storico dell'Esercito: Un secolo di storiografia militare (Rome, 1987).

15. Messick, Frederick M., ed. Primary Sources in European Diplomacy, 1914-1945: A Bibliography of Published Memoirs and Diaries. Westport, CT, & London, 1987.

Extremely useful guide for scholars of diplomacy of era bounded by two world wars. Memorialists of some 30 nations listed in alphabetical order; brief identifications, annotations. Indices of authors by nation and by topic.

BIBLIOGRAPHICAL AIDS

16. Milza, Pierre, and Dreyfus, Michel. Un siècle d'immigration italienne en France: Bibliographie. Paris, 1987.

    Italian anti-Fascist exiles in France were a live political issue between the wars.

17. Schröder, Josef. Italien im Zweiten Weltkrieg: Eine Bibliographie. L'Italia nella seconda guerra mondiale: Una bibliografia. Stuttgart, Bibliothek für Zeitgeschichte Schriften no. 14, 1978.

    One volume with titles and introductory material in both German and Italian; strongest in works of those languages. Massive compilation of 10,000 entries without annotation. Includes all kinds of printed sources, some relating to entire period, 1918-1945. Intricately subdivided by topic with various indices, including author list.

18. Smith, Myron J. World War II: The European and Mediterranean Theaters: An Annotated Bibliography. New York, 1984.

    Over 2,800 English-language items, with concentration on U.S. military history, briefly annotated; author and subject indices. Aims to supplement Ziegler (#22).

19. ———. The Secret Wars: A Guide to Sources in English, 3 vols. Santa Barbara, CA, 1980.

    Some 9,000 books, articles, theses, government documents in English language on intelligence operations; vol. 1 for 1939-45, other vols. post-1945. Frank L. Schaf, ed., Intelligence, Espionage, Counterespionage, and Covert Operations: A Guide to Information Sources (Detroit, 1978), is concerned almost exclusively with the post-World War II era. Marjorie W. Cline, et al., eds., Scholar's Guide to Intelligence Literature (Frederick, MD, 1983) lists 6,000 published items on the subject in Georgetown University Library, Washington, DC.

20. Toscano, Mario. The History of Treaties and International Politics. Vol. 1. Baltimore, 1966.

    Very important bibliographical tool for students of twentieth-century Italian foreign policy. After a general introduction on the nature of diplomatic documentary sources, the bulk of the book consists of extended descriptions of published documentary collections and memoirs relative to the diplomatic origins and conduct of both world wars. All major powers, and some minor, are comprehended in this sweeping analysis, obviously the fruit of a research team. But given the author's eminence as a historian of Italian diplomacy, documentary and memoir sources for Italy's foreign policy receive a lion's share of attention. The unusual and misleading title derives from the formal name of the course that Toscano taught at the University of Rome and that provided the framework for his investigations.

The book has dated slightly, although the great documentary series were launched and the most revelatory memoirs produced within twenty years of the end of the Second World War, and were therefore taken into account in this revised English-language edition of earlier Italian sketches and versions: "Fonti documentarie e memorialistiche per la storia diplomatica della seconda guerra mondiale," Rivista Storica Italiana 60 (1948): 83-126; "Fonti per la storia diplomatica della seconda guerra mondiale," in Questioni di storia contemporanea, ed. Ettore Rota, vol. 1 (Milan, 1952), pp. 531-92; Lezioni di storia dei trattati e politica internazionale (Turin, 1958, 1963).

At his death in 1968 Toscano was the unquestioned doyen of Italian diplomatic historians. His position as director of the Italian Foreign Ministry archives gave him access to material then denied to other scholars, and bestowed on his numerous books and articles a unique authoritative character. A valuable list of titles by Toscano is included in an obituary tribute by William L. Langer, "Mario Toscano," Clio, 5 (1969): 141-55.

21. Wright, Moorhead; Davis, Jane; Clarke, Michael, eds. Essay Collections in International Relations: A Classified Bibliography. New York, 1977.

    More theoretical, analytical international relations than diplomatic history. Comprehends international affairs since 1870 and publications in English, 1945-75.

22. Ziegler, Janet, ed. World War II: Books in English, 1945-1965. Palo Alto, CA, 1971.

    List of about 4,500 secondary works and memoirs restricted fairly rigorously to wartime events; arranged topically with author index. See also the same author's "Bibliographie sur la seconde guerre mondiale," Revue d'Histoire de la Deuxième Guerre Mondiale, no. 81 (1971): 95-104, which includes non-English titles.

Retrospective Bibliographies

See also Foreign Affairs Bibliography (#10).

23. Bibliografia Fascista. Rome, 1926-1935. Reprint, 10 vols. Nendeln, Liechtenstein, 1975.

    Monthly, then fortnightly, synopsis of literature for and against Fascist movement printed in Italy and abroad. Articles on Italian colonialism in 1930's.

24. Gnirss, Christa, ed. Internationale Bibliographie der Reprints, 2 vols. Munich, 1976-80.

BIBLIOGRAPHICAL AIDS

Vol. 1 for books, serials; vol. 2 newspapers, etc. Of self-evident value in tracing older and out-of-print titles. For latest reprints, see Guide to Reprints (#42).

25. Gregory, Winifred, ed. List of the Serial Publications of Foreign Governments, 1815-1931. New York, 1932. Reprint, Nendeln, Liechtenstein, 1973.

Arranged by country; useful for identifying Italian governmental publications, parliamentary papers, etc., and their location in North America.

26. Italy, Biblioteca della Camera Fascista. Bibliografia dell'impero fascista, 2d ed. Rome, 1938.

Lists over 3,000 titles of books, periodicals, articles, speeches, etc. on Italian colonialism including much propaganda material; topically subdivided with author index. A companion and more general volume is Opere sul fascismo (Rome, 1935), which has a few pages on foreign policy.

27. Italy, Ministero delle Finanze (now Ministero del Tesoro): Provveditorato Generale dello Stato. Pubblicazioni edite dallo stato e col suo concorso, 1861-1923. Rome, 1924. Supplements (1924-1940), Rome, 1931-40. Supplement (1941-44), Rome, 1969.

Contains section "Affari esteri," and until 1923 cataloged parliamentary libri verdi; useful for government handbooks, documentary publications, printed speeches, etc. Another title from the same governmental source is Elenco delle legi e dei decreti emanati dal 1851 al 31 dicembre 1941 (Rome, 1942).

28. Kramm, Heinrich, ed. Bibliographie historischer Zeitschriften, 1939-1951, 3 parts. Marburg, 1952-54.

Italian journals of interwar years in part 2.

29. Màdaro, Luigi, ed. Bibliografia fascista. Milan, 1935.

Section on "Politica estera"; useful list of Italian and pro-Italian foreign publications.

30. Mosca, Rodolfo, ed. Bibliografia del fascismo. Milan, 1930.

Short section "Rapporti internazionali" lists books published in late 1920's, mainly of nationalistic stamp.

31. Ragatz, Lowell J., ed. A Bibliography for the Study of European History, 1815-1939. Ann Arbor, MI, 1942. Supplements, 1943, 1945, 1956.

Once the standard bibliography of main-language books and articles in the field; now useful for out-of-print items. Lists without annotation, divided by topic; no indices.

32. Weltkriegsbücherei, Bibliographische Vierteljahrshefte no. 19. <u>Bibliographie zur Geschichte Italiens in der Nachkriegszeit</u>. Stuttgart, 1938.

    Thorough list of some 3,000 official publications, documentary collections, books, and periodical literature. A section devoted to foreign affairs; arranged alphabetically within topics.

Current Bibliographies

In this category it should be noted that many scholarly journals provide excellent up-to-date bibliographical information by way of books reviewed and lists of books received. Recommended particularly on this score: <u>American Historical Review</u> (#123); <u>Historische Zeitschrift</u> (#129); <u>International History Review</u> (#133); <u>Nuova Rivista Storica</u> (#114); <u>Quellen und Forschungen aus italienischen Archiven und Bibliotheken</u> (#137).

33. American Historical Association. <u>Doctoral Dissertations in History</u>. Washington, 1976- . Biannual.

    Useful specialist serial. For more comprehensive dissertation guides, see <u>Dissertation Abstracts International</u> (#103), <u>Historical Abstracts</u> (#104).

34. ———. <u>Recently Published Articles</u>. Washington, 1976- . Triennial.

    Comprehensive and valuable listing of periodical literature, formerly included in issues of <u>American Historical Review</u> (#123), now published separately. Has a section on Italian history and is more up to date than <u>Historical Abstracts</u> (#104).

35. <u>Arts and Humanities Citation Index</u>. Philadelphia, 1978- . Biannual, annual vols.

    Covers 1,300 journals. Useful for identifying related writings by indicating sources in which work(s) cited. In the same genre, <u>Social Sciences Citation Index</u> (Philadelphia, 1973-) comprehends 2,000 journals triannually and annually. Both titles served by data base for computer searching of recent titles.

36. Associazione Italiana Editori. <u>Catalogo dei libri in commercio</u>. Milan, 1970- . Irregular.

    Trade publication of Italian books in print; issued frequently, on recent average triennially. Indexed in three separate volumes, by author, title, and subject.

BIBLIOGRAPHICAL AIDS

37. Bibliographie zur Zeitgeschichte. Stuttgart, Munich, 1953-Annual.

Formerly published quarterly, then biannually, in separate volumes; now appears with fourth issue of Vierteljahrshefte für Zeitgeschichte (#142). Very thorough listing of secondary works, including articles, in various languages. Index to issues 1953-80, ed. Thilo Vogelsang and Hellmuth Auerbach, 3 vols. (Munich 1982-83); vol. 2 for titles on the twentieth century before 1945.

38. Bibliothek für Zeitgeschichte. Jahresbibliographie. Stuttgart, 1961- . Irregular.

Continues Bücherschau der Weltkriegsbücherei: Katalog, 1929-60, 31 vols. (Boston, 1961). Gives some 10,000 titles accessioned by library on annual basis; arranged by topic and country with author index. Also contains thematic review articles.

39. Book Review Index. Detroit, 1965- . Bimonthly.

Standard listing of English-language reviews from 450 publications; see also cumulative vol., 1969-79, ed. Gary C. Tarbert, 7 vols. (Detroit, 1980). The annual Index to Book Reviews in the Humanities (Williamston, MI, 1960-) lists English and foreign-language reviews, but concentration is on literary and artistic titles. A now discontinued annual publication was John W. Brewster et al., eds., Index to Book Reviews in Historical Journals, 4 vols. (Metuchen, NJ, & London, 1972-77), 3,000 reviews including foreign-language titles from 100 English-language periodicals. See also Humanities Index (#44), and for full international coverage of book reviews, Zeller (#53).

40. Deutsches Historisches Institut in Rom (Istituto Storico Germanico in Roma). Bibliographische Informationen zur italienischen Geschichte im 19. und 20. Jahrhundert. Rome, 1974- . Quarterly.

Annotated list of latest Italian historical publications in alphabetical order by author; not restricted to works on Italo-German relations. Thorough, up to date, and deserves to be better known; often has titles some time before their appearance in standard Italian guides.

See also the same institution's Storia e Critica: Die italienische Zeitgeschichte im Spiegel der Tages- und Wochenpresse (Rome, 1979-), quarterly, which reprints bibliographical items from the press. An Indici 1979-1985 lists book reviews noted by Storia e Critica, with cross references to citation of the work reviewed in Bibliographische Informationen. Both above titles obtainable through membership in the Istituto Storico Germanico in Rome or in the Gruppo di Studio per la Storia Contemporanea Italiana, University of Trier, West Germany.

41. Guide to Microforms in Print. Westport, CT, 1961- . Annual.

Continues Union List of Microfilms, 3 vols. (Ann Arbor, MI, 1951-61), and incorporates International Microforms in Print, eds. A.B. Veaner and A.M. Meckler (Weston, CT, 1974-75). In view of the proliferation of documentary and press material in microform, this is an increasingly important research tool. Cumulative, world-wide coverage, though most microforms of U.S. provenance. Appears in two volumes (one an author, the other a subject index) and a supplement. Subject categories by number; Italy represented by no. 330.

42. Guide to Reprints. Washington, 1967- . Annual.

    For older, discontinued titles. Cumulative alphabetical list of books, journals, and other reprinted material. Now provides international coverage.

43. Historical Association. Annual Bulletin of Historical Literature. London, 1912- . Annual.

    General and selective bibliography in form of historiographical essays; organization by period and country.

44. Humanities Index. New York, 1974- . Quarterly, annual vols.

    Formerly International Index (1907-65) and Social Sciences and Humanities Index (1966-74); historical items now allocated to humanities division. Lists English-language, mostly North American, articles from 300 journals; alphabetical organization embraces both authors and subjects. Also contains list of book reviews in journals, arranged by author reviewed.

    United Kingdom equivalent is British Humanities Index (London, 1962-), quarterly, annual vols., which continues British Humanities Subject Index to Periodicals (1915-61). Lists articles from 400 British and Commonwealth journals. For international coverage, see Zeller (#54).

45. Informazione Bibliografica. Bologna, 1975- . Quarterly.

    General cultural periodical includes lengthy section "I libri pubblicati nel trimestre passato," with subsection "Storia moderna e contemporanea."

46. International Committee of Historical Sciences. International Bibliography of Historical Sciences. Washington, Paris, New York, 1926- . Annual.

    Unannotated list of documentary works, books, and articles in several languages; far-ranging but not always up to date. Organization by subject with author index. Publication interrupted, 1940-46, which gap can be filled by Pier Fausto Palumbo, Bibliografia storica internazionale, 1940-1947 (Rome, 1950), which is strong in Italian titles.

47. Internationale Jahresbibliographie der Festschriften. International Bibliography of Festschriften with Subject Index. Osnabrück, 1982- . Annual.

   Now regular publication that continues Otto Leistner, ed., International Bibliography of Festschriften, 2d ed., 3 vols. (Osnabrück, 1984-89). General list arranged by name of scholar or institution honored; also subject index.

48. Italy, Centro Nazionale per il Catalogo Unico delle Biblioteche Italiane e per le Informazioni Bibliografiche. Bibliografia Nazionale Italiana. Nuova serie del Bollettino delle publicazioni italiane ricevute per diretto di stampa. Florence, 1958- , monthly. Catalogo alphabetico annuale, 1958- . Florence, 1961- .

   Monthly title formerly Bollettini delle Pubblicazioni Italiane; see Catalogo cumulativo, 1886-1957, 41 vols. (Nendeln, Liechtenstein, 1968-69). Lists all titles copyrighted in Italy, including official publications. Italian equivalent of American and British lists of copyrighted titles, namely, U.S. National Union Catalog, American Publishing Record, and the British National Bibliography.

   Annual volume cumulates most but not all information in monthly issues; thus it cannot serve as a comprehensive guide despite index of secondary authors and subjects.

49. Italy, Giunta Centrale per gli Studi Storici. Bibliografia Storica Nazionale. Rome-Bari, 1939-42, 1949- . Several yearly issues in one vol.

   Key reference work for students of Italian history; comprehensive listing of Italian titles, published in Italy and elsewhere, including important articles. Chronological and topical subdivisions, e.g. part G (Storia contemporanea, 1871-1945) includes sections "Prima guerra mondiale," "Seconda guerra mondiale," "Relazioni internazionali." Also has an author index.

50. Italy, Presidency of the Council of Ministers Information and Copyright Services. Italian Books and Periodicals. Rome, 1958- . Quarterly, annual vols.

   Useful English-language edition of monthly Libri e Riviste d'Italia (1950-). In two parts for books and articles, respectively; each part contains historical section. Selected titles accorded signed book review, other titles in bibliographical list by author; articles listed under journal title with occasional description.

51. Public Affairs Information Service (PAIS). Bulletin. New York, 1915- . Fortnightly, triannual vols.

Lists books, articles, documents, etc. on "contemporary public issues." Hence, a historian must go back to earlier issues for his material; see Cumulative Subject Index to PAIS Annual Bulletins, 1915-1974, 15 vols. (Arlington, VA, 1977-78). Data base for online computerized searching.

Too recent to interest the historian, although containing Italian material, is PAIS, Foreign Language Index (New York, 1972-); quarterly, annual vols.

52. U.N.E.S.C.O. Index Translationum: International Bibliography of Translations. Paris, 1932-40, 1949- . Annual.

Multilingual listings by subject, with index of authors translated. Approx. 75 countries covered. See also Cumulative Index to English Translations, 1948-1968, 2 vols. (Boston, 1973).

53. Zeller, Otto, ed. Internationale Bibliographie der Rezensionen wissenschaftlicher Literatur. Osnabrück, 1971- . Biannual.

Continues Bibliographie der Rezensionen (Leipzig, 1900-43). Book reviews in all disciplines and languages listed under periodical title, subject, book author, and reviewing author. In German, French, and English.

54. ———. Internationale Bibliographie der Zeitschriften aus allen Gebeiten des Wissens. Osnabrück, 1965- . Irregular (most frequent pub. monthly).

Continues in combined form Bibliographie der deutschen Zeitschriftenliteratur (1896-1964) and Bibliographie der fremdsprachigen Zeitschriftenliteratur (1911-64). Lists articles drawn from 4,000 journals in all disciplines, languages; subject and author indices. In German, French, and English.

Selected Bibliographical Essays

See also Ceva (#907); Delzell (#11).

55. Albrecht-Carrié, René. "Italian Foreign Policy, 1914-1922." Journal of Modern History, 20 (1948): 326-39.

56. Burgwyn, H. James. "Recent Books on Italian Foreign Policy in the 1930's: A Critical Essay." Journal of Italian History, 1 (1978): 523-53.

57. Conzemius, Victor. "Pius XII and Nazi Germany in Historical Perspective." Historical Studies, 7 (1969): 97-124.

And by same author, "Le concordat du 20 juillet 1933 entre la Saint Siège et l'Allemagne: Esquisse d'un bilan de la recherche historique," Archivum Historiae Pontificiae, 15 (1977): 333-62.

BIBLIOGRAPHICAL AIDS

58. Cunsolo, Ronald S. "Italian Nationalism: Recent Literature." Canadian Review of Studies in Nationalism, 10 (1979): 85-89.

   Update of the same author's "Modern Italian Nationalism to 1945," ibid., 6 (1979): 139-47.

59. Debyser, Félix. "Sur la diplomatie italienne, 1937-1939." Revue d'Histoire de la Deuxième Guerre Mondiale, no. 34 (1959): 27-38.

60. Garbari, Maria. "La storiografia sull'irredentismo apparsa in Italia dalla fine della prima guerra mondiale ai giorni nostri." Studi Trentini di Scienze Storiche, 58 (1979): 149-221, 301-57.

61. Giannini, Amadeo. "Gli studi di storia diplomatica in Italia, 1860-1950." Rivista di Studi Politici Internazionali, 17 (1950): 607-32.

62. Nuti, Leopoldo. "I problemi storiografici connessi con l'intervento italiano nella seconda guerra mondiale." Storia delle Relazioni Internazionali, I (1985): 369-91.

63. Pastorelli, Pietro. "La storiografia italiana del dopoguerra sulla politica estera fascista." Storia e Politica, 10 (1971): 575-614.

   Good selection of authors considered; some of their views tested against published documentary evidence.

64. Perona, Gianni. "Richerche archivistiche e studi sulle relazioni tra gli alleati e l'Italia." Italia Contemporanea, no. 142 (1981): 89-101.

65. Petersen, Jens. "La politica estera del fascismo come problema storiografico." Storia Contemporanea, 3 (1972): 661-706.

   Thorough survey of literature on Fascist diplomacy to 1935; themes are Salvemini's view of Fascist diplomacy as purposeless agitation (#678), and interplay of foreign and domestic policy. Slightly revised version is "Die Aussenpolitik des faschistischen Italien als historiographisches Problem," Vierteljahrshefte für Zeitgeschichte, 22 (1974): 417-57.

66. Rumi, Giorgio. "Tendenze e caratteri degli studi sulla politica estera fascista, 1945-1966." Nuova Rivista Storica, 51 (1967): 149-68.

   Examines debate whether pattern discernible in Fascist foreign policy. Also by the same author, "I 'documenti diplomatici italiani' e la recente storiografia," Rassegna degli Archivi di Stato, 29 (1969): 360-410, which considers the dimensions of diplomatic history and the role of public opinion.

67. Senesi, Liliana. "Recente letteratura sulla svolta politica del 1933 nella politica estera di Mussolini." Storia e Politica, 23 (1984): 19-52.

68. Smyth, Denis. "Duce Diplomatico." Historical Journal, 21 (1978): 981-1000.

69. Toscano, Mario. "Gli ebrei in Italia dall'emancipazione alle persecuzioni." Storia Contemporanea, 17 (1986): 905-54.

   Extensive review of works on question at the nub of Rome-Berlin Axis.

70. Tsirpanlis, Zacharias N. "The Italian View of the 1940-1941 War: Comparisons and Problems." Balkan Studies, 23 (1982): 27-79.

   Conflicting interpretations of Italo-Greek diplomacy and war advanced in each country.

71. Vaussard, Maurice. "Quelques aspects des rapports diplomatiques et militaires allemands d'après les derniers diplomates de l'Axe." Revue d'Histoire de la Duexième Guerre Mondiale, no. 4 (1951): 33-46.

2. Works of Reference

Two general guides to reference works stand out: Eugene P. Sheehy, ed., Guide to Reference Works, 10th ed. (Chicago, 1986), and Albert J. Walford, ed., Guide to Reference Material, 4th ed., 3 vols. (London, 1980-87). Both provide copious annotations to citations international in scope. Sheehy is the more comprehensive and is geared more to North American requirements, Walford to British. For historical titles in Walford, consult his second volume.

In the particular field of historical reference books, several guides are available. Helen J. Poulton, The Historian's Handbook: A Descriptive Guide to Reference Works (Norman, OK, 1972), is a standard work that mentions some 700 titles in the course of a series of bibliographical essays subdivided into general, chronological, and national categories (though there is no section reserved for Italian items). John Brown Mason, ed., Research Resources: Annotated Guide to the Social Sciences, 2 vols. (Santa Barbara, CA, 1968-71), takes an interdisciplinary approach and focuses mostly on current events. Very relevant by reason of its restricted subject matter is Gwyn M. Bayliss, ed., Bibliographic Guide to the Two World Wars: An Annotated Survey of English Language Reference Material (London & New York, 1977). This provides a wide mixture of about 2,400 reference and documentary items that are divided topically; indices by author, title, subject, and geographic region are supplied.

Encyclopedias and Dictionaries

72. Académie Diplomatique Internationale. Dictionnaire diplomatique, 8 vols. Paris, 1933-73.

   Monumental set of reference books on diplomatic history and practice since 1918; later volumes update earlier. Information on states, regions, and diplomatic events. Vol. 5 contains biographical sketches of diplomats from Middle Ages to the 1950's.

WORKS OF REFERENCE

73. Cannistraro, Philip V., ed. An Historical Dictionary of Fascist Italy. Westport, CT, 1982.

    Brief, descriptive essays on events, issues, personalities.

74. Coppa, Frank J., ed. A Dictionary of Modern Italian History. Westport, CT, 1983.

    Same formula as previous entry but of wider historical scope.

75. Dizionario storico politico italiano, ed. Ernesto Sestan. Florence, 1971.

    Updated version of Dizionario storico italiano, ed. Orlando Freri and Alberto Malatesta (Milan, 1940). Given its specialization and overall quality, new edition constitutes invaluable reference work for students of modern Italian history; welcome biographical entries have been added.

76. Enciclopedia biografica e bibliografica "Italiana." Milan, 1936-44.

    Uncompleted project planned in 48 topical series. Most relevant series to reach fruition was no. 43: Alberto Malatesta, ed., Ministri, deputati, senatori dal 1848 al 1922, 3 vols. (Milan, 1940-41), which contains biographical sketches.

77. Enciclopedia italiana di scienze, lettere ed arti, 36 vols. incl. index. Appendices: 1 (1938); 2 (1938-48), 2 vols.; 3 (1949-61), 2 vols.; 4 (1961-81), 3 vols. Published for Istituto della Enciclopedia Italiana fondata da Giovanni Trecanni. Rome, 1929- .

    Italy's standard national encyclopedia. Volume 14 of the original Trecanni series contains the famous definition of Fascism written in part by Mussolini.

78. Haensch, Günther, ed. Dictionary of International Relations and Politics, 2d ed. Munich, 1975.

    Basic vocabulary of diplomacy and international law, grouped according to topic. In English, French, German, Spanish.

79. Plano, Jack C., and Olton, Roy, eds. The International Relations Dictionary, 3d ed. Santa Barbara, CA, 1982.

    General dictionary of both words and phrases; definitions and exegeses subdivided in a dozen topical chapters.

80. Seth, Ronald. Encyclopedia of Espionage. London, 1972.

    Mostly biographical information, heavily oriented to Soviet espionage.

Biographical Directories

Overall guides to biographical directories are led by Robert B. Slocum, ed., Biographical Dictionaries and Related Works, 2d ed. (Detroit, 1986). This has, besides general works, titles listed by nation and vocation, with a modicum of annotation. Several guides index individual biographical entries. The Biography and Genealogy Master Index, 2d ed., 8 vols. (Detroit, 1980), has citations to biographical sketches in 350 works; multiple citations for many names. The same publisher (Gale) issues "Bio-base," a periodic cumulative master index on microfiche to 500 current and historical biographical dictionaries, though limited to North American publications. Somewhat broader coverage is provided by Biography Index (New York, 1947-), issued quarterly and annually, which contains biographical material from current English-language books wherever published and 2,000 periodicals. Relevant to the latter end of the period 1918-1945 is Current Biography (New York, 1940-), in quarterly, annual issues; see also a published cumulative index for 1940-70 (New York, 1973). Promise of a valuable biographical service on an international scale is offered by Index Bio-Bibliographicus Notorum Hominum, ed. Jean-Pierre Lobies (Osnabrück, 1972-), in English, French, and German. This covers 2,000 works from all countries in all periods, but while Pars B contains a full list of biographical dictionaries, the alphabetical index of individual names in Pars C is appearing depressingly slowly.

Much biographical information may also be extracted from encyclopedias, etc., cited in the previous section and from some handbooks in the next section.

81. Almanach de Gotha: Annuaire généalogique, diplomatique et statistique. Gotha, 1763-1944.

    Famous source on the genealogies of noble families; also contains information on states and governments, and most useful of all, lists diplomatic and consular officials serving abroad by country in which stationed.

82. Chi È? Dizionario degli italiani d'oggi. Rome, 1928- . Published intermittently.

    The Italian Who's Who; biographical sketches of public figures. Most relevant editions for period 1918-1945: 1st (1928), and supplement (1929); 2d (1931); 3rd (1936); 4th (1940).

    See also Great Britain, Ministry of Economic Warfare, Who Was Who in Fascist Italy, 4th ed. (London, 1943), short biographical lists and annotations issued soon after Mussolini's fall to assist Allied propagandists in Italy.

83. Codignola, Arturo, ed. L'Italia e gli italiani di oggi. Genoa, 1947.

    A single-issue Who's Who with very brief entries, but useful because at date of publication necessarily included individuals prominent between 1918 and 1945.

WORKS OF REFERENCE

Other biographical indices in this category are Centomila: Dizionario storico enciclopedico di molti italiani d'oggi (Rome, 1949); Panorama biografico degli italiani d'oggi, ed. Gennaro Vaccaro, 2 vols. (Rome, 1956).

84. Dizionario biografico degli italiani. Rome, 1960- .

   Comprehensive coverage of famous Italians throughout the ages; full and authoritative articles with bibliographical references. Unfortunately, entire project will take many years to complete; at present, 33 published volumes have reached names beginning De; index to vols. 1-10.

85. Grassi, Fabio, ed. La formazione della diplomazia nazionale: Repertorio bio-bibliografico dei funzionari del Ministero degli Affari Esteri. Rome, 1987.

   Very full biographies of 800 Italian career diplomats serving between 1861-1918. Useful for the early career of many Foreign Ministry functionaries prominent after World War I.

86. International Who's Who. London, 1935- . Annual.

   Approximately 10,000 short biographical entries; strong on world statesmen and includes prominent diplomats.

87. Italy, Ministero degli Affari Esteri. Annuario diplomatico del regno d'Italia. Florence, Rome, 1865- .

   Counterpart of the U.S. Department of State's Foreign Service List and British Foreign Office List, this occasional publication provides statistical and biographical data on Italy's foreign service personnel. For the period covered by this guide, see the issues of 1926, 1931, and 1937.

   A similar biographical tool also published irregularly by the Italian Foreign Ministry is Elenchi del personale (Rome, 1931-).

   The Vatican's occasional biographical handbook is the Annuario pontificio (Rome, 1716-).

88. Italy, Ministero dell'Interno. Governi, alte cariche dello stato e prefetti del regno d'Italia, ed. Mario Missori, 2d ed. Rome, 1973.

   Catalogs Italian ministers and public servants. Supplemented by M. Missori, Gerarchie e statuti del P.N.F. (Rome, 1988), biographies of Fascist party officials; of use for those involved in foreign policy.

89. Kuehl, Warren F., ed. Bibliographical Dictionary of Internationalists. Westport, CT, 1983.

Brief sketches of figures from many countries and walks of life; some Italian politicians and diplomats qualify.

Handbooks

90. Annuario d'Italia: Guida generale del regno. Rome, 1886-1955.

    Manual of governmental organization, charts, lists of officials. Available on 602 microfiche (Chadwick-Healey); see selections from Guida, 1920, 1925, 1930, 1936, 1939.

91. Cook, Christopher P., and Paxton, John. European Political Facts, 1918-1984. New York, 1986.

    In the same category of handbook, see also Alan Palmer, The Facts on File Dictionary of Twentieth-Century History, 1900-1978 (New York, 1979), and with an emphasis on Italian events, Maria Luisa Rizzatti, Dizionario di storia: Il 20. secolo (Milan, 1986).

92. Italy, Istituto Centrale di Statistica. Sommario di statistiche storiche dell'Italia, 1861-1965. Rome, 1968.

    Data to support or refute Italy's claim to major-power status. The same source publishes intermittently the Annuario statistico italiano (Rome, 1878-).

93. Italy, Ministero degli Affari Esteri. Il Ministero degli Affari Esteri al servizio del popolo italiano, 1943-1949, ed. Giuseppe Brusasca, 2d ed. Rome, 1949.

    Although printed under the editorial imprimatur of the then undersecretary for foreign affairs, the work was actually compiled by Mario Toscano. In part a justificatory explanation of the foreign ministry's role after Mussolini's fall, it also describes the ministry's internal administration over the years and gives extensive lists of Italy's principal diplomatic personnel from 1861.

94. Mitchell, Brian R., ed. European Historical Statistics, 1750-1950, 2d ed. New York, 1980.

    For comparison amongst the powers; arranged by topic.

95. Satow, Ernest M. Satow's Guide to Diplomatic Practice, 5th ed. by Lord Gore-Booth. London, 1978.

    Updated classic of diplomatic precedents and custom.

96. Serra, Enrico. La diplomazia in Italia. Milan, 1984.

    Excellent handbook, more oriented to the historical development of Italy's Foreign Ministry than the same author's also valuable Manuale di storia dei trattati e di diplomazia, 5th ed. (Milan, 1985). Both titles,

WORKS OF REFERENCE

composed by the head of the Foreign Ministry's historical archive, contain a wealth of useful information on Ministero degli Esteri administration, past and present, and Italian diplomatic sources.

97. Steiner, Zara, ed. The Times Survey of Foreign Ministries of the World. London, 1982.

   Descriptive essays of present foreign ministries; limited historical observation. Chap. on Italy by Enrico Serra.

News Digests and Surveys

98. Annual Register: A Record of World Events. London, 1761- . Annual.

   Survey articles on current issues; texts of some documents, speeches published. In early twentieth century contained much biographical information in obituaries.

99. Keesing's Contemporary Archives. London, 1931- . Weekly to 1983, now monthly.

   Day-by-day digest of world happenings, useful for dating and placing visits, meetings, speeches, etc. Cumulative name and subject indices. Another daily digest of international affairs is The Bulletin of International News, 22 vols. (London, 1922-45).

100. Royal Institute of International Affairs. Survey of International Affairs, 45 vols. London, 1925-77.

   Continuation of H.W.V. Temperley's A History of the Peace Conference of Paris, 6 vols. (London, 1920-24). First volume embraces the years 1920-23, thereafter regular annual publications in one or more volumes to 1966. Scholarly, documented factual essays; dated but very helpful to beginning students for establishing outline of a problem. Most famous author/editor in interwar period was Arnold Toynbee.

   Companion series is Documents on International Affairs (#217). There is a Consolidated Index to the Survey of International Affairs, 1920-1938, and Documents on International Affairs, 1920-1938, ed. E.M.R. Ditmas (London, 1967).

101. The Statesman's Year-Book: Statistical and Historical Annual of the States of the World, 1864- . London & New York, 1864- . Annual.

   Most useful of the yearbooks. Prints governmental statements and statistics from all over the world. Divided into three parts: Britain and Commonwealth, United States, other nations.

ITALIAN FOREIGN POLICY, 1918-1945

Abstracts

102. Book Review Digest. New York, 1905- . Monthly, annual vols.

   Aimed at public libraries rather than scholarly community. Nevertheless, contains review abstracts of major historical monographs and general works. See also cumulated author-title index, 1905-1974, ed. Leslie Dunmore-Leiber, 4 vols. (New York, 1976). For review indices, see Farber (#2); Book Review Index (#39); Zeller (#53).

103. Dissertation Abstracts International. Ann Arbor, MI, 1938- . Monthly, annual vols.

   The word "international" was added in 1969 to indicate inclusion of dissertations written outside North America, but majority listed and described still emanate from U.S. and Canadian institutions. Abstracts 600 words in length (actual theses available on microfilm). Most useful source, although worth to historians pre-empted by expanded coverage of Historical Abstracts (next entry). Work subdivided along disciplinary lines; theses in history found in Section A: "Humanities and Social Sciences." Annual author index supplied. Entire undertaking serviced by multivolume sets of Comprehensive Dissertation Index, 1861- , (Ann Arbor, MI, 1973-). As in the regular serial publications, historical theses listed together, with separate vols. of author indices. Data base for online computer searching.

104. Historical Abstracts. Santa Barbara, CA. 1955- . Quarterly.

   Invaluable reference work, providing succinct English-language summaries of articles from many countries. Originally devoted solely to periodical literature, beginning with vol. 31 (1980) it now includes unannotated references to books, single-subject journal issues, and theses drawn from the historical and allied disciplinary sections of Dissertations Abstracts International (above). Annual coverage: over 4,000 articles from almost 100 journals; more than 1,000 books; about 700 dissertations. First three issues per year divided into Parts A and B; part A for world history, 1775-1914, part B for subject matter after 1914. Each part sectioned by topic and geographical area; see especially "International Relations," "World War II," "Europe-Italy." Last issue of year is subject and author index. Cumulative subject-author indices published every five years. Data base for online computerized searching.

3. Scholarly Journals

There is no dearth of guides to periodicals. One may begin with bibliographies of periodical bibliographies. The most extensive is Paul E. Vesenyi, An Introduction to Periodical Bibliography (Ann Arbor, MI, 1974), a lengthy essay followed by annotated lists. More specialized is the same

SCHOLARLY JOURNALS

author's European Periodical Literature in the Social Sciences and Humanities (Metuchen, NJ, 1969), which contains twenty pages of bibliographies published in Italy over half a century. Also for Italian periodical bibliographies, see Maria Tentori Califano, ed., Elenchi e cataloghi di periodici in Italia, 1946-1966 (Rome, 1967), and Gertrude Nobile Stolp, ed., Cataloghi a stampa di periodici delle biblioteche italiane, 1859-1967 (Florence, 1968).

Probably, however, the historical researcher will rest content with reference works that list periodical titles themselves. A standard guide is Eric H. Boehm, Barbara H. Pope, Marie S. Ensign, eds., Historical Periodicals Directory, 5 vols. (Santa Barbara, CA, 1981-86). This is a comprehensive overview organized by nation, including a good section on Italian journals in vol. 2. For current information one must turn to Ulrich's International Periodicals Directory (New York, 1932-) and Ulrich's Irregular Serials and Annuals: An International Directory (1967-). These are unannotated listings by topic and title, but are cumulated biennially and both can be further updated by Ulrich's Quarterly (1977-).

For exclusively Italian serial titles, consult Centro Nazionale per il Catalogo Unico delle Biblioteche Italiane e per le Informazione Bibliografiche, Periodici italiani, 1886-1957, 1968-1981 (Rome, 1980-83), titles drawn from the catalog of the Biblioteca Nazionale Centrale (#49). The gap in this listing, more apparent than real, is filled by Repertorio analitico della stampa italiana: Quotidiani e periodici (Milan, 1963-69). For current Italian serials there is Roberet Maini, ed., Catalogo dei periodici italiani, 3d ed. (Milan, 1988), which cites over 10,000 serials arranged by title, subject matter, and place of publication.

To locate runs of journals in North American institutions, one should have recourse to the National Union List of Serials: A Bibliography, 5 vols. (New York, 1965), which lists acquisitions before 1949, and New Serial Titles, 1950- (Washington, 1953), which appears in eight monthly, four quarterly, and one annual issue, as well as in five-year cumulations; it is also data-based. For journal locations in the U.K., consult the British Library's British Union Catalogue of Periodicals, 4 vols. and supplements (London, 1955-81), continued by Serials in the British Library (London, 1981-), which covers most British libraries; it is published quarterly with an annual cumulative vol. on microfiche. Unfortunately, there is no equivalent Italian publication.

Generally speaking, periodical articles lose their scholarly relevance and worth more quickly than books. It appears sensible, therefore, to restrict the journals cited below to those serials currently in print.

Italian Serial Titles

105.   Affari Esteri. Rome, 1969- . Quarterly.

   Published for Associazione Italiana per gli Studi di Politica Estera. Mostly contemporary international relations; occasional articles on diplomatic history.

106.   Altreitalie. Turin, 1989- . Biannual.

   Product of the Agnelli Foundation, reflects growing interest in migration studies, especially, of course, re Italian populations worldwide.

107. Analisi Storica. Fasano, 1983- . Biannual.

 Journal of historians at universities in Bari and Lecce. Modern and contemporary history of military-diplomatic nature prominent.

108. Clio. Rome, 1965- . Quarterly.

 Lively magazine of general modern history.

109. Il Mulino. Bologna, 1951- . Bimonthly.

 Popular political and cultural periodical, but has published some substantial historical articles.

110. Il Politico. Pavia, 1928- . Quarterly.

 Published by Istituto di Scienze Politiche dell'Università di Pavia. Carries a number of essays on diplomatic history. Some articles in English; all have an English-language summary.

111. Il Ponte. Florence, 1945- . Monthly.

 General cultural and political magazine; occasional historical pieces.

112. Italia Contemporanea. Milan, 1974- . Quarterly.

 Until volume 25 called Il Movimento di Liberazione in Italia (1949-73). History of anti-Fascist resistance and related topics. Index vols. 1-15 (1949-65).

113. Nuova Antologia di Lettere, Arti e Scienze. Rome, 1866- . Monthly.

 Highly esteemed journal of general culture; occasional diplomatic reminiscences, diaries. Indices 1886-1930, 1931-50, 1966-85.

114. Nuova Rivista Storica. Rome, 1917- . Triennial.

 Despite title, few essays on twentieth-century history. Most useful for book reviews, list of books received. Index 1917-66.

115. Passato e Presente. Florence, 1982- . Biannual.

 Concentration on modern history; encourages innovative approaches; strong on historiographical debates. Brief English-language summary of contents.

116. Relazioni Internazionali. Milan, 1933- . Weekly.

 Issued by the Istituto per gli Studi di Politica Internazionale. Emphasis on current international scene; short articles, documentary synopses, speeches, etc.; useful for items published 1933-45.

SCHOLARLY JOURNALS

117. Rivista di Storia Contemporanea. Turin, 1972- . Quarterly.

 Occasional essays in diplomatic history.

118. Rivista di Studi Politici Internazionali. Florence, 1934- . Quarterly.

 Very relevant journal that has published many items, including documentary texts and memoirs, on interwar Italian foreign policy. Indices 1934-58, 1959-78.

119. Rivista Storica Italiana. Naples, 1884- . Quarterly.

 Oldest and most prestigious of Italy's scholarly journals of history. Covers all historical fields, frequent articles on Italian history of this century. Book reviews and list of books received, mostly Italian.

120. Storia Contemporanea. Bologna, 1970- . Six issues per year.

 Has become the leading scholarly journal of Italian history of this century, particularly the Fascist period. Prints frequent articles in foreign policy area; a few book reviews. Vol. 15 contains cumulative index, 1970-84.

121. Storia delle Relazioni Internazionali. Florence, 1985- . Biannual.

 Scholarly journal devoted exclusively to international affairs over the past century or so. Articles in both Italian and English on diplomatic history, rather than international relations theory as journal title might imply. Small section of book reviews.

122. Studi Storici. Rome, 1959- . Quarterly.

 Journal of modern history with strongest emphasis on economic studies.

Non-Italian Serial Titles

123. American Historical Review. Washington, 1895- . Five issues per year.

 Organ of the American Historical Association spans all historical fields, though articles on political-diplomatic history rare of late. Remains essential for bibliographical service: wide-ranging book review section, extensive lists of books and essay collections received (see also AHA's Recently Published Articles issued separately, #34). Several cumulated indices covering 1895-1970.

124. European History Quarterly. London, 1984- . Quarterly.

 Was European Studies Review, 1970-83. European history and historical thought from 1500; some diplomatic history. Occasional thematic volume.

125. Foreign Affairs. New York, 1922- . Quarterly.

House journal of Council on Foreign Relations; mostly current international affairs. Sometimes forum for public figures to air personal views.

126. Guerres Mondiales et Conflits Contemporains. Paris, 1987- . Quarterly.

Continues Revue d'Histoire de la Deuxième Guerre Mondiale et des Conflits Contemporains (1950-82, 1982-86). Scholarly journal specializing in international history of this century; most likely of French periodicals to carry material pertinent to this guide.

127. The Historian. Allentown, PA, 1938- . Quarterly.

Journal of American scholarly fraternity, Phi Alpha Theta; articles, book reviews in most fields of history. Five-year cumulative indices 1938-78.

128. Historical Journal. Cambridge, 1958- . Quarterly.

Formerly Cambridge Historical Journal, 1923-57. Major British scholarly journal interested in all phases of British and European history since the fifteenth century. Publishes more articles than most perodicals, a high proportion on diplomatic history. Review articles rather than reviews. Index 1923-74.

129. Historische Zeitschrift. Munich, 1859- . Bimonthly.

Oldest and principal German scholarly historical journal; embraces main historical fields; very strong bibliographical service, including lists of articles. Series of cumulated indices up to 1977.

130. History. London, 1912- . Triannual.

Journal of British Historical Association. Broad coverage of all fields of history; superior book reviews. Index 1916-65.

131. Intelligence and National Security. London, 1986- . Quarterly.

Journal of new dimension to diplomatic history - study of espionage and deception in international politics. Mainly, though not exclusively, Anglo-American intelligence.

132. International Affairs. London, 1922- . Quarterly.

Journal of Royal Institute of International Affairs; comparable to the American Foreign Affairs in its concentration on current world affairs. Prints speeches given before the association.

133. International History Review. Burnaby, BC, 1979- . Quarterly.

SCHOLARLY JOURNALS

Periodical devoted expressly to international history, interpreted broadly, throughout the ages. Exceptionally valuable to the historian of foreign policy. Occasional issues on single theme. Standard format of articles and book reviews.

134. Italian Quarterly. New Brunswick, NJ, 1957-77, 1980- . Quarterly.

    English-language magazine of general Italian culture; occasional contributions on Italian historical subjects.

135. Journal of Contemporary History. London, 1966- . Quarterly.

    Specializes in twentieth-century history. Originally each issue devoted to one theme; some issues still follow this pattern. Some diplomatic historical essays but not journal's stock-in-trade. Prints more than average number of articles; no book reviews. Index vols. 1-21 (1966-87).

136. Journal of Modern History. Chicago, 1929- . Quarterly.

    Best-known U.S. scholarly journal of general modern history since the Renaissance, though foreign policy articles not frequent. Substantial book reviews; most issues carry review articles.

137. Quellen und Forschungen aus italienischen Archiven und Bibliotheken. Tübingen, 1898- . Irregular.

    Journal of the Deutsches Historisches Institut in Rome. All aspects of Italo-Germanic relationship throughout the ages; long articles, reviews of both books and articles. Index 1898-1971.

138. Relations Internationales. Paris, 1973- . Quarterly.

    Published for La Société d'Etudes Historiques des Relations Internationales Contemporaines. International affairs from late nineteenth century on, though most essays on post-1945 topics; theme issues, few book reviews.

139. Review of Politics. Notre Dame, IN, 1929- . Quarterly.

    Political science journal that has published a number of historical articles.

140. Revue d'Histoire Diplomatique. Paris, 1887- . Quarterly.

    Journal of Société d'Histoire Générale et d'Histoire Diplomatique. Mostly on pre-twentieth-century diplomacy. Index 1887-1963.

141. Times Literary Supplement. London, 1902- . Weekly.

    Influential magazine of long, critical reviews of books in all disciplines and languages, once anonymous, now signed. Cumulative indices: 1902-39, 2 vols.; 1940-80, 3 vols.; 1981-85. Closest American analogue is the bimonthly New York Review of Books (New York, 1963-).

142. Vierteljahrshefte für Zeitgeschichte. Munich, 1953- . Quarterly.

Highly respected scholarly journal of Institut für Zeitgeschichte; concentrates on study of Nazism and Fascism, including foreign policy aspects. Most relevant of German serials to this guide. Article summaries in English; book review essays with bibliographical items in last annual issue (see Bibliographie zur Zeitgeschichte, #37). Index vols. 1-22 (1952-74).

B. DOCUMENTARY AND OFFICIAL PUBLICATIONS

Although relevant documentary aids are cited in the preceding section of this guide (see especially #25, #27), there also exist reference works to documentary bibliographies at large. Useful and international in scope is Vladimir M. Palic, Government Publications: A Guide to Bibliographic Tools, 4th ed. (Washington, 1975). See also J.B. Childs, "Government Publications (Documents)," in Encyclopedia of Library and Information Science, vol. 10 (1973), pp. 36-140, and U.N.E.S.C.O., International Committee for Social Sciences Documentation, A Study of Current Bibliographies of National Official Publications: Short Guide and Inventory, comp. Jean Meyriat (Paris, 1958), in both French and English. F. Gothier, Initiation à la documentation écrite contemporaine (Liège, 1970), is brief but good on European guides.

For the location of both U.S. and foreign documentary holdings in North America, see Barbara Kile and Audrey Taylor, eds., Directory of Government Document Collections and Librarians, 4th ed. (Bethesda, MD, 1984).

1. Italian Documents

With each passing year more and more material from diplomatic archives finds its way into print. Quantitatively, Italian published documentation of this nature is less than that of most other western powers. Yet it is not inconsiderable, and certainly it behooves the researcher to investigate published Italian diplomatic documents before venturing into the archives. Not only can time and duplicated effort be avoided, but the printed documents can often give pointers to archival organization and archival treasures.

Two further observations: Included in the following section are documentary essays that print fragmentary or complete documents. In addition, memoirs and secondary works often have documents integrated into their text or placed in appendices; cases in point will be noted later in sections C and D.

Italian Treaty Texts: Collections

See also Grenville (#213); Keith (#215); League of Nations (#266).

143. Giannini, Amadeo, ed. Documenti per la storia dei rapporti fra l'Italia e la Jugoslavia, 2d ed. Rome, 1934.

Collection of public accords, one of several edited by this scholar diplomat. Others concerning Italy: I trattati commerciali del regno d'Italia, 2 vols. (Rome, 1924-25); I trattati di conciliazione e di regolamento giudizario del regno d'Italia (Rome, 1928).

More general collections edited by Giannini, though still very pertinent to Italian foreign policy: Trattati ed accordi per la pace con la Germania, 1918-1924 (Rome, 1929); Documenti per la storia della pace orientale, 1913-1934 (Rome, 1934); Trattati ed accordi per l'Europa Orientale (Rome, 1934); Trattati ed accordi per l'Europa danubiana e balcanica, 2d ed. (Rome, 1936).

144. Italy, Ministero degli Affari Esteri. Raccolta dei Trattati e delle convenzioni conchiuse fra il regno d'Italia ed i governi esteri. Turin, Florence, Rome, 1865-19 .

After the Second World War series title changed to Trattati e convenzioni fra l'Italia e gli altri stati. Standard source for all Italy's diplomatic accords.

A minor collection published by the Italian Foreign Ministry is Convenzioni consolari tra l'Italia e gli altri Stati (Rome, 1932). See also Ministero dell'Economia Nazionale, Trattati di Commercio e Navigazione tra l'Italia e gli altri Stati per il periodo 1914-1929, 3 vols. (Rome, 1929).

145. Panhuys Polman Gruys, Pompejus van, ed. Trattati e convenzioni bilaterali fra il regno d'Italia e gli altri stati in vigore al 1 gennaio 1933. Leiden, 1934.

Handy list of bilateral agreements in chronological order with index by country.

Italian Documentary Series

146. Italy, Ministero degli Affari Esteri. Collana di testi diplomatici. Rome, 1974- .

Ongoing documentary series, each volume reflective of the work of a well-known Italian diplomat. Prepared within and for the Foreign Ministry, they are not printed for public sale, although they are obtainable from the Ministero degli Esteri. Volumes begin with a short biography, followed by a score of reports, notes, etc., penned by the diplomat in question. Diplomats prominent between 1918 and 1945 treated so far in the series include: vol. 1, Pietro Quaroni; vol. 2, Renato Prunas; vol. 5, Leonardo Vitetti; vol. 7, Augusto Rosso; vol. 9, Raffaele Guariglia; vol. 11, Bernardo Attolico.

147. ———. Libri verdi. Rome, 1861- .

Generic title of Italy's series of "colored books," typical of such publications that evolved in most European states during the nineteenth century in imitation of British "blue books." Collections of documents on specific international issues, they were technically laid

ITALIAN DOCUMENTS

before parliament though, in reality, printed for public consumption. Sometimes a libro verde text was agreed with the foreign ministry of another power, which would simultaneously publish the same documents in its own language - in which case the contents were guaranteed to be inoffensive. But when no consultation with foreign chancelleries was involved, the public record was composed with an eye to enhancing the national or governmental image. Although pre-1914 Italy issued over a hundred libri verdi, only a handful were published after World War I before Fascism put a stop to this parliamentary exercise. During the Fascist era the government did publish occasional diplomatic documentary selections (#171, #172, #174), but strictly speaking no libri verdi.

One of the first libri verdi to appear after 1918 was Accordo di Londra del 26 aprile 1915 (Rome, 1920). The Treaty of London was, of course, the basis of most of Italy's postwar claims. The central issue in Italian postwar diplomacy was the relationship with Yugoslavia and the attempt to find a modus vivendi through the Treaty of Rapallo, 1920, documented in Negoziati diretti fra il Governo italiano e il Governo Serbo-Croato-Sloveno per la pace adriatica (Rome, 1921). Parallel with this libro verde the Foreign Ministry issued Il trattato di Rapallo nei commenti della stampa (Roma, 1921). Amadeo Giannini edited two semiofficial publications: Il trattato di Rapallo al Parlamento italiano (Rome, 1920); La questione di Porto Baros e gli accordi di Santa Margherita al Parlamento italiano (Rome, 1923), speeches pronounced in the Chamber of Deputies and Senate. Other libri verdi from the post-World War I years: Conferenza di Washington, 1921-1922 (Rome, 1922); Verbali e documenti delle Conferenze interalleate di Londra e di Parigi sulle questioni delle riparazioni tedesche e dei debiti interalleati (Rome, 1923); Documenti diplomatici relativi alla pace con la Turchia, 4 vols. (Rome, 1923); also available in English as British parliamentary "blue books": Cmd. 1627; Cmd. 1812; Cmd. 1814.

148. ———. Commissione per la Pubblicazione dei Documenti Diplomatici Italiani. I documenti diplomatici italiani, 9 series. Rome, 1952- .

Quite simply, the one indispensable printed source for modern Italian foreign policy. While many other countries in the interwar years published documentary collections on the outbreak of World War I, Italy without the need to refute any charge of war guilt did not. Not until 1946 was an official commission established to rehabilitate war-torn diplomatic archives and publish selections therefrom. Arriving late on the scene, Italian editors have profited from the experience and mistakes of others to produce work of outstanding quality.

Unlike other national documentary collections, the Italian encompasses the origins of both world wars in one project. I documenti diplomatici italiani assays a record of Italian diplomacy, 1861-1943, divided into 9 chronological series. Series relevant to this guide: series 6 (1918-22); 7 (1922-35); 8 (1935-39); 9 (1939-43).

Each series has its own editorial team, and rate of publication varies widely from one series to another. At the moment of writing the following volumes for 1918-43 have appeared: series 6, vols. 1-2 (4 Nov. 1918 - 23 Mar. 1919); series 7, vols. 1-12 (31 Oct. 1922 - 31 Dec. 1932); series 8, vols. 12-13 (23 May 1939 - 3 Sept. 1939); series 9, vols. 1-8 (4 Sept. 1939 - 20 July 1942). About 120 volumes are in prospect before every series is complete; one wonders whether the twentieth century will witness the total enterprise fulfilled.

Over 90 percent of the documentation printed is drawn from the files of the Ministero degli Affari Esteri, but appropriate material from ACS, service ministry archives, and unpublished private diplomatic papers are also deployed. The avvertenza, or foreword, to each volume indicates the most heavily used sources, and specifies the most pertinent files in ASME. Also, at the start of each volume, a table of documents gives a brief description of every item. For reasons of space many more telegraphic communications than full reports are published. Footnotes supply minutes or marginalia appended to incoming documents, information on composition of outgoing messages, and valuable cross-references within the Italian documentary collection and to other national collections and printed sources. Documents are arranged in sensible chronological order; to assist in tracing the course of a single question, every volume contains an enumerated index of documents sectioned by nation and topic. Several appendices per volume identify the incumbents of Italy's foreign service posts at home and abroad, as well as foreign embassies and legations in Rome and their chief personnel. A general index of names rounds off each volume.

149. ———. Comitato per la Documentazione delle Attività Italiane in Africa (formerly Comitato per la Documentazione dell'Opera dell'Italia in Africa). L'Italia in Africa: Serie storica. Rome, 1958- .

Series aspires to cover Italy's African policy, 1859-1943. A mix of volumes of authoritative narrative and documents; latter material drawn mostly from Ministry of Colonies, later Ministry of Italian Africa, files housed in ASME; cross-referenced to I documenti diplomatici italiani (previous entry). But publication of colonial historical series slow; no volumes yet for 1918-45.

150. Italy, Parlamento. Atti parlamentari. Turin, Florence, Rome, 1848-19-.

Massive series in three parts each for Chamber of Deputies and Senate: Disegni di legge - Relazioni comprised of draft legislation and committee hearings; Discussioni, Italian equivalent of U.S. Congressional Record and British Hansard, provide verbatim debate accounts; Documenti consist of parliamentary papers, including libri verdi, which are thus published in Atti parlamentari as well as separately (#147). Italian parliamentary records are worth consulting for the immediate post-World War I period but lose value under

ITALIAN DOCUMENTS

Fascism, particularly after 1925. Available on microfilm (U.S. Library of Congress, 959 reels).

The Camera dei Fasci e delle Corporazioni, which took parliament's place in 1939, published a record of deliberations and legislative achievements, 1934-43, but nothing of substance on foreign policy.

151. Italy, Partito Nazionale Fascista. Atti del P.N.F. Rome, Bologna, 1926-43.

General directives to party members and organizations, including those charged with overseeing Fascism abroad. The Fascist party also published Il Gran Consiglio del Fascismo nei primi quindici anni dell'era fascista (Bologna, 1938), abstracts of proceedings of the supreme body in the P.N.F. and, in effect, in government. Grand Council minutes have not been printed, but see p. 42.

152. Mussolini, Benito. Opera omnia, ed. Edoardo and Duilio Susmel, 44 vols. Florence, Rome, 1951-80.

By far the most comprehensive and authoritative collection of Duce's words and writings, replacing an old series of Scritti e discorsi, 12 vols. (Milan, 1934-39). Mussolini's Opera omnia originally ran to 36 vols. (Florence, 1951-63), which consist in the main of speeches and public pronouncements as printed in Popolo d'Italia and Grand Fascist Council communiqués. Volumes chronologically ordered, final one a cumulated index of names.

In 1978 the editors reopened publication with "appendices," actually supplementary volumes, composed from newly accessible material. Vol. 37 gives an essential key to all sources used in the supplementary volumes, and also contains scritti riservati, many of a diplomatic nature from I documenti diplomatici italiani and ASME. Vols. 38-43 print Mussolini's carteggio in chronological sequence, 1903-45, drawn from many archival sources, notably ACS. Vol. 44 offers more attività oratoria. The new volumes increase markedly the stature of what has long been a standard work from which scholars have quoted copiously.

Post-Fascist Judicial Inquests

Italy underwent nothing like the trials of the German Nazis at Nuremberg. Nevertheless, after Mussolini's fall, the Italian state lodged a number of politico-juridical indictments against individuals on the grounds of their complicity with Fascism. Some were charged with promoting a criminal Fascist foreign policy.

153. Aloisi, Pompeo. La mia attività al servizio della pace: Fatti nuovi e nuovi elementi probatori sottoposto all'esame dell'Alta corte di giustizia. Rome, 1946.

Brief explanation of Aloisi's role in the Ethiopian affair supported by telegrams sent in 1934-35 from League of Nations. Cf. Aloisi's Journal (#282).

154. Graziani, Rodolfo. Processo Graziani, 3 vols. Rome, 1948-50.

Principal charge that of collaboration with Nazis when minister of defence in Salò government, 1943-45. Vol. 1 has marshal's self-exculpation; vols. 2 and 3 for trial documents and testimony.

155. Lanza d'Ajeta, Blasco. Documenti prodotti a corredo della memoria presentata al Consiglio di Stato. Rome, 1946.

Documents on mission to Lisbon, August 1943, in pursuit of peace negotiations with Allies. See also Lanza d'Ajeta's "Relazione sulla missione a Lisbona," Rivista di Studi Politici Internazionali, 13-14 (1946-47): 578-85.

On the larger issue of this diplomat's service under Fascism, see Italy, Consiglio di Stato, Memoria a svolgimento del ricorso del Consigliere di Legazione Blasco Lanza d'Ajeta contro la decisione della Commissione per l'epurazione del personale dipendente dal Ministero degli Affari Esteri (Rome, 1946).

156. Roatta, Mario. Il processo Roatta. Rome, 1945.

Trial with important diplomatic connotations. Investigation of Fascist Italian subversion and terrorism abroad in Ethiopia, Spain, France, Albania, and Yugoslavia (involving collusion with Croatian separatists). Chief defendants General Roatta and Foreign Undersecretaries Suvich and Benini; diplomats charged included Anfuso and Jacomini. Documents consist of interrogations, depositions, memorials by Suvich and Benini, etc.

An account of Fascist Italy's subversive foreign policy based largely on revelations of the Roatta-Suvich trial is Clara Conti, Servizio segreto (Rome, 1945), which includes a documentary appendix of interrogations conducted in 1944 by the Alto Commissariato per la punizione dei delitti del fascismo.

Miscellaneous Italian Documents

157. Adami, Vittorio, ed. Storia documentata dei confini del regno d'Italia, 4 vols. in 6 parts. For Stato Maggiore dell'Esercito: Ufficio Storico. Rome, 1919-31.

Documentation concerning Italy's frontiers with France, Switzerland, Austria, and Yugoslavia.

158. Askew, William C. "The Secret Agreement between France and Italy on Ethiopia, January 1935." Journal of Modern History, 25 (1953): 47-48.

ITALIAN DOCUMENTS

>Summarizes the Italian Foreign Ministry's annual report on France for 1935.

159. Bianchi, Gianfranco. Rivelazioni sul conflitto italo-etiopico. Milan, 1967.

>Excerpts from General De Bono's papers and diary.

160. Bruccoleri, Giuseppe, ed. L'opera dei delegati italiani nella Società delle Nazioni, 4 vols. For L'Associazione Italiana per la Società delle Nazioni. Rome, 1935-37.

>Memoranda and other documents as well as speeches before the League's Council and Assembly; vol. 4 for the Ethiopian dispute, 1933-36. In French.

161. Ceva, Lucio. "1927: Una riunione fra Mussolini e i vertici militari." Il Politico, 50 (1985): 329-37.

>Text of discussion of military preparations against Yugoslavia. Other Italian military documents, from 1942, printed by the same author in "L' 'intelligence' britannico nella seconda guerra mondiale e la sua influenza sulla strategia e sulle operazioni," Storia Contemporanea, 13 (1982): 99-122.

162. Ciuffoletti, Zeffiro, and Degl'Innocenti, Maurizio. L'emigrazione nella storia d'Italia, 1868-1975: Storia e documenti, 2 vols. Florence, 1978.

>Vol. 2 for material on fasci all'estero.

163. Colapietra, Raffaele. "Documenti dell'Archivio Colosimo in Catanzaro." Stora e Politica, 20 (1981): 584-627.

>Reproduces 25 documents on Italian colonial claims, 1917-19, not listed in Gasbarri or Pastorelli (p. 48).

164. Colarieti, Mirella, ed. "Umori e asperazioni in Serbia dopo il primo conflitto mondiale." Balcanica, 2/1 (1983): 108-22.

>Prints report, 5 Dec. 1918, by Consalvo Summonte, Italian diplomatic expert on Yugoslav affairs. Other documentary publications by the same author on Italo-Yugoslav relations: "L'altra Italia sull'altra Jugoslavia," ibid., 1/2 (1982): 93-99, two intelligence reports on Yugoslavia 1920; "L'Italia fascista e l'attentato a Marsiglia," ibid., 3/3 (1984): 52-116, documents from ASME.

165. Deambrosis, Marcella. "Conversazioni Johnson-Deambrosis (1918) sul confine italiano." Rassegna Storica del Risorgimento, 73 (1986): 300-306.

Records found in ASME of exchanges between Italian colonel and U.S. major, September 1918.

166. De Felice, Renzo, ed. Autobiografia del fascismo, 1919-1945. Bergamo, 1978.

Anthology of Fascist texts including foreign policy material from the 1930's, presented as counterpart to Costanzo Casucci, ed., Il fascismo: Antologia di scritti critici (Bologna, 1961).

167. Goglia, Luigi, and Grassi, Fabio, eds. Il colonialismo italiano da Adua all'impero. Bari, 1981.

Recommended anthology of documents on Italian imperialism in Africa, on the fringe of diplomatic history. Also Aldo A. Mola, ed., L'imperialismo italiano: La politica estera dall'Unità al fascismo (Rome, 1980); Giorgio Rochat, ed., Il colonialismo italiano (Turin, 1973).

Documentary articles on colonialism by L. Goglia are "Una diversa politica razziale coloniale in un documento inedito di Alberto Pollera del 1937," Storia Contemporanea, 16 (1985): 1071-92; "Il Mufti e Mussolini: Alcuni documenti sui rapporti tra nazionalismo palestine e fascismo negli anni trenta," ibid., 17 (1986): 1201-53. In this genre see also Biancamara Scarcia Amoretti, "Alcuni documenti sulla posizione italiana nei confronti della Siria tra il 1919 e il 1925," Il Veltro, 28 (1982): 413-36.

168. Grandi, Dino. La guerra di Spagna nel comitato di Londra, luglio 1936 - aprile 1939. Vol. 1, luglio 1936 - ottobre 1937. For Istituto per gli Studi di Politica Internazionale. Varese, 1943.

Italian position before Nonintervention Committee seen in verbali and other documents; withdrawn from circulation immediately after publication of first volume. For documentation from the other side in the Spanish Civil War, see #276.

169. Guariglia, Raffaele. Primi passi in diplomazia e rapporti dall'ambasciata di Madrid, 1932-34, ed. Ruggero Moscati. Naples, 1972.

Some slight essays but over 100 important documents from ASME and ACS. For Guariglia's later ambassadorships in Buenos Aires (1936-38) and Paris (1938-40), see his Scritti storico-eruditi e documenti diplomatici (Rome, 1981).

170. Guerri, Giordano B., ed. Rapporto al Duce (il testo stenografico inedito dei colloqui tra i federali e Mussolini nel 1942). Milan, 1978.

ITALIAN DOCUMENTS

Located incongruously among files on Spain in the fondo Lancellotti of the Foreign ministry; testimony from local officials on Italian people's distaste for war and the Axis.

171. Italy, Governo. Memoria del Governo Italiano circa la situazione in Etiopia. Rome, 1935. Eng. trans. Memorandum of the Italian Government on the Situation in Ethiopia. Rome, 1935.

    Official statement of the Italian case against Ethiopia. See also Renato Mori, "Come Mussolini giustificò l'azione armata contro l'Etiopia," Nuova Antologia, 535 (Oct.-Dec., 1978): 217-25 - Mussolini's instructions to Grandi, 2 Oct. 1935, how to explain Italy's conduct in London; excluded from Mori (#752).

172. Italy, Ministero degli Affari Esteri. Accordi fra l'Italia e la Germania relativi al transferimento di allogeni e cittadini germanici. Rome, 1940.

173. ———. La conferenza della pace, 12 gennaio 1919 - 4 marzo 1920 (Documenti sulla questione adriatica). Rome, 1946?

174. ———. Raccolta di provvedimenti di carattere legislativa riguardanti l'Albania, ed. Romolo Bertùccioli. Rome, 1941

175. Italy, Stato Maggiore dell'Esercito: Ufficio Storico. Verbale delle reunioni tenute del capo di stato maggiore generale. Rome, 1985.

    Useful for interplay of military and political factors in World War II. Similarly, see Fortunato Minniti, "Il Diario storico del Comando Supremo: Considerazioni e ipotesi sul ruolo del capo di Stato Maggiore Generale nell'estate del 1940," Storia Contemporanea, 18 (1987): 171-90.

176. Mazzetti, Massimo. "I contatti del governo italiano con i conspiratori spagnoli prima del luglio 1936." Storia Contemporanea, X (1979): 1181-94.

    Prints documents from ASME. Another documentary text is William C. Askew, "Italian Intervention in Spain: The Agreements of March 31, 1934, with the Spanish Monarchist Parties," Journal of Modern History, 24 (1952): 181-83.

177. Rivista di Studi Politici Internazionali, 13-14 (1946-47): 541-88. "Documenti."

    Documentary miscellany, mostly translations from German Auswärtiges Amt records, though several items originally Italian, e.g. Italo-Spanish protocol, 28 Nov. 1936, Mussolini-Franco letters, 1943. Also records of Mussolini-Hitler conferences, 1943. On peace negotiations with the Allies in 1943, Lanza d'Ajeta's deposition (#155) reprinted, pp. 578-85, together with Alberto Berio, "Relazione del console generale a Tangeri Alberto Berio sulle sue trattative armistiziale tra l'Italia e gli Alleati, 5-20 agosto 1943," pp. 586-88; cf. latter's Missione segreta (#324).

178. Rochat, Giorgio. Militari e politici nella preparazione della campagna d'Etiopia: Studi e documenti, 1932-1936. Milan, 1971.

Extremely valuable for tracing Mussolini's growing determination on Ethiopian conquest.

179. Sabine, Candido M. Le fond d'une querelle: Documents inédits sur les relations franco-italiennes, 1914-1921. Paris, 1921.

Documents provided by commercial attaché, Paris embassy.

180. Schuster, Ildefonso. Gli ultimi tempi di un regime. Milan, 1946.

So-called white book of 93 documents, prepared by the Archbishop of Milan active in negotiations for the surrender of Nazi forces in Italy in 1945.

181. Steffanson, Borg G., and Starrett, K., eds. Documents on Ethiopian Politics. Salisbury, NC, 1976.

First parts on European powers' relationship with Ethiopia, 1920-36; final section "A Diplomatic Study" on Italo-Ethiopian war, 1935-36.

Personal Papers and Letters

182. Albertini, Luigi. Epistolario, 1911-1926, ed. Ottavio Barié, 4 vols. Milan, 1968.

Correspondence of editor of Corriere della Sera and confidant of Italian liberal statesmen; some items on foreign affairs.

183. Ciano, Galeazzo. L'Europa verso la catastrofe: 184 colloqui di Mussolini, Franco, Chamberlain, ecc., ed. Rodolfo Mosca. Milan, 1948. Eng. trans. Ciano's Diplomatic Papers, ed. Malcolm Muggeridge, London, 1948.

Early source for researchers, and still valuable, notwithstanding more recent documentary publications. Minutes of important conversations, 1936-42, originally assembled by Ciano to buttress his diary when published (#287). Contents go further back in time than diary, though most material concerns 1939-42; almost identical with Lisbon and Rose Garden papers in archives and on microfilm (see pp. 35, 47). For the papers' discovery, authenticity, and inventory, see H.M. Smyth, Secrets of the Fascist Era, appendix (p. 55).

184. De Stefani, Alberto. Vent'anni di economia e politica: Le carte De Stefani, 1922-1941, ed. Franco Marcoaldi. Milan, 1986.

More letters to than from Mussolini's first finance minister; discussion of lira exchange rate, etc.

185. Frassati, Alfredo. *Un uomo: Un giornale: Alfredo Frassati*, ed. Luciana G. Frassati, 3 vols. Rome, 1978-83.

Project edited by Frassati's daughter deploys documents and letters freely in text and appendices; *leitmotiv* is editorial career, but vol. 2 has long chap. on Frassati as ambassador in Berlin. See John A. Thayer, "Alfredo Frassati in the History and Historiography of Modern Italy," *Journal of Modern History*, 55 (1983): 284-96.

186. Giolitti, Giovanni. *Quarant'anni di vita politica: Dalle carte di Giovanni Giolitti, 1885-1928*, ed. Piero D'Angiolini, Giampiero Carocci, Claudio Pavone, 3 vols. Milan, 1962.

Vol. 3 covers 1910-1928; contains some correspondence, e.g. with Frassati, Sforza, on foreign policy during Giolitti's ministry, 1920-21. See also G. Giolitti, "Verbale di un incontro a Lucerne," *Nuova Antologia*, 445 (Jan.-Apr., 1949): 111-30, minutes of a talk with Lloyd George, 22 Aug. 1920, regarding Yugoslavia, German reparations, Russia, Turkey, etc.

187. Grandi, Dino. "Grandi-Mussolini Letters." *Il Borghese*, 21, 28 April 1966, pp. 859-63.

Text of miscellaneous letters, 1932-35, regarding Grandi's management of Italy's London embassy.

188. Mussolini, Benito. *Corrispondenza inedita*, ed. Duilio Susmel. Milan, 1972.

Superseded by Mussolini's *Opera omnia* (#152), as indeed are all other selections of the Duce's correspondence.

Nevertheless, worth mentioning are collections of correspondence with certain individuals. Most spectacular, at least when it first appeared, *Hitler: Mussolini, lettere e documenti*, ed. Vittorio Zincone (Milan, 1946), 67 items dated 1939-43 - messsages exchanged and minutes of Duce-*Führer* conferences. Probably from Mussolini's files, which disappeared in April 1945, their publication remains still a mystery, although their genuineness is confirmed by copies in ministerial archives. From this latter source Mario Toscano supplemented the Zinconi collection, publishing further Hitler-Mussolini correspondence of 1938-43 in *Epoca*, nos. 188-95 (8 May-27 June, 1954), all of which have now been reprinted in *I documenti diplomatici italiani* (#148) or *Akten zur deutschen Politik* (#244). Some Duce-*Führer* exchanges are included in Max Domarus, *Mussolini und Hitler: Zwei Wege - Gleiches Ende* (Wurzburg, 1977), and see also F.W. Deakin, "Una lettera di Mussolini a Hitler, 2 giugno 1944," *Rassegna degli Archivi di Stato*, 43 (1983): 401-9, Early contacts between the two dictators are documented in Renzo De

Felice, ed., <u>Mussolini e Hitler: I rapporti segreti, 1922-1933, con documenti inediti</u>, 2d ed. (Florence, 1983).

Some dozen documents on Austro-Italian relations, 1933-34, were discovered by Paul R. Sweet who printed them in English as an appendix to Julius Braunthal, <u>The Tragedy of Austria</u> (London, 1948); published in Italian by Agostino Renda, "Carteggio segreto Dollfuss-Mussolini," <u>Il Mondo</u>, 2 April 1949, in German by Karl Hans Sailer, <u>Geheimer Briefwechsel Mussolini-Dollfuss</u> (Vienna, 1949). In fact, only half of the brief collection consists of Mussolini-Dollfuss messages.

Naturally, the nationalistic foundations of Italian interwar foreign policy find expression in <u>Carteggio D'Annunzio-Mussolini, 1919-1938</u>, 2d ed. by Renzo De Felice and Emilio Mariano (Milan, 1971), which supersedes an official edition of D'Annunzio's <u>Lettere a Mussolini</u> (Verona, 1941).

<u>Carteggio Arnaldo-Benito Mussolini</u>, ed. D. Susmel (Florence, 1954), contains letters from 1923 until the death of the Duce's brother in 1931, but with only vague references to foreign policy.

189. Salandra, Antonio. <u>Salandra inedito</u>, ed. Giambattista Gifuni. Milan, 1973.

Liberal extracts from unpublished letters and documents woven into the text. Chapter of Salandra's comments during Corfu crisis, 1923, not published in his <u>Memorie politiche</u> (#344). For Salandra's diary, see #300.

190. Sonnino, Sidney. <u>Carteggio, 1914-1922</u>, ed. Pietro Pastorelli, 2 vols. Bari, 1974-75.

Vol. 2 for correspondence, 1916-1922, from huge archive of Sonnino's wartime papers buttressed by material from other deposits of Sonnino records. Bulk of material concerns war years, but useful chapter for 1919 gives information on post-World War I peace negotiations. See also Sonnino's <u>Diario</u> (#303).

On publications derived from Sonnino's papers, see Enrico Serra, " 'Opera omnia' di Sidney Sonnino," <u>Rivista Storica Italiana</u>, 90 (1978): 143-59.

Speeches

See also Bruccoleri (#160).

191. Bonomi, Ivanoe. <u>Discorsi Politici, 1901-1950</u>. Rome, 1954.

For speeches on foreign policy made when premier, 1921-22.

ITALIAN DOCUMENTS

192. Ciano, Galeazzo. <u>Italy's Foreign Policy: A Speech to the Italian Chamber of Deputies, 13 May 1937</u>. Rome, 1937.

    Pro-Axis statement contrasts interestingly with Ciano's veiled call for continued Italian neutrality in World War II: <u>L'Italia di fronte al conflitto</u>, 2d ed. (Milan, 1940); Eng. trans. <u>Speech in the Chamber of Fasces and Corporations, 16 Dec. 1939: An Account of the International Situation in Recent Years</u> (Rome, 1940).

193. Corradini, Enrico. <u>Discorsi politici, 1902-1923</u>. Florence, 1923.

    By one of the founders of the Italian Nationalist movement. In same nationalist vein by the Fascist minister of colonies, Luigi Federzoni, <u>Presagi alla nazione</u> (Milan, 1924).

194. Giannini, Amadeo, ed. <u>Tommaseo Tittoni e Vittorio Scialoja. L'Italia alla conferenza della pace: Discorsi e documenti</u>. Rome, 1921.

    On Tittoni's role as titular head of Italian delegation.

195. Giolitti, Giovanni. <u>Discorsi parlamentari</u>, 4 vols. Rome, 1953-54.

    Vol. 4 for pronouncements made during Giolitti's last premiership, 1920-21. Nothing relevant to post-World War I diplomacy in his <u>Discorsi extraparlamentari</u> (Turin, 1952).

196. Grandi, Dino. <u>La politica estera dell'Italia, 1929-1932</u>, ed. Paolo Nello, 2 vols. Rome, 1985.

    Useful collection of speeches, some made privately, during Grandi's tenure of foreign ministry, though in some cases text has been doctored; see MacGregor Knox, "I testi 'aggiusti' dei discorsi segreti di Grandi," <u>Passato e Presente</u>, (Jan.-April 1987): 97-117. Two Grandi speeches of 1930 were published contemporaneously in Italian and English: <u>L'Italia fascista nella politica internazionale</u>; <u>Two Speeches on Italy's Foreign Policy</u> (Rome, 1930).

197. Lessona, Alessandro. <u>Scritti e discorsi coloniale</u>. Milan, 1935.

    By the undersecretary for colonies, 1929-36, then minister, 1936-37.

198. Mussolini, Benito. <u>Storia d'Italia nei discorsi di Mussolini, 1915-1945</u>, comp. Pino Rauti and Giuseppe Carlucci, 3d ed. Rome, 1966.

    Handy one-volume selection of the Duce's speeches; more comprehensive collection in his <u>Opera omnia</u> (#152).

199. Nitti, Francesco Saverio. <u>Discorsi parlamentari</u>, 5 vols. Rome, 1973-75.

ITALIAN FOREIGN POLICY, 1918-1945

Final volume for foreign policy statements, mostly on reparations and Adriatic questions, made when premier, 1919-20.

200. Orlando, Vittorio Emanuele. Discorsi parlamentari, 4 vols. Rome, 1965.

Vol. 4 for reports by Premier Orlando to Italian parliament on peace negotiations in Paris 1919.

201. Scialoja, Vittorio. Discorsi alla Società delle Nazioni. Rome, 1932.

Speeches delivered, 1921-31, by long-serving Italian spokesman at Geneva.

202. Sonnino, Sidney. Discorsi parlamentari, 3 vols. Rome, 1925.

Vol. 3 for post-World War I period but little on foreign affairs, and nothing in Scritti e discorsi extraparlamentari, 1870-1922, ed. Benjamin F. Brown, 2 vols. (Bari, 1972).

203. Volpi di Misurata, Giuseppe. Il consolidamento dei debiti con i governi degli Stati Uniti d'America e della Gran Bretagna. Rome, 1926.

Speeches to Chamber of Deputies and Senate by chief Italian negotiator of war debt settlements.

Vatican Diplomatic Documentation

See also Di Nolfo (#218), Ludlow (#234).

204. Albrecht, Dieter, ed. Der Notenwechsel zwischen dem Heiligen Stuhl und der deutschen Reichsregierung. 2 vols. Mainz, 1965-69.

Basic documentation from German archival sources of vexed question of Papal Concordat with Nazi Germany, 1933. In same series, see Alfons Kupper, ed., Staatliche Akten über die Reichskonkordatsverhandlungen, 1933 (Mainz, 1969).

205. Friedlander, Saul. Pius XII and the Third Reich: A Documentation, rev. ed. New York, 1966.

Documents from German Auswärtiges Amt files regarding the Vatican failure to oppose openly the Nazi "final solution" of the Jewish question.

206. Graham, Robert A. "Il Giappone e il Vaticano in tempo di guerra: Corrispondenza diplomatica inedita." Civiltà Cattolica, no. 3127 (Oct.-Dec., 1980): 11-25.

ITALIAN DOCUMENTS

Synopsis of 80 documents; brief verbatim excerpts from "Magic - Diplomatic Summary" (see p. 60), intercepted messages between Tokyo and Japanese plenipotentiary in Vatican, 1942-45.

207. Pius XI. Discorsi di Pio XI, ed. Domenico Bartetto, 3 vols. Turin, 1960.

Veiled comments on Fascist Italian policy in Albania and East Africa; criticism of Axis racism.

For Pius XII's observations on World War II, see annual publications of his Discorsi e radiomessagi (Rome, 1940-58); index to first 15 vols. (1939-54).

208. Vatican, Secrétairerie d'Etat. Actes et documents du Saint Siège relatifs à la seconde guerre mondiale, ed. Pierre Blet, Robert A. Graham, Angelo Martini, Burkhart Schneider, 11 vols. Rome, 1965-80.

In response to accusations advanced, for example, in Friedlander's work (#205) of silence during Nazism's slaughter of European Jewry, the Papacy authorized publication of extensive selections from its Archivio Segreto. Valuable collection arranged chronologically with tables of both published documents and those not printed but mentioned; also an index of names and topics. Dwells heavily on events in Italy, illuminates Nazi-Fascist relations during World War II.

Because vol. 1 documenting Vatican diplomacy during Italian neutrality was considered of exceptional importance, it has been translated into English: Records and Documents of the Holy See relating to the Second World War, vol. 1, The Holy See and the War in Europe, March 1939 - August 1940, ed. Gerard Noel (London, 1968). Complements earlier documentary publication on Vatican attempts to keep Italy out of war: L'opera di pace della Santa Sede e l'Italia (Vatican City, 1945).

2. Non-Italian Documents

For the same reasons that the student of Italy's diplomacy, 1918-1945, can benefit from the archives of other powers, so too it behooves him to give heed to non-Italian printed documents. Of course, this category encompasses a vast range of titles. All that it is possible to list below are the official series of diplomatic documents sponsored by national governments, a few outstanding collections of international documents, and such works as have a direct bearing on Italy's role in world affairs.

International Documentary Collections

209. Adamthwaite, Anthony, ed. The Lost Peace: International Relations in Europe, 1918-1939. London, 1980.

Some 70 significant documents in English. See also the same author's Making of the Second World War (London, 1977), which includes translations of Italian documents on Ethiopia, Anschluss, and neutrality, 1939.

210. Albrecht-Carrié, René. "Italy and Her Allies, June 1919." American Historical Review, 46 (1940-41): 837-43.

Text of Allied note rejecting Italy's claim to Fiume.

211. Anchiere, Ettore, ed. Diplomazia Contemporanea: Raccolta di documenti diplomatici, politici, 1815-1956. Padua, 1959.

Useful documentary collection weighted to Italy's international role, particularly in the interwar years.

212. Delzell, Charles F., ed. Mediterranean Fascism, 1919-1945. New York, 1970.

Contains sections of translated Italian documents on foreign policy after 1935 - intervention in Spain, surrender to the Allies, 1943, etc.

213. Grenville, J.A.S. The Major International Treaties, 1914-1945: A History and Guide with Texts, 2d ed. New York, 1987.

Deservedly well-known reference work; good selection of texts and commentary.

214. Jacobsen, Hans-Adolf, and Smith, Arthur L., eds. World War II: Policy and Strategy. Santa Barbara, CA, & Oxford, 1980.

Agreements, reports, memos, speeches, etc., both Allied and Axis, 1939-45.

215. Keith, Arthur B., ed. Speeches and Documents on International Affairs, 1918-1937, 2 vols. London, 1938.

Standard reference work for texts of treaties, speeches, communiqués, and so on.

216. Mantoux, Paul, ed. Les délibérations du Conseil des Quatre, 24 mars - 28 juin 1919, 2 vols. Paris, 1955. Eng. trans. Paris Peace Conference, 1919: Proceedings of the Council of Four, Geneva, 1964.

Comptes rendus transcribed by official interpreter. Minutes taken by Sir Maurice Hankey, secretary to the Big Four, are published in Foreign Relations of the United States: Paris Peace Conference, 1919, vols. 5-6 (#225). The two sets of records match closely.

Processed minutes of the Conference of Ambassadors, 1920-1931, which devolved from the Council of Four, are available on microfilm,

NON-ITALIAN DOCUMENTS

99 reels (Hoover Institution on War, Revolution and Peace, Palo Alto, CA).

217. Royal Institute of International Affairs. <u>Documents on International Affairs</u>, 31 vols. London, 1928-73.

Useful reference source, originally published annually, for texts of state papers, speeches, exchanges of diplomatic notes, etc. For index and companion series, see <u>Survey of International Affairs</u> (#100).

U.S. Documents

218. Di Nolfo, Ennio. <u>Vaticano e Stati Uniti, 1939-1952: Dalle carte di Myron C. Taylor</u>. Milan, 1978.

From the papers of President Roosevelt's personal representative to the Vatican in World War II; 362 documents, most not previously printed. For further excerpts from Taylor's papers, see Elena Aga Rossi, "La politica del Vaticano durante la seconda guerra mondiale," <u>Storia Contemporanea</u>, 6 (1977): 881-928.

219. Eisenhower, Dwight D. <u>The Papers of Dwight David Eisenhower: The War Years</u>, ed. Alfred D. Chandler, 9 vols. Baltimore, 1970-78.

Vol. 2 for negotiations of the Italian armistice, 1943.

220. House, Edward M. <u>The Intimate Papers of Colonel House</u>, arr. Charles M. Seymour, 4 vols. Boston-New York, 1926-28.

Vol. 4 for peace negotiations, 1919, and the Fiume question.

221. MacVeagh, Lincoln. <u>Ambassador MacVeagh Reports: Greece, 1933-1947</u>, ed. John O. Iatrides. Princeton, 1979.

U.S. ambassador in Athens supplies information on Mussolini's "parallel war," 1940.

222. Moffat, Jay Pierrepoint. <u>The Moffat Papers</u>, ed. Nancy Harvison Hooker. Cambridge, MA, 1956.

Author a member of Sumner Welles mission to Italy, spring 1940; cf. Welles (#405).

223. Ribuoli, Patrizia. "Italia e Stati Uniti dal 1943 al 1945 in 'The Charles Poletti Papers.' " <u>Aevum</u>, 57/3 (1983): 474-79.

Contents of the archive, located in the School of International Affairs, New York, of commissioner of Allied Military Government in Italy. See also Fiorentino (#870).

ITALIAN FOREIGN POLICY, 1918-1945

224. Roosevelt, Franklin D. The Public Papers and Addresses of Franklin Delano Roosevelt, ed. Samuel I. Rosenman, 13 vols. New York, 1938-50.

For World War II diplomacy, see also F.D.R.: His Personal Letters, 1928-1945, ed. Elliott Roosevelt, 4 vols. (New York, 1947-50); Wartime Correspondence between President Roosevelt and Pope Pius XII, intro., notes by Myron C. Taylor (New York, 1947); Churchill and Roosevelt: The Complete Correspondence, ed. Warren F. Kimball, 3 vols. (1984).

225. U.S. Department of State. Foreign Relations of the United States: Diplomatic Papers. Washington, 1861- .

Continues Papers Relating to the Foreign Relations of the United States, so-called to 1931. Official record of American diplomacy; first regular documentary series to be published by a nation state. Volumes for entire period 1918-45; each set of annual volumes arranged by topic and country.

226. ―――. United States and Italy, 1936-1946: Documentary Record. Washington, 1946.

Convenient collection of 101 documents, mostly official U.S. pronouncements drawn from State Department Bulletin.

227. Wilson, Woodrow. The Papers of Woodrow Wilson, ed. Arthur S. Link. Princeton, 1966- .

Massive ongoing publishing venture; supersedes all previous collections of Wilson's papers, letters, etc. Organized chronologically; vol. 53ff. for post-World War I peace negotiations.

228. Wrigley, David W. "The United States and the Italian Influence in Albania: Six Diplomatic Documents, 1928-1939." Balkan Studies, 25/1 (1984): 81-108.

In spite of America's desire to preserve the open door for trade in Albania, until 1939 Washington acquiesced in Italian penetration and control.

British Documents

See also League of Nations (#264); Petrie (#704).

229. Great Britain, Cabinet. Principal War Telegrams and Memoranda, 1940-1943. Nendeln, Liechtenstein, 1976.

Summary record of the War Cabinet's activity in all spheres.

NON-ITALIAN DOCUMENTS

230. Great Britain, Foreign Office. <u>Anglo-Vatican Relations, 1914-1939: Confidential Annual Reports of the British Ministers to the Holy See</u>, ed. Thomas E. Hachey. Boston, 1972.

    Britain was the only major power to have diplomatic representation at the Vatican throughout these years; a useful compendium.

231. ——. <u>British Documents on Foreign Affairs: Reports and Papers from the Foreign Office Confidential Print</u>, general editors Kenneth Bourne and D. Cameron Watt, 420 vols. Frederick, MD, 1988- .

    From the mid nineteenth to mid twentieth century the F.O. printed its most important papers for limited internal circulation within government circles and kept them in the <u>Confidential Print</u>. Few sets have survived. A current publishing enterprise by University Publications of America will provide liberal selections divided into 18 series within a two-part framework - before and after World War I. In Part II the most relevant series to this guide are <u>Europe, 1919-1939</u>, ed. Christopher Seton Watson et al., 60 vols.; <u>The Paris Peace Conference of 1919</u>, ed. M.L. Dockrill, 15 vols.; <u>The League of Nations</u>, ed. Peter S. Beck, 10 vols.

232. ——. <u>Documents on British Foreign Policy, 1919-1939</u>, 3 series, 65 vols. London, 1947- .

    Major documentary series drawn mainly from F.O.'s general correspondence files. In reality, 4 rather than 3 series: series 1 (1919-1925); 1A (1925-1930); 2 (1929-1938); 3 (1938-1939). Final vol. an index of names and lists of diplomats in 1938-39. At start of each volume an analytical table of documents, but no index or listing of offices and personnel. Although a rough chronology is maintained, organization of chapters in each volume is often by topic. Collection lacks minutes appended to documents, an outstanding feature of its British predecessor on the origins of the First World War.

233. Great Britain, Parliamentary Papers. <u>Accounts and Papers</u>. London, 1918-45.

    Search for command papers on foreign policy laid before parliament and printed as "blue books" facilitated by Robert Vogel, <u>A Breviate of British Diplomatic Blue Books, 1919-1939</u> (Montreal, 1963).

234. Ludlow, Peter. "Dokumentation: Papst Pius XII, die britische Regierung und die deutsche Opposition im Winter 1939-1940." <u>Vierteljahrshefte für Zeitgeschichte</u>, 22 (1974): 299-341.

    Eighteen documents from British archival sources on the Papacy's intermediary role, with commentary.

235. Mercuri, Lamberto. "La situazione dei partiti italiani vista dal Foreign office, dicembre 1943." <u>Storia Contemporanea</u>, 11 (1980): 1049-60.

Includes several F.O. documents.

French Documents

236. Blum, Léon. L'oeuvre de Léon Blum, 1934-1937, 6 vols. Paris, 1954-72.

    Writings and speeches of the head of France's Popular Front government, 1936-37, at odds with Mussolini over Ethiopia and Spanish Civil War. Blum's L'Histoire jugera, 2d ed. (Montreal, 1973), contains speeches and diary extracts, 1932-42. See also Léon Blum devant la Cour de Riom, février-mars 1942 (Paris, 1945).

237. Briand, Aristide. Sa vie, son oeuvre, avec son journal, ed. Georges Suarez, 6 vols. Paris, 1938-52.

    Vol. 5 for post-World War I diplomacy; vol. 6 on Briand's failure as foreign minister, 1925-32, to achieve détente with Fascist Italy.

238. France, Assemblée Nationale. Les événements survenus en France de 1933 à 1945: Témoignages et documents recueillis par la Commission d'Enquête Parlementaire, 10 vols. Paris, 1947-54.

    Famous inquest into the reasons for France's collapse, 1940; French diplomatic posture faced with Nazi Germany and Fascist Italy put under scrutiny.

239. France, Ministère des Affaires Etrangères. Documents diplomatiques français, 1932-1939, 3 series. Paris, 1963- .

    Disruption of France's diplomatic archives in 1940 has caused French to lag behind other powers in printing an official series. Introductory series (1919-32) still to come; series 1 (1932-35), 13 vols.; series 2 (1936-39), 19 vols. Documents drawn principally from Correspondence Politique et Commerciale, but also contain extracts from private papers. Items arranged in strict chronological order, while table of documents at beginning of each volume divided topically; there are also indices of names.

240. Laval, Pierre. Le procès Laval: Compte rendu sténographique. Paris, 1946.

    French foreign minister, 1935-36, accused at post-World War II trial of appeasing Mussolini in Ethiopian crisis. See also Laval's Diary (#314).

    Similar foreign policy issues surfaced in the trial of France's premier, 1935, and Laval's successor at the Foreign Ministry: Le procès Flandin devant la Haute Cour de Justice, 23-26 juillet 1946 (Paris, 1947).

NON-ITALIAN DOCUMENTS

241. Valiani, Leo. "Documenti francesi sull'Italia e il movimento jugoslavo." Rivista Storica Italiana, 80 (1968): 351-64.

    Synopsis of contents of documents found in French Foreign Ministry archives on Italo-Yugoslav tension at the end of World War I.

242. Watt, D. Cameron. "The Secret Laval-Mussolini Agreement of 1935 on Ethiopia." Middle Eastern Journal, 15 (1961): 69-78.

    Franco-Italian exchanges deriving from French Senate Committee on Foreign Affairs; originals seized by Nazi Germany and unearthed among German records captured in 1945.

German Documents

243. Collotti, Enzo. Le potenze dell'Asse e la Jugoslavia: Saggi e documenti, 1941-1943. Milan, 1974.

    Axis documentation, a mix of German and Italian records. Records from German sources comprise much of E. Collotti, L'amministrazione tedesca dell'Italia occupata, 1943-1945: Studio e documenti (Milan, 1963).

244. Germany, Auswärtiges Amt. Akten zur deutschen auswärtigen Politik, 1918-1945, 5 series. Baden-Baden, Göttingen, 1950- .

    Best-known and probably most-used of all European national collections. Unusual in that initiation lay not with the nation of provenance, Germany, but with an Anglo-French-American commission given access to Auswärtiges Amt files captured by the Western Allies in 1945. At the outset, the commission resolved to concern itself solely with printing documents for 1933-41 (series C, D). Hence, these published in German and English; latter entitled Documents on German Foreign Policy, 1918-1945, from the Archives of the German Foreign Ministry, 6, 13 vols. (Washington & London, 1949-83), plus index to series D prepared by James E. McSherry (Arlington, VA, 1976). French publication, Les archives secrètes de la Wilhelmstrasse (Paris, 1950-), is only a selection. With return of the original files to Bonn in 1959 the Federal Republic has assumed responsibility for completing the project.

    The five series are: A (1918-25), still in publication, 14 vols. planned; B (1925-33), 21 vols.; C (1933-37), 6 vols.; D (1937-41), 13 vols.; E (1941-45), 8 vols. Arrangement of documents mainly chronological with analytical table of documents at front of each volume sectioned by country and topic. Useful appendices detail German Foreign Office personnel and administration. Individual documents carry file numbers that can be related to the microfilm of records made before their return to Germany, available in Washington and London; see Kent (p. 67).

ITALIAN FOREIGN POLICY, 1918-1945

245. ———. Nazi-Soviet Relations, 1939-1941, ed. Raymond J. Sontag and James S. Beddie. Washington, DC, 1948.

Selections from captured German records published during the Cold War to indict the Soviet Union for the nonaggression pact with Nazi Germany, 1939. To which the Soviets replied with Documents and Materials relating to the Eve of the Second World War, 2 vols. (Moscow, 1948), German, Czech, and other documents chosen to illustrate Western appeasement. See also U.S.S.R., Ministry of Foreign Affairs, Soviet Peace Efforts on the Eve of World War II (Moscow, 1973), which continues the polemic and even includes some Italian material.

246. Germany, Reichskanzlei. Akten der Reichskanzlei, Weimarer Republik, ed. Karl-Dietrich Erdmann. Boppard, 1968- .

Supplemented by Akten der Reichskanzlei, Regierung Hitler, 1933-1938, ed. Konrad Repgen (Boppard, 1983-). Both series still in course of publication. Records of cabinet meetings include foreign policy discussions, naturally of more substance in the pre-1933 democratic years.

247. Hillgruber, Andreas, ed. Staatsmänner und Diplomaten bei Hitler: Vertrauliche Aufzeichnungen über Unterredungen mit Vertretern des Auslandes, 2 vols. Frankfurt, 1967-70.

Records of the Führer conversations, 1939-44, including a number with Mussolini, Ciano, and Italy's successive representatives in Berlin; drawn from published and unpublished sources.

248. Hitler, Adolf. Hitler: Reden und Proklamationen, 1932-1945, ed. Max Domarus, new ed., 4 vols. Leonberg, 1988.

Most complete collection of Hitler's public utterances; Eng. trans. in preparation. See also The Speeches of Adolf Hitler, April 1932 - August 1939, ed. Norman H. Baynes, 2 vols. (London, 1942).

Off-the-cuff remarks by the Führer during World War II are recorded in overlapping publications: Tischgespräche im Führerhauptquartier, ed. Henry Picker, 3d ed. (Stuttgart, 1976); Adolf Hitler: Monologe im Führerhauptquartier, 1941-1944. Die Aufzeichnungen Heinrich Heims, ed. Werner Jochmann (Hamburg, 1980); Hitler's Table Talk, 1941-1944, intro. by Hugh Trevor Roper, 2d ed. (London, 1973).

For Hitler's exchanges with Mussolini, see Zinconi (#188).

249. International Military Tribunal. Trial of the Major War Criminals before the International Military Tribunal, Nuremberg, 14 November 1945 - 1 October 1946, 42 vols. Nuremberg, 1947-49.

Comprehensive documentary selection known as the "Blue Series" of Nuremberg Trials publications. Printed in English, French, Russian,

NON-ITALIAN DOCUMENTS

German editions. Emphasizes indictment of planning and waging war; vols. 9, 10, 14-17, 25 for most information on foreign policy. Vol. 23 an index to testimony, vol. 24 an index to documents. A summary, though with supplementary documentation, is the "Red Series": Nazi Conspiracy and Aggression, 10 vols. (Washington, 1946-48).

Subsequent trials of some 200 lesser war criminals were conducted by the American Military Tribunal at Nuremberg. A selected documentary record comprises the "Green Series": Trials of War Criminals before the Nuremberg Military Tribunals under Control Council Law No. 10, October 1946 - April 1949, 15 vols. (Washington, 1949-53); vols. 12-14 for foreign affairs.

All series available in microform; consult Guide to Microforms in Print (#41). For archival records from which printed collections drawn, see p. 69.

250. Krausnick, Helmut, ed. "Himmler über seinen Besuch bei Mussolini vom 11-14 Oktober 1942." Vierteljahrshefte für Zeitgeschichte, 4 (1956): 423-26.

Document printed from S.S. Reichsführer files.

251. Poliakov, Léon, and Sabille, Jacques. Jews under the Italian Occupation. Paris, 1955.

Contains mainly German documentation, accompanied by some Italian and French pieces, concerning the hindrance of Nazism's antisemitic Holocaust in France, Greece, and Croatia by Italian military and diplomats.

252. Robertson, Esmonde M. "Zur Wiederbesetzung des Rheinlandes 1936." Vierteljahrshefte für Zeitgeschichte, 10 (1962): 178-205.

Exchanges between Berlin and the German embassy in Rome, Jan.-Mar. 1936, from Auswärtiges Amt files and Hassell's diary (#312).

253. Rommel, Erwin. Krieg ohne Hass: Afrikanischen Memoiren. Heidenheim, 1950. Expanded Eng. trans. The Rommel Papers, ed. B. Liddell Hart, London & New York, 1953.

For Italo-German relations during World War II.

254. Stresemann, Gustav. Vermächtnis, ed. Henry Bernhard, 3 vols. Berlin, 1932-33. Eng. trans. His Diaries, Letters and Papers, ed. Eric Sutton, 3 vols., New York & London, 1935-40.

Carefully edited records of Weimar Germany's foreign minister, 1923-29, concealing revisionist sentiment apparent in archival Nachlass. Chronicles Italo-German arguments over Alto Adige.

255. Watt, D. Cameron. "An Earlier Model for the Pact of Steel: The Draft Treaties Exchanged between Germany and Italy during Hitler's Visit to Rome in May 1938." International Affairs [London], 33 (1957): 185-97.

Documentary article based on Auswärtiges Amt files.

256. Weizsäcker, Ernst von. Die Weizsäcker Papiere, 1900-32, 1933-50, 2 vols., ed. Leonidas E. Hill. Berlin, Frankfurt, 1974-82.

Papers of state secretary in Germany's Foreign Ministry, 1938-43, and ambassador to the Vatican, 1943-45.

257. Whealey, Robert H. "Mussolini's Ideological Diplomacy: An Unpublished Document." Journal of Modern History, 39 (1967): 432-37.

Mussolini interviewed by a Völkischer Beobachter correspondent, 31 Mar. 1936, regarding the Duce's recent overture to Germany.

Russian Documents

See also Germany, Nazi-Soviet Relations (#245).

258. Degras, Jane, ed. Communist International, 1919-1943, 3 vols. London, 1956-65.

Official publications, communiqués, etc. of covert arm of Soviet foreign policy. More extensive Comintern records drawn from the Fondazione Giangiacomo Feltrinelli, Milan, are available on microfiche (Clearwater): The Congresses of the Communist International, 1919-1935; The Executive Committees: Its Presidium and Commissions, 1921-1934; The Activity of the Comintern; material in various languages.

259. ———. Soviet Documents on Foreign Policy, 1917-1941, 3 vols. London, 1951-53.

Collections of press releases, speeches, etc. For a listing, see J. Degras, ed., Calendar of Soviet Documents on Foreign Policy, 1917-1941 (London, 1948).

260. U.S.S.R., Ministry of Foreign Affairs. Correspondence between the Chairman of the Council of Ministers of the U.S.S.R. and the Presidents of the U.S.A. and the Prime Ministers of Great Britain during the Great Patriotic War of 1941-1945. Moscow, 1957.

Occasional references to postwar plans for Italy. See also Andrew Rothstein, ed., Soviet Foreign Policy during the Patriotic War: Documents and Materials, 2 vols. (London, 1946?).

261. ———. Dokumenty vneshnei Politiki SSSR. Moscow, 1957- .

NON-ITALIAN DOCUMENTS

Important Soviet series of documents from Russia's Foreign Ministry archives, available only in Russian. In theory an ongoing publication but no vols. issued for over ten years; 21 vols. so far published span 1917-1938.

262. ⸺. International Affairs [Moscow].

English-language edition of journal Mezhdurnarodnaia Zhizn'. Until 1988 commentary along standard Moscow foreign policy lines, but interspersed with valuable excerpts (in translation) from Soviet diplomatic archives. Documentation on such topics as disarmament and collective security in 1930's, though nothing directly pertinent to Italy.

263. ⸺. SSSR-Italii: Stranitsy istorii, 1917-1984, dokumenty i materialy. Ministerstvo inostrannykh del SSSR, Ministerstvo inostrannykh del Italii. Moscow, 1985.

Public documents on Italo-Russian relations assembled to celebrate sixtieth anniversary of Italian de jure recognition of Soviet Union, 1924.

League of Nations Documentation

264. League of Nations. Dispute between Ethiopia and Italy. London, 1936.

Handy compilation of British diplomatic "blue books": Cmds. 5071, 5072, 5094.

265. ⸺. Official Journal, 20 vols., 194 supplements. Geneva, 1920-39.

League council minutes, assembly debates, committee records, etc., also printed in French. In addition, the League published a mass of documentation; see Mary Eva Birchfield, comp., Consolidated Catalog of League of Nations Publications Offered for Sale (Dobbs Ferry, 1976). Many records, including Official Journal and supplements, have been filmed; consult League of Nations Documents, 1919-1946: A Descriptive Guide and Key to the Microfilm Collection, ed. Edward A. Reno, 3 vols. (New Haven, CT, 1973-75).

266. ⸺. Recueil des traités et des engagements registrés par le Secretariat de la Société des Nations, 205 vols. Geneva, 1920-46.

Basic international treaty collection for period 1918-45; French and English texts of almost 5,000 diplomatic agreements registered at Geneva. Includes accords signed by Italy to 1937 when Fascist Italy left the League.

267. World Peace Foundation. Pamphlets, 12 vols. Boston, 1917-29.

Series of documentary pamphlets related to work of the League of Nations. Most relevant to Italian diplomacy: "The Corfu Crisis," ed. A. Lawrence Lowell, 6/3 (1923): 169-210.

Miscellaneous National Documentation

268. Adám, Magda, et al. Allianz Hitler-Horthy-Mussolini: Dokumente zur ungarischen Aussenpolitik, 1933-1944. Budapest, 1966.

Substantial work consisting of introductory essay followed by 136 documents from Hungarian Foreign Ministry files.

269. Belgium, Académie Royale. Documents diplomatiques belges: La politique de sécurité extérieure, 1920-1940, 5 vols. Brussels, 1964-66.

Belgium's authorized selections from Foreign Ministry archives.

270. Greece, Ministère des Affaires Etrangères. Documents diplomatiques: Différend italo-grec, août-sept. 1923 (Affaire Kakavia). Athens, 1923.

Greek "white book" on the Corfu affair.

271. Greece, Royal Greek Ministry for Foreign Affairs. The Greek White Book: Diplomatic Documents relating to Italy's Aggression against Greece. London, 1942.

Issued by the Greek government in exile during World War II; 183 documents from Italo-Greek treaty of 1928 to Italian invasion of Greece, 1940.

272. Horthy, Miklós. The Confidential Papers of Admiral Horthy, ed. Miklós Szinai and Laszlo Szücs. Budapest, 1965.

English translation of 65 documents; disappointingly little on Italy from the Hungarian regent's papers.

273. Hungary, Ministry of Foreign Affairs. Papers and Documents relating to the Foreign Relations of Hungary, 2 vols. Budapest, 1939-46.

Hungary's authorized diplomatic documentary series, mostly in English, interrupted by the turmoil at the end of World War II; only documents for 1919-21 published. Project was resumed by postwar regime in 1959 with a documentary series for 1936-45, but printed in Magyar.

274. Jedlicka, Ludwig, ed. "Mussolini und Österreich 1936: Niederschrift des österreichischen Militärattachés in Rom, General Dr. E.

NON-ITALIAN DOCUMENTS

Liebitzky, über seine Unterhaltung mit Mussolini am 12. August 1936." Österreich in Geschichte und Literatur, 6 (1962): 415-18.

Mussolini urges Austrian self-reliance and rearmament.

275. Kerekes, Lajos, ed. "Akten des ungarischen Ministeriums des Ausseren zur Vorgeschichte der Annexion Österreichs." Acta Historica Hungarica, 7 (1960): 355-90.

Reports from the Hungarian envoy in Rome, talks with the Italian minister in Budapest; 16 documents, Jan. 1936 - April 1938. Mussolini's involvement with Austria's Heimwehr documented in L. Kerekes, "Akten zu den geheimen Verbindungen zwischen der Bethlen Regierung und der österreichischen Heimwehrbewegung," ibid., 11 (1965): 299-339.

276. Spain, Ministry of Foreign Affairs. Documents on the Italian Intervention in Spain. London, 1937. U.S. ed. Spanish White Book. The Italian Invasion of Spain: Official Documents and Papers from Italian Units in Action at Guadalajara. Washington, DC, 1937.

Spanish Republican government's submission of some 100 documents to the League of Nations. Further documents on the Italian and German role in Spain in Seeds of Conflict: series 3, The Spanish Civil War, 1936-1939; vol. III, Non Intervention and Intervention (reprint, Nendeln, 1975). From the Italian side, see Grandi (#168).

277. Switzerland, Commission Nationale pour la Publication des Documents Diplomatiques. Documents diplomatiques suisses; Diplomatische Dokemente der Schweiz; Documenti diplomatici svizzeri, 1848-1945. Bern, 1979- .

Ongoing documentary series drawn from Swiss diplomatic archives; vols. 7, 9, 10 so far published on 1918-1945.

278. Szabo, Laszlo. "Papers." English-language edition in preparation by Brian R. Sullivan.

Originals in Hungarian National Archives, Budapest. Colonel Szabo was Hungarian military attaché in Rome, 1932-41, and confidant of Mussolini; papers detail Italo-Hungarian politico-military collaboration in late 1930's.

279. Zermeli, S. "Deux rapports du directeur du protocole sur deux visites à son altesse le bey." Revue d'Histoire Maghrebine, 9 (1982): 367-70.

Two reports of Italian démarches to protect Italy's interests in Tunisia, 1943.

280. Zervos, Skevos G., ed. La question du Dodécanèse et ses documents diplomatiques, 2d ed. Athens, 1928.

Twenty-three documents in Greek and French run from 1835 to 1923, when Italian possession of the Dodecanese Islands was recognized in the Treaty of Lausanne.

C. DIARIES AND MEMOIRS

Diplomatic reminiscences can be revelatory, although many that promise much deliver disappointingly little. Moreover, it must be remembered that in one degree or another they all represent an author's apologia pro la sua vita. In other words, memoirs constitute an essential research tool, but must be used with care and in conjunction with less subjective evidence. The same thing can be said of those diaries published by their author some time after the events they describe. Indeed, many a self-serving memoir is based on a diary tailored for the purpose. On the other hand, diaries edited by a third party from unpublished papers may deserve more credence as a quasi-documentary source.

The best guides to relevant diaries and memoirs are Messick (#15); Toscano (#20).

1. Diaries

Italian Diaries

Diary material woven into a memoir found in Caviglia (#358); Graziani (#335); Mellini Ponce de Leon (#373); Pini (#342); Varè (#348). See also Bianchi (#159).

281. Aldrovandi Marescotti, Luigi. Guerra diplomatica: Ricordi e frammenti di diario, 1914-1919, 6th ed. Milan, 1937.

   Together with the same author's Nuovi ricordi e frammenti di diario per far seguito a Guerra Diplomatica, 2d ed. (Milan, 1938), constitutes an important source for Italy's role in the post-World War I peace negotiations.

282. Aloisi, Pompeo. Journal: 25 juillet 1932 - 14 juin 1936, trans. by Maurice Vaussard. Paris, 1957.

   Invaluable first-hand account of Fascist Italy's move to imperialist aggression in Ethiopia. See commentary by Mario Toscano, "Il diario di Barone Aloisi," Rassegna Italiana di Politica e di Cultura, 34 (1957): 427-35, who also supplied edition's notes and introduction.

283. Armellini, Quirino. Diario di guerra: Nove mesi al Commando Supremo. Milan, 1946.

Provides some information on the political background in Rome from May 1940. See also the same author's Con Badoglio in Ethiopia (Milan, 1937).

284. Bonomi, Ivanoe. Diario di un anno, 2 giugno 1943 - 10 giugno 1944. Milan, 1947.

On the pre-Fascist premier's resumption of political activity; for Italy's efforts to achieve Allied cobelligerent status.

285. Bottai, Giuseppe. Diario, 1935-1944, ed. Giordano B. Guerri. Milan, 1976.

Fascist hierarch who vainly opposed Italian intervention in World War II. See also his Vent'anni e un giorno, 24 luglio 1943 (Cernusco, 1949), partially in diary form.

286. Cavallero, Ugo. Diario 1940-1943, ed. Giovanni Buccianti. Rome, 1984.

Italy's chief of staff was involved in some wartime political decision-making.

287. Ciano, Galeazzo. Diario, 1937-1943, ed. Renzo De Felice. Milan, 1980.

This is the diary Ciano, his wife, and friends tried unsuccessfully to use in bargaining for his life in 1944. Demonstrates frankly Ciano's early enthusiasm for Axis but later entries full of barbs against the Nazis. Appearing soon after the Second World War, the diary has comprised a basic source of accounts, scholarly and popular, of the declining years of Fascist foreign policy. Still essential testimony, it may be used in conjunction with papers Ciano collected as supporting evidence (L'Europa verso la catastrofe, #183).

Originally, the diary appeared in two parts - the first covering 1939-1943, the other the earlier years. Principal early editions in Italian and English: Diario, 1939-1943, 2 vols. (Milan, 1946), Eng. trans. The Ciano Diaries, 1939-1943, ed. Hugh Gibson (New York, 1946), ed. Malcolm Muggeridge (London, 1947); Diario, 1937-1938 (Bologna, 1948), Eng. trans. Ciano's Hidden Diary, 1937-1938, ed. Andreas Mayor (London, 1952; New York, 1953). Texts of these, and other, editions do not coincide, and the diary original is still not available (that for 1937-38 destroyed, that for 1939-43 in the hands of Ciano family). De Felice's one-volume edition is not therefore definitive. His compilation from earlier versions occasioned an authoritative article on the diary's vicissitudes, various texts, editions by Marco Palla, "La fortuna di un documento: Il diario di Ciano," Italia Contemporanea, no. 142 (1981): 31-54.

288. Crespi, Silvio. Alla difesa d'Italia in guerra e al Versaglio: Diario, 1917-1919, 2d ed. Milan, 1938.

DIARIES

Italy's wartime minister of supply and delegate to the Paris Peace Conference makes perceptive observations; useful documentary appendix.

289. Croce, Benedetto. Croce, the King and the Allies: Extracts from a Diary by Benedetto Croce, July 1943 - June 1944. London, 1950.

Accounts of Italian cabinet meetings but not much on diplomacy; some documents concern Italian military help to the Allies. See also Zeno Zencovich (#613).

290. D'Aroma, Nino. Mussolini segreto. Rome, 1958.

Author a journalist who spoke frequently with Mussolini, 1930-45; nothing directly on foreign affairs but offers pen portraits of Ciano, etc.

291. Dolfin, Giovanni. Con Mussolini nella tragedia: Diario del Capo della Segreteria Particolare del Duce, 1943-1944, 3d ed. Milan, 1950.

General information on Salò's relations with Germany.

292. Galli, Carlo. Diari e lettere: Tripoli, 1911; Trieste, 1918. Florence, 1951.

Diary stops in 1918, but followed by reminiscences of the Paris Peace Conference where the author was a member of Italy's delegation.

Galli's diary also the basis for accounts of diplomatic service in Yugoslavia: "Jugoslavia tragica, 1928-1934," Nuova Antologia, 458 (May-Aug. 1953): 137-56, 302-17, 432-54; "La politica serba per un accordo con l'Italia," Mondo Europeo, Jan.-Feb. 1946. See also Pavlowitch (#734).

293. Grandi, Dino. "Pagine di diario del 1943," ed. Renzo De Felice. Storia Contemporanea, 14 (1983): 1037-75.

Excerpt from Grandi's famous diary relating events leading up to the Fascist Grand Council's vote of no confidence in Mussolini.

294. Jannelli, Pasquale. "Preludio balcanica della guerra russo-germanica: Pagine di diario, Berlino, 13 aprile 1941," Rivista di Studi Politici Internazionali, 31 (1964): 210-20.

Jannelli also viewed World War II from Moscow briefly and Tokyo: "A Mosca alla vigilia dell'attacco tedesco," Nuova Antologia, 488 (May-Aug. 1963): 347-68; "L'intervento dell'Italia contro l'Unione Sovietica nel 1941," ibid., 487 (Jan.-Apr. 1963): 355-76, 502-20; "La guerra nel Pacifico dal diario di un diplomatico italiano," Storia e Politica, 3 (1964): 20-49, 351-79; "Italia e Giappone dopo l'armistizio dell'8 settembre 1943," ibid., 2 (1963): 157-82.

295. Justus, V. [Macchi di Cellere, Dolores]. Macchi di Cellere all'ambasciata di Washington: Memorie e testimonianze, 2d ed. Florence, 1921.

   Based on a diary of the Paris Peace Conference; includes some documents. Edited by the ambassador's widow soon after his death, October 1919, under the cloud of imminent recall to Rome.

296. Nenni, Pietro. Tempo di guerra fredda: Diari, 1943-1956, ed. Domenico Zucaro. Milan, 1981.

   First of a multivolume series of Nenni diaries. Returned to Italy from exile, the socialist leader had some dealings with the victorious powers.

297. Ortona, Egidio. "La caduta di Eden nel 1938." Storia Contemporanea, 15 (1984): 477-91.

   Ortona was a member of the Italian embassy in London, 1938; diary extract concerns resignation of the British foreign secretary, Mussolini's bête noire. Account may be measured against that of Ambassador Grandi (#334).

   Later, Ortona served under Bastianini in Dalmatia; see "Diario sul Governo della Dalmazia, 1941-1943," ibid., 18 (1987): 1365-1403. A further diary excerpt gives the view of the eventful summer of 1943 from the Foreign Ministry where the writer was head of the secretariat of first Bastianini, then Guariglia: "Il 1943 da Palazzo Chigi: Note di diario," ed. Renzo De Felice, ibid., 14 (1983): 1076-1147.

298. Pirelli, Alberto. Taccuini, 1922-1943, ed. Donato Barbone. Bologna, 1984.

   Supplements Dopoguerra, 1919-1932: Note ed esperienze (Milan, 1961). Important diary and notes of Italy's representative in international economic matters, president of the Istituto per gli Studi di Politica Internazionale (p. 74); illustrative of the nexus between Italian business and foreign policy-making in Rome.

299. Puntoni, Paolo. Parla Vittorio Emanuele III. Milan, 1958.

   Royal aide-de-camp's diary, discovered after his death, recounts the king's words and attitude during World War II.

300. Salandra, Antonio. I retroscena di Versailles, ed. Giambattista Gifuni. Milan, 1971.

   Continuation of Il diario di Salandra, (Milan, 1969), ed. G.B. Gifuni, which stops in 1918. Valuable for Salandra's role in Italy's delegation at the Paris Peace Conference and his resignation on nationalistic grounds in May 1919. Cf. Salandra inedito (#189).

DIARIES

301. Sforza, Carlo. "Dalle pagine del diario." Nuova Antologia, 501 (Sept.-Dec. 1967): 447-76; 502 (Jan.-Apr. 1968): 47-74; 524 (May-Aug. 1975): 311-39.

    Brief entries reveal little of substance; first excerpts for years 1915-18, second and third, 1923-27. See also Sforza (#345).

302. Simoni, Leonardo [Lanza, Michele]. Berlino, ambasciata d'Italia, 1939-1943. Rome, 1946.

    Second secretary of Italy's Berlin embassy probably composed this diary some time after the events described; includes documents since published in I documenti diplomatici italiani. See also Da Baranca (#361).

303. Sonnino, Sidney. Diario, ed. Benjamin F. Brown and Pietro Pastorelli, 3 vols. Bari, 1972.

    Vol. 3 for years 1916-22; many more entries for war years than postwar era, though some detailed accounts of peace negotiations. See also Sonnino's Carteggio (#190).

304. Vitetti, Leonardo. "Diario." Nuova Antologia, 519 (Sept.-Dec. 1973): 493-501.

    Extracts from a diary kept 1939-41, now in ASME; printed here as addendum to Enrico Serra, "Leonardo Vitetti e una sua testimonianza," ibid., pp. 487-92.

Non-Italian Diaries

See also Blum (#236); Briand (#237); Child (#397); Nicolson (#423); Phillips (#404); Stresemann (#254).

305. Baudouin, Paul. Neuf mois au Gouvernement, avril-décembre 1940. Paris, 1948. Eng. trans. The Private Diaries, March 1940 to January 1941, of Paul Baudouin, London, 1948.

    French foreign minister under Pétain discusses both German and Italian armistices, 1940; armistice texts in appendix.

306. Butcher, Harry C. My Three Years with Eisenhower. New York, 1946.

    Diary covers events leading up to Cassibile armistice, 1943.

307. Cadogan, Alexander. Diaries, 1938-1945, ed. David J. Dilks. London, 1971.

    Diary of the British Foreign Office's permanent undersecretary charts growing British disillusionment with Mussolini, distrust of Ambassador Grandi, etc.

308. Dawes, Charles G. A Journal of Reparations. New York, 1939.

On the making of the Dawes Plan, 1924, with references to work of Italian delegation led by Pirelli (#298).

309. Goebbels, Joseph. Tagebücher aus den Jahren 1942-1943, ed. Louis P. Lochner (Zurich, 1948). Eng. trans. The Goebbels Diaries, 1942-1943, London & Garden City, NY, 1948.

Continued by Goebbels Tagebücher: Die letzen Aufzeichnungen (Hamburg, 1977), Eng. trans. The Goebbels Diaries, the Last Days, ed. Hugh Trevor Roper (London, 1978), Final Entries, 1945: The Diaries of Joseph Goebbels (New York, 1978). Volumes show the Nazi propaganda minister's opinion of Italy in the Axis years growing progressively more contemptuous. A definitive version of all Goebbels's diaries, 1924-45, is in preparation in two parts by the Institut für Zeitgeschichte: Part 1, Aufzeichnungen, 1924-41, 4 vols. and index vol. (Munich, 1987).

310. Grew, Joseph C. Turbulent Era: A Diplomatic Record of Forty Years, 1904-1945, 2 vols. Boston, 1952.

American career diplomat's recollections, mostly in diary form; germane to Italian diplomacy is eyewitness account of the Lausanne Conference, 1922-23, in vol. 1.

311. Harvey, John, ed. The Diplomatic Diaries of Oliver Harvey, 1937-1940. London, 1970.

Prominent British F.O. official and private secretary to Eden during latter's tenure of the Foreign Office; his sentiments parallel those in Cadogan's Diaries (#307).

312. Hassell, Ulrich. Vom andern Deutschland: Aus den nachgelassenen Tagebüchern, 1938-1944. Zurich, 1946. Eng. trans. Diaries, 1938-1944: Story of the Forces against Hitler inside Germany, London, 1948.

Account of anti-Nazi resistance activities; frequent reference to Mussolini, Ciano, etc., but regrettably little on Hassell's earlier ambassadorship in Rome.

313. Hore-Belisha, Leslie. The Private Papers of Hore-Belisha, ed. Rubeigh J. Minney. London, 1960.

Diary within text recounts the author's term at the British War Office, 1937-40, dealings with Ambassador Grandi, and visit to Rome in April 1938.

314. Laval, Pierre. Laval parle: Notes et mémoires rédigés à Fresne d'août à octobre 1945. Paris, 1948. Eng. trans. The Unpublished Diary of Pierre Laval, London & New York, 1948.

DIARIES

Prison diary prepared for Laval's upcoming trial (see #240); general chapter on his stance towards Italy, 1934-40.

315. Macmillan, Harold. War Diaries: Politics and War in the Mediterranean, January 1943 - May 1945. London, 1984.

British minister-resident in North Africa on Italian armistice, liberation. See also Macmillan memoirs (#422).

316. Miller, David H. My Diary at the Conference of Paris, 1918-1919, with Documents, 22 vols. New York, 1924-26.

Work of the Italian delegation subsumed in massive publication by a U.S. participant.

317. Speranza, Gino. Italy, 1915-1919, 2 vols. New York, 1941.

Vol. 2 for the author's role as press attaché in U.S. Rome embassy, 1919; useful for the temper of Italian nationalist opinion.

318. Szembek, Jean. Journal, 1933-1939. Paris, 1952.

Polish undersecretary for foreign affairs records talks with Italian ambassador, Bastianini (#323).

2. Italian Memorialists

General Italian Memoirs

319. Alessandrini, Adolfo. Valigia diplomatica. Suzzari, 1984.

Memoirs span 1925-67, mostly apropos postings in Middle and Far East.

320. Anfuso, Filippo. Da Palazzo Venezia al lago di Garda, 3d rev. ed. Bologna, 1957.

Originally published in French as Du Palais de Venise au lac de Garde (Paris, 1949); first Italian edition, Roma-Berlino-Salò (Cernusco, 1950). Main theme is Rome-Berlin Axis, but also has useful information on Hungary, 1942

321. Badoglio, Pietro. L'Italia nella seconda guerra mondiale: Memorie e documenti, 2d ed. Verona, 1946. Eng. trans. Italy in the Second World War: Memoirs and Documents, London, 1948.

Best-known of Badoglio's memoirs; on military conduct of World War II, politics of Mussolini's overthrow, and Italy's switch to the Allied side. Book has a number of inaccuracies; see Gaetano Salvemini, "Pietro Badoglio's Role in the Second World War," Journal of Modern History, 21 (1949): 326-32.

First-hand accounts of two other international crises in which Badoglio was involved are Rivelazioni su Fiume (Rome, 1946), including appendix of 83 documents on negotiations with D'Annunzio 1919; La guerra d'Etiopia, 7th ed. (Rome, 1936), Eng. trans. The War in Abyssinia (London, 1937), which gives some account of political planning, 1934-35, before turning to military campaigning, and also prints some documents.

322. Barzilai, Salvatore. Luci ed ombre del passato. Milan, 1937.

Author deputy, journalist, and member of Italy's delegation to the Paris Peace Conference. Sketchy account of peacemaking; essays on Fascist diplomacy and diplomatic figures.

323. Bastianini, Giuseppe. Uomini, cose, fatti: Memorie di un ambasciatore. Milan, 1959.

On the author's tenure of Italy's Warsaw embassy and undersecretary's post in the Palazzo Chigi, 1943; in latter capacity Bastianini involved in attempts to persuade Germany to relinquish Russian campaign and to disentangle Italy from Nazi net.

324. Berio, Alberto. Dalle Ande all'Himalaya. Naples, 1961.

Superficial survey of varied diplomatic life. More meaty accounts of specific episodes in "L'affare etiopico," Rivista di Studi Politici Internazionali, 25 (1958): 181-219, on Berio's role as liaison between the League of Nations secretariat and Italy; Missione segreta: Tangeri, agosto 1943 (Milan, 1947), on his peace mission to the Western Allies after Mussolini's fall. See also #177.

325. Bissolati, Leonida. La politica estera dell'Italia dal 1897 al 1920. Milan, 1920.

Wartime cabinet minister who resigned, December 1918; last chap. a good example of rinunciatari argument.

326. Bova Scoppa, Renato. La pace impossibile. Turin, 1961.

Surveys in general terms seven diplomatic posts held 1920-43. Most important those in Portugal (1940-41), Rumania (1941-44), which are more fully described in R. Bova Scoppa, Colloqui con due dittatori (Rome, 1949).

327. Cerruti, Elisabetta. Vista da vicino. Milan, 1951. Eng. trans. Ambassador's Wife, London, 1952.

Social rather than political side of husband's diplomatic postings around the globe.

328. Ciano, Edda. Mia testimonianza, ed. Albert Zarca. Milan, 1975. Eng. trans. My Truth, New York, 1977.

Personal more than political memoir; no substantive issues until story reaches trial and execution of the author's husband, 1944.

329. Cora, Giuliano. "Un diplomatico durante l'era fascista." Storia e Politica, 5 (1966): 88-98.

Interesting if brief encounters with Mussolini, 1922-35, reflects atmosphere within Italy's diplomatic service under Fascism. See also G. Cora, "Il problema coloniale italiano," Rivista di Studi Politici Internazionali, 12 (1945): 3-20; "Il trattato italo-etiopico del 1928," ibid., 15 (1948): 205- 26.

330. Donosti, Mario [Luciolli]. Mussolini e l'Europa: La politica estera fascista. Rome, 1945.

Ostensibly a secondary survey, but since written from a position within Italy's Foreign Ministry, usually regarded as a memoir. An early and perceptive account.

Under his own name the author draws an authentic picture of the Ministero degli Esteri and its personalities in the Fascist and post-Fascist eras: Mario Luciolli, Palazzo Chigi: anni roventi. Ricordi di vita diplomatica italiana dal 1933 al 1948 (Milan, 1978).

331. Federzoni, Luigi. Italia di ieri per la storia di domani. Milan, 1967.

General account of Italian history, 1909-43, and part played by the author, an old-style nationalist and Mussolini's minister of colonies, 1923-24, 1926-29.

332. Giannini, Amadeo. Saggi di storia diplomatica, 1921-1940. Florence, 1942.

Essays based in part on personal observation by a long-serving prominent Foreign Ministry functionary. See also his L'ultima fase della questione orientale, 1913-1939, 2d ed. (Milan, 1941), and "Profili di uomini politici," Rivista di Studi Politici Internazionali, 20 (1953): 433-39; 21 (1954): 317-28, 688-96.

As head of the Palazzo Chigi's commercial department during World War II, Giannini was responsible for Italo-German economic co-operation: "L'accordo italo-germanico per il carbone, 1940," ibid., 21 (1954): 462-69; "Il convegno italo-germanico di Assisi, 20 agosto - 8 settembre 1943," ibid., 17 (1950): 3-18. See also his "L'armistizio italo-francese." ibid., 18 (1951): 7-24.

333. Giolitti, Giovanni. Memorie della mia vita, 3d ed. Monza, 1945. Eng. trans. Memoirs, London, 1923.

Concluding chapters on post-World War I peacemaking, Fiume crisis, and other diplomatic issues of Giolitti's premiership, 1920-21, but in no great detail.

334. Grandi, Dino. Il mio paese: Ricordi autobiografici, ed. Renzo De Felice. Bologna, 1985.

Most comprehensive of several versions of Grandi memoirs published in the final years of his life; essentially the same material as printed in 25 luglio: Quarant'anni dopo, ed. R. De Felice (Bologna, 1983). Important memoirs but very self-serving and far from reliable, e.g. on Grandi's role in promoting the Munich Conference. No substitute therefore for his private papers (p. 49). See also Dino Grandi racconta l'evitabile "Asse": Memorie raccolta e presentate da Gianfranco Bianchi (Milan, 1984), letters exchanged between Grandi and an Italian historian.

335. Graziani, Rodolfo. Ho difeso la patria, 5th ed. Milan, 1948.

Covers the marshal's military and political career in Libya, Ethiopia, and Salò Republic; includes several documentary texts. Other memoirs by Graziani mix military and political recollections: Il fronte sud (Milan, 1938) on his part in the Ethiopian campaign with diary extracts; Africa Settentrionale, 1940-1941 (Rome, 1948) also containing diary material and appendix of documents. See also Emilio Canevari, Graziani mi ha detto (Rome, 1947), which is based on Graziani's oral reminiscences in prison after World War II and includes documents.

336. Guariglia, Raffaele. Ricordi, 1922-1946. Naples, 1950.

Celebrated Italian diplomatic memoir. Its merit lies partly in coverage of the entire interwar period, partly in detailed descriptions and analysis deriving from the author's prominent position within Italy's diplomatic corps. The Foreign Ministry's relationship and cooperation with Mussolini is frankly discussed. Also valuable for Guariglia's own short tenure as foreign minister after Mussolini's dismissal. Worth noting that the French edition, La diplomatie difficile: Mémoires, 1922-1946 (Paris, 1955), although often quoted, is an abbreviated version. See also in response to De Monzie's Ci-devant (#447) Guariglia on his efforts for a Franco-Italian accord to keep Italy out of World War II: "Diario di un 'Ex,' " Nuova Antologia, 418 (Nov.-Dec. 1941): 342-47, and #169.

337. Lessona, Alessandro. Memorie, 2d ed. Rome, 1963.

Recounts activities as Mussolini's diplomatic emissary to Albania, 1925-26, and at Ministry of Colonies, 1929-37, when the main business was Ethiopia. His Un ministro di Mussolini racconta (Milan, 1973), a broad survey of events, 1922-43, seeks to analyze Mussolini, and L'Africa settentrionale nella politica mediterranea, 2d ed. (Rome, 1942), consists of miscellaneous essays.

338. Mussolini, Benito. Il tempo del bastone e della carota: Storia di un anno, ottobre 1942 - settembre 1943. Milan, 1944. Eng. trans. The Fall of Mussolini: His Own Story by Benito Mussolini, ed. Max

Ascoli, New York, 1948; Memoirs, 1942-1943, with Documents relating to the Period, ed. Raymond Klibansky, London, 1949.

Memoirs composed after his fall in self-justification; sweeping review of Mussolini's political career with no real substance. Similarly superficial is Mussolini's My Autobiography, rev. ed. (London, 1939), whose composition was aided by the onetime U.S. ambassador to Italy, R.W. Child (#397).

Several records of what purport to be the Duce's own words have been been published, including Testamento politico di Mussolini (Rome, 1948), an interview given on 22 April 1945 to the newspaper editor, Gian Gaetano Cabella. Other oral memoirs are: Ottavio Dinale, Quarant'anni di colloqui con Lui (Milan, 1953); Emil Ludwig, Mussolinis Gespräche mit Emil Ludwig (Berlin, 1932), Eng. trans. Talks with Mussolini (London, 1932), Ital. trans. Colloqui con Mussolini (Milan, 1932); Franco Maugeri, Mussolini mi ha detto: Confessioni di Mussolini durante il confino a Ponza e alla Maddalena (Rome, 1944), reprinted in the same author's From the Ashes of Disgrace, ed. Victor Rosen (New York, 1948); Cesare Rossi, Trentatre vicende mussoliniane (Milan, 1958); Georg Zachariae, Als Arzt und vertrauter Freund bei Mussolini, Ital. trans. Mussolini si confessa: Rivelazioni del medico tedesco inviato da Hitler al Duce, new ed. (Milan, 1966). On international affairs none offers much beyond general remarks. See also Hoettl (#456).

339. Mussolini, Rachele. La mia vita con Benito. Verona, 1948. Eng. trans. My Life with Mussolini, London, 1959.

The Duce's wife not a political figure, but she gives the background of visits to Rome by Hitler and other luminaries. See also her Mussolini sans masque, ed. Albert Zarca (Paris, 1973), Eng. trans. The Real Mussolini (Farnborough, 1974), Ital. trans. Mussolini privato (Milan, 1980).

340. Mussolini, Vittorio. Vita con mio padre. Milan, 1957.

Mussolini's youngest son recounts some political conversations with his father, including one regarding a proposed Mussolini-Roosevelt meeting, 1938.

341. Navarra, Quinto. Memorie del commesso di Mussolini. Milan, 1983.

Reprint of Memorie del cameriere di Mussolini (Milan, 1946). The Duce's valet supplies some interesting tidbits, especially regarding Mussolini's conference experiences.

342. Pini, Giorgio. Filo diretto con Palazzo Venezia. Bologna, 1950.

Author, editor of Popolo d'Italia, 1936-43, describes manipulation of the press and attempts to sell the Rome-Berlin Axis to Italy's public; some diary extracts. See also the same author's Itinerario tragico,

1943-1945 (Milan, 1950), recollections as undersecretary of Salò's Ministry of the Interior.

343. Quaroni, Pietro. Ricordi di un ambasciatore. Milan, 1954.

Tandem volume to his Valigia diplomatica (Milan, 1956); selections from both works have appeared in English as Diplomatic Bags (London, 1966). Quaroni, a long-serving career diplomat, specializes in biographical portraits of fellow Italian diplomats, e.g. Aldrovandi Marescotti, Contarini, as well as foreign statesmen and ambassadors. Most substantial information on Albanian question in late 1920's and Stesa Conference, 1935.

344. Salandra, Antonio. Memorie politiche, 1916-1925. Milan, 1951.

Useful for explanation of collaboration with early Fascism, especially as Italy's delegate to League of Nations during Corfu affair, 1923. Cf. Salandra (#189, #300).

345. Sforza, Carlo. L'Italia dal 1914 al 1944 quale io la vidi, 2d ed. Rome, 1944.

Nearest to general memoir composed by prolific political author; naturally most informative on 1920-21 when Sforza was foreign minister in Giolitti's cabinet. Also based on personal recollection of post-World War I diplomacy, especially Adriatic issues, are C. Sforza, Pensiero e azione di una politica estera italiana (Bari, 1924); Jugoslavia: Storia e ricordi (Milan, 1948). Sforza's secondary works also rest in part on personal memory (#513, #540, #552).

346. Soleri, Marcello. Memorie. Turin, 1949.

Financial expert marginally involved in interwar diplomacy, e.g. Franco-Italian exchanges, 1939.

347. Tolomei, Ettore. Memorie di vita. Milan, 1948.

Tolomei present at the Paris Peace Conference where Italy given the Alto Adige, and moving spirit behind Italianization of the region under Fascism.

348. Varè, Daniele. Laughing Diplomat. London & New York, 1938.

Lightweight contribution by career diplomat covers the years 1900-32; describes the ready welcome accorded Mussolini's arrival at the Foreign Ministry, 1922. Varè's later reminiscences, The Two Imposters (London, 1949), provide some information from his diary on the nonintervention committee in the Spanish Civil War. The same author's Twilight of the Kings (London, 1948) is anecdotal with hardly anything on foreign affairs. See also Varè's talk at London's Chatham House defending Italy's Ethiopian policy: "British Foreign Policy through Italian Eyes," International Affairs, 15 (1936): 80-102.

ITALIAN MEMORIALISTS

Italian Memoirs: Specific Topics

349. Alfieri, Dino. Due dittatori di fronte. Milan, 1948. Eng. trans. Dictators Face to Face, London, 1954.

    One of several standard memoirs on the Axis written from the perspective in Berlin, 1940-43.

350. Amè, Cesare. Guerra segreta in Italia, 1940-1943. Rome, 1954.

    By the general in command of Italian military intelligence.

351. Belloni, Maurizio. Uno come tanti. Rome, 1948.

    Author military attaché in Berlin, 1942-43; for the Italo-German breach in latter year, fate of Berlin embassy staff.

352. Bolla, Nino. Il segreto di due re. Milan, 1951.

    Author, confidant of King Vittore Emanuele III, details the royal posture between Nazis and Allies in World War II.

353. Borra, Eduardo. Prologo di un conflitto: Colloqui con secretario del Negus, dicembre 1934 - ottobre 1935. Milan, 1965.

    By a medical doctor in Ethiopia, involved in informal negotiations to avert an Italo-Ethiopian war after the Wal Wal incident.

354. Calabrò, Lino. Intermezzo africano: Ricordi di un Residente di Governo in Etiopia, 1937-1941 (Rome, 1988).

    On the colonization of Italian East Africa; diplomatic reverberations of Ethiopian crisis in background.

355. Cantalupo, Roberto. Fu la Spagna: Ambasciata presso Franco, febbraio - aprile 1937. Milan, 1948.

    Important memoir of the special envoy who unavailingly counseled Italy's disengagement from Spain's civil war.

    Less significant is the same author's Racconti politici dell'altra pace (Rome, 1940), a survey of Italy's post-World War I position from the Nationalist viewpoint, though it contains useful information on Mussolini's attitude to the export of Fascism.

356. Carboni, Giacomo. Più che il dovere: Memorie segrete, 1935-1948. Florence, 1955.

    General Carboni was in charge of Italy's military intelligence service, 1939-40. A further military memoir is his Storia di una battaglia italiana, 1937-1951 (Rome, 1952).

Later, as commandant of Italian troops protecting Rome, 1943, Carboni became the center of a postwar investigation into the capital's easy surrender to the Germans. His defence: L'armistizio e la difesa di Roma: Verità e menzonge (Rome, 1945), supplemented by L'Italia tradita dall'armistizio alla pace, 2d ed. (Rome, 1947).

357. Castellano, Giuseppe. Come firmai l'Armistizio di Cassibile, 2d ed. Rome, 1945.

Covers the events of February 1942 - September 1943; includes procès-verbal of talks between General Castellano and the Allies. See also same author's La guerra continua: La vera storia dell'8 settembre con documenti inediti (Milan, 1963).

358. Caviglia, Enrico. Il conflitto di Fiume: Memorie e documenti. Milan, 1948.

Author in command of Italian troops charged with expelling D'Annunzio from Fiume; information on diplomatic as well as military action. Publication prevented by the Fascists, whereupon Marshal Caviglia began to keep his Diario, Aprile 1925 - Marzo 1945 (Rome, 1952), though it has very little on public life.

359. Colosimo, Gaspare. Opera tratta dagli scritti di Gaspare Colosimo, 1916-1919, ed. Maurizio Colosimo. Pompei, 1959.

Colonial minister's memoir on colonial questions at the end of World War I; publication prevented by Fascists, later edited by son.

360. Constantini, Francesco. "Gli occhi del S.I.M. nell'ambasciata inglese." Candido, 10, 17, 24 November, 1 December 1957.

His own story by the Italian spy in Britain's Rome embassy.

361. Da Baranca, Mario. [Lanza, Michele]. Germania e Russia, 1921-1941: Vent'anni di storia diplomatica. Milan, 1942.

Withdrawn from circulation on publication. Italian career diplomat's observations based on service in the Soviet Union; reflects mood at the time of writing. See also Simoni (#302).

362. De Bono, Emilio. La preparazione e le primi operazioni, 3d ed. Rome, 1937. Eng. trans. Anno XIII: The Conquest of an Empire, London, 1937.

Italy's initial commander-in-chief in the Ethiopian campaign; first chapter has a little on the political background.

363. Depoli, Attilio. "Incontri con Facta e Mussolini: Pagine fiumane da ricordi di un dittatore involuntario." Fiume, 4 (July-Dec. 1956).

Spokesman for Italians in Fiume describes his links with Rome prior to Italy's acquisition of the port in 1924.

364. Di Nola, Carlo. "Italia e Austria dall'armistizio di Villa Giusti (nov. 1918) all'Anschluss (marzo 1938)." Nuova Rivista Storica, 44 (1960): 221-96.

Very general account by Italian commercial attaché in Vienna and Budapest, 1921-38, as is his "L'Anschluss nei ricordi di uno pseudo-diplomatico," Nuova Antologia, 463 (Jan.-Apr. 1955): 477-95. On Di Nola's career before 1921, see "Ricordi di uno pseudo-diplomatico," ibid., 461 (May-Aug. 1954): 327-44.

365. Foschini, Antonio. La verità sulle cannonate di Corfu: Un mese di storia, 29 agosto - 29 settembre 1923. Rome, 1953.

Author second-in-command of Corfu expedition. See also his briefer "A trent'anni dall'occupazione di Corfu," Nuova Antologia, 458 (Sept.-Dec. 1959): 401-12.

366. Grazzi, Emanuele. Il principe della fine: L'impresa di Grecia. Rome, 1945.

Detailed memoir of Italian minister to Greece prior to Italian attack, 1940; based on documents in the author's possession, though many now published in I documenti diplomatici italiani (#148).

367. Guarneri, Felice. Battaglie economiche tra le due grandi guerre, 2 vols. Milan, 1953.

Author businessman in charge of Italian foreign currency exchange, 1936-40, part of Fascism's autarchy drive.

368. Jacomini di San Sevino, Francesco. La politica dell'Italia in Albania. Rocca San Casciano, 1965.

Comprehensive first-hand account of Italy's gradual absorption of Albania, 1926-43, by diplomat imprisoned after 1945 for service to Mussolini in that country; includes appendix of documents.

369. Lanfranchi, Ferrucio. La resa degli ottocentomila, con le memorie autografe del barone L. Parilli. Milan, 1948.

On negotiations for German surrender to Allies, spring 1945.

370. Magistrati, Massimo. L'Italia a Berlino, 1937-1939. Milan, 1956.

Very valuable series of essays written from the author's vantage point in the Berlin embassy on Italo-German relations during Austrian, Czech, and Polish crises leading to World War II. His account of earlier Ethiopian and Rhineland episodes in Magistrati's Il prologo del dramma: Berlino, 1934-1937 (Milan, 1971), which prints several documents. See also the same author's general essay, "Venti anni fa: Roehm e Dollfuss," Rivista di Studi Politici Internazionali, 21 (1954): 375-88.

371. Malagodi, Olindo. Olindo Malagodi: Conversazioni della guerra, 1914-1919, ed. Brunello Vigezzi, 2 vols. Milan-Naples, 1960.

Notes of talks held by an Italian editor of Giolittian persuasion with many Italian statesmen; vol. 2 very informative on the Paris Peace Conference.

372. Masotti, Pier Marcello. Ricordi d'Etiopia di un funzionario coloniale. Milan, 1981.

Author in Ethiopia, 1934-39, views Italo-Ethiopian crisis from colonial service perspective. Also by Masotti, "Il rimpatrio di donne, bambini, vecchi ed invalidi italiani dall'Etiopia nel 1942-1943." Storia Contemporanea, 15 (1983): 463-73.

373. Mellini Ponce de Leon, Alberto. Guerra diplomatica a Salò, ottobre 1943 - aprile 1945. Bologna, 1950.

Almost exclusively on relations with Germany. Mussolini's capo di gabinetto quotes extracts from his own diary, a diary of Undersecretary Serafino Mazzolini, and some reports from Anfuso in Berlin.

374. Mondini, Luigi. Prologo del conflitto italo-greco. Rome, 1945.

Author sent by Ciano as military attaché to Italy's legation in Athens, 1938-40, in preparation for Albanian coup and attack on Greece.

375. Nitti, Francesco Saverio. Rivelazioni, dramatis personae. Bari, 1963.

Italy's premier, 1919-20, gives his version of Fiume crisis, San Remo Conference, etc., as well as some biographical sketches. See also "Europa e sistema europeo in 22 articoli inediti di F.S. Nitti, 10 settembre 1921 - 28 aprile 1924," ed. Paolo Alatri, Rivista di Studi Politici Internazionali, 48 (1981): 375-94, 565-77; 49 (1982): 37-80, 217-42, and Edizione nazionale delle opere di Francesco Saverio Nitti (Bari-Rome, 1958-).

376. Orlando, Vittorio Emanuele. Memorie, 1915-1919, ed. Rodolfo Mosca. Milan, 1960.

Italian premier gives general description of peacemaking in Paris with pen portraits. Appendix contains some letters exchanged with Lloyd George.

377. Ortona, Egidio. Anni d'America: La ricostruzione, 1944-1951. Bologna, 1954.

ITALIAN MEMORIALISTS

On the rehabilitation of Italian diplomacy at the end of World War II. Memoir begins with Mattioli-Quintiari mission to U.S., Nov. 1944, preparing the way for appointment of Ambassador Tarchiani, 1945 (#388). Ortona himself ambassador to Washington, 1967-75; for his prewar and World War II reminiscences, see diary excerpts (#297).

378. Parri, Feruccio. "L'armistizio, gli alleati e il governo Badoglio." Movimento di Liberazione in Italia, nos. 54 (1959): 64-75; 55 (1959): 41-57; 56 (1959): 22-51; 58 (1960): 24-41.

Recollections of resistance politician who became Italy's first post-World War II premier.

379. Pietromarchi, Luca. "Spagna, guerra tra spagnoli e conflitto tra dittature." Politica Estera, special issue (1970): 34-41.

Brief, general remarks by head of special Palazzo Chigi office for Spanish Civil War policy.

380. Pricolo, Francesco. Ignavia contro eroismo: L'avventura italo-greca, ottobre 1940 - aprile 1941. Rome, 1946.

Mainly military memoir, but some information on political planning.

381. Ridòmi, Cristano. La fine dell'ambasciata a Berlino, 1940-1943. Milan, 1972.

Author cultural attaché in Berlin embassy. Rather slight contribution, though information from attendance at Hitler-Mussolini meetings.

382. Roatta, Mario. Otto milioni di baionetti: L'esercito italiano in guerra dal 1940 al 1944. Milan, 1946.

Mostly on military affairs but, as Italian chief of staff in summer 1943, Roatta deeply involved in armistice negotiations with the Allies.

383. Rossi, Francesco. Mussolini e lo Stato Maggiore. Rome, 1951.

Italian general's account of Axis wartime cooperation; prints verbali and memoranda of Italo-German military conferences, 1940. His Come arrivammo all'armistizio: Memorie e documenti (Cernusco, 1946) describes Italy's balancing act between the Germans and Allies, summer 1943, and also contains notes of Italo-German staff meetings.

384. Rosso, Augusto. "Obiettivi e metodi della politica estera sovietica." Rivista di Studi Politici Internazionali, 13 (1946): 3-49.

Two public lectures on Russian policy from the Finnish war to summer 1940, and Italy's confused reaction to the changing Russo-German relationship; draws on the author's own experience in Moscow.

ITALIAN FOREIGN POLICY, 1918-1945

385. Senise, Carmine. Quando ero capo della polizia, 1940-1943. Rome, 1946.

Background memoir; indicates degree of German penetration of Italian life in World War II, Italian public's attitude to war, etc.

386. Silvestri, Carlo. Mussolini, Graziani e antifascismo, 1943-1945. Milan, 1945.

Journalist approached by Mussolini regarding disposal of Segreteria Particolare del Duce files; exchanges touch on Italo-German relations at the close of World War II.

387. Suvich, Fulvio. Memorie, 1932-1936, ed. Gianfranco Bianchi. Milan, 1984.

Undersecretary for Foreign Affairs covers events from Four-Power Pact to Ethiopian affair. A native of Trieste, Suvich understandably dwells on relations with Yugoslavia and Austria. Some documents included, but Suvich not a confidant of Mussolini; volume not very revealing.

388. Tarchiani, Alberto. Dieci anni fra Roma e Washington. Milan, 1955.

For resumption of Italo-American diplomatic ties, 1945.

389. Tassoni Estense, Alessandro. "Un incunabolo dell'Asse." L'Osservatore Politico e Letterario, 23 (Aug. 1977): 91-96.

Recounts visit of head of Italian Ballila to Germany, January 1936, foreshadowing Axis.

390. Tomasi della Torretta, Pietro. "Ministero degli Affari Esteri 1921." La Pace, June 1951.

On Italy's role in solving the Burgenland dispute.

391. Tuminetti, Dante Maria. La mia missione segreta in Austria, 1937-1938. Milan, 1946.

By Mussolini's emissary dispatched to Vienna, February 1937, to stabilize relations between the Austrian government party and Austria's Nazis.

392. Umiltà, Carlo. Jugoslavia e Albania: Memorie di un diplomatico. Milan, 1947.

Useful memoir reporting talks with Mussolini, Grandi, Contarini, etc. by Italian consular official during the interwar years in Split and Zagreb, and later administrator of Kossovo province, Yugoslavia, 1941-43.

ITALIAN MEMORIALISTS

393. Visconti Prasca, Sebastiano. <u>Io ho aggredito la Grecia</u>, 2d ed. Milan, 1946.

General in charge of Italian attack on Greece, 1940, discusses mostly military matters, but with some comment on the diplomatic dimension.

394. Zanussi, Giacomo. <u>Guerra e catastrofe dell'Italia</u>, 2 vols. Rome, 1945-46.

Vol. 2 of a military memoir of greater interest; as deputy chief of staff General Zanussi helped negotiate the Cassibile armistice, 1943.

3. Non-Italian Memorialists

The following entries fall into two categories. First, memoirs of non-Italian statesmen, diplomats, and officials who were directly involved in or close observers of the conduct of Italian diplomacy. Second, more general reminiscences of large events in which Italy simply played a part. As a general rule, the former are annotated, the latter not.

U.S. Memoirs

395. Baker, Ray Stannard. <u>Woodrow Wilson and the World Settlement</u>, 3 vols. New York, 1923.

396. Bowers, Claude G. <u>My Mission to Spain: Watching the Rehearsal for World War II</u>. New York, 1954.

U.S. ambassador observes Italian intervention in the Spanish Civil War.

397. Child, Richard Washburn. <u>A Diplomat Looks at Europe</u>. New York, 1925.

Very insubstantial account by U.S. ambassador in Rome; some diary extracts on Genoa and Lausanne Conferences, 1922-23. Sympathetic to the Duce, leading to the author's cooperation in compiling Mussolini's <u>My Autobiography</u> (#338).

398. Dulles, Allen. <u>The Secret Surrender of the Nazis in Italy, 1945</u>. New York, 1966.

399. Eisenhower, Dwight D. <u>Crusade in Europe</u>. New York, 1948.

400. Hull, Cordell. <u>The Memoirs of Cordell Hull</u>, 2 vols. New York, 1948.

401. Johnson, Douglas W. "Fiume and the Adriatic," in <u>What Really Happened at Paris: The Peace Conference</u>, ed. Edward M. House and Charles M. Seymour, pp. 112-39. New York, 1921.

402. Lansing, Robert. <u>The Peace Negotiations: A Personal Narrative</u>. Boston-New York, 1921.

See also R. Lansing, <u>The Big Four and Others of the Peace Conference</u> (Boston-New York, 1921).

403. Murphy, Robert D. <u>Diplomat among Warriors</u>. New York, 1964.

By President Roosevelt's personal emissary involved in negotiations for Italian surrender, 1943.

404. Phillips, William. <u>Ventures in Diplomacy</u>. Boston, 1952.

Based on diary kept during the author's tenure of the U.S. Rome embassy, but end product disappointing in view of the crucial events observed, 1936-41.

405. Welles, Sumner. <u>The Time for Decision</u>. New York, 1944.

For author's special mission to Italy, spring 1940, in vain attempt to prevent Italian entry into World War II.

406. Wilson, Hugh R. <u>Diplomat between the Wars</u>. New York, 1941.

By U.S. observer at the League of Nations, 1927-37, not altogether extraneous to diplomatic action in the Ethiopian crisis.

British Memoirs

407. Carton de Wiart, Adrian. <u>Happy Odysseus</u>. London, 1950.

Chatty military memoir; author briefly involved with Italian General Zanussi (#394) for Italy's surrender, 1943.

408. Cecil, Robert. <u>A Great Experiment</u>. London, 1941.

For Corfu and Ethiopian crises at the League of Nations. See also R. Cecil, <u>All the Way</u> (London, 1949).

409. Chatfield, Alfred Ernle. <u>The Navy and Defence</u>, 2 vols. London, 1942-47. Vol. 2, <u>It Might Happen Again</u>.

First Sea Lord on British naval posture in the Mediterranean during the Italo-Ethiopian affair.

410. Churchill, Winston S. <u>The Second World War</u>, 6 vols. London, 1948-54.

For Churchill on the First World War, see his <u>The World Crisis</u>, 5 vols. (London, 1923-31), especially vol. 5, <u>The Aftermath</u>.

NON-ITALIAN MEMORIALISTS

411. Dixon, John Pierson. Double Diploma, ed. Piers Dixon. London, 1968.

    Author in Britain's Rome embassy, 1938-40, a participant in negotiations for Easter Accord.

412. Eden, Anthony (Avon, Earl of). The Eden Memoirs: Facing the Dictators. London, 1962.

    Spans 1931-38, and deals with Ethiopian affair, Spanish Civil War, Anglo-Italian Gentleman's Agreements when Eden undersecretary, then secretary for foreign affairs; also his resignation, 1938, over Chamberlain's Italian policy. For Eden's memoirs beyond 1938, covering his foreign secretaryship during World War II, see The Reckoning and Full Circle (London, 1960, 1965).

413. Gladwyn, Lord (Jebb, Hubert M.G.). The Memoirs of Lord Gladwyn. London, 1972.

    Second secretary at Britain's Rome embassy, 1931-35, but conveys little of substance.

414. Halifax, Lord (Wood, Edward F.L.). Fullness of Days. London, 1957.

    Not a very revealing memoir by the foreign secretary, 1938-40. More in Earl of Birkenhead, Halifax: The Life of Lord Halifax (London, 1965), based on Halifax's personal papers.

415. Hankey, Maurice. Diplomacy by Conference: Studies in Public Affairs, 1920-1946. London, 1946.

    More illumination in Stephen Roskill, Hankey: Man of Secrets, 3 vols, (London, 1970-74), which focuses on the cabinet secretary's private papers.

416. Headlam Morley, James. A Memoir of the Paris Peace Conference, 1919, ed. Agnes Headlam Morley. London, 1972.

417. Henderson, Nevile. Water under the Bridges. London, 1945.

    Information on Italo-Yugoslav relations, 1929-34, when the author was British minister in Belgrade. Henderson's more famous Failure of a Mission: Berlin, 1937-1939 (London, 1940) has little on Italy in the Munich and Danzig crises.

418. Hoare, Samuel (Viscount Templewood). Nine Troubled Years. London, 1954.

    Covers 1931-40, including Hoare's role as foreign secretary in Ethiopian crisis, but very unrewarding.

419. Kirkpatrick, Ivone. The Inner Circle: Memoirs. London, 1959.

   Author posted to British embassy in Rome, 1930-32, Vatican, 1932-33; more on Papal than Italian affairs.

420. Lansbury, George. My Quest for Peace. London, 1938.

   By British pacifist socialist who interviewed Mussolini and Ciano in 1937.

421. Lloyd George, David. The Truth about the Peace Treaties, 2 vols. London, 1938; reprint, New York, 1972.

   Slightly different edition is Memoirs of the Peace Conference, 2 vols. (London, 1939); useful on Italian post-World War I claims.

422. Macmillan, Harold. The Blast of War, 1939-1945. London & New York, 1968.

   Second volume of Macmillan's memoirs based on his War Diaries (#315); concentrates on Mediterranean theater, Italian surrender, liberation, and efforts to win Allied cobelligerent status.

423. Nicolson, Harold. Peacemaking, 1919. London, 1933.

   Author a member of British delegations at the Paris Peace Conference, 1919, and Lausanne Conference, 1922-23; his account of latter, Curzon: The Last Phase: A Study in Postwar Diplomacy (London, 1934; reprint, New York, 1974) in effect also a memoir. See too H. Nicolson, Diaries and Letters, ed. Nigel Nicolson, 3 vols. (London, 1966-68), vol. 1 of which relates Nicolson's visit to Italy with Sir Oswald Mosley, 1932.

424. Peterson, Maurice. Both Sides of the Curtain. London, 1950.

   By the head of a special office created within the F.O. to deal with the Ethiopian crisis, 1935.

425. Randall, Alec. Vatican Assignment. London, 1956.

   Mostly on Italian church-state relations and Maltese affairs by secretary of the British legation, 1925-30.

426. Rodd, James Rennell. Social and Diplomatic Memories, 1884-1919, 3 vols. London, 1922-25.

   By long-serving British ambassador in Rome; only general observations in vol. 3 on Italy in post-World War I peace negotiations.

427. Selby, Walford. Diplomatic Twilight, 1930-1940. London, 1953.

NON-ITALIAN MEMORIALISTS

Author British minister in Vienna, 1932-37, Lisbon, 1937-40; useful for Austro-Italian relations before Anschluss.

428. Simon, Lord John. Retrospect. London, 1952.

British foreign secretary, 1931-35, gives sketchy account of disarmament and Stresa conferences.

429. Steed, Henry Wickham. Through Thirty Years, 1892-1922, 2 vols. London, 1924.

Vol. 2 includes journalist's attempt to arbitrate between Italian and Yugoslav representatives at Paris Peace Conference, 1919.

430. Strong, Kenneth. Intelligence at the Top: The Recollections of an Intelligence Officer. London, 1968.

Author military attaché, British embassy, Berlin, 1937-39; present at negotiations for Italian surrender, 1943, then served as liaison with Badoglio.

431. Thompson, Geoffrey. Front-Line Diplomat. London, 1959.

Account from Foreign Office's special section on Ethiopia (cf. Peterson, #424) and the League of Nations, 1935-36.

432. Vansittart, Lord Robert. The Mist Procession: The Autobiography of Lord Vansittart. London, 1958.

By advocate of appeasing Mussolini to keep Italy out of Hitler's camp. As permanent undersecretary for foreign affairs Vansittart cooperated with Grandi in drafting Hoare-Laval Plan for an Ethiopian settlement, Dec. 1935.

French Memoirs

433. Barrère, Camille. "La conférence de San Remo." Revue des Deux Mondes (July-Aug. 1938): 510-14.

Criticism of Nitti, whose reply is in Rivelazioni, dramatis personae (#375).

434. Baudouin, Paul. "Un voyage à Rome, février 1939." Revue des Deux Mondes (May-June 1962): 69-85.

Exercise in appeasement; failure of special mission to reach Franco-Italian colonial accord.

435. Blondel, Jules-François. Au fil de la carrière: Récit d'un diplomat, 1911-1938. Paris, 1960.

Counselor, then chargé, of French embassy in Rome, 1935-38, during Franco-Italian quarrel over new ambassadorial appointment. More on personalities than politics.

436. Bonnet, Georges. Défense de la paix, 2 vols. Geneva, 1946-48.

Vol. 2 has appeared in revised form as De Munich à la guerre: Défense de la paix (Paris, 1967). French foreign minister's justification of efforts to appease both Axis dictators.

437. Chambrun, Count Charles Pineton de. Traditions et souvenirs. Paris, 1952.

French ambassador to Italy concentrates on the Laval-Mussolini agreement and sanctions dispute over Ethiopia, 1935; quotes verbatim some conversations with the Duce.

438. Charles-Roux, François. Souvenirs diplomatiques: Rome-Quirinal, février 1916 - février 1919. Paris, 1958.

Prolific memorialist of Franco-Italian relations, although this work treats postwar peace talks very generally. Other titles by Charles-Roux: Souvenirs diplomatiques: Une grande ambassade à Rome, 1919-1925 (Paris, 1961), and his anonymously published articles, "La France et l'Italie des armistices à Locarno," Revue des Deux Mondes (Jan.-Feb. 1926): 803-25; (Mar.-April 1926): 188-207, which chronicle Franco-Italian-Yugoslav complications; Cinq mois tragiques aux affaires étrangères, 21 mai-1 novembre 1940 (Paris, 1949), which deals with the author's tenure of the Quai d'Orsay's secretary generalship, Italy's attack on France, armistice, etc.

See also F. Charles-Roux, Huit ans au Vatican, 1932-1940 (Paris, 1947). Author, ambassador to the Holy See, claims his embassy better informed on Italian affairs than its counterpart to the Quirinale; provides information on Vatican's attitude to Ethiopian crisis, Rome-Berlin Axis, Anschluss, and Italian neutrality, 1939-40.

439. Dampierre, Robert de. "Dix années de politique française à Rome, 1925-1935." Revue des Deux Mondes (Nov.-Dec. 1953): 14-38, 258-83.

Author first secretary in France's Rome embassy, recounts fruitless attempts of successive French ambassadors to achieve détente in Franco-Italian relations. See also the same author's "Une entente italo-yougoslave, mars 1937," ibid. (Sept.-Oct. 1955): 126-36, in which Dampierre sent as ambassador to Belgrade, May 1935, to foster an Italo-Yugoslav rapprochement following the Mussolini-Laval agreements.

440. Elie, Hubert. Souvenirs d'un diplomate, 1920-1950. Paris, 1978.

General account of service in France's Rome embassy in 1930's.

NON-ITALIAN MEMORIALISTS

441. Flandin, Pierre-Etienne. Politique française, 1919-1940. Paris, 1947.

    Author premier, then foreign minister, 1935-36, describes Franco-Italian understanding on Tunisia before the Ethiopian affair.

442. François-Poncet, André. Au Palais Farnese: Souvenirs d'une ambassade à Rome, 1938-1940. Paris, 1961.

    Account of talks with Ciano and other diplomats in Rome, but not very perceptive memoir. Descriptions of Mussolini in Berlin, 1937, and at Munich Conference, 1938, found in François-Poncet's Souvenirs d'une ambassade à Berlin, septembre 1931 - octobre 1938 (Paris, 1946), Eng. trans. The Fateful Years: Memoirs of a French Ambassador in Berlin, 1931-1938 (New York, 1949), Ital. trans. Ricordi di un ambasciatore a Berlino (Milan, 1947).

443. Gamelin, Maurice. Servir, 3 vols. Paris, 1946-47.

    Vol. 2 for French military talks with Italy, 1935.

444. Garnier, Jean-Paul. Excellences et plumes blanches, 1922-1946. Paris, 1961.

    General reminiscences embrace term in the French embassy in Rome, 1934-39.

445. Herriot, Edouard. Jadis, 2 vols. Paris, 1948-52.

    Vol. 2 of French premier's memoirs covers negotiations regarding Mussolini's Four-Power Pact, 1933.

446. Lagardelle, Hubert. Mission à Rome: Mussolini. Paris, 1955.

    Valuable memoir by special emissary attached to French embassy in Rome, 1932-36, charged with promoting Franco-Italian rapprochement. Information on Four-Power Pact, Austria, and Mussolini-Laval accords with an exchange of letters printed in appendix.

447. Monzie, Anatole de. Ci-devant. Paris, 1941.

    French cabinet minister's recollection of drôle de guerre and Italian declaration of war, 1940.

448. Noel, Léon. Les illusions de Stresa: L'Italie abandonnée à Hitler. Paris, 1975.

    Noel a member of the French delegation to the Stresa Conference, 1935; memoir contains an appendix of documents, including proposed Franco-Italian air pact. The same author has essays on Stresa and other diplomatic episodes of the 1930's in La guerre de 39 a commencé quatre ans plus tôt (Paris, 1979). See also L. Noel, Un tèmoignage: Le diktat de Rethondes et l'armistice franco-italien de juin

1940 (Paris, 1945), an eyewitness account originally published anonymously.

449. Paul-Bancour, Joseph. Entre deux guerres: Souvenirs sur la IIIe République, 3 vols. Paris, 1945-46.

French foreign minister, 1932-34, 1938, comments on the Four-Power Pact, Ethiopian crisis, Spanish Civil War, etc.

450. Reynaud, Paul. Au coeur de la mêlée, 1930-1945. Paris, 1951. Abridged Eng. trans. In the Thick of the Fight, 1930-1945, London & New York, 1955.

Original version, written without access to documentation, entitled La France a sauvé l'Europe, 2 vols. (Paris, 1947); most interesting on Premier Reynaud's attempt to buy off Italian declaration of war, May-June 1940. See also the same author's Mémoires, 2 vols. (Paris, 1960-63); vol. 2 prints some correspondence with Mussolini.

451. Sarraz-Bournet, Marius. Témoignage d'un silencieux. Paris, 1948.

Present at negotiations for Franco-Italian armistice, 1940.

452. Weygand, Maxime. Mémoires, 3 vols. Paris, 1950-57. Eng. trans. of vol. 3, Recalled to Service, London, 1952.

Military memoirs; author at Lausanne Conference, 1922-23, in vol. 2; French military situation at time of Italian attack, 1940, in vol. 3.

German Memoirs

453. Doenitz, Karl. Zehn Jahre und Zwanzig Tage. Bonn, 1958. Eng. trans. Memoirs: Ten Years and Twenty Days, London, 1959.

Recounts author's visit to Italy, summer 1943, discussion with Hitler on Italo-German naval cooperation and Italian situation at large.

454. Dollmann, Eugenio. Roma Nazista. Milan, 1951.

S.S. colonel and interpreter for many German dignitaries in Italy, 1937-45, including on occasion Hitler; emphasis on services to the German military, 1943-45. A mixture of social gossip and solid political information, but on balance of considerable importance. Broader, more autobiographical is Dolmetscher der Diktatoren (Bayreuth, 1963), Eng. trans. The Interpreter (London, 1967), Ital. trans. Un libero schiavo (Bologna, 1968). In L'eroe della paura (Milan, 1955), Eng. trans. Call Me Coward (London, 1956), Dollmann recounts his capture by and escape from the Allies in 1945, with flashbacks to his career as interpreter.

455. Hitler, Adolf. Mein Kampf. Munich, 1925. Eng. trans. by Ralph Manheim, My Struggle, new ed. London, 1969.

Hitler's attitude to Italy occurs, along with a myriad other details of his credo, in this rambling work - a memoir only in the loosest sense. More pointed directly towards international affairs is a book Hitler finished 1928, but never published in his lifetime: Hitlers Zweites Buch, ed. Gerhard L. Weinberg (Stuttgart, 1961), Eng. trans. Hitler's Secret Book, ed. Telford Taylor (New York, 1962). In both books Germany's need for an Italian alliance is asserted and its price - recognition of Italy's possession of the Alto Adige - unequivocally accepted. Hitler's views in this vital matter were also expressed in a pamphlet: Die südtiroler Frage und das deutsche Bündnisproblem (Munich, 1926).

456. Hoettl, Wilhelm [Hagen, Walter]. Die Geheime Front: Organisation, Personen und Aktionen des deutschen Geheimdienstes, 2d ed. Linz & Vienna, 1950. Eng. trans. The Secret Front: The Story of Nazi Political Espionage, 2d ed., London, 1954. Ital. trans. La guerra delle spie, Milan, 1952.

English edition the most comprehensive of these accounts of intelligence work, which include German secret service activity in Italy culminating in the surrender of German forces in Italy, 1945. Italian edition contains Mussolini's notes made in captivity, Aug.-Sept. 1943.

457. Kesselring, Albert. Soldat bis zum letzten Tag. Bonn, 1953. Eng. trans. The Memoirs of Field-Marshal Kesselring, London, 1953; Kesselring: A Soldier's Record, New York, 1954, reprint, 1970.

Commander of German forces in Italy, 1943-45, supplies some information on Nazi relations with the Salò Republic.

458. Kordt, Erich. Nicht aus den Akten: Die Wilhelmstrasse in Frieden und Krieg. Erlebnisse, Begegnungen und Eindrücke, 1928-1945. Stuttgart, 1950.

Memoir by Ribbentrop's cabinet chief, mostly on prewar years. See also the same author's less personal Wahn und Wirklichkeit: Die Aussenpolitik des Dritten Reiches. Versuch einer Darstellung (Stuttgart, 1948).

459. Ludecke, Kurt G.W. I Knew Hitler: The Story of a Nazi who Escaped the Blood Purge. New York, 1937.

Interesting memoir by an intermediary in the first Hitler-Mussolini contacts from 1922. See Roland V. Layton, "Kurt Ludecke and I Knew Hitler: An Evaluation," Central European History, 12 (1979): 372-86.

460. Moellhausen, Eitel F. La carte perdente: Memorie diplomatiche, 25 luglio 1943 - 2 maggio 1945. Rome, 1948. Germ. trans. Die gebrochene Achse, Alfeld/Leine, 1949.

Author counselor and chargé of German embassy in Rome after Mussolini's fall and later accredited to the Salò regime. Detailed account of Nazi Rome and information on surrender of German forces in Italy, 1945. Moellhausen's earlier memoirs of diplomatic service mostly in North Africa, 1940-43, though like his first book published in Italy, have only marginal relevance to Italian affairs: Il giucco è fatto (Florence, 1951).

461. Papen, Franz von. Der Wahrheit eine Gasse. Munich, 1952. Eng. trans. Memoirs, London, 1952.

German plenipotentiary in Austria, 1934-38, on the prologue to Anschluss.

462. Plehwe, Friedrich-Karl von. Als die Axis zerbrach: Das Ende des deutsch-italienischen Bündnisses im Zweiten Weltkrieg. Berlin, 1967; rev. ed., Wiesbaden, 1980. Eng. trans. The End of an Alliance: Rome's Defection from the Axis in 1943, London, 1971.

Author chief of staff to German military attaché in Rome, Rintelen (#466); account made up of own recollection supplemented by published documents.

463. Prittwitz und Gaffron, Friedrich von. Zwischen Petersburg und Washington: Ein Diplomatenleben. Munich, 1952.

Author counselor and chargé of Germany's Rome embassy, 1921-27.

464. Rahn, Rudolf. Ruheloses Leben: Aufzeichnungen und Erinnerungen. Düsseldorf, 1949. Ital. trans. Ambasciatore di Hitler a Vichy e a Salò, Milan, 1950.

German ambassador to Salò describes the final Nazi-Fascist relationship and German military surrender to the Allies in northern Italy.

465. Ribbentrop, Joachim von. Zwischen London und Moskau: Erinnerungen und letzte Aufzeichnungen, ed. Annelies von Ribbentrop. Leoni, 1953. Eng. trans. The Ribbentrop Memoirs, London, 1954.

Nazi foreign minister's memoirs notoriously unreliable.

466. Rintelen, Enno von. Mussolini als Bundesgenosse: Erinnerungen des deutschen Militärattachés in Rom, 1936-1943. Tübingen, 1951. Ital trans. Mussolini l'alleato: Ricordi dell'addetto militare tedesco a Roma, 1936-1943, Rome, 1952.

Part military, part diplomatic memoir; offers some accurate observation of Rome-Berlin Axis. See also the same author's "Mussolinis Parallelkrieg im Jahre 1940," Wehrwissenschaftliche Rundschau, 12 (1962): 16-38.

NON-ITALIAN MEMORIALISTS

467. Schmidt, Paul. Statist auf diplomatischer Bühne, 1923-1945: Erlebnisse des Chefdolmetschers im Auswärtigen Amt mit den Staatsmannern Europas. Bonn, 1949. Abridged Eng. trans. Hitler's Interpreter, ed. R.H.C. Steed, London, 1950.

    Valuable summaries of Hitler's talks with a wide variety of statesmen, including Mussolini and Italian diplomats; also interesting background information.

468. Skorzeny, Otto. Geheimkommando Skorzeny. Hamburg, 1950. Abridged Eng. trans. Skorzeny's Secret Missions, New York, 1950. Ital. trans. Skorzeny: Missioni segrete, 2d ed., Milan, 1951.

    By S.S. officer best known for his rescue of Mussolini and transport of the Duce to meet Hitler, September 1943.

469. Weizsäcker, Ernst von. Erinnerungen. Munich, 1950. Eng. trans. Memoirs, London, 1951.

    Self-justificatory, rather thin memoir by German state secretary for foreign affairs, 1938-43, then ambassador to the Vatican, 1943-45. Weizsäcker Papiere (#256) more important.

Miscellaneous Memoirs

470. Barbul, Georgiu. Mémorial Antonescu: Le troisième homme de l'Axe. Paris, 1950.

    Rumanian diplomat's memoirs for 1938-43; verbatim conversations of Antonescu with Hitler and Axis diplomats, including Bova Scoppa (#326).

471. Beneš, Eduard. Memoirs: From Munich to New War and New Victory. London, 1954.

472. Beyens, Napoléon Eugène Louis. Quatre ans à Rome, 1921-1926: Fin du Pontificat du Benoît XV; Pie XI; Le début du fascisme. Paris, 1934.

    Belgian diplomat's reminiscences of the advance of Fascism; a general treatment of foreign affairs, e.g. Ruhr occupation, Corfu crisis, Locarno Pacts.

473. Commène, Nicolas P. Preludi del grande dramma: Ricordi e documenti di un diplomatico. Milan, 1947.

    Author Rumanian diplomat and foreign minister briefly, 1938. Other titles by Commène: I responsabili (Milan, 1949); Luci e ombre sull'Europa, 1914-1950 (Milan, 1957). All mix personal reminiscence with historical reconstruction based on unpublished documents; pen portraits of European statesmen, including Mussolini and Ciano.

ITALIAN FOREIGN POLICY, 1918-1945

474. Fotič, Constantin. The War We Lost: Jugoslavia's Tragedy and the Failure of the West. New York, 1948.

    Yugoslav minister to Washington in Second World War; more on U.S. than Italian attitude to his country.

475. Gafencu, Grigore. Derniers jours de l'Europe: Un voyage diplomatique en 1939. Paris, 1946. Eng. trans. Last Days of Europe: A Diplomatic Journey in 1939, London, 1947. Ital. trans. Ultimi giorni dell'Europa: Viaggio diplomatico nel 1939, Milan, 1947.

    Valuable account of Rumanian foreign minister's peace mission to European capitals, including Rome, on the eve of World War II. By the same author: Préliminaires de la guerre à l'est (Paris, 1944), Ital. trans. Preliminari della guerra all'est (Milan, 1946), complemented by Gafencu's talks with the Italian historian, Mario Toscano, both refugees in Switzerland, 1944: M. Toscano, "Colloqui con Gafencu," Rivista di Studi Politici Internazionali, 12 (1945): 85-100.

476. Goldmann, Nahum. Staatsmann ohne Staat: Autobiographie. Berlin, 1970. Eng. trans. Memories, London, 1969.

    Conversations between leading Zionist and the Duce, 1933-34; Mussolini, scornful of Hitler's antisemitism, suggests Goldmann mediate between the Nazis and world Jewry.

477. Horthy, Miklós. Ein Leben für Ungarn. Bonn, 1953. Eng. trans. Memoirs, 1920-1944, London, 1956.

    Not very enlightening memoir by Hungarian regent, but some commentary on relations with Italy in the 1930's.

478. Kállay, Miklós. Hungarian Premier: A Personal Account of a Nation's Struggle in the Second World War. New York, 1954.

    Kállay includes account of his visit to Rome, April 1943.

479. Kybal, Vlastomil. "Czechoslovakia and Italy; My Negotiations with Mussolini, 1922-1924." Journal of Central European Affairs, 13 (1953-54): 352-68; 14 (1954-55): 65-76.

    By Czech minister to Rome who negotiated Italo-Czech treaty of 1924; tone is pro-Mussolini, anti-Beneš.

480. Lipski, Józef. Diplomat in Berlin: Papers and Memoirs, ed. Waclaw Jedrzejewicz. New York, 1968.

    Polish ambassador to Berlin throws some light on Axis relations; includes a number of documents.

481. Litvinov, Maxim. Notes for a Journal. London, 1955.

NON-ITALIAN MEMORIALISTS

Probably spurious memoirs of Soviet foreign minister who advocated collective security in 1930's.

482. Maček, Vladko. <u>In the Struggle for Freedom</u>. New York, 1957.

A Croatian member of Yugoslav cabinet, then vice-premier, provides information on Italo-Croatian ties in the Second World War.

483. Papagos, Alexandros. <u>The Battle for Greece, 1940-1941</u>. Athens, 1949. Ital. trans, <u>La Grecia in guerra, 1940-1941</u>, Milan, 1950.

Memoir by commander-in-chief of the Greek army has some reflections on the diplomatic background.

484. Pierre II de Yougoslavie. <u>La vie d'un roi: Mémoires</u>. Paris, 1955. Eng. trans. <u>Peter II, King of Jugoslavia, A King's Heritage: Memoirs</u>, London, 1955.

485. Reynoso, Francisco De. <u>Reminiscences of a Spanish Diplomat</u>. London, 1933.

By Spain's ambassador in Rome, 1923-24, when Mussolini imagined General Primo De Rivera to be a Spanish Duce.

486. Rintelen, Anton. <u>Erinnerungen an österreichs Weg: Versailles, Berchtesgaden, Grossdeutschland</u>. Munich, 1941.

Author Austrian minister in Rome, 1933-34, but kept on the periphery of the Mussolini-Dollfuss relationship.

487. Schuschnigg, Kurt von. <u>Im Kampf gegen Hitler: Die überwindung der Anschlussidee</u>. Vienna, 1969, Munich, 1988. Eng. trans. <u>The Brutal Takeover</u>, London & New York, 1971.

Austrian chancellor's recital of steps towards <u>Anschluss</u>, 1934-38; very useful on Italian attitude and includes <u>verbali</u> of Schuschnigg-Mussolini exchanges. More comprehensive and fully documented than his <u>Ein Requiem in Rot-Weiss-Rot</u> (Zurich, 1946), Eng. trans. <u>Austrian Requiem</u> (London, 1946).

488. Serrano Suñer, Ramón. <u>Entre les Pyrénées et Gibraltar: Notes et réflexions sur la politique espagnole depuis 1936</u>. Geneva, 1947. Fr. trans. of <u>Entre Hendaya y Gibraltar: Noticia y reflexión, frente a una legenda, sobre nuestra politica en dos guerras</u>, Madrid, 1947, Barcelona, 1973.

Spanish foreign minister concentrates on Spain's decision to remain neutral in World War II; good coverage of Italo-Spanish relations, including his trip to Rome, spring 1940.

489. Starhemberg, Prince Ernst Rüdiger von. Between Hitler and Mussolini: Memoirs of Ernst Rüdiger Prince Starhemberg. London, 1942.

   Leader of the Austrian Heimwehr who entered into agreement with Fascist Italy recounts meetings with Mussolini, 1930-36. Essential source for Fascist Italy's Austrian policy.

490. Wagnière, Georges. Dix-huit ans à Rome. Geneva, 1944.

   General observations on Italian diplomacy by Swiss minister in Rome, 1918-36.

491. Zernatto, Guido. Die Wahrheit über Österreich. New York, 1938.

   Austrian cabinet minister relates how Anschluss came about and gives details of Mussolini's heavy involvement in Austrian domestic politics.

D. SECONDARY LITERATURE

1. European International Affairs, 1918-1945

Surveys and General Topics

492. Bell, P.M.H. The Origins of the Second World War in Europe. London, 1986.

    Sophisticated textbook that examines ideological, economic, and strategic factors behind interwar conflicts; the diplomatic narrative concentrates on 1932-41.

493. Carr, Edward H. The Twenty Years' Crisis, 2d ed. London, 1946.

    Elegant classic discussion of the balance between power and morality in interwar world politics.

494. Ceplair, Larry. Under the Shadow of War: Fascism, Antifascism, and Marxists, 1918-1939. New York, 1987.

    On the failure to develop a coherent international antifascist front; deals with Popular Front and western diplomacy in the 1930's.

495. Craig, Gordon. "The Historian and the Study of International Relations." American Historical Review, 88 (1983): 1-11.

    President of the American Historical Association offers sound advice on the importance and scope of diplomatic history. On the same topic, see Alexander De Conde, "On the Nature of International History, "International History Review, 10 (1988): 282-301, and from the Italian perspective, Ennio Di Nolfo, "Gli studi di storia delle relazioni internazionali in Italia," Storia delle Relazioni Internazionali, 2 (1986): 189-97.

496. Fink, Carole. The Genoa Conference: European Diplomacy, 1921-1922. Chapel Hill, NC, 1984.

    Authoritative study of post-World War I conference on Italian soil with Italian participation. See also Stephen White, The Origins of Détente: The Genoa Conference and Soviet-Western Relations, 1921-1922 (Cambridge & New York, 1985).

497. Jacobson, Jon. "Is There a New International History of the 1920s?" American Historical Review, 88 (1983): 617-45.

498. Kent, Bruce. The Spoils of War: The Politics, Economics, and Diplomacy of Reparations, 1918-1932. New York, 1989.

499. Kolko, Gabriel. The Politics of War: Allied Diplomacy and the World Crisis of 1943-1945. New York, 1968.

   An economic-determinist emphasis on western capitalism.

500. Kulischer, Eugene M. Europe on the Move: War and Population Changes, 1917-1947. New York, 1948.

501. Lamb, Richard A. Ghosts of Peace: Failed Peace Efforts, 1935-1945. Salisbury, 1987.

   Criticism of British appeasement of both Mussolini and Hitler, and alleged failure to exploit opposition to the dictators within Italy and Germany. The same thesis that World War II was potentially avoidable expressed in R.A. Lamb, The Drift to War, 1922-1939 (London, 1989).

502. Maier, Charles S. Recasting Bourgeois Europe: Stabilization in France, Germany, and Italy in the Decade after World War I. Princeton, 1975. Ital. trans. La rifondazione dell'Europa borghese, Bari, 1979.

   Not strictly diplomatic history, but interesting transnational study of business-political practices embracing Italy. See also the same author's "The Two Postwar Eras and the Conditions for Stability in Twentieth-Century Western Europe," American Historical Review, 86 (1981): 327-52.

503. Marks, Sally. The Illusion of Peace: International Relations in Europe, 1918-1933. London & New York, 1976.

504. Mayer, Arno J. Politics and Diplomacy of Peacemaking: Containment and Counterrevolution at Versailles, 1918-1919. New York, 1967.

   Well-known study of the Paris Peace Conference continuing the same author's Wilson vs. Lenin: Political Origins of the New Diplomacy, 1917-1918 (New Haven, CT, 1959).

505. Moulton, Harold G., and Pasvolsky, Leo. World War Debt Settlements. New York, 1926.

   By the same authors, War Debts and World Prosperity (Washington, 1932).

506. Mowat, Charles L. The Shifting Balance of World Forces, 1898-1945, 2d ed. Cambridge, 1968.

EUROPEAN INTERNATIONAL AFFAIRS

Vol. 12 of the New Cambridge Modern History.

507. Murray, Williamson. The Change in the European Balance of Power, 1938-1939: The Path to Ruin. Princeton, 1984.

Ambitious and only partly successful work. Assays a calculation of the military balance on the eve of World War II and the powers' perception of each others' strength. Inter alia, discloses a widespread overestimate of Italy's capability for war.

508. Nolte, Ernst. Der europäische Bürgerkrieg, 1917-1945: Nazionalsozialismus und Bolschewismus. Frankfurt, 1987.

Work of some notoriety on Europe's twentieth-century civil war; not the clash of states but of ideologies.

509. Northedge, F.S. The League of Nations: Its Life and Times, 1920-1946. Leicester & New York, 1986.

An older account by a League undersecretary general is still useful: Francis P. Walters, A History of the League of Nations, 2 vols. (London, 1952).

510. Overy, Richard, and Wheatcroft, Andrew. The Road to War. London, 1989.

Eight studies of different countries, including Mussolini's Italy.

511. Pink, Gerhard P. The Conference of Ambassadors: Paris, 1920-1931. Geneva, 1942.

512. Potemkin, Vladimir, ed. Histoire de la diplomatie, 3 vols. Paris, 1946-47. German edition, Geschichte der Diplomatie, vols. 2 and 3. Moscow & Berlin, 1947-48.

For the standard Stalinist line on diplomatic history; vol. 3 for period 1919-39.

513. Sforza, Carlo. Makers of Modern Europe. Indianapolis, 1930. Ital. trans. Costruttori e distruttori, Rome, 1945.

Also by C. Sforza, Europe and the Europeans: A Study in Historical Psychology and International Politics (New York, 1936); The Totalitarian War and After (Chicago, 1941).

514. Sontag, Raymond J. A Broken World, 1919-1939. New York, 1971.

A volume in the worthy "Rise of Modern Europe" series. Supplemented by the next title in the series: Gordon Wright's splendid The Ordeal of Total War (New York, 1968).

ITALIAN FOREIGN POLICY, 1918-1945

515. Taylor, A.J.P. The Origins of the Second World War. London, 1961.

    Brilliantly perverse work; once highly controversial, now somewhat less so. See "The Origins of the Second World War" Reconsidered: The A.J.P. Taylor Debate after Twenty-Five Years, ed. Gordon Martel (London, 1986); chap. on Italy by Alan Cassels, "Switching Partners," pp. 73-96.

516. Watt, D. Cameron. How War Came: The Immediate Origins of the Second World War, 1938-1939. London, 1989.

    Thirty years in the writing and perhaps the most authoritative account of European diplomacy from the Munich to the Danzig crises. Like Weinberg (next entry), considers 1939 to be Hitler's war.

517. Weinberg, Gerhard L. The Foreign Policy of Hitler's Germany, 2 vols. Chicago, 1970-80.

    Heavily documented and by far the best English-language treatment of Nazi diplomacy before the Second World War. In refutation of A.J.P. Taylor (#515), re-establishes Hitler's responsibility for the outbreak of war, 1939. Supplement for the World War II period with Norman Rich, Hitler's War Aims, 2 vols. (New York, 1973-74).

Collected Essays

518. Andrew, Christopher, and Dilks, David J, eds. The Missing Dimension. London, 1984.

    Essays on espionage in international affairs; see in particular Dilks, "Flashes of Intelligence," pp. 101-25, on Italian breaches of British security, 1937-39. See also Constantini (#360); Dilks (#805).

519. Aquarone, Alberto, and Vernazza, Maurizio, eds. Il regime fascista. Milan, 1974.

    Includes several essays on Fascist foreign policy.

520. Becker, Josef, and Hildebrand, Klaus, eds. Internationale Beziehungen in der Weltwirtschaftskrise, 1929-1933. Munich, 1980.

    Papers delivered at a symposium in Augsburg, 1979. See especially the contribution by Jens Petersen, "Italien und Südosteuropa," pp. 393-411.

521. Craig, Gordon A., and Gilbert, Felix, eds. The Diplomats, 1919-1939. Princeton, NJ, 1953.

    Valuable essays on the status of career diplomats faced by the twin challenges of democratic diplomacy and totalitarian dictatorships. In particular, H. Stuart Hughes, "The Early Diplomacy of Italian Fascism," pp. 210-33; F. Gilbert, "Ciano and His Ambassadors," pp. 512-36.

522. Ecole Française de Rome. Opinion publique et poltique extérieure, 2 vols. Rome, 1984.

Vol. 2 has essays on the interplay of mass opinion and foreign policy-making in Italy, France, and other nations, 1915-1940.

523. Gatzke, Hans, ed. European Diplomacy between Two Wars, 1919-1939. Chicago, 1972.

524. May, Ernest R., ed. Knowing One's Enemies: Intelligence Assessment before the Two World Wars. Princeton, 1984.

Chapter by MacGregor Knox, "Fascist Italy Assesses Its Enemies, 1935-1940," pp. 347-72, a very good summary of the accomplishments of the Servizio Informazioni Militari, etc.

525. Millett, Allan R., and Murray, Williamson, eds. Military Effectiveness, 3 vols. Boston & London, 1988.

Vol. 1 on the First World War, vol. 2 on the interwar years, vol. 3 on World War II. Authoritative, well-documented essays, one on Italy per volume: John Gooch, "Italy in the First World War," vol. 1: 157-89; Brian R. Sullivan, "The Italian Armed Forces, 1918-1940," vol. 2: 169-217; MacGregor Knox, "The Italian Armed Forces, 1940-1943," vol. 3: 136-79.

526. Petricioli, Marta, ed. Le relazioni internazionali nell'età contemporanea: Saggi di storia contemporanea, 1915-1975. Florence, 1981.

Festschrift in honor of Rodolfo Mosca.

527. Sarkissian, Arshag O., ed. Studies in Diplomatic History and Historiography for G.P. Gooch. London, 1961.

528. Toscano, Mario. Pagine di storia diplomatica contemporanea, 2 vols. Milan, 1963.

Some articles from vol. 2, Origini e vicende della seconda guerra mondiale, trans. and pub. in revised form as Designs in Diplomacy: Pages from European Diplomatic History in the Twentieth Century, ed. George A. Carbone (Baltimore, 1970). Overall, valuable compilation of essays originally published elsewhere by quondam director of ASME who used Italian Foreign Ministry files to great effect. Hence most pieces are on Italian policy, and include early attempts to evaluate intelligence gathering in diplomatic decision-making.

529. Watt, D. Cameron. Too Serious a Business: European Armies and the Approach of the Second World War. London & Los Angeles, 1975.

   Essays on the general staffs of Britain, France, Germany, Italy, and Poland.

Regional Studies

See also Giannini, De Luca (#627).

530. Alcock, Antony Evelyn. History of the South Tyrol Question. London, 1970.

   Judicious survey of a heated topic. See also Gisela Framke, Im Kampfe um Südtirol: Ettore Tolomei (1865-1952) und das "Archivio per l'Alto Adige" (Tübingen, 1987); Karl Heinz Ritschel, Diplomatie um Südtirol: Politische Hintergrunde eines europaïschen Versagens (Stuttgart, 1966); Leopold Steurer, Südtirol zwischen Rom und Berlin, 1919-1939 (Vienna, 1980). From the Italian side, Mario Toscano, Storia diplomatica della questione dell'Alto Adige, 2d ed. (Bari, 1968), Eng. trans. Alto Adige - South Tyrol: Italy's Frontier with the German World (Baltimore, 1975).

   Interwar denunciation of Italian discrimination against the German minority may be sampled in Hans Fingeller, Die Wahrheit über Südtirol, 1918-1926, Eng. trans. The Case of German South Tyrol against Italy, ed. Charles H. Herford. London, 1927; S. Miles Bouton, Robert Dell, C.H. Herford, English and American Voices about the South German Tyrol (New York, 1925); Eduard Reut-Nicolussi, Tirol unterm Beil (Munich, 1928), Eng. trans. Tyrol under the Axe of Italian Fascism (London, 1930).

531. Andri, Adriano. "Gli italiani in Dalmazia tra le due guerre mondiale." Clio, 24 (1988): 83-116

   Employs ASME documentation.

532. Ara, Angelo, and Magris, Claudio. Trieste: Un'identità di frontiera, 2d ed. Turin, 1987.

533. Boveri, Margret. Das Weltgeschehen am Mittelmeer. Zurich, 1936. Eng. trans. Mediterranean Cross-Currents, London, 1938.

534. Cermelj, Lavo. Life-and-Death Struggle of a National Minority: The Jugoslavs in Italy, 2d ed. Ljubljana, 1945.

   See also Carlo Schiffrer, Historic Glance at the Relations between Italians and Slavs in Venezia Giulia, rev. ed. (Trieste, 1946); Manlio Udina, "La questione della Venezia Giulia nelle relazioni internazionali, 1915-1950," Rivista di Studi Politici Internazionali, 19 (1952): 14-28.

EUROPEAN INTERNATIONAL AFFAIRS

535. Hodgkinson, Harry. The Adriatic Sea. London, 1955.

536. Monroe, Elizabeth. The Mediterranean in Politics. London & New York, 1938.

537. Moodie, Arthur E. The Italo-Yugoslav Boundary. London, 1945.

 See also Franco Stefani, Senza pace: L'incerto confine orientale italiano in trent'anni di storia, 1915-1945 (Udine, n.d.).

538. Ránki, György. Economy and Foreign Policy: Struggle for Hegemony in the Danube Valley. Boulder, CO, 1983.

 English translation of an important work by a distinguished Hungarian scholar. See also La Marca (#595).

539. Rusinow, Dennison I. Italy's Austrian Heritage, 1919-1946. Oxford & New York, 1969.

 Best scholarly treatment of the vexed issue of Italy's entire northeastern border - with both Yugoslavia and Austria.

540. Seton Watson, Hugh. Eastern Europe between the Wars, 1918-1941. Cambridge, 1945.

 See also Carlo Sforza, Fifty Years of War and Diplomacy in the Balkans (New York, 1940).

541. Stuart, Graham H. The International City of Tangier, rev. ed. Palo Alto, CA, 1955.

542. Tsakalakis, Antoine. Le Dodecanese. Alexandria, 1928. Eng. trans. The Dodecanese: A Study in International Law, London, 1942.

2. History of Italy, 1918-1945

General Works of Italian History

543. Candeloro, Giorgio. Storia d'Italia moderna. 11 vols., Milan, 1975-86.

 Standard multivolume textbook series; vols. 8-10 cover 1914-45. Similar though aimed at more popular audience is Indro Montanelli and Mario Cervi, Storia d'Italia, 45 vols. (Milan, 1971-84); vols. 38-47 for 1918-45. See also Ernesto Ragionieri, Dall'Unità a oggi: La storia politica e sociale (Turin, 1976), a volume in the series Storia d'Italia put out by Einaudi publishers.

544. Clark, Martin. Modern Italy, 1871-1982. London, 1984.

More than a mere textbook; an incisive survey strongest on social history. For a more politically oriented account of Italy since unification, see Denis Mack Smith, Italy: A Modern History, rev. ed. (Ann Arbor, 1969), Ital. trans. Storia d'Italia dal 1861 al 1969, new ed. (Bari, 1987).

545. Clough, Shepard B. The Economic History of Modern Italy. New York, 1964.

Relevance lies in the shaping of Italian foreign and colonial policies by, first, the country's limited economic development and, second, pressure from domestic economic forces. On the former phenomenon, see Rosario Romeo, Breve storia della grande industria in Italia, 1861-1961 (Bologna, 1972); Giulio Sapelli, Organizzazione lavoro e innovazione industriale nell'Italia tra le due guerre (Turin, 1978). For the latter, a number of works recount the history of influential business enterprises: Franco Bonelli, Sviluppo di una grande impresa in Italia: La Terni dal 1884 al 1962 (Milan, 1975); Valerio Castronovo, Giovanni Agnelli: La FIAT dal 1899 al 1945 (Turin, 1977); Luigi De Rosa and Gabriele De Rosa, Storia del Banco di Roma, 3 vols, (Rome, 1982-84); Paride Rugafiori, Uomini, macchine, capitale: L'Ansaldo durante il fascismo (Milan, 1981).

Two case studies of British capitalism in Italy by Luciano Segreto are "More Trouble than Profit: Vickers' Investment in Italy, 1905-1939," Business History, 27 (1985): 316-37; "La City e la 'dolce vita' romana: La storia della Banca Italo-britannica, 1916-1930," Passato e Presente, (Jan.-April 1987): 63-95. On Italo-American economic relations, Ferdinando Fasce, "Strategie imprenditoriali e mercato mondiale degli armamenti: I rapporti tra l'Ansaldo e la siderurgia USA nel primo Novecento," Società Storica, (Oct.-Dec. 1987): 1915-47, and Migone (#817). See also Giuseppe Tattara, "External Trade in Italy, 1922-1938," Rivista di Storia Economica, 5 (Feb. 1988): 102-20.

546. Cunsolo, Ronald S. Modern Italian Nationalism: From Its Origins to World War II. Melbourne, FL, 1989.

On the same topic, Franco Gaeta, Nazionalismo italiano, new ed. (Rome-Bari, 1981).

547. De Lutiis, Giuseppe. Storia dei servizi segreti in Italia. Reprint, Rome, 1985.

Account runs from 1922 to the present, but rather thin on Fascist intelligence. So too is Giorgio Pillon, Spie per l'Italia (Rome, 1968).

548. Hughes, H. Stuart. The United States and Italy, 3d ed. Cambridge, MA, 1979.

Lucid survey of modern Italian history aimed at the literate but nonspecialist North American audience.

HISTORY OF ITALY

549. La Palombara, Joseph. Democracy, Italian Style. New Haven, 1987. Ital. trans. Democrazia all'italiana, Milan, 1989.

   Intriguing examination of the Italian national character.

550. Mack Smith, Denis. Italy and Its Monarchy. New Haven, CT & London, 1989. Ital. trans., forthcoming, Milan, 1989.

   Critique of four Italian kings, 1861-1946, detailing the monarchs' political follies, not least in foreign policy.

551. Seton Watson, Christopher. Italy from Liberalism to Fascism, 1870-1925. London, 1967.

   Large, detailed, solid work.

552. Sforza, Carlo. Contemporary Italy. New York, 1944.

   See also C. Sforza, Italy and Italians (London, 1948).

Biographies

For biographies of diplomats and foreign ministers other than Mussolini, see under Italy in International Affairs: Foreign Ministry and Ministers.

553. Alatri, Paolo. Gabriele D'Annunzio. Turin, 1983.

   Complemented by the same author's D'Annunzio negli anni del tramonto, 1930-1938 (Venice, 1984). Also on the spokesman of Italian nationalism, Piero Chiara, Vita di Gabriele D'Annunzio (Milan, 1978); A.R.E. Rhodes, The Poet as Superman: Life of D'Annunzio (London, 1959); Vito Salierno, D'Annunzio e Mussolini: Storia di una cordiale inimicizia (Milan, 1988). See also De Felice (#647).

554. Albertini, Alberto. Vita di Luigi Albertini. Milan, 1945.

555. Barbagallo, Francesco. Francesco Saverio Nitti. Turin, 1984.

556. Bertoldi, Silvio. Vittorio Emanuele III. Milan, 1970.

   See also Nino D'Aroma, Vent'anni insieme: Vittorio Emanuele e Mussolini (Bologna, 1957); Aldo A. Mola, "Vittorio Emanuele III, il Re isolato," Studi Piemontesi, 17 (Mar. 1988): 155-65; Mack Smith (#550).

557. Cordova, Ferdinando, ed. Uomini e volti del fasismo. Rome, 1980.

   Biographical essays of leading Fascist hierarchs.

558. De Felice, Renzo. Mussolini. 3 of 4 vols. to date (in 6 parts). Turin, 1965- .

Stands out from multifarious biographies of Mussolini, both for its vast scope and the contentiousness of some arguments advanced. In attempting to set the Duce in his environment the work goes beyond conventional biography to become a magisterial analysis of Italy in the Mussolinian era viewed from every perspective, not excepting that of foreign policy. Volumes published so far: 1, Mussolini il rivoluzionario, 1883-1920; 2, part 1, Mussolini il fascista: La conquista del potere, 1921-1925; 2, part 2, Mussolini il fascista: L'organizzazione dello Stato Fascista, 1925-1929; 3, part 1, Mussolini il duce: Gli anni del consenso, 1929-1936; 3, part 2, Mussolini il duce: Lo Stato totalitario, 1936-1940. De Felice intends a one-volume summary in conclusion of his monumental labors.

De Felice has been criticized for accepting Fascist sources too uncritically, thereby presenting too complaisant a view of the Duce. His interpretations in earlier volumes stirred acrimonious debate; see Michael A. Ledeen, "Renzo De Felice and the Controversy over Italian Fascism," Journal of Contemporary History, 11 (1976): 269-82. The most recent volume dwells heavily on foreign policy, advancing the argument that, the Rome-Berlin Axis notwithstanding, Mussolini struggled to find a middle diplomatic road; for comment see Adrian Lyttleton, Jens Petersen, and Gianpasquale Santomassimo, "Il Mussolini di Renzo De Felice," Passato e Presente, (Jan.-June 1982): 5-30; Raffaele Quartaro, "La 'politica estera fascista' negli scritti di Renzo De Felice," Analisi Storica, 5 (1987): 101-24.

Best-known of English-language biographies is Denis Mack Smith, Mussolini (London, 1981), Ital. trans. Mussolini (Milan, 1981). Strongly narrative and very readable, it presents a much harsher picture than does De Felice. Other biographical studies worth attention are Ivone Kirkpatrick, Mussolini: Study of a Demagogue (London, 1964), U.S. edition, Mussolini: A Study in Power (New York, 1964), which emphasizes foreign policy because of the author's diplomatic background and service in Rome and the Vatican, 1930-33; Giorgio Pini and Duilio Susmel, Mussolini: L'uomo ed l'opera, 3d ed., 4 vols. (Florence, 1953-55), a sympathetic work by writers regarded as Mussolini's authorized biographers.

559. Guerri, Giordano B. Giuseppe Bottai: Un fascista critico. Milan, 1976.

Although the holder of domestic portfolios, Bottai joined other prominent Fascists in questioning Italian intervention in the Second World War.

560. Pieri, Piero, and Rochat, Giorgio. Pietro Badoglio. Turin, 1974.

Authoritative study of significant military politician and shadow foreign minister, 1943-44. See also Silvio Bertoldi, Badoglio, 2d ed. (Milan, 1982).

561. Romano, Sergio. Giuseppe Volpi: Industria e finanza tra Giolitti e Mussolini. Milan, 1979. Fr. trans. Giuseppe Volpi et l'Italie moderne, Rome, 1980.

   Good account of a career spent on the frontier of business and politics, based partly on unpublished material.

562. Santarelli, Enzo. Pietro Nenni. Turin, 1988.

   See also Giuseppe Tamburrano, Pietro Nenni (Bari, 1986).

563. Segrè, Claudio. Italo Balbo: A Fascist Life. Berkeley, CA, 1987.

   Balbo, ex-minister of air and governor of Libya until his death in 1940, was another Fascist hierarch with qualms about the Ethiopian adventure and even more about Italy's intervention in World War II. See too Giordano B. Guerri, Italo Balbo (Milan, 1984); Giorgio Rochat, Italo Balbo (Turin, 1986); Meir Michaelis, "Il marasciallo dell'aria Italo Balbo e la politica mussoliniana: Il frondismo di Balbo alla luce di alcune documenti e testimonianze inediti," Storia Contemporanea, 14 (1983): 333-57.

564. Valeri, Nino. Giovanni Gioliti. Turin, 1971.

Fascism

See also De Felice (#558).

565. Cassels, Alan. Fascist Italy, 2d ed. Arlington Heights, IL, 1985.

   Succinct survey of what happened in Mussolini's Italy. Complemented by Alexander De Grand's Italian Fascism: Its Origins and Development, 2d ed. (Lincoln, NE, 1982), a brief analysis of the nature of Italian Fascism.

566. Chabod, Federico. L'Italia contemporanea, 1918-1948. Turin, 1961. Eng. trans. History of Italian Fascism, London, 1963.

567. De Grand, Alexander. The Italian Nationalist Association and the Rise of Fascism in Italy. Lincoln, NE, 1978

   A case study of Nationalist-Fascist relations is Giuseppe Parlati, "Vittorio Cian: Un intelletuale nazionalista durante il fascismo," Storia Contemporanea, 14 (1983): 603-48.

568. Delzell, Charles F. Mussolini's Enemies: The Italian Anti-Fascist Resistance. Princeton, NJ, 1961. Ital. trans. I nemici di Mussolini, Turin, 1966.

   Standard account of the fuorusciti, anti-Fascists who took refuge abroad; their impact was greatest on Franco-Italian relations, see Milza (#670), Tombaccini (#680).

569. Germino, Dante. The Italian Fascist Party in Power: A Study in Totalitarian Rule. Minneapolis, 1959.

For the ideology of a Third Rome. On the same topic see also Dino Cofrancesco, "Appunto per un'annalisi del mito romano nell'ideologia fascista," Storia Contemporanea, 11 (1980): 383-411.

570. Hamilton, Alastair. The Appeal of Fascism. London, 1971.

On the attraction of fascism for certain intellectuals, mostly English-speaking.

571. Knox, MacGregor. "Conquest, Foreign and Domestic, in Fascist Italy and Nazi Germany." Journal of Modern History, 56 (1984): 1-57.

This thought-provoking lengthy article finds a symbiotic relationship between domestic revolution and expansion abroad, which, it is argued, both Mussolini and Hitler pursued more or less consistently.

572. La Francesca, Salvatore. La politica economica del fascismo. Bari, 1972.

573. Ledeen, Michael A. Universal Fascism: The Theory and Practice of the Fascist International, 1928-1936. New York, 1972.

Reveals the gulf between racist national socialists from Eastern Europe and Italian corporativists that prevented the launch of an international fascist movement at Montreux, 1934. See also Neulen, Cofrancesco (#827). For consideration of Italian Fascism's ideological place in universalfascismo, see Alan Cassels, Fascism (New York, 1975); Jens Petersen. "La dimensione europea del fascismo," Problemi di Ulisse, no. 82 (1976): 69-78.

On the spread of fascist ideas beyond Italy: Theodore I. Armon, "Fascismo italiano e Guardia di Ferro," Storia Contemporanea, 20 (1989): 561-98; Jerzy W. Borejsza, "L'Italia e le tendenze fasciste nei paesi baltici, 1922-1940," Annali della Fondazione Luigi Einaudi, 8 (1974): 279-316; Luigi Bruti Liberati, "Il Canada, l'Italia e il fascismo, 1919-1945 (Rome, 1984); Gianfranco Cresciani, Fascismo, antifascismo e gli italiani in Australia, 1922-1945 (Rome, 1979). See also Blatt (#670); Hoepke (#708).

574. Lyttleton, Adrian. The Seizure of Power: Fascism in Italy, 1919-1929, 2d ed. Princeton, NJ, 1988.

The authoritative account.

575. Natali, Claudio. La Terza Internazionale e il fascismo, 1919-1923. Rome, 1982.

A case study of transnational interplay between communism and fascism is Alexander De Grand, Angelo Tasca: Un politico scomodo (Milan, 1985), Eng. trans. In Stalin's Shadow: Angelo Tasca and the Crisis of the Left in Italy and France (DeKalb, IL, 1986).

576. Nolte, Ernst. Der Faschismus in seiner Epoche. Munich, 1963. Abridged Eng. trans. Three Faces of Fascism: Action Française, Italian Fascism, National Socialism, New York, 1966.

A seminal but dense work; fascism as antitranscendentalism.

577. Poulantzas, Nicos. Fascism and Dictatorship. London, 1974.

For a modern Marxist, or Gramscian, view of fascism as a capitalist, imperialist phenomenon.

578. Revue d'Histoire de la Deuxième Guerre Mondiale et des Conflits Contemporaines, nos. 139 (July 1985), 143 (July 1986): "Sur l'Italie fasciste."

579. Salvatorelli, Luigi, and Mira, Giovanni. Storia d'Italia nel periodo fascista, 5th rev. ed. Turin, 1976.

Long recognized as a standard account. Cf. L. Salvatorelli, Nazional-fascismo (Turin, 1923), an early and perceptive interpretation.

580. Salvemini, Gaetano. Under the Axe of Fascism. London & New York, 1936; reprint, New York, 1971.

Classic critique by one of Mussolini's most articulate and persistent enemies.

581. Santarelli, Enzo. Storia di movimento e del regime fascista, 2 vols. Rome, 1967.

Written from a proletarian viewpoint. By the same author, Richerce sul fascismo (Urbino, 1971), collected essays, some on diplomatic and colonial questions.

582. Secchi, Salvatore, ed. Fascismo ed esilio: Aspetti della diaspora intelletuale di Germania, Spagna e Italia. Pisa, 1988.

Some refugees fled from Italian Fascism to Weimar Germany; later, others escaped Nazism by taking refuge in Italy. See Lönne (#668); Voigt (#795).

583. Vivarelli, Roberto. Il dopoguerra in Italia e l'avvento del fascismo, 1918-1922. Vol. 1, Dalla fine della guerra all'impresa di Fiume. Naples, 1967.

Important study depicting the clash between Wilsonianism and Italian nationalism. A sequel, in lieu of vol. 2, is Il fallimento di liberalismo: Studi sulle origine del fascismo (Bologna, 1981).

3. Italy in International Affairs, 1918-1945

General Works on Italian Diplomacy

584. Albrecht-Carrié, René. "Foreign Policy since the First World War," in Modern Italy: A Topical History, ed. Edward R. Tannenbaum and Emiliana P. Noether, pp. 337-54. New York, 1974.

585. Barclay, Glen St. J. The Rise and Fall of the New Roman Empire: Italy's Bid for World Power, 1890-1943. London & New York, 1973.

586. Blatt, Joel. "Franco-Italian Relations, 1880-1940," in Studies in Modern Italian History in Honor of A.W. Salamone, ed. F.J. Coppa, pp. 171-96. New York, 1986.

587. Bosworth, R.J.B., and Romano, Sergio, eds. Il problema della politica estera italiana. Bologna, forthcoming, 1990.

588. Currey, Muriel I. Italian Foreign Policy, 1918-1932. London, 1932.

Well known between the wars as an English-language statement of Italian nationalist viewpoint. See also the same author's A Woman at the Abyssinian War (London, 1936).

589. Decleva, Enrico. L'alleato incerto: Ricerche sugli orientamenti internazionali dell'Italia unita. Milan, 1987.

Essays, all but one published previously, on Italian diplomacy, 1870-1970.

590. Del Bo, Dino, et al. Inchiesta sulla politica estera italiana. Rome, 1970.

Useful collection of essays on twentieth-century Italian diplomacy.

591. Duroselle, Jean-Baptiste, and Serra, Enrico, eds. Italia e Francia dal 1919 al 1939. Milan, 1981.

Papers read at the Istituto per gli Studi di Politica Internazionale, Milan. The same institute and editors have published a sequel: Italia e Francia, 1939-1945, vol. 1 (Milan, 1984); for vol. 2, see Serra (#881). Also J-B. Duroselle and E. Serra, eds. Il vincolo culturale fra Italia e Francia negli anni trenta e quaranta (Milan, 1986).

592. Fischer, Bernd J. "Italian Policy in Albania, 1894-1943." Balkan Studies, 26 (1985): 101-12.

ITALY IN INTERNATIONAL AFFAIRS

593. Giannini, Amadeo. I Rapporti italo-inglese. Milan, 1940.

> Survey of a century of Anglo-Italian relations paralleled by Giannini's "I rapporti italo-spagnoli" and "I rapporti italo-ellenici," Rivista di Studi Politici Internazionali, 24 (1957): 8-63, 389-445.

594. International History Review, 8/1 (1986): "Italy in the Aftermath of the First World War."

> A half-dozen diplomatic historical essays; none present really fresh information or interpretation.

595. La Marca, Nicola. Italia e Balcani fra le due guerre: Saggio di una ricerca sui tentativi italiani di espansione economica nel Sud Est europeo fra le due guerre. Rome, 1979.

> See also Francesco Leoncini, "Rapporti tra l'Italia ed i paesi dell'Europa orientale." Rivista di Studi Politici Internazionali, 41 (1974): 369-74, and "Italia e Cecoslovacchia, 1919-1939," ibid., 45 (1978): 357-72.

596. Lowe, Cedric J., and Marzari, Frank. Italian Foreign Policy, 1870-1940. London, 1975.

> A general but scholarly survey.

597. Macartney, Maxwell H.H., and Cremona, Paul. Italy's Foreign and Colonial Policy, 1914-1937. London, 1938.

> Dated of course, but stands the test of time very well.

598. McGuire, Constantine E. Italy's International Economic Position. New York, 1926.

> Still useful for reference.

599. Rossini, Giuseppe, comp. La politica estera italiana dal 1914 al 1943. Turin, 1963.

> Collection of essays by eminent scholars first presented over Italy's radio-television network on twentieth anniversary of Fascism's collapse.

600. Sierpowski, Stanislaw, "I rapporti italo-polacchi nel periodo tra le due guerre mondiali: Tentativo di un bilancio," Rassegna degli Archivi di Stato, 47 (1987): 321-38.

601. Sori, Ercole. L'emigrazione italiana dall'unità alla seconda guerra mondiale. Bologna, 1979.

> Studies of Italian emigration to particular countries include: Alexander De Conde, Half-Bitter, Half-Sweet: An Excursion in Italian-American

History (New York, 1971); Renzo De Felice, ed., Cenni storici sull'emigrazione italiana nelle Americhe e in Australia (Milan, 1979); Grazia Dore, La democrazia italiana e l'emigrazione in America (Brescia, 1964); Luigi De Rosa, "L'emigrazione italiana in Brasile: Un bilancio," Rassegna Economica, 50/1 (1986): 11-30; Pierre Milza, ed., Les italiens en France de 1914 à 1940 (Rome, 1986). See also under Fascist Foreign Policy and Second World War for the political dimension of emigration, and Cannistraro and Rossoli (#967).

602. Spini, Giorgio; Migone, Gian Giacomo; Teodori, Massimo, eds. Italia e America dalla grande guerra a oggi. Venice, 1976.

See also G.G. Migone, Problemi di storia nei rapporti tra l'Italia e gli Stati Uniti (Turin, 1971), and #817.

603. Storia e Politica. Vols. 12/3 (1973), 13/1 and 2 (1974). "1° e 2° Convegno Storico Italo-Austriaco."

Papers delivered in Innsbruck, Oct. 1971, and Venice, Oct. 1972, on Austro-Italian relations over the past century. A similar range of essays found in Angelo Ara, Fra Austria e Italia: Dal Cinque Giornate alla questione alto-atestina (Udine, 1987).

604. Valsecchi, Franco. "Italia e Germania da Bismarck a Hitler," Il Veltro, 6 (1962): 349-76.

One of several surveys of Italy's relations with another country to appear in Veltro. Others include Francesco Guida, "Italia e Grecia dalla formazione del regno di Grecia ai giorni nostri," 27 (1983): 27-55; Luigi Bruti Liberati, "Le relazioni tra Italia e Canada nel Novecento," 29 (1985): 91-106.

605. Vedovato, Giuseppe. "La politica estera italiana." Rivista di Studi Politici Internazionali, 44 (1977): 59-76, 373-400, 579-90; 45 (1978): 59-78, 337-56.

606. Vigezzi, Brunello. "Politica estera e opinione pubblica in Italia dal 1870 al 1945." Nuova Rivista Storica, 63 (1979): 548-69.

Foreign Ministry and Ministers

See also Craig and Gilbert (#521); De Felice (#558); Italy, Ministero degli Affari Esteri (#93, #146); Serra (#96).

607. Cantalupo, Roberto [Legatus]. Vita diplomatica di Salvatore Contarini. Rome, 1947. Reprinted as La "belle époque" della diplomatica italiana, Rome, 1965.

An unsatisfactory sketch but the only life we have of this important diplomat.

608. Carrillo, Elisa. *Alcide De Gasperi: The Long Apprenticeship*. Notre Dame, IN, 1966.

609. Collotti, Enzo. "Fulvio Suvich e l'apporto dei nazionalisti giuliani all'espansionismo fascista." *Bolletino dell'Istituto Regionale per la Storia del Movimento di liberazione in Friuli-Venezia Giulia*, 2/2 (May 1974): 20-24.

610. Cora, Giuliano. "Vittorio Cerrutti." *Rivista di Studi Politici Internazionali*, 28 (1961): 473-76.

611. D'Amelio, Mariano. "Vittorio Scialoja." *Nuova Antologia*, 370 (Nov.-Dec. 1933): 396-404.

    On Scialoja, see too Giannini, "Profili" (#332).

612. Ferraris, Luigi V. *L'Amministrazione Centrale del Ministero degli esteri italiano nel suo sviluppo storico, 1848-1954*. Florence, 1955.

    Essential administrative study, also published in *Rivista di Studi Politici Internazionali*, 21 (1954): 426-61, 605-63.

613. Giordano, Giancarlo. *Carlo Sforza: la diplomazia, 1896-1921*. Milan, 1987.

    Vol. I of a definitive life, drawn from Sforza papers in ASME and ACS, covers the subject's tenure of Italy's Foreign Ministry, 1920-21. See also Melchionni, Brogi, Marsico (#650).

    Livio Zeno Zencovich, *Ritratto di Carlo Sforza: Col carteggio Croce-Sforza e altri documenti inediti* (Florence, 1975), stresses Sforza's role at the close of World War II but without access to his private papers in ASME. See also Antonio Varsori, "La politica inglese e il Conte Sforza, 1941-1943," *Rivista di Studi Politici internazionali*, 43 (1976): 31-57; Giorgio Petracchi, "Carlo Sforza e il mondo sovietico, 1917-1950: Apparenze diplomatiche e realtà psicologiche" *Il Politico*, 49 (1984): 381-404.

614. Guerri, Giordano B. *Galeazzo Ciano: Una vita 1903-1944*. Milan, 1979.

    Workmanlike, but Ciano's definitive biography remains to be written. See also Diulio Susmel, *Vita sbagliata di Galeazzo Ciano* (Milan, 1962).

615. Nello, Paolo. *Dino Grandi: La formazione di un leader fascista*. Bologna, 1987.

    First volume of authoritative biography, based on Grandi's papers, takes the story to 1929, thus embracing the first four years of Grandi's diplomatic career; interpretation is arguably oversympathetic to Grandi.

616. Vedovato, Giuseppe. "Amadeo Giannini." Rivista di Studi Politici Internazionali, 28 (1961): 477-79.

4. The Foreign Policy of Liberal Italy, 1918-1922

Postwar Peace Negotiations

See also Buccianti (#738); Vivarelli (#583); and the next section on the Adriatic problem.

617. Albrecht-Carrié, René. Italy at the Peace Conference. New York, 1938.

618. Barié, Ottavio. "Luigi Albertini, il 'Corriere della Sera' e la 'politica della nazionalità,' 1917-1919." Storia e Politica, 8 (1969): 43-87.

619. Blatt, Joel. "The Parity that meant Superiority: French Naval Policy towards Italy at the Washington Conference, 1921-1922." French Historical Studies, 12 (1981): 223-48.

See also Matteo Pizzigallo, "L'Italia alla conferenza di Washington, 1921-1922," Storia e Politica, 14 (1975): 408-48, 550-89.

620. Bosworth, R.J.B. "Sir Rennell Rodd e l'Italia." Nuova Rivista Storica, 54 (1970): 420-36.

621. Caroli, Giuliano. "L'Italia e il problema nazionale romeno alla Conferenza della pace di Parigi." Storia e Politica, 22 (1983): 435-79.

See also Francesco Guida, "Il compimento dello Stato nazionale romeno e l'Italia: Opinione pubblica e iniziative politio-diplomatiche," Rassegna Storica del Risorgimento, 70 (1983): 387-409.

622. Clodomiro, Vanni. "Il ministro delle Colonie Colosimo e la conferenza di Versailles." Storia Contemporanea, 16 (1985): 1001-42.

623. Coppa, Frank J. "Francesco Saverio Nitti: Early Critic of the Treaty of Versailles." Risorgimento [Brussels], 1 (1980): 211-19.

Also Edgar R. Rosen, "Francesco Nitti und die deutsche Frage zwischen den Weltkriegen," in Faschismus-Nationalsozialismus: Ergebnisse und Referate der 6. italienisch-deutschen Historiker-Tagung in Trier, ed. G. Eckert and O-E. Schüdekopf (Braunschweig, 1964), pp. 42-59.

624. D'Amoja, Fulvio. La politica estera italiana da Caporetto alla conferenza per la pace di Parigi: Le premesse. Messina, 1970.

625. De Courten, Ludovica. "Marina mercantile e politica estera: L'Ansaldo di Pio Perrone nel primo dopoguerra." Analisi Storica, 1 (July-Dec. 1983): 7-38.

626. De Vergottini, Tomaso. "L'Italia e il plebiscito per l'Alta Silesia." Storia e Politica, 11 (1972): 22-49.

627. Giannini, Amadeo. La questione orientale alla Conferenza della pace. Rome, 1921.

 Complemented by the same author's L'ultima fase della questione orientale (#332), and Anthony R. De Luca, Great Power Rivalry at the Turkish Straits: The Montreux Conference and Convention of 1936 (Boulder, CO, 1981).

628. Guida, Francesco. "Ungheria e Italia dalla fine del primo conflitto mondiale al Trattato di Trianon." Storia Contemporanea, 19 (1988): 381-418.

 Also by the same author, La Bulgaria dalla guerra di liberazione sino al trattato di Neuilly, 1877-1919: Testimonianze italiane (Rome, 1984).

629. Lindeck-Pozza, Irmtraut. "Die Burgenland in der italienischen Aussenpolitik: Ein Vermittlungsversuch Italiens zu Ende 1920." Römische Historische Mitteilungen, 14 (1972): 123-53.

630. Lönne, Karl-Egon. "Italien und das Deutschland des Versailler Vertrages: Zur diplomatischen Berichterstattung des italienischen Botschafters Alfredo Frassati aus Berlin, 1921-1922." Quellen und Forschungen aus italienischen Archiven und Bibliotheken, 53 (1973): 318-84.

631. Macfie, A.L. "The Revision of the Treaty of Sèvres: The First Phase, August 1920 - September 1922." Balkan Studies, 24 (1983): 57-88.

632. Malfèr, Stefan. Wien und Rom nach dem Ersten Weltkrieg: österreichisch-italienische Beziehungen, 1919-1923. Vienna, 1978.

 Also relevant, Renata Schulla, "Karl Renner als Leiter des Staatsamtes für Ausseres, 1919-1920," Österreich in Geschichte und Literatur, 17 (1973): 458-66; Gertrude Bercel, "Politische und ökonomische Aspekte des Renner-Nitti Abkommens vom april 1920," Zeitgeschichte, 7 (1980): 115-27; Johann Rainer, "Il ricupero dei beni culturali italiani dall'Austria dopo la prima guerra mondiale," Studi Trentini di Scienze Storiche, 67 (1988): 237-50. See also Storia e Politica (#603).

633. Melchionni, Maria Grazia. La vittoria mutilata: Problemi ed incertezza della politica estera italiana sul finire della Grande guerra, ottobre 1918 - gennaio 1919. Rome, 1981.

See also M.G. Melchionni, Il confine orientale italiano, 1918-1920 (Rome, 1981), and "La convenzione antiasburgica del 12 novembre 1920," Storia e Politica, 11 (1972): 224-64, 374-417.

634. Minerbi, Sergio I. L'Italie et Palestine, 1914-1920. Paris, 1970.

By the same author, "The Italian Activity to Recover the 'Cenalco,' " Risorgimento [Brussels], 1 (1980): 181-209. Further on Palestine, see Frank E. Manuel, "The Palestine Question in Italian Diplomacy, 1917-1920," Journal of Modern History, 27 (1955): 263-80.

635. Pastorelli, Pietro. "L'Italia e la nazione finlandese, 1917-1919." Clio, 2 (1983): 571-80.

636. Petracchi, Giorgio. La Russia rivoluzionaria nella politica italiana: Le relazioni italo-sovietiche, 1917-1925. Rome-Bari, 1982.

Well-documented study culminating in Fascist Italy's de jure recognition of the Soviet Union. Takes account of economic and ideological as well as political dimensions. By the same author, "Ideology and Realpolitik: Italo-Soviet Relations, 1917-1933," Journal of Italian History, 2 (1979): 473-519. Antonello Venturi, Rivoluzionari russi in Italia, 1917-1921 (Milan, 1979), has a chapter on the first Comintern agents in Italy.

On the impact of communism on Italian party politics, see for the immediate post-World War I period Serge Noiret, "Nitti e Bombacci: Aspetti di un dialogo impossibile. I bolscevichi contro la rivoluzione italiana, novembre 1919 - febbraio 1920," Storia Contemporanea 17 (1986): 397-441, and "Le origini della ripresa delle relazioni tra Roma e Mosca. Idealismo massimalista e realismo bolscevico: La missione Bombacci-Cabrini a Copenhagen nell'aprile 1920," ibid., 19 (1988): 797-850; and over the longer term Joan Barth Urban, Moscow and the Italian Communist Party: From Togliatti to Berlinguer (Ithaca, NY, 1986); Paolo Spriano, I communisti europei e Stalin (Turin, 1983), Eng. trans. Stalin and the European Communists: Relations between the Stalinist C.P.S.U. and the French and Italian Parties, 1935-1947 (London, 1985); Spencer Di Scala, Renewing Italian Socialism: From Nenni to Craxi (New York, 1989). See also Natali, De Grand (#575).

637. Petricioli, Marta. L'occupazione italiana del Caucaso: Un ingrato servizio da rendere a Londra. Pavia, 1972.

638. ———. "La resa di conti: Diplomazia e finanza di fronte alle aspirazioni italiane in Anatolia, 1918-1923." Storia delle Relazioni Internazionali, 2 (1986): 63-93.

Also for the beginning and end of Italy's hopes in Asia Minor, see Luciano Flussio, "La diplomazia delle cannoniere: Gli sbarchi italiani in Anatolia nel 1919," Analisi Storica, 1 (July-Dec. 1983): 39-56; Matteo Pizzigallo, "L'ultimo accordo con la Sublime Porta e la fine dell'occupazione italiana in Anatolia, 1922, ibid., 57-86. On the same topic, Louis A. Cretella, "A Lost Opportunity: Italian Banks and Anatolian Railways in 1920," Risorgimento [Brussels], 1 (1980): 333-52.

639. Petsales-Diomedes, N. Greece at the Paris Peace Conference, 1919. Thessalonika, 1978.

Occasion of a documentary review by Maria Grazia Melchionni, "Accordi italo-greci a Parigi," Rivista di Studi Politici Internazionali, 48 (1981): 465-80.

640. Serra, Enrico. Camille Barrère e l'intesa italo-francese. Milan, 1950.

See also Léon Noel, Camille Barrère, ambassadeur de France (Paris, 1948).

641. ———. Nitti e la Russia. Bari, 1975.

642. Staderini, Alessandra. "Rivendicazioni territoriali e mobilitazione nazionale nei documenti del 1919 di Giovanni Giurati e Oscar Sinigaglia." Storia Contemporanea, 14 (1983): 89-140.

Case study of a nationalist-irredentist pressure group. On the general background, Roberto Chiarini, "Il nazionalismo e il problema delle rivendicazioni territoriali nell'Italia del primo dopoguerra," Annali della Facoltà di scienze politiche dell'Università degli Studi di Milano, 2 (1982): 262-96.

643. Toscano, Mario. Patto di Londra. Bologna, 1934.

Authoritative Italian treatment of the document that conditioned Italy's position at the Paris Peace Conference, supplemented by the same author's "Rivelazioni e nuovi documenti sul negoziato di Londra per l'ingresso dell'Italia nella prima guerra mondiale," Nuova Antologia, 494 (May-Aug. 1965): 433-57; 495 (Sept.-Dec. 1965): 15-37, 150-65, 295-312; "Il negoziato di Londra del 1915," ibid., 501 (Sept.-Dec. 1967): 313-26; "Le origini diplomatiche dell'Art. 9 del Patto di Londra relativo agli eventuali compensi all'Italia in Asia Minore," Storia e politica, 4 (1965): 339-84. See also William A. Renzi, In the Shadow of the Sword: Italy's Neutrality and Entrance into the Great War, 1914-1915 (New York, 1988).

644. Valiani, Leo. La dissoluzione dell'Austria-Ungheria. Milan, 1966; new ed., Milan, 1985. Eng. trans. The End of Austria-Hungary, London, 1973.

For the achievement of Italy's prime aim in World War I. See also François Fejto, Requiem pour un empire défunt: Histoire de la destruction de l'Autriche-Hongrie (Paris, 1988); Nicola La Marca, "Conseguenze politiche, economiche e sociali per l'Italia del crollo dell'impero austro-ungarico," Economia e Storia, 2d series, 1 (1980): 221-41.

645. Walworth, Arthur. Wilson and his Peacemakers: American Diplomacy at the Paris Peace Conference. New York, 1986.

With specific reference to Italy, see Sterling J. Kernek, "Woodrow Wilson and National Self-Determination along Italy's Frontier: A Study of the Manipulation of Principles in the Pursuit of Political Interests," Proceedings of the American Philosophical Association, 126/4 (1982): 243-300; Louis J. Nigro, "Wilsonian Propaganda and Italian Politics during the First World War, 1917-1919: Data and Hypotheses," in The United States and Italy: The First Two Hundred Years, ed. Humbert S. Nelli (New York, 1977), pp. 63-80.

The Adriatic Problem

See also under Regional Works for studies of Venezia Giulia and the Italo-Yugoslav border.

646. Alatri, Paolo. Nitti, D'Annunzio e la questione adriatica, 1919-1920. Milan, 1976.

See also Michael A. Ledeen, D'Annunzio a Fiume (Bari, 1975), Eng. trans. The First Duce: D'Annunzio at Fiume (Baltimore, 1977).

647. De Felice, Renzo. D'Annunzio politico, 1918-1938. Rome-Bari, 1978. First two parts a well-documented account of the Fiume enterprise; part 3 on D'Annunzio and Mussolini.

648. Gerra, Ferdinando. L'impresa di Fiume, 2 vols. Milan, 1974-75.

A good narrative of events. See also Guglielmo Salotti, "Gli 'intrighi balcani' del 1919-1920 in un memorandum a Mussolini del 1932 di Vladimiro Petrovich-Saxe," Storia Contemporanea, 20 (1989): 685-93.

649. Lederer, Ivo. Yugoslavia at the Peace Conference. New Haven, CT, 1963.

650. Melchionni, Maria Grazia. "La politica estera di Carlo Sforza nel 1920-1921." Rivista di Studi Politici Internazionali, 36 (1969): 537-70.

See also Alessandro Brogi, "Il trattato di Rapallo del 1920 e la politica danubiano-balcanica di Carlo Sforza," Storia delle Relazioni Internazionali, 5 (1989): 3-46; Giorgio Marsico, "L'Italia e la preparazione della conferenza di Portorose, 24 ottobre - 23 novembre 1921." Risorgimento [Milan], 30 (1978): 55-74; Giordano (#613).

651. Paoli, Germano. "Lo sbarco di D'Annunzio a Zara, 14 novembre 1919, in un rapporto riservatissimo dell'ammiraglio Millo al

presente del Consiglio dei Ministri." Rivista Dalmatica, 29 (1982): 7-49.

Lengthy disquisition with brief documentary excerpts.

652. Pastorelli, Pietro. L'Albania nella politica estera italiana, 1914-1920. Naples, 1970.

Definitive work documented from a wide variety of published and unpublished sources. Supplemented by the same author's Italia-Albania, 1924-1927: Origini diplomatiche del Trattato di Tirana del 22 novembre 1927 (Florence, 1967). See too Rosselli (#676); Zamboni (#719).

From the Albanian side, see Studia Albanica, 3/1 (1966): several papers delivered "à l'occasion du 1er Congrès International des Etudes Balkaniques et Sud-Est Européennes" recount Albania's resistance to Italian penetration, 1912-45. Also Bobi Bobev, "Le conflit entre l'Albanie et le Royaume des Serbes, des Croates et des Slovenes et la position de l'Italie," Etudes Balkaniques, 16/1 (1980): 87-100.

653. Riosa, Alceo. L'interventismo democratico e la questione adriatica tra l'armistizio e la marcia su Roma." Storia e Politica, 4 (1965): 514-65.

654. Valiani, Leo. "Documenti francesi sull'Italia e il movimento jugoslavo." Rivista Storica Italiana, 80 (1968): 351-64.

655. Zivojinovič, Dragan. America, Italy, and the Birth of Yugoslavia, 1917-1919. New York, 1972

Employs Serbian Foreign Ministry papers. See also Fritz Fellner, "George D. Herron and the Italian-Yugoslav Rivalries during the Final Stages of World War I, 1917-1919," in The Creation of Yugoslavia, 1914-1918, ed. Dimitrije Djordjevic (Santa Barbara, CA, 1980), pp. 125-36.

5. Fascist Foreign Policy

Overviews and Interpretations of Fascist Diplomacy

See also Aquarone and Vernazza (#519); Donosti (#330); Rossini (#599); Schmitz (#817); Shorrock (#819).

656. Adler, Winfried. "Die Kulturpolitik des italienischen Faschismus in Südtirol." Quellen und Forschungen aus italienischen Archiven und Bibliotheken, 61 (1981): 305-61.

On the basis of Italian primary sources considers Fascist nationalization policy in Alto Adige, a perennial bone of contention between Rome and Vienna. See also Enzo Collotti, "Il fascismo e la questione austriaca," Movimento di Liberazione in Italia, no. 81 (Oct.-Dec. 1965): 3-25; Ludwig Jedlicka, "Österreich und Italien 1922 bis 1938," Wissenschaft und Weltbild, 26 (1973): 45-69; Klaus Weiss, Das Südtirol-Problem in der Ersten-Republik: Dargestellt an österreichs Innen-und Aussenpolitik im Jahre 1928, Munich, 1989.

Fascist discrimination against Italy's French-speaking minority created fewer diplomatic waves: W. Adler, "La politica del fascismo in Valle d'Aosta," Bollettino Storico Bibliografico Subalpino, 78/1 (1980): 223-75.

657. Bessis, Juliette. La Méditerranée fasciste: L'Italie mussolinienne et la Tunisie. Paris, 1981.

Based mostly on French and Arabic North African press. See also William I. Shorrock, "The Tunisian Question in French Policy toward Italy, 1881-1940," International Journal of African Historical Studies, 16 (1983): 631-51.

658. Borejsza, Jerzy W. Il fascismo e l'Europa orientale: Dalla propaganda all'aggressione, trans. from Polish. Rome-Bari, 1981.

Takes account of Fascist-Nazi rivalry.

659. Cannistraro, Philip V., and Wynot, Edward D. "On the Dynamics of Anti-Communism as a Function of Fascist Foreign Policy, 1933-1943." Il Politico, 38 (1973): 645-81.

660. Cassels, Alan. "Was There a Fascist Foreign Policy?: Tradition and Novelty." International History Review, 5 (1983): 255-68; Ital. trans. "E esistita una politica estera fascista?" Rassegna degli Archivi di Stato, 43 (1983): 419-29.

661. Casucci, Costanzo. "La politica estera fascista nel giudizio di Carlo Rosselli." Il Mulino, 33 (1984): 231-65.

Appraisal of a speech given by the most famous of the fuorusciti at the Royal Institute of International Affairs, London, 16 March 1933, printed ibid., pp. 241-61.

662. Certutti, Mauro. Fra Roma e Berna: La svizzera italiana nel ventennio fascista. Milan, 1986.

663. Cresciani, Gianfranco. "Italian Fascism in Australia." Studi Emigrazione, 25 (1988): 237-46.

664. De Felice, Renzo. Il fascismo e l'oriente: Arabi, ebrei e indiani nella politica di Mussolini. Bologna, 1988.

Takes the story up to 1935. Then see Storia Contemporanea, 17/6 (1986): "Ebrei e arabi nella politica mediterranea del fascismo," 8 essays mainly diplomatic historical.

FASCIST FOREIGN POLICY

665. Di Nolfo, Ennio. "Il revisionismo nella politica estera di Mussolini." Il Politico, 19 (1954): 85-100.

666. Dumoulin, Michael, and Willequest, Jacques, eds. Aspects des relations de la Belgique, du Grand-Duché de Luxembourg et des Pays-Bas avec l'Italie, 1925-1940. Brussels, 1983.

667. Gentile, Emilio. "L'emigrazione italiana in Argentina nella polticia di espansione del nazionalismo e del fascismo." Storia Contemporanea, 17 (1986): 355-96.

668. Lönne, Karl-Egon. "Die politische Rolle antifascistischer italenischer Emigranten in Deutschland zwischen 1918 und 1943." Risorgimento [Brussels], 4 (1983): 109-22.

    In the same context by Lönne see, Il fascismo come provocazione: 'Rote Fahne' e 'Vorwärts' a confronto con il fascismo italiano tra il 1920 e il 1933 (Naples, 1985); "Il fascismo italiano nel giudizio del cattolicesimo politico della Repubblica di Weimar," Storia Contemporanea, 2 (1971): 697-716.

669. Mack Smith, Denis. Mussolini's Roman Empire. London, 1976. Ital. trans. Le guerre del Duce, Bari, 1979.

    Factual and anecdotal survey centered on the Ethiopian adventure; devastating critique of the Duce's pretensions.

670. Milza, Pierre. L'Italie fasciste devant l'opinion française, 1920-1940. Paris, 1967.

    See also the same author's "Le fascisme italien à Paris," Revue d'Histoire Moderne et Contemporaine, 30 (1983): 420-52; Pierre Guillen, "Le role politique de l'emigration italienne en France dans l'entre-deux-guerre," Risorgimento [Brussels], 4 (1983): 109-22, and Tombaccini (#680).

    A case study of Fascist influence in France is Joel Blatt, "Relatives and Rivals: The Responses of the Action Française to Italian Fascism," European Studies Review, 11 (1981): 263-93.

671. Montenegro, Angelo. "Politica estera e organizzazione del Consenso: Note sull'Istituto per gli Studi di Politica Internazionale, 1933-1943." Studi Storici, 19 (1978): 777-817.

    ISPI operated at home and abroad. A case study of its role outside Italy is Enrico Decleva, "Politica estera, storia, propaganda: L'ISPI di Milano e la Francia, 1934-1943," Storia Contemporanea, 13 (1982): 697-757.

    Another Fascist organization for foreign policy propaganda, founded 1931, was the Istituto per l'Asia media ed Estrema; see Valdo Ferretti,

"Politica e cultura: Origini e attività dell'IsMeo durante il regime fascista," ibid., 17 (1986): 779-820.

672. Morelli, Anne. Fascismo e antifascismo nell'emigrazione italiana in Belgio, 1922-1940. Rome, 1987.

See also Benito Gallo, "Le role politique de l'immigration italienne au Grand-Duché de Luxembourg de 1922 au lendemain de la duexième guerre mondiale," Risorgimento [Brussels], 4 (1983): 123-37.

673. Petersen, Jens. "Gesellschaftssystem, Ideologie und Interesse in der Aussenpolitik des Faschistischen Italien." Quellen und Forschungen aus italienischen Archiven und Bibliotheken, 54 (1974): 428-70.

Valuable, wide-ranging article discusses not just the clash of ideology and interests but also the interplay of domestic and foreign policies.

674. Rainero, Romain. "I rapporti italo-turchi nel periodo fascista." Il Veltro, 23 (1979): 391-97.

675. Romano, Sergio. "Diplomazia nazionale e diplomazia fascista: Continuità e rottura." Affari Esteri, 16 (1984): 440-54.

676. Rosselli, Alessandro. Italia e Albania: Relazioni finanziarie nel ventennio fascista. Bologna, 1986.

677. Salvatorelli, Luigi. Il fascismo nella politica internazionale. Modena-Rome, 1946.

Still a useful, balanced survey.

678. Salvemini, Gaetano. Preludio alla seconda guerra mondiale, in Opere, III, Scritti di politica estera, vol. 3, ed. Augusto Torre, pp. 1-689. Milan, 1967.

Celebrated denunciation alleging that Fascist Italy had no coherent foreign policy. First published as Mussolini diplomatico (Paris, 1932); present definitive edition based on an English-language version, Prelude to World War II (London, 1951).

679. Togliatti, Palmiro. Opere, 4 vols. Rome, 1972-79.

Veteran Italian communist leader gives a traditional Marxist interpretation of Fascist diplomacy, particularly in vol. 3, part 2 (1919-35), pp. 199-207.

680. Tombaccini, Simonetta. Storia dei fuorusciti italiani in Francia. Milan, 1988.

See also Aldo Garosci's biography of the most famous fuoruscito, Vita di Carlo Rosselli, 2 vols. (Florence, 1945), and Enrica Decleva,

FASCIST FOREIGN POLICY

"Le delusioni di una democrazia: Carlo Rosselli e la Francia," <u>Nuova Rivista Storica</u>, 63 (1979): 570-602.

681. Villari, Luigi. <u>Italian Foreign Policy under Mussolini</u>. New York, 1956.

Best-known apology in English for Fascist diplomacy. In the same vein, L. Villari, <u>The Expansion of Italy</u> (London, 1930).

682. Zani, Luciano. <u>Fascismo, autarchia, commercio estero</u>. Bologna, 1988.

Study centers on Felice Guarneri (#367).

Fascist and Nationalist Writings

In the interwar years the Fascists and their Nationalist allies produced endless books, pamphlets, and articles, all stating Italy's international grievances and claims. Without exception, their scholarly value is minimal or nonexistent. Nevertheless, their propaganda affords an insight into what Mussolini was supposed to accomplish. In addition, they recapture the mood of much contemporary Italian opinion. For these reasons a selection of the more celebrated titles of this genre follows:

683. Bastianini, Giuseppe. <u>Gli Italiani all'estero</u>. Milan, 1939.

684. Cantalupo, Roberto. <u>Fatti europei e politica italiana, 1922-1924</u>. Milan, 1924.

685. Coppola, Francesco. <u>La pace coatta</u>. Milan, 1929.

686. Corradini, Enrico. <u>La rinascita nazionale</u>. Florence, 1929.

687. D'Annunzio, Gabriele. <u>Scritti politici</u>, ed. Paolo Alatri. Milan, 1980.

Brief selection from the voice of neoromantic Italian nationalism.

688. Federzoni, Luigi. <u>A.O.: Il 'Posto al Sole.'</u> Bologna, 1936.

689. Forges Davanzati, Roberto. <u>Premesse fasciste di politica estera</u>. Milan, 1926.

690. Gayda, Virginio. <u>Che cosa vuole l'Italia?</u>, 6th ed. Rome, 1940.

Perhaps the definitive statement of Fascist overseas aspirations by a prominent newspaper editor.

691. Gravelli, Asvero. <u>Verso l'internazionale fascista</u>. Rome, 1932.

692. Lessona, Alessandro. <u>Verso l'impero</u>. Florence, 1939.

693. Orano, Paolo. <u>Gli ebrei in Italia</u>. Rome, 1937.

Antisemitic tract commissioned by Mussolini to prepare the way for anti-Jewish legislation. See also Telesio Interlandi, Contra Judaeos (Rome-Milan, 1938); Giovanni Preziosi, Come il giudaismo ha preparato la guerra, 2d ed. (Rome, 1940), and Giudaismo, bolscevismo, plutocrazia, massoneria, 4th ed. (Milan, 1944).

Early Fascist Diplomacy

See also Jedlicka, Weiss (#656); Malfèr (#632); Pastorelli (#652); Petracchi (#636). For Mussolini's first dealings with Ethiopia, consult Buccianti (#738).

694. Angelini, Maria. "La politica estera italiana e il patto renano del 1925." Università di Perugia: Annali della Facoltà di Scienze Politiche, no. 10 (1968-70), pp. 201-56.

On the same topic, see also Sally Marks, "Mussolini and Locarno: Fascist Foreign Policy in Microcosm," Journal of Contemporary History, 14 (1979): 423-39.

695. Barros, James. The Corfu Incident of 1923. Princeton, NJ, 1965.

Best contemporary accounts of the Corfu affair are Pierre Lasturel, L'affaire gréco-italienne de 1923 (Paris, 1925), and Konstantin von Neurath, Der italienisch-griechische Konflikt vom Jahre 1923 und seine völkerrechtliche Bedeutung (Berlin, 1929). Scholarly appraisals include: Ettore Anchiere, "L'affare di Corfu alla luce dei Documenti diplomatici italiani," Il Politico, 20 (1955): 374-95; Joel Blatt, "France and the Corfu-Fiume Crisis of 1923," The Historian 50 (1988): 234-59; Vera Torunsky, "Der Korfu-Konflikt von 1923: Grossmachtinteressen und das System der Kollektiven Sicherheit," in Inseln als Brennpunkte internationaler Politik, ed. Jost Dülffer et al. (Cologne, 1986), pp. 60-96; Peter J. Yearwood, " 'Consistently with Honour': Great Britain, the League of Nations and the Corfu Crisis," Journal of Contemporary History, 21 (1986): 559-79. See also Cassels (#702); Pizzigallo (#714).

696. Berselli, Aldo. L'opinione pubblica inglese e l'avvento del fascismo, 1919-1925. Milan, 1971.

Also on western public response to Fascism's rise to power, see R.J.B. Bosworth, "The British Press, Conservatives and Mussolini, 1920-1934," Journal of Contemporary History, 5/2 (1970): 163-82; Charles Keserich, "The British Labour Press and Italian Fascism, 1922-1925," ibid., 10 (1975): 579-90; Elena Fasano Guarini, " 'Il Times' di fronte al fascismo, 1919-1932," Rivista Storica del Socialismo, 8 (1965): 155-85; Corrado Vivanti, "La stampa francese di fronte al fascismo, 1922-1925," ibid., pp. 52-92. See also Di Nolfo (#703); Milza (#670).

697. Bosmans, Jac. "Ausländische Präsenz in Österreich während des Genfer Sanierungswerkes, 1922-1926," Österreichisches Staatsarchiv Mitteilungen, 34 (1981): 286-332.

Also on the Austrian question, Stefan Malfèr, "Ein österreichisch-italienischer Zwischenfall 1925 ausgelöst durch eine Rede Wilhelm Ellenbogens gegen Mussolini." Risorgimento [Brussels], 1 (1980): 221-33.

698. Breccia, Alfredo. "La politica estera italiana e l'Ungheria, 1922-1933." Rivista di Studi Politici Internazionali, 47 (1980): 93-112.

See also Giorgio Rumi, "Mussolini,'Il Popolo d'Italia' e l'Ungheria, 1918-1922," Storia Contemporanea, 4 (1975): 675-96; R. John Rath, "Mussolini, Bethlen, and the Heimwehr in 1928-1930," in The Mirror of History: Essays in Honor of Fritz Fellner, ed. Solomon Wank et al. (Santa Barbara, CA, 1988). From the Hungarian side, György Réti, "Sulla politica italiana del regime di Horthy," Clio, 22 (1986): 671-82; Maria Ormos, "L'opinione del conte Stefano Bethlen sui rapporti italo-ungheresi, 1927-1931," Storia Contemporanea, 2 (1971): 283-314. See also next entry.

699. Burgwyn, H. James. Il revisionismo fascista: La sfida di Mussolini alle grande potenze nei Balcani e sul Danubio, 1925-1933. Milan, 1979.

Depicts the Duce ready to undermine the post-World War I settlement in order to promote Italian influence in southeastern Europe. Also on Fascist Italy's Balkan and Danubian policies, see Giuliano Caroli, "Un amicizia difficile: Italia e Romania, 1926-1927," Analisi Storica, 2 (1984): 277-316; Luca Riccardi, "Il trattato italo-romeno del 16 settembre 1926," Storia delle Relazioni Internazionali, 3 (1987): 39-72; Constantin Iordan, "La Roumanie et la Yougoslavie face à face à l'Italie fasciste, 1926-1928: Une solidarité défaillante?" Revue des Etudes Sud-Est Européennes, 22/2 (1984): 159-70, and "Antirévisionisme et diplomatie: Nicolae Titulescu chez Benito Mussolini, janvier 1928," in Académie des Sciences Sociales et Poltiques, Nouvelles Etudes d'Histoire (Bucharest, 1985), pp. 253-65. See also Sadkovich, Troebst (#717).

700. Cannistraro, Philip V., and Rosoli, Gianfausto. "Fascist Emigration Policies in the 1920's: An Interpretative Framework." International Migration Review, 13 (1979): 673-92.

701. Carocci, Giampiero. La politica estera dell'Italia fascista, 1925-1928. Bari, 1969.

Well-documented account of the pivotal years of early Fascist diplomacy.

702. Cassels, Alan. Mussolini's Early Diplomacy. Princeton, NJ, 1970.

Challenges the notion of Mussolini as a "good European" in his first five years in office.

703. Di Nolfo, Ennio. Mussolini e la politica estera, 1919-1933. Padua, 1960.

704. Dutton, David. Austen Chamberlain: Gentleman in Politics. Bolton, 1985.

   Also on the Anglo-Italian entente over which Sir Austen presided as foreign secretary, 1925-29, see Life and Letters of Sir Austen Chamberlain, 2 vols., ed. Sir Charles Petrie (London, 1939-40), and articles by Peter G. Edwards: "The Foreign Office and Fascism, 1924-1929," Journal of Contemporary History, 5/2 (1970): 153-61; "The Austen Chamberlain-Mussolini Meetings," Historical Journal, 14 (1971): 153-64; "Britain, Mussolini and the 'Locarno-Geneva System,' " European Studies Review, 10 (1980): 1-16.

705. Fabiano, Domenico. "La Lega Italiana per la tutela degli interessi nazionali e le origini dei Fasci italiani all'estero, 1920-1923." Storia Contemporanea, 16 (1985): 203-50.

706. Heineman, John L. Hitler's First Foreign Minister: Constantin Freiherr von Neurath. Berkeley, CA, 1979.

   Only a brief discussion of Neurath's tenure of Weimar Germany's Rome embassy.

707. Hermon, Elly. "L'Italia di fronte all'occupazione franco-belga della Ruhr, 1923." Storia Contemporanea, 10 (1979): 697-766.

   By the same author, "La crise de l'Entente du mois de novembre 1923 à la lumière des documents diplomatiques italiens," Mélange de l'Ecole Française de Rome, 92 (1980): 663-90.

708. Hoepke, Klaus-Peter. La destra tedesca e il fascismo. Bologna, 1971. Rev. Ital. trans. of Die deutsche Rechte und der italienische Faschismus: Ein Beitrag zum Selbstverständnis und zur Politik von Gruppen und Verbänden der deutschen Rechten, Düsseldorf, 1968.

   Details early Fascist association with a broad spectrum of German right-wing groups, including the Nazis. On the latter, see Silvana Casmirri, "Il viaggio di Mussolini in Germania nel marzo del 1922," Storia e Politica, 12 (1973): 86-112; Karl-Egon Lönne, "Der 'Völkische Beobachter' und der italienischen Faschismus," Quellen und Forschungen aus italienischen Archiven und Bibliotheken, 51 (1971): 539-84; Meir Michaelis, "I rapporti tra fascismo e nazismo prima dell'avvento di Hitler al potere, 1922-1928," Rivista Storica Italiana, 85 (1973): 544-600, and "I nuclei nazisti in Italia e la loro funzione nei rapporti tra fascismo e nazismo nel 1932: La Landesgruppe Italien del partito nazionalsocialista tedesco alla luce di alcuni documenti inediti," Nuova Rivista Storica, 57 (1973): 422-38; Michael Palumbo, "Goering's Italian Exile, 1924-1925," Journal of Modern History, 50 (1978): offprint only. Also Cassels (#702).

FASCIST FOREIGN POLICY

709. Lestz, Michael E. "Chinese Perceptions of Italian Fascism, 1922-1934." Italian Quarterly, no. 93 (1983): 109-20. Ital. trans. "Percezione cinesi del fascismo italiano, 1922-1934," Storia Contemporanea, 15 (1984): 245-61.

710. Manning, A.F. "Reports of the British Embassy in Rome on the Rise of Fascism." Risorgimento [Brussels], 1 (1980): 33-45.

711. Massagrande, Danilo L. Italia e Fiume, 1921-1924: Dal 'Natale di sangue' all'annessione. Milan, 1982.

712. Migone, Gian Giacomo. "La stabilizzazione della lira, la finanza americana e la lira." Rivista di Storia Contemporanea, 2 (1973): 145-85.

713. Minardi, Salvatore. Le trattative Mussolini-Beaumarchais per un accordo italo-francese, 1928-1929. San Scascia, 1982.

   A short but useful monograph.

714. Pizzigallo, Matteo. Mediterraneo e Russia nella politica estera italiana, 1922-1924. Milan, 1983.

   Wide-ranging study that embraces the Corfu crisis, de jure recognition of Soviet Russia, and the search for oil (cf. Pizzigallo #917).

715. Poulain, Marc. "L'Italie, la Yugoslavie, la France et le pacte de Rome, janvier 1924: La comédie de l'accord à trois." Balkan Studies, 16 (1975): 93-116.

716. Rumi, Giorgio. Alle origini della politica estera fascista, 1918-1923. Bari, 1968.

   Perceptive study of the roots of Fascist diplomacy.

717. Sadkovich, James J. Italian Support for Croatian Separatism, 1927-1937. New York, 1987.

   For Fascist Italy's efforts to subvert neighboring Yugoslavia. Similar Mussolinian intrigues in Stefan Troebst, Mussolini, Makedonien und die Mächte, 1922-1930: Die 'Innere Makedonische Revolutionäre Organisation' in der Südosteuropapolitik des fascistischen Italien (Cologne, 1987). See also Salotti (#648).

718. Spindler, Katherina. Die Schweiz und der italienische Faschismus, 1922-1930: Der Verlauf der diplomatischen Beziehungen und die Beurteilung durch das Bürgertum. Basel & Stuttgart, 1976.

719. Zamboni, Giovanni. Mussolinis Expansionspolitik auf dem Balkan: Italiens Albanienpolitik vom I. bis zum II. Tiranapakt im Rahmen des italienisch-jugoslawischen Interessenkonflikts und der

italienischen 'imperialen' Bestrebungen in Südosteuropa. Hamburg, 1970.

See also Marc Poulain, "L'Albanie dans la politique des puissances, 1921-1926," Revue d'Histoire Moderne et Contemporaine, 25 (1978): 530-55; Pastorelli (#652); Rosselli (#676).

The Great Depression and Hitler's Advent: Mussolini's Response

See also Weinberg, vol. 1 (#517) and relevant titles on Anschluss under the Rome-Berlin Axis.

720. Arisi Rota, Arianna. "La politica del 'peso determinante': Nota su un concetto di Dino Grandi." Il Politico, 53/1 (1988): 99-113.

 On Grandi's tenure of the foreign ministry, 1929-32. See also H. James Burgwyn, "Grandi e il mondo teutonico, 1929-1932," Storia Contemporanea, 19 (1988): 197-223, which is based on Grandi's diary.

721. Bloch, Charles. Hitler und die europaïschen Machte, 1933-1934: Kontinuität oder Bruch. Frankfurt, 1966.

 On the key Italo-German issue, see Paolo Polimadei, "Il partito nazionale-socialista NSDAP e la questione dell'Alto Adige, 1933-1936," Venetica, (July-Dec. 1987): 5-51.

722. Brügel, Johann W. "Hitler und Mussolini feilschen um Österreich: Eine Erinnerung an 1934." Die Zukunft (1960), no. 10, pp. 285-90.

723. Clemente, Vincenzo. "La questione austriaca dalla diplomazia del 'Patto a quattro' alla diplomazia della 'Wacht am Brenner.' " Storia e Politica, 4 (1965): 263-303.

 Continued by M. De Vincentiis, "Il problema dell'Austria: Preludio all'Anschluss," ibid., 5 (1966): 66-87, 194-222, 390-424, 564-80.

724. Collotti, Enzo. "Fascismo e Heimwehren: La lotta antisocialista nella crisi della prima repubblica austriaca." Rivista di Storia Contemporanea, 12 (1983): 301-37.

 For Fascist Italy's attempt to control Austria by patronizing the Heimwehr. See also Kerekes (#728); Burgwyn (#781).

725. D'Amoja, Fulvio. Declino e prima crisi dell'Europa di Versailles, 1931-1933. Milan, 1967.

 Important, detailed study based on extensive documentation, including copies of Aloisi's papers (p. 47).

726. Di Roberto, Federico. "La conferenza del disarmo di Ginevra, 1932-1934." Rivista di Studi Politici Internazionali, 25 (1958): 511-84.

727. Giordano, Giancarlo. Il Patto a Quattro nella politica estera di Mussolini. Bologna, 1976.

Compact work but based on wide published and unpublished documentation. Konrad H. Jarausch, The Four Power Pact, 1933 (Madison, WI, 1965), is a solid treatment. For contemporary defences of the Duce's efforts to stabilize the European situation, see Francesco Salata, Il Patto Mussolini: Storia di un piano politico e di un negoziato diplomatico (Verona, 1933); Pietro Quaroni, "Il Patto a Quattro," Rivista di Studi Politici Internazionali, 1 (1934): 49-67; Francesco Jacomini di San Sevino, "Il Patto a Quattro," ibid., 18 (1951): 25-66.

On Franco-Italian relations and the Four-Power Pact, see Emile Roche, "Le pacte à quatre et Henri de Jouvenel," Revue des Deux Mondes (July-Sept. 1978), pp. 577-85; Enrico Serra, "La Francia, l'Italia ed il Patto a Quattro," Affari Esteri, 3 (1971): 138-55.

728. Kerekes, Lajos. Abenddämmerung einer Demokratie: Mussolini, Gombos und die Heimwehr. Vienna, 1966.

On Mussolini's attempt to create an Italo-Austro-Hungarian bloc; prints a number of documents. See also, György Ránki, "Il patto tripartito di Roma e la politica estera della Germania, 1933-1934," Studi Storici, 3 (1962): 343-75.

729. Kindermann, Gottfried-Karl. Hitlers Niederlage in Österreich. Hamburg, 1984. Eng. trans. Hitler's Defeat in Austria, 1933-1934: Europe's First Containment of Nazi Expansionism (Boulder, CO, & London, 1988).

Treatment of the failed Anschluss that Mussolini helped to thwart prints a number of documents. But for more comprehensive accounts, see Gerhard Jagschitz, Der Putsch: Die Nationalsozialisten 1934 in Österreich (Graz, Vienna & Cologne, 1976); Dieter Ross, Dollfuss und Hitler: Die deutsche österreich-Politik, 1933-1934 (Hamburg, 1966).

730. Lopez Celly, Arrigo. "Le origini del patto di non aggressione italo-sovietico del 2 settembre 1933." Storia e Politica, 19 (1980): 71-113.

See also Anne Morelli, "Due missioni techniche italiane in U.R.S.S., 1930-36," Storia Contemporanea, 18 (1987): 731-65.

731. ———. "L'Italia, Barthou e il progetto di una Locarno orientale nel 1934," Storia e Politica, 17 (1978): 48-90, 241-78.

By the same author, "Il fallimento del progetto di una Locarno orientale nel 1934," Rivista di Studi Politici Internazionali, 44 (1977): 235-61.

732. Minardi, Salvatore. Italia e Francia: Alla Conferenza navale di Londra del 1930. Caltanisetta, 1989.

See also Francesco Lefebvre D'Ovidio, "L'Italia e la Conferenza navale di Londra di 1930," Storia e Politica, 17 (1978): 612-62.

733. Mugnaini, Marco. "L'Italia e l'America Latina, 1930-1936: Alcuni aspetti della politica estera fascista." Storia delle Relazioni Internazionali, 2 (1986): 199-244.

Supplement with Ricardo Silva Seitenfus, "Ideology and Diplomacy: Italian Fascism and Brazil, 1935-1938," Hispanic American Historical Review, 64 (1984): 503-34.

734. Pavlowitch, Stevan K. "La Yougoslavie et l'Italie entre les deux guerres: Les conversations Marinkovitch-Grandi, 1930-1931." Revue d'Histoire Diplomatique, 81 (1967): 254-67.

Based on an interview with Yugoslav foreign minister, Marincovič, regarding talks held mainly at the League of Nations, complementing other negotiations conducted by Galli (#292). See also on Italo-Yugoslav relations, H.J. Burgwyn, "Conflict or Rapprochement: Grandi, France, and Its Protegé Yugoslavia," Storia delle Relazioni Internazionali, 3 (1987): 73-98, and Dassovich (#804).

Ethiopia and the League of Nations

See also Bandini (#927); Currey (#588); Kent (#970); Mockler (#938); Salvemini (#975); and under Colonial Questions.

735. Baer, George W. The Coming of the Italian-Ethiopian War. Cambridge, MA, 1967. Ital. trans. La guerra italo-etiopica e la crisi dell'equilibrio europeo, Bari, 1970.

Recommended scholarly account. Continued by G.W. Baer, Test Case: Italy, Ethiopia, and the League of Nations (Palo Alto, CA, 1976).

736. Barker, A.J. The Civilizing Mission: A History of the Italo-Ethiopian War, 1935-1936. London, 1968.

General account, strongest on the military aspect.

737. Barros, James. Betrayal from Within: Joseph Avenol, Secretary-General of the League of Nations, 1933-1940. New Haven, CT, 1969.

See also the same author's study of Avenol's predecessor, Office without Power: Secretary-General Sir Eric Drummond, 1919-1933 (Oxford, 1979). More directly on the Ethiopian affair is J. Barros, Britain, Greece and the Politics of Sanctions: Ethiopia, 1935-1936 (London, 1982).

738. Buccianti, Giovanni. L'egemonia sull'Etiopia, 1918-1923: Lo scontro diplomatico tra Italia, Francia e Inghilterra. Milan, 1977.

For the background and prelude to the Italo-Ethiopian crisis of 1935-36. See also Maria G. Caravaglios, "Le relazioni politiche, economiche e finanziarie tra Etiopia, Italia e Francia all'inizio del XX secolo," Africa [Rome], 34 (1979): 67-103; Antoinette Iadarola, "Ethiopian Admission into the League of Nations: An Assessment of Motives," Journal of African Studies, 8 (1975): 601-22; Peter J. Beck, "Looking to Geneva for Protection against the Great Powers: The Example of Ethiopia in 1925-1926," Genève-Afrique, 19/1: 81-102; Peter G. Edwards, "Britain, Fascist Italy and Ethiopia, 1925-1928," European Studies Review, 4 (1974): 359-74; Giorgio Rochat, "La missione Malladra e la responsibilità della preparazione militare in Africa orientale nel 1926," Risorgimento [Milan], 22/3 (1970): 135-48; Giuseppe Vedovato, Gli accordi italo-etiopici dell'agosto 1928 (Florence, 1956).

739. ———. Verso gli accordi Mussolini-Laval: Il riavvicinamento italo-francese fra il 1931 e il 1934. Milan, 1984.

Important piece of scholarship based partly on the Lancellotti files in ASME. See also Francesco Perfetti, "Alle origini degli accordi Laval-Mussolini: Alcuni contatti italo-francese del 1932 in materia coloniale," Storia Contemporanea, 8 (1977): 638-716, and Lefebvre D'Ovidio (#748).

740. Caroli, Giuliano. "La Romania e il conflitto italo-etiopico, 1935-1936." Rivista di Studi Politici Internazionali, 49 (1982): 243-70.

Based on ASME records and Titulescu papers. See also Antonina Kuzmanova, "La Roumanie face aux actes agressifs de l'Allemagne et de l'Italie, octobre 1935 - mars 1936," Etudes Balkaniques, 13/2 (1977): 5-19; N.Z. Lupu, "Romania and the Italo-Ethiopian Conflict," Analele Universitatii Bucuresti: Istorie, no. 30 (1981): 117-32; George C. Potra, "Romania's Foreign Policy, 1932-1936, and Mussolini's Regime," Romania: Pages of History, 11/2-3 (1986): 190-219. See also Manchev (#750).

741. Chukumba, Stephen U. The Big Powers against Ethiopia: Anglo-French, American Maneuvers during the Italo-Ethiopian Dispute, 1934-1938. Washington, 1977.

A Third World account gives understandable vent to anti-imperialist sentiment. See also Richard Pankhurst, "The Italo-Ethiopian War and

League of Nations Sanctions, 1935-1936," Genève-Afrique, 13 (1974): 5-29.

742. Cialdea, Basileo. "L'impresa etiopica, le sanzioni e l'opinione pubblica italiana," in Trent'anni di storia politica italiana, pp. 277-95. Turin, 1967.

743. Funke, Manfred. Sanktionen und Kanonen: Hitler, Mussolini und der Abessinienkonflikt, 1934-1936. Düsseldorf, 1970.

Authoritative work on a much debated topic. See also Esmonde M. Robertson, "Hitler and Sanctions: Mussolini and the Rhineland," European Studies Review, 7 (1977): 409-31; Germ. trans. "Hitler und die Sanktionen des Völkerbunds: Mussolini und die Besetzung des Rheinlands," Vierteljahrshefte für Zeitgeschichte, 26 (1978): 237-64.

744. Goglia, Luigi. "Un aspetto dell'azione politica italiana durante la campagna d'Etiopia, 1935-1936: La missione del senatore Jacopo Gasparini nell'Amhara." Storia Contemporanea, 8 (1977): 791-822.

See also Alain Rouaud, "Les contacts italo-ethiopiens du printemps 1936 d'après les archives françaises," Africa [Rome], 37 (1982): 400-11.

745. Hardie, Frank M. The Abyssinian Crisis. London, 1974.

Solid, reliable narrative.

746. Highley, Albert E. The Actions of the States Members of the League of Nations in Application of Sanctions against Italy, 1935-1936. Geneva, 1938.

747. Laurens, Franklin D. France and the Italo-Ethiopian Crisis, 1935-1936. The Hague, 1967.

748. Lefebvre D'Ovidio, Francesco. L'intesa italo-francese del 1935 nella poltica estera di Mussolini. Rome, 1984.

Substantial study, privately printed, which employs Grandi's papers, Lancellotti records in ASME (cf. Buccianti, #739). See also A.J. Crozier, "Philippe Berthelot and the Rome Agreements of January 1935," Historical Journal, 26 (1983): 413-22; Salvatore Minardi, "Mussolini, Laval e il désistement della Francia in Etiopia," Clio, 22 (1986): 77-107; Charles O. Richardson, "The Rome Accords of January 1935 and the Coming of the Italian-Ethiopian War," The Historian, 41 (1978): 41-58.

749. Legnani, Massimo. "Sul finanziamento della guerra fascista." Italia Contemporanea, no. 160 (1985): 25-42.

FASCIST FOREIGN POLICY

750. Manchev, Krastjo. "Le conflit italo-ethiopien et l'entente balkanique." Etudes Balkaniques, 22/1 (1986): 42-56.

    A companion piece by Antonia Kuzmanova is "L'aggression de l'Italie fasciste contre l'Ethiopie et les pays balkaniques," ibid., pp. 31-41.

751. Minardi, Salvatore. "L'accordo militare segreto Badoglio-Gamelin del 1935." Clio, 23 (1987): 271-300.

    For the Franco-Italian military pact that followed the Laval-Mussolini agreements. See also Robert J. Young, "Soldiers and Diplomats: The French Embassy and Franco-Italian Relations, 1935-1936," Journal of Strategic Studies, 7 (1984): 74-91; "French Military Intelligence and the Franco-Italian Alliance, 1933-1939," Historical Journal, 28 (1985): 143-68.

752. Mori, Renato. Mussolini e la conquista dell'Etiopia. Florence, 1978.

    Scholarly account based on Italian published and unpublished documents.

753. Parker, R.A.C. "Great Britain, France and the Ethiopian Crisis of 1935-1936." English Historical Review, 89 (1974): 293-332.

754. Procacci, Giuliano. Il socialismo internazionale e la guerra d'Etiopia. Rome, 1978.

755. Quartararo, Rosaria. "L'altra faccia della crisi mediterranea, 1935-1936." Storia Contemporanea, 13 (1982): 759-820.

    On the possibility of a direct Anglo-Italian confrontation. Also on the strategic situation, see Arthur J. Marder, "The Royal Navy and the Ethiopian Crisis of 1935-1936," American Historical Review, 75 (1970): 1327-56; Mariano Gabriele, "Mediterraneo 1935-1936: La situazione militare marittima nella visione britannica," Rivista Marittima, 119/5 (1986): 21-36. See too Chiavarelli (#938).

756. Robertson, Esmonde M. Mussolini as Empire-Builder: Europe and Africa, 1932-1936. London, 1977. Ital. trans. Mussolini fondatore dell'Impero, Bari, 1979.

    Argues that Mussolini's perception of a European balance of power favorable to Italy caused him to launch the Ethiopian venture when he did.

757. Robertson, James C. "The Hoare-Laval Plan." Journal of Contemporary History, 10 (1975): 433-64.

    Further on the Hoare-Laval Plan, see Henderson B. Braddick, "The Hoare-Laval Plan: A Study in International Politics," Review of Politics, 24 (1962): 342-64; Enrico Serra, "Mussolini, l'Etiopia ed un segreto di Sir Samuel Hoare," Nuova Antologia, 478 (Jan.-April

1960): 481-88; Norman Rose, Vansittart: Study of A Diplomat (London, 1978); Aaron L. Goldman, "Sir Robert Vansittart's Search for Italian Co-operation against Hitler, 1933-1936," Journal of Contemporary History, 9/3 (1974): 93-130.

758. Rouad, Alain. "La guerre d'Ethiopie e l'opinion mondiale." Afrique et l'Asie Modernes, no. 156 (1988): 56-61.

759. Sbacchi, Alberto. "Italian Mandate or Protectorate over Ethiopia in 1935-1936." Rivista di Studi Politici Internazionali, 42 (1975): 559-92.

See also by A. Sbacchi, "Towards the Recognition of the Italian Empire: Period 1936-1937," ibid., pp. 52-63; "Legacy of Bitterness: Poison Gas and Atrocities in the Italo-Ethiopian War, 1935-1936," Genève-Afrique, 13 (1974): 30-53.

760. Serra, Enrico. "La questione italo-etiopica alla conferenza di Stresa." Affari Esteri, 9 (1977): 313-39.

See also the same author's "Dalle trattative sul confine meridionale della Libia al baratto sull'Etiopia," Nuova Antologia, 542 (July-Sept. 1980): 164-74.

761. Sullivan, Brian A. "Roosevelt, Mussolini e la guerra d'Etiopia: Una lezione sulla diplomazia americana." Storia Contemporanea, 19 (1988): 85-105.

An older standard work is Brice Harris, The United States and the Italo-Ethiopian Crisis (Palo Alto, CA, 1964).

762. Tillett, Lowell R. "The Soviet Role in League Sanctions against Italy, 1935-1936." American Slavic and East European Review, 15 (1956): 11-16.

763. Toscano, Mario. "Eden a Roma alla vigilia del conflitto italo-etiopico." Nuova Antologia, 478 (Jan.- April 1960): 21-44.

Reprinted in Toscano, Pagine, 2: 133-59 (#528), and as "Eden's Mission to Rome on the Eve of the Italian-Ethiopian Conflict," in Sarkissian, pp. 126-52 (#527).

764. Waley, Daniel P. British Public Opinion and the Abyssinian War. London, 1975.

See also Luigi Goglia, "La propaganda italiana a sostegno della guerra contro l'Etiopia svolta in Gran Bretagna nel 1935-1936," Storia Contemporanea, 15 (1984): 845-908; James C. Robertson, "The Origins of British Opposition to Mussolini over Ethiopia," Journal of British Studies, 9 (1969-70): 122-42, and "The British General Election of 1935," Journal of Contemporary History, 9 (1974): 149-

64; Michael Pugh, "Peace with Italy: B.U.F. Reactions to the Abyssinian War," Wiener Library Bulletin, 27 (1974): 11-18.

The Spanish Civil War

765. Aquarone, Alberto. "La guerra di Spagna e l'opinione pubblica italiana." Il Cannonchiale, nos. 4-6 (1966): 3-36.

For Catholic opinion, see Rumi, Campanini (#974).

766. Attanasio, Sandro. Gli italiani e la guerra di Spagna. Milan, 1974.

Account of Italians on both sides in the war.

767. Catalano, Franco. "La politica europea nei mesi centrali del 1936." Nuova Rivista Storica, 51 (1967): 79-106.

768. Cattell, David. Soviet Diplomacy and the Spanish Civil War. Berkeley, CA, 1957.

See also Luigi Chiodini, Roma o Mosca: Storia della guerra civile spagnola (Rome, 1966).

769. Cortada, James W. "Ships, Diplomacy and the Spanish Civil War: Nyon Conference, September 1937." Il Politico, 37 (1972): 673-89.

On the conference that curbed Italian submarine activity off the Spanish coast. For the British angle, see Peter Gretton, "The Nyon Conference - The Defence Aspect," English Historical Review, 90 (1975): 103-12. See also Frank (#933).

770. Coverdale, John F. Italian Intervention in the Spanish Civil War. Princeton, NJ, 1976. Ital. trans. I fascisti italiani alla guerra di Spagna, Rome-Bari, 1977.

Most authoritative monograph on the subject. See also Leo Valiani, "L'intervento in Spagna," in Trent'anni di storia italiana, 1915-1945, ed. Franco Antonicelli, pp. 214-35 (Turin, 1961).

771. Edwards, Jill. The British Government and the Spanish Civil War, 1936-1939. London, 1979.

On London's unavailing efforts to persuade Fascist Italy to abide by the nonintervention agreement. For British public opinion, see John Foreman, "L'attitude de la Grande Bretagne envers l'Italie et l'Espagne, 1936-1938," Relations Internationales, no. 6 (1974): 147-63.

772. Faldella, Emilio. Venti mesi di guerra in Spagna, luglio 1936 - febbraio 1938. Florence, 1939.

General history of Italian intervention by a participant, with concentration on the military contribution.

773. Graham, Helen, and Preston, Paul, eds. The Popular Front in Europe. London, 1978.

774. Payne, Stanley. Falange: A History of Spanish Fascism. Palo Alto, CA, 1961.

775. Puzzo, Dante A. Spain and the Great Powers, 1936-1941. New York, 1962.

See also Patricia Van der Esch, Prelude to War: The International Repercussions of the Spanish Civil War, 1936-1939 (The Hague, 1951); Willard C. Frank, "The Spanish Civil War and the Coming of the Second World War," International History Review, 9 (1987): 368-409.

776. Thomas, Hugh. The Spanish Civil War, 3d ed. London, 1986.

Best-known English-language account of all aspects of the war. See also Gabriel Jackson, The Spanish Republic and the Civil War (Princeton, NJ, 1965).

777. Vedovato, Giuseppe. "Il non intervento in Spagna, 31 luglio 1936 - 19 aprile 1937." Rivista di Studi Politici Internazionali, 49 (1982): 529-54.

778. Whealey, Robert H. Hitler and Spain: The Nazi Role in the Spanish Civil War, 1936-1939. Lexington, KY, 1989.

Italo-German cooperation in Spain, though limited, served to nourish the Rome-Berlin Axis. Several essays in Der spanische Burgerkrieg in der Internationalen Politik, 1936-1939, ed. Wolfgang Schieder and Christof Dipper (Munich, 1976), also deal with the burgeoning Nazi-Fascist relationship.

The Rome-Berlin Axis

See also Deakin (#891); Hoepke (#708); Weinberg, vol. 2 (#517); and titles on the Alto Adige-South Tyrol under Regional Studies and Early Fascist Diplomacy.

779. Anchiere, Ettore. "Les rapports italo-allemands pendant l'ère nazi-fasciste." Revue d'Histoire de la Deuxième Guerre Mondiale, no. 26 (1975): 1-23.

Synoptic essay. More specific articles by Anchiere based on I documenti diplomatici italiani are: "Dal patto d'acciaio al convegno di Salisburgo," Il Politico, 18 (1953): 54-65; "Dal convegno di Salisburgo alla nonbelligeranza italiana," ibid., 19 (1954): 23-43; and analogous series of articles: "Das grosse Missverständnis des deutsch-italienischen Bündnisses," "Der deutsche 'Bündnisverrat' an Italien," "Italiens Ausweichen vor dem Krieg," <u>Aussenpolitik</u>, 5 (1954): 509-19, 588-95, 653-62.

780. Borgogni, Massimo. <u>I rapporti italo-tedeschi dalla firma del Patto d'Acciaio alla non belligeranza</u>. Siena, 1982.

781. Burgwyn, H. James. "Italy, the Heimwehr, and the Austro-German Agreement of 11 July 1936." <u>Österreichisches Staatsarchiv Mitteilungen</u>, 38 (1985): 305-25.

782. Celovsky, Boris. <u>Das Münchener Abkommen von 1938</u>. Stuttgart, 1958.

Standard scholarly study of the Munich crisis, resolved by Mussolini's eleventh-hour appeal to Hitler. For English-language treatment, see Telford Taylor, <u>Munich: The Price of Peace</u> (Garden City, NY, 1979). A good account how an Italian plan became the Sudeten settlement reached at Munich is in Leonidas E. Hill, "Three Crises, 1938-1939," <u>Journal of Contemporary History</u>, 3/1 (1968): 113-44.

783. D'Amoja, Fulvio. <u>La politica estera dell'impero dall'conquista dell'Etiopia all'Anschluss</u>, 2d ed. Padua, 1967.

Sound, scholarly treatment of the crucial years of Fascist Italy's foreign policy.

784. Dimitrov, Ilco. "L'Italie et la Bulgarie, de Munich au début de la deuxième guerre mondiale," <u>Bulgarian Historical Review</u>, 9/1 (1981): 36-45.

785. Ferretti, Valdo. <u>Il Giappone e la politica estera italiana, 1935-1941</u>. Milan, 1983.

The author's prologue to this important study is "La politica estera italiana e il Giappone imperiale, gennaio 1934 - giugno 1937, <u>Storia Contemporanea</u>, 10 (1979): 873-924. Also by the same author on Italy and Far Eastern affairs, "Il patto cino-sovietico del 21 agosto 1938 e i suoi riflessi nella politica estera italiana," <u>Storia e Politica</u>, 19 (1980): 309-43.

786. Funke, Manfred. "Die deutsch-italienischen Beziehungen: Antibolschewismus und aussenpolitische Interessenkonkurrenz als Strukturprinzip der Achse," in <u>Hitler, Deutschland und die Mächte: Materialien zur Aussenpolitik des Dritten Reiches</u>, ed. M. Funke, pp. 823-46. Düsseldorf, 1976.

787. Israelien, Viktor L., and Kutakov, Leonid N. <u>Diplomacy of Aggression. Berlin-Rome-Tokyo Axis: Its Rise and Fall</u>. Moscow, 1970.

788. Low, Alfred D. The Anschluss Movement, 1931-1938, and the Great Powers. Boulder, CO, 1985.

Scholarly study expressly geared to the international dimension of Anschluss. See also Jürgen Gehl, Austria, Germany and the Anschluss, 1931-1938 (London, 1963); Lajos Kerekes, Anschluss, 1938: Österreich und die internationale Diplomatie, 1933-1938 (Budapest, 1963).

789. Michaelis, Meir. Mussolini and the Jews: German-Italian Relations and the Jewish Question in Italy, 1922-1945. Oxford, 1978. Rev. Ital. trans. Mussolini e la questione ebraica: Le relazioni italo-tedesche e la politica razziale in Italia, Milan, 1982.

The most up-to-date edition of this authoritative work is a Hebrew version published in Jerusalem, 1989. Another magisterial work is Renzo De Felice, Storia degli ebrei italiani sotto il fascismo, 4th ed. (Turin, 1988). Susan Zuccotti, The Italians and the Holocaust: Persecution, Rescue, and Survival (New York, 1987), is both readable and scholarly. On the prelude to Fascist Italian antisemitism, see Sergio I. Minerbi, "Gli ultimi due incontri Weizmann-Mussolini, 1933-1934," Storia Contemporanea, 5 (1974): 431-77; Gene Bernardini, "The Origins and Development of Racial Anti-Semitism in Fascist Italy," Journal of Modern History, 69 (1977): 431-53; see also Preti, Goglia, Del Canuto, Robertson (#899).

With specific reference to antisemitism in Nazi-Fascist relations, Helmut Heiber, "Die deutsche Beeinflussung der Rassenpolitik des faschistischen Italien bis 1943," Gutachten des Instituts für Zeitgeschichte, 2 (1966): 80-92; Reiner Pommerin, "Rassenpolitische Differenzen im Verhältnis der Achse Berlin-Rom, 1938-1943," Vierteljahrshefte für Zeitgeschichte, 27 (1979): 646-60, Ital. trans. "La controversia di politica razziale nei rapporti dell'Asse Roma-Berlino, 1938-1943," Storia Contemporanea, 10 (1979): 925-40; M. Michaelis, "Fascism, Totalitarianism and the Holocaust," European History Quarterly, 19 (1989): 85-103. See too Mayda (#894).

790. Petersen, Jens. Hitler-Mussolini: Die Entstehung der Achse Berlin-Rom, 1933-1936. Tübingen, 1973. Rev. Ital. trans. Hitler e Mussolini: La difficile alleanza, Bari, 1975.

Extremely thorough study that regards a Mussolini-Hitler association as always likely. By the same author, "Vorspiel zum 'Stahlpakt' und Kriegsallianz: Das deutsche-italienische Kulturabkommen vom 23. November 1938," Vierteljahrshefte für Zeitgeschichte, 36 (1988): 41-77.

Also on the antecedents of the Axis, see Meir Michaelis, "Il Conte Galeazzo Ciano di Cortellazo quale antesignano dell'Asse Roma-Berlino: La linea 'germanofilia' di Ciano dal 1934 al 1936 alla luce di alcuni documenti inediti," Nuova Rivista Storica, 61 (1977): 116-49, and "La prima missione del Principe d'Assia presso Mussolini, agosto 1936," ibid., 55 (1971): 367-70; Renato Mori, "Verso il riavvicinamento tra Hitler e Mussolini, ottobre 1935 - guigno 1936," Storia e Politica, 15 (1976): 70-120.

791. Romano Avezzana, Camillo. "Funzione dell'Italia nei rapporti franco-tedeschi." Rassegna di Politica Internazionale, 3 (1936): 859-76.

Former prominent diplomat's vain pleading for Italy to preserve equidistance between the power blocs.

792. Sakmyster, Thomas L. Hungary, the Great Powers, and the Danube Crisis, 1936-1939. Athens, GA, 1980.

Indicates declining Italian influence on the Danube in face of Germany's advance. See also György Réti, "Le relazioni ungaro-italiane dall'Anschluss all'occupazione della Rutenia sub-Carpatica, 1938-1939," Il Politico, 52 (1987): 577-619; M. Musat, C. Popisteaunu, V. Dobrinescu, "The Fascist Vienna Award: An Expression of the Policy of Force," Romania: Pages of History, 12/4 (1987): 168-88.

793. Stuhlpfarrer, Karl. Umsiedlung Südtirol, 1939-1940. Vienna & Munich, 1985.

Authoritative study of proposed resettlement of South Tyrolean Germans. Also on the Alto Adige question in the Axis period, see Conrad F. Latour's still useful Südtirol und die Achse Berlin-Rom, 1938-1945 (Stuttgart, 1962); Renzo De Felice's volume of essays, Il problema dell'Alto Adige nei rapporti italo-tedeschi dall'Anschluss alla fine della seconda guerra mondiale (Bologna, 1973); Veronika M. Rubatscher, Le opzioni del 1939 in Alto Adige (Trent, 1987); Mario Toscano, "Le origini del 'Testamento spirituale' di Hitler per la frontiera del Brennero," Nuova Antologia, 497 (May-Aug. 1960): 315-36, reprinted in Toscano, Pagine, 2: 161-86 (#528).

794. Toscano, Mario. Le origini diplomatiche del Patto d'Acciaio, 2d rev. ed. Florence, 1956. Eng. trans. The Origins of the Pact of Steel, Baltimore, 1967.

Most authoritative work on the subject, based on Italian Foreign Ministry files.

795. Voigt, Klaus. "Gli emigranti in Italia dai paesi sotto la dominazione nazista: Tollerati e perseguitati, 1933-1940." Storia Contemporanea, 16 (1985): 45-87.

By the same author, "Refuge and Persecution in Italy, 1933-1945, " Simon Wiesenthal Center Annual, 4 (1987): 3-64.

796. Watt, D. Cameron. "The Rome-Berlin Axis, 1936-1940: Myth and Reality." Review of Politics, 22 (1960): 519-43.

797. Wiskemann, Elizabeth. The Rome-Berlin Axis, 3d rev. ed. London, 1969.

Once the recognized authority, now somewhat dated; written mainly from German documentation.

The Western Democracies, Their Allies, and Appeasement

See also Rainero (#919), and relevant works under Ethiopia and the League of Nations.

798. Aster, Sidney. 1939: The Making of the Second World War. London, 1973.

On Britain's movement away from appeasement of Nazi Germany and Fascist Italy in the last six months of peace.

799. Binion, Rudolph. Defeated Leaders: The Political Fate of Caillaux, Jouvenel, and Tardieu. New York, 1960.

For Jouvenel's mission to Rome in 1933; see also Shorrock (#819).

800. Bolech Cecchi, Donatella. Non bruciare i ponti con Roma: Le relazioni fra l'Italia, la Gran Bretagna e la Francia dall'accordo di Monaco allo scoppio della seconda guerra mondiale. Milan, 1986.

In effect, continues account of the triangular relationship of Rome, London, and Paris begun by Brundu Olla (next entry) and Bolech Cecchi herself in L'accordo di due imperi: L'accordo italo-inglese del 16 aprile 1938 (Milan, 1977). Both works by Bolech Cecchi heavily documented, conventional political-diplomatic history. Latter volume critical of France for refusing to reach a colonial détente with Fascist Italy; compare indictment of British policy by Lamb (#501) and Quartararo (#814).

801. Brundu Olla, Paola. L'equilibrio difficile: Gran Bretagna, Italia e Francia nel Mediterraneo, 1930-1937. Milan, 1980.

Based on a good array of published and unpublished documents. Contends that France sought a Mediterranean Locarno but that Britain preferred bilateral pacts with Italy - hence the Gentleman's Agreements; see Seton Watson (#818); Bolech Cecchi (previous entry).

802. Centre National de la Recherche Scientifique. Les relations franco-britanniques, 1935-1939. Paris, 1975.

See especially among these papers delivered in London, 1971, and Paris, 1972, D. Cameron Watt, "Britain, France and the Italian problem, 1937-1939," pp. 277-94, and Pierre Renouvin, "Les relations de la Grande Bretagne et de la France avec l'Italie, 1938-1939," pp. 295-318. Both describe British pressure on France to accommodate Italian colonial demands. On the same theme, François Bédarida, "Le gouvernement anglais," in Edouard Daladier, ed. René Rémond and Janine Bourdin (Paris, 1977), pp. 228-40.

803. Costa Bona, Enrica. "La visita del colonello Beck a Roma nel marzo del 1938." Il Politico, 44 (1979): 316-36.

804. Dassovich, Mario. "Involuzioni della politica adriatica da Laval a Stojadinovic, 7 gennaio 1935 - 25 marzo 1938." Rivista Dalmatica, 30 (1983): 59-72.

805. Dilks, David J. "Appeasement and Intelligence," in Retreat from Power, ed. D.J. Dilks, vol. 1, pp. 139-39. London, 1981.

On the Anglo-Italian contest in espionage.

806. Duroselle, Jean-Baptiste. La décadence, 1932-1939. Paris, 1979.

Continued by the same author's L'abîme, 1939-1945 (Paris, 1982). Definitive studies of French diplomacy before and during the Second World War, founded on impressive quantity of archival and published sources.

807. Feiling, Keith. Life of Neville Chamberlain. London, 1946

Since the author had access to Chamberlain's private papers, this is still the best biography of the prime minister bent on appeasing Mussolini, either to detach him from the Axis or to act as a restraint on Hitler. But due to be surpassed by David J. Dilks's Neville Chamberlain in preparation, of which vol. I (Cambridge, 1984) takes the life to 1929.

808. Funderbark, David B. "Nadir of Appeasement: British Policy and the Demise of Albania, April 7, 1939." Balkan Studies, 11 (1970): 299-304.

809. James, Robert Rhodes. Anthony Eden. London, 1987.

Authoritative biography of British foreign secretary at odds with Mussolini, whose resignation, February 1938, elicited joy in Rome. Also Norman Rose, "The Resignation of Anthony Eden," Historical Journal, 25 (1982): 911-31.

810. Lukowitz, David. "George Lansbury's Peace Missions to Hitler and Mussolini in 1937." Canadian Journal of History, 15 (1980): 67-82.

811. MacDonald, Callum A. "Radio Bari and Italian Propaganda in the Middle East and British Counter Measures, 1934-1938," Middle Eastern Studies, 13 (1977): 195-207.

812. Pottecher, Frédéric. Le procès de la défaite: Riom, février-avril 1942. Paris, 1989.

For the accusation that the French Popular Front failed to cultivate Fascist Italy. See also Henri Michel, Le Procès de Riom (Paris, 1979); Joel Colton, Léon Blum: Humanist in Politics (New York, 1966). For the countercharge of French appeasement of Mussolini, consult Geoffrey Warner, Pierre Laval and the Eclipse of France (London, 1968); Shorrock (#819) proffers a modest rehabilitation of Laval.

813. Pratt, Lawrence R. East of Malta, West of Suez: Britain's Mediterranean Crisis, 1936-1939. London, 1975.

Very useful study, documented mainly from cabinet and military records, linking British strategic planning to foreign policy; traces Britain's gradual recognition of Fascist Italy as a potential enemy. In the same vein, Williamson Murray, "The Role of Italy in British Strategy, 1938-1939," Journal of the Royal United Services Institute for Defence Studies, 124/3 (1979): 43-49.

814. Quartararo, Rosaria. Roma tra Londra e Berlino: Politica estera fascista dal 1930 al 1940. Rome, 1980.

On the basis of a wide variety of unpublished and published sources places the blame for the failure to reach an Anglo-Italian entente at London's door. The same debatable proposition is advanced from the British perspective by Lamb (#501).

Also by Quartararo, "Inghilterra e Italia: Dal Patto di Pasqua a Monaco (con un'appendice sul 'canale segreto' italo-inglese)," Storia Contemporanea, 7 (1976): 607-716. Of particular interest is the lengthy appendix, an exegesis on the Dingli memorial found in Grandi's papers (p. 49).

815. Rainero, Romain H. "Le Coup d'Etat de Metaxos et ses échos dans l'Italie fasciste." Revue d'Histoire Moderne et Contemporaine, 35 (1989): 438-49.

816. Rapone, Leonardo. "Le alleanze politiche dell'emigrazione antifascista italiana, 1937-1940." Storia Contemporanea, 19 (1988): 873-934.

817. Schmitz, David F. The United States and Fascist Italy, 1922-1940. Chapel Hill, NC, & London, 1988.

Based on U.S. primary sources and concentrates on the American side of the relationship; demonstrates U.S. complaisance towards Fascist Italy over two decades. So too does John P. Diggins, Mussolini and Fascism: The View from America (Princeton, 1972), Ital. trans. L'America, Mussolini e il fascismo (Bari, 1982), more a study in popular culture and attitudes. See also Philip V. Cannistraro and

Theodore P. Kovaleff, "Father Coughlin and Mussolini: Impossible Allies," Journal of Church and State, 13 (1971): 427-43.

A controversial study of the influence of American capitalism, on the margins of diplomatic history, is Gian Giacomo Migone, Gli Stati Uniti e il fascismo: Alle origini dell'egemonia americana in Italia (Milan, 1980). See also Maurizio Vaudagna, "Il corporativismo nel giudizio dei diplomatici americani a Roma," Studi Storici, 16 (1975): 764-96.

818. Seton Watson, Christopher. "The Anglo-Italian Gentleman's Agreement of January 1937," in The Fascist Challenge and the Policy of Appeasement, ed. Wolfgang J. Mommsen and Lothar Kettenacker, pp. 266-82. London, 1983.

Based on Documents on British Foreign Policy.

819. Shorrock, William I. From Ally to Enemy: The Enigma of Fascist Italy in French Diplomacy, 1920-1940. Kent, OH, 1988.

As the title implies, written from the French side of the Franco-Italian relationship. Well-presented and well-documented study; high point the refroidissement between Rome and Paris, 1936-38.

820. Stafford, P.R. "The Chamberlain-Halifax Visit to Rome: A Reappraisal." English Historical Review, 98 (1983): 61-100.

Analysis of the British failure to impress Mussolini. The same author's "The French Government and the Danzig Crisis: The Italian Dimension," International History Review, 6 (1984): 48-87, concerns Italy's last-ditch mediation overture, which some French, but no British, ministers welcomed.

821. Waterfield, Gordon. Professional Diplomat: Sir Percy Loraine. London, 1973.

Rather pedestrian biography of the last British ambassador to Fascist Italy.

6. The Second World War

See also appropriate titles under Fascist Foreign Policy: The Rome-Berlin Axis, and Military Matters: World War II.

Surveys of World War II

822. Battaglia, Roberto. La seconda guerra mondiale: Problemi e nodi cruciali, 6th ed. Rome, 1971.

Popular general work as is Guido Gigli, La seconda guerra mondiale, 2d ed. (Bari, 1964). Arguably, the best short English-language account of World War II is R.A.C. Parker, Struggle for Survival: The History of the Second World War (London & New York, 1989). See also Wright (#514).

823. Colarizi, Simona. La seconda guerra mondiale e la Repubblica. Turin, 1984.

Vol. 21 in an ongoing series of 23 intended volumes, Storia d'Italia, ed. Giuseppe Galasso. Although general studies, they are compiled in very professional historical way.

824. Collotti, Enzo; Sala, Teodoro; Vaccarino, Giorgio. L'Italia nell'Europa danubiana durante la 2a guerra mondiale. Monza, 1968.

825. De Felice, Renzo, ed. Italia fra tedeschi e alleati: La politica estera fascista e la seconda guerra mondiale. Bologna, 1973.

Broad range of essays.

826. Ferrantini Tosi, F.; Grassi G.; Legnani M., eds. L'Italia nella seconda guerra mondiale e nella resistenza. Milan, 1987.

Includes essays on wartime diplomacy.

827. Neulen, Hans Werner. Eurofaschismus und der Zweite Weltkrieg: Europas verratene Söhne. Munich, 1980. Ital. trans. L'eurofascismo e la seconda guerra mondiale, Rome, 1982.

See also Dino Cofrancesco, "Il mito europeo del fascismo, 1939-1945," Storia Contemporanea, 14 (1983): 5-45.

828. Revue d'Histoire de la Deuxième Guerre Mondiale, no. 92 (Oct. 1973): "L'Italie dans la deuxième guerre mondiale."

Mostly on the Italian home front.

829. Storia Contemporanea, 7/4 (Dec. 1976): "Aspetti e momenti della crisi europea e della seconda guerra mondiale"; 18/6 (1987): "L'Italia nella seconda Guerra Mondiale."

Seven valuable articles all on Italy's international position on the eve of and during World War II, including Quartararo (#814).

830. Toscano, Mario. "Considerazioni sulle origini e vicende diplomatiche della seconda guerra mondiale." Rivista di Studi Politici Internazionali, 22 (1955): 52-94.

A general essay reprinted in Toscano, Pagine, 2: 89-132 (#528).

831. Woodward, E. L. British Foreign Policy in the Second World War, 5 vols. London, 1971.

SECOND WORLD WAR

Since Britain was Italy's principal opponent in World War II and the Mediterranean theater was a British political preserve, this volume in the series of official British histories of the Second World War is very relevant. For the same reasons so are: F.H. Hinsley, et al., British Intelligence in the Second World War, 5 vols. (Cambridge, 1979-90); Randolph S. Churchill and Martin Gilbert, Winston S. Churchill, 8 vols. (London, 1966-88), vols. 6 and 7 for 1939-45.

Italy's Nonbelligerency and Intervention, 1939-1943

832. Aquarone, Alberto. "Lo spirito pubblico in Italia alla vigilia della seconda guerra mondiale." Nord e Sud, 11 (Jan. 1964): 117-25.

On wartime public opinion there is a regional study by Leonida Balestreri, Stampa e opinione pubblica a Genova tra il 1939 e il 1943 (Florence, 1965), and Mario Isnenghi, "Russia e la campagna di Russia nella stampa italiana, 1940-1943," Italia Contemporanea, no. 138 (1980): 25-47.

833. Breccia, Alfredo. Jugoslavia, 1939-1941: Diplomazia della neutralità. Milan, 1978.

An important publication. See also Perich (#852).

834. Browning, Christopher R. The Final Solution and the German Foreign Office: A Study of Referat D III of Abteilung Deutschland, 1940-1943. New York, 1978.

Discusses German pressure on Italy to cooperate in Nazi antisemitic measures in Axis-occupied territories; resisted by, among others, Italian Foreign Ministry officials.

Italian obstruction of the Final Solution in specific countries is recounted in David Carpi, "The Recue of Jews in the Italian Zone of Occupied Croatia," in Rescue Attempts during the Holocaust, ed. Yisrael Gutman and Efraim Zuroff (Jerusalem, 1977), pp. 465-525, which prints a few Italian documents, and "Notes on the History of the Jews in Greece during the Holocaust Period: The Attitude of the Italians, 1941-1943," in Festschriften in Honor of Dr. George S. Wise (Tel Aviv, 1981): 25-62; Michael Marrus and Robert Paxton, Vichy France and the Jews (New York, 1981); Anne Morelli, "Les diplomates italiens en Belgique et la 'Question Juive,' 1938-1943," Bulletin de l'Institut Belgique de Rome (1983-84): 53-54, 357-407. See also Michaelis, De Felice, Zuccotti (#789).

835. Caroli, Giuliano. "I rapporti italo-romeni nel 1940: La visita di Antonescu a Roma." Rivista di Studi Politici Internazionali, 45 (1978): 373-404.

836. Carpi, David. "The Mufti of Jerusalem, Amin El-Husseini, and his Diplomatic Activity during World War II, October 1941 - July 1943," Studies in Zionism, no.7 (1983): 101-32.

For the Mufti's visits to Italy.

837. Catalano, Franco. L'economia di guerra: La politica economico-finanziaria del fascismo della guerra d'Etiopia alla caduta del regime, 1935-1943. Milan, 1969.

An authoritative study. On Italy's limited economic capacity for war, see also Fortunato Minniti, "Il problema degli armamenti nella preparazione militare italiana dal 1935 al 1943," Storia Contemporanea, 9 (1978): 5-61; "La politica industriale del Ministero dell'Aeronautica: Mercato, pianificazione, sviluppo, 1935-1943," ibid., 12 (1981): 271-312; and "Le materie prime nella preparazione bellica dell'Italia, 1935-1943," ibid., 16 (1986): 5-40, 245-76; James J. Sadkovich, "The Development of the Italian Air Force prior to World War II," Military Affairs, 51/3 (1987): 128-36. And on the Axis economic partnership, Angela Raspin, Some Aspects of Italian Economic Affairs, 1940-1943, with Particular Reference to Italian Relations with Germany (New York, 1986).

838. Cavallo, Antonio. "Il movimento per l'indipendenza della Sicilia, 1940-1943," Analisi Storica, 5 (1987): 221-36.

See also Edgar R. Rosen, "Andrea Finocchiaro Aprile und die Anfänge des sizilianischen separatismus, 1941-1943: Zur Innen-und Aussenpolitik eines Regionalproblems im Zweiten Weltkrieg," in Innen-und Aussenpolitik: Primat oder Interdependenz, ed. Urs Altermatt and Judit Garamvölgyi (Bern, 1980), pp. 619-33.

839. Cliadakis, Harry. "Neutrality and War in Italian Policy, 1939-1940." Journal of Contemporary History, vol. 9/3 (1974): 171-90.

Reply by Birdsall S. Viault, "Mussolini et la recherche d'une paix négociée, 1939-1940," Revue d'Histoire de la Deuxième Guerre Mondiale, no. 107 (1977): 1-18. Lynn H. Curtwright, "Great Britain, the Balkans, and Turkey in the Autumn of 1939," International History Review, 10 (1988): 433-55, contends that Mussolini's nonbelligerency, 1939-40, kept Turkey out of war. See also Marzari (#852).

840. De Risio, Carlo. Generali, servizi segreti e fascismo: La guerra nella guerra, 1940-1943. Milan, 1978.

See also Aldo Giambartolomei, "I servizi segreti militare italiani," Rivista Militare, 106/3 (1983): 57-72; Alberto Santoni, "La guerra nel Mediterraneo: Aspetti e momenti dell'attività dei servizi informativi," Analisi Storica, 2 (1984): 125-435.

841. De Robertis, Anton Giulio. Le grande potenze e il confine giuliano, 1941-1947. Bari, 1983.

Also Pierluigi Pallante, Il PCI e la questione nazionale Friuli-Venezia Giulia, 1941-1945 (Udine, 1980). See too Novak (#850).

SECOND WORLD WAR

842. Di Nolfo, Ennio; Rainero, Romain; Vigezzi, Brunello, eds. L'Italia e la politica di potenze in Europa, 1938-1940. Milan, 1985.

843. Herde, Peter. Italien, Deutschland und der Weg in den Krieg im Pacifik, 1941. Wiesbaden, 1983.

    See also Orazio Ciccarelli, "La diplomazia italiana nella guerra del Pacifico," Storia Contemporanea, 17 (1986): 43-66.

844. Knox, MacGregor. Mussolini Unleashed, 1939-1941: Politics and Strategy in Fascist Italy's Last War. Cambridge & New York, 1982. Ital. trans. La guerra di Mussolini, 1939-1941, Rome, 1984.

    Fine study of Italian diplomacy and military strategy from the summer 1939 to New Year 1941, based on an impressive range of source material. Links up the Duce's domestic and foreign policy ambitions in a fashion more fully developed in #571.

845. Linsenmeyer, William S. "Italian Peace Feelers before the Fall of Mussolini." Journal of Contemporary History, 16 (1981): 649-62.

    See too Antonio Varsori, "Italy, Britain and the Problem of a Separate Peace during the Second World War, 1940-1943," Journal of Italian History, 1 (1978): 455-91; "Aspetti della politica inglese verso l'Italia, 1940-1941," Nuova Antologia, 552 (July-Sept. 1983): 271-98. Consult also Lamb (#501).

846. Lukac, Dusan. "Aggression of Italy against Greece and the Consequences of Failure of Italian Expansion." Balkan Studies, 23 (1982): 81-99.

847. Medlicott, W.N. The Economic Blockade, 2 vols. London, 1952.

    Vol. I of this official history for the Allied use of blockade as a means to keep Italy neutral, 1939-40. From the Italian side, see Carlo De Risio, "Aspetti della crisi politico-militare nel 1939-1940: La non belligeranza italiana e il blocco navale anglo-francese," Rivista Marittima, no. 117/4 (1984): 17-35; Gabriele Mariano, "L'Italia nel Mediterraneo fra tedeschi e alleati," ibid., no. 117/12 (1984): 17-36.

848. Mellini Ponce de Leon, Alberto. L'Italia entra in guerra: Gli eventi diplomatici dal 10 gennaio al giugno 1940. Bologna, 1963.

    A former career diplomat reconstructs events from published sources, not his own memory.

849. Miller, James Edward. The United States and Italy, 1940-1950: The Politics and Diplomacy of Stabilization. Chapel Hill, NC, & London, 1986.

    Theme is U.S. motivation and maneuverings between Italy's Right tainted by cooperation with Fascism and the Italian Left dominated by the communists. On this topic, see also Ennio Di Nolfo, "The United States and Italian Communism, 1942-1946: World War II to the Cold War," Journal of Italian History, 1 (1978): 74-94, and Harper (#873).

850. Novak, Bogdan C. Trieste, 1941-1954: The Ethnic, Political, and Ideological Struggle. Chicago, 1970.

Sound scholarly survey of an emotional topic, as is Giampaolo Valdevit, La questione di Trieste, 1941-1954: Politica internazionale e contesto locale (Milan, 1986). All works on Trieste concentrate on the postwar situation. See also De Castro (#868).

851. Pavlowitch, Stevan K., ed. Unconventional Perceptions of Yugoslavia, 1940-1945. New York, 1985.

One of four essays deals with the Duke of Spoleto's "monarchy" in Croatia, 1941-43. See also Gian Nicola Amoretti, La vicenda italo-croata nei documenti di Aimone di Savoia (Rapallo, 1980); Ladislaus Hory and Martin Broszat, Der kroatische Ustascha-Staat, 1941-1945, 2d ed. (Stuttgart, 1965).

852. Perich, Giorgio. Mussolini nei Balcani: I retroscena politici dell'intervento militare italiano in Jugoslavia, Grecia e Albania. Milan, 1966.

Also on Mussolini's Balkan policy, Frank Marzari, "Projects for an Italian-led Balkan Bloc of Neutrals, September-December 1939," Historical Journal, 13 (1970): 767-88; Stevan K. Pavlowitch, "The Balkan Union Agreement of 1942," Storia delle Relazioni Internazionali, 3 (1987): 99-118. See also Breccia (#833).

853. Rosen, Edgar. "Viktor Emanuel III. und die Schweiz während des Zweiten Weltkriegs." Schweizerische Zeitschrift für Geschichte, 10 (1960): 533-49.

854. Sala, Teodoro. "1939-1943: Jugoslavia 'neutrale' e Jugoslavia occupata." Italia Contemporanea, no. 138 (1980): 85-105.

See also Jovan Vujosevič, "L'occupation italienne," Revue d'Histoire de la Deuxième Guerre Mondiale, no. 87 (1972): 33-52; Breccia (#833); Perich (#852).

855. Sebastian, Peter. I servizi segreti speciale britannici e l'Italia, 1940-1945. Rome, 1986.

See too Lamberto Mercuri, ed., Intelligence: Propaganda, missioni e operazioni speciali degli alleati in Italia (Rome, 1979), and Hinsley (#831).

856. Siebert, Ferdinand. Italiens Weg in den Zweiten Weltkrieg. Frankfurt, 1962.

Still a useful account of Italian diplomacy between the Munich Conference and Italy's intervention in World War II.

857. Sierpowski, Stanislaw. "L'Italia e l'aggressione hitleriana alla Polonia nel 1939." Italia Contemporanea, no. 128 (1977): 35-55; Eng. trans. "Italy and the Nazi Aggression on Poland in 1939," Polish Western Affairs, 19 (1978): 34-57.

858. Todorovski, Gilgor. "Le relazioni internazionali fra Italia e Bulgaria negli anni 1941-1943 e il problema nella Macedonia occidentale." Balkanica, 2/1 (1983): 24-43.

859. Toscano, Mario. L'Italia e gli accordi tedesco-sovietici dell'agosto 1939. Florence, 1955.

Complemented by the same author's Una mancata intesa italo-sovietica nel 1940 e 1941 (Florence, 1955). Both works documented from Palazzo Chigi records, and published in revised English-language versions in Toscano, Designs, pp. 48-252 (#528).

Toscano's other studies of Russo-Italian relations, 1939-41, include "La politique russe d'Italie au printemps 1939," Revue d'Histoire de la Deuxième Guerre Mondiale, no. 7 (1952): 1-15, and "L'intervento dell'Italia contro l'Unione Sovietica nel 1941 visto dalla nostra Ambasciata a Mosca," Nuova Antologia, 484 (Jan.-Apr. 1962): 299-312, 445-62, reprinted in Toscano, Pagine, 2: 359-444 (#528).

860. Varsori, Antonio. Gli alleati e l'emigrazione democratica antifascista, 1940-1943. Florence, 1982.

861. Woolf, Stuart J. "Inghilterra, Francia e Italia, settembre 1939 - giugno 1940." Rivista di Storia Contemporanea, 1 (1972): 477-95. Eng. trans. "Britain, France and Italy, September 1939 - June 1940," in Altro Polo: A Volume of Italian Studies, ed. R.J.B. Bosworth and Gianfranco Cresciani, Sydney, 1979, pp. 141-60.

Based on British cabinet papers.

The Armistice of 1943 and the Allies in Italy

See also Deakin (#891); De Felice (#825); Miller (#849).

862. Acciaiolo, Niccolò. "Umberto, luogotenente e re, di fronte al problema internazionale." Rivista di Studi Politici Internazionali, 50 (1983): 183-97.

863. Aga Rossi, Elena. L'Italia nella sconfitta: Politica interna e situazione internazionale durante la seconda guerra mondiale. Naples, 1985.

A half-dozen collected essays on Italian problems, 1943-45, written by an expert in the field.

864. Albònico, Aldo. "La Spagna tra Badolglio e Mussolini, 1943-1945." Nuova Rivista Storica, 49 (1985): 217-76.

Also by Albònico, "La ripresa delle relazioni tra Italia e America Latina dopo il fascismo," Clio, 24 (1988): 435-53.

865. Arcidiacono, Bruno. Le "précédent italien" et les origines de la guerre froide. Brussels, 1984.

Argues that Anglo-American policy in Italy, 1943-45, provided a model for future dealings with Soviet Russia. By the same author, "La politique soviétique en Italie, 1943-1945," Relations Internationales, no. 45 (1986): 35-49; "Gli Alleati e l'armistizio della Romania: Variazioni su un tema italiano," Storia delle Relazioni Internazionali, 4 (1988): 317-54. See also Marco Altherr, "L'armistice italien de 1943 et les origines de la Guerre Froide," Risorgimento [Brussels], 1 (1980): 353-65; Moshe Gat, "The Soviet Factor in British Policy towards Italy, 1943-1945," The Historian, 50 (1988): 535-57; Morozzo della Rocca, Pettracchi (#878).

866. Bertoldi, Silvio. Contro Salò: Vita e morte del Regno del Sud. Milan, 1984.

A standard, reliable account; cf. Bertoldi (#888).

867. Cecace, Paolo. Vent'anni di politica estera italiana, 1943-1963. Rome, 1987.

Scholarly essay. See also Luigi Bonante, "L'Italia nel nuovo sistema internazionale, 1943-1948," Communità, no. 170 (1973): 13-75.

868. De Castro, Diego. La questione di Trieste: L'azione politica e diplomatica italiana dal 1943 al 1954, 2 vols. Trieste, 1981-82.

A comprehensive study. See also Roberto Rabel, "Prologue to Containment: The Truman Administration's Response to the Trieste Crisis of May 1945," Diplomatic History, 10/2 (1986): 141-60; Novak, Valdevit (#850).

869. De Leonardis, Massimo. La Gran Bretagna e la resistenza partigiana in Italia, 1943-1945. Milan, 1988.

For British policy on the future role of Italy's monarchy; the U.S. stand on this issue is found in Carlo Pinzani, "Gli Stati Uniti e la questione istituzionale in Italia, 1943-1946," Italia Contemporanea, no. 134 (1979): 3-44.

870. Ellwood, David W. L'alleato nemico: La politica d'occupazione anglo-americano in Italia, 1943-1946. Milan, 1977. Rev. Eng. trans. Italy, 1943-1945, Leicester & New York, 1985.

Authoritative study based on a good range of primary and secondary sources. Norman Kogan's Italy and the Allies (Cambridge, MA, 1956) is still a most informative survey. See also Lamberto Mercuri, 1943-1945: Gli alleati e l'Italia (Naples, 1975); Fiorenza Fiorentino, La Roma di Charles Poletti, giugno 1944 - aprile 1945 (Rome, 1986).

871. Filippone Thaulero, Giustino. La Gran Bretagna e l'Italia dalla conferenza di Mosca a Potsdam, 1943-1945. Rome, 1980.

Employs papers of the first post-Fascist Italian ambassador to Britain.

872. Garland, Albert N., and Smyth, Howard M. Sicily and the Surrender of Italy. Washington, 1965.

Authoritative account of 1943 armistice negotiations in the official series "The U.S. Army in World War II." Further on the Cassibile armistice: Mario Belardinelli, "L'armistizio di 1943: Problemi politici e diplomatici," Cultura e Scuola, no. 18 (April-June 1979): 113-28; Ennio Di Nolfo, "L'armistizio dell'8 settembre 1943 come problema internazionale," Nuova Antologia, 552 (Oct.-Dec. 1983): 141-54, and "La svolta di Salerno come problema internazionale," Storia delle Relazioni Internazionali, 1 (1985): 5-28; Italy, Stato Maggiore dell'Esercito: Ufficio Storico, Otto Settembre 1943: L'armistizio italiano 40 anni dopo (Rome, 1985), conference papers; Carlo Pinzani, "L'8 settembre 1943: Elementi e ipotesi per un giudizio storico," Studi Storici, 14 (1972): 289-337; Mario Toscano, Dal 25 luglio all'8 settembre: Nuove rivelazioni sugli armistizi fra l'Italia e la Nazioni Unite (Florence, 1966), based on Foreign Relations of the United States, 1943.

873. Harper, John L. America and the Reconstruction of Italy, 1945-1948. New York & Cambridge, 1986. Ital. trans. L'America e la ricostruzione dell'Italia, 1945-1948, Bologna, 1987.

Primarily on post-World War II Italo-American relations, as is Rosaria Quartararo, Italia e Stati Uniti: Gli anni difficile, 1945-1952 (Naples, 1986). See also Ottavio Barié, "La politica italiana verso gli Stati Uniti dalla caduta del fascismo al Patto Atlantico;" Verifiche, 10/4 (1981): 415-36; Ronald L. Filipelli, American Labor and Postwar Italy, 1943-1953 (Palo Alto, CA, 1989).

874. Harris, C.R.S. Allied Military Administration in Italy, 1943-1946. London, 1957.

One of the British official histories of World War II. For an Italian official account of cooperation with the Allied occupation authorities, see next entry.

875. Italy, Stato Maggiore dell'Esercito: Ufficio Storico. I rapporti fra Alleati e Italiani nella cobelligeranza, ed. Loi Salvatore. Rome, 1986.

For both the political and military relationship. See also papers presented at a symposium sponsored by Italy's Ministero della Difesa, La cobelligeranza italiana nella lotta di liberazione dell'Europa, ed. Aldo A. Mola (Rome, 1986). On Italy's uncertain status, 1943-45, Antonio Varsori, " 'Senior' o 'Equal' Partner," Rivista di Studi Politici Internazionali, 45 (1978): 229-60.

876. Lussu, Emilio. La difesa di Roma, new ed. by Gian Giacomo Ortu and Luia Maria Plaisant. Sassari, 1987.

Well-known survey of Italy in the summer of 1943, including the diplomatic scene.

877. Mercuri, Lamberto. Guerra psicologica: La propaganda anglo-americana in Italia, 1942-1946. Rome, 1983.

See also Pietro Cavallo, "America sognata, America desiderata. Mito e immagini: Uso in Italia dal sbarco alla fine della guerra, 1943-1945," Storia Contemporanea, 16 (1985): 1001-42.

878. Morozzo della Rocca, Roberto. La politica estera italiana e l'Unione Sovietica, 1944-1948. Rome, 1985.

See also Giorgio Petracchi, "Le relazioni tra l'Unione Sovietica e il regno del sud: Una riconsiderazione della politica sovietica in Italia, 1943-1944," Storia Contemporanea, 15 (1984): 1171-1206, which includes some documents, and "Russofilia e russophobia: Mito e antimito del'URSS in Italia, 1943-1948," ibid., 19 (1988): 225-47; Salvatore Secchi, "Tra neutralismo ed equidistanza: La politica estera italiana verso l'URSS, 1944-1948," ibid., 18 (1987): 665-712; Mario Toscano, "La ripresa delle relazioni diplomatiche tra l'Italia e l'Unione Sovietica nel corso della seconda guerra mondiale," Communità Internazionale, 1 (Jan. 1962): 34-73, based on Italian Foreign Ministry records and reprinted in Italian and English, respectively, in Toscano, Pagine, 2: 299-358, and Designs, pp. 253-304 (#528).

879. Musso, Carlo. Diplomazia partigiana: Gli alleati, i rifugiati italiani e la delegazione del CLNAI in Svizzera, 1943-1945. Milan, 1983.

On the same topic, Elisa Signori, La Svizzera e i fuorusciti italiani: Aspetti e problemi dell'emigrazione politica, 1943-1945 (Milan, 1983).

880. Pupo, R. La rifondazione della politica estera italiana: La questione giuliana, 1944-1946. Udine, 1979.

See also Guglielmo Salotti, "Il dramma di Fiume nel secondo dopoguerra," Storia Contemporanea, 14 (1983): 47-65; Coceani (#890); Stuhlpfarrer (#897).

881. Serra, Enrico. La diplomazia italiana e la ripresa dei rapporti con la Francia, 1943-1945. Milan, 1984.

Vol. 2 of Italia e Francia, 1939-1945 (#591) illuminates the work of Secretary General Prunas. See also Mario Toscano, "La ripresa delle relazioni diplomatiche fra l'Italia e la Francia nel corso della seconda guerra mondiale," Storia e Politica, 1 (1962): 523-604, reprinted in Pagine, 2: 359-444, and Designs, pp. 305-72 (#528).

882. ———. "La politica estera dei governi Bonomi, 1944-1945." Il Politico, 52 (1987): 473-84.

883. Smith, Bradley F., and Aga Rossi, Elena. Operation Sunrise: The Secret Surrender. London & New York, 1979.

Good account of the surrender of German forces in Italy, 1945. Also on this subject, Ennio Di Nolfo, "L'operazione 'Sunrise': Spunti e documenti," Storia e Politica, 14 (1975): 345-76, 501-22; Jon Kimche, Spying for Peace: General Guisan and Swiss Neutrality (London, 1961).

884. Visconti Venosta, Giovanni. "La politica estera della liberazione nel 1944 e 1945." Movimento di Liberazione in Italia, no. 48 (1957): 52-57.

885. Warner, Geoffrey. "Italy and the Powers, 1943-1949," in The Rebirth of Italy, 1943-1950, ed. Stuart J. Woolf, pp. 30-56. London, 1972. Ital. trans. "L'Italia e le potenze alleate," in L'Italia 1943-1950: La ricostruzione, Bari, 1974, pp. 49-85.

See also Ennio Di Nolfo, "Problemi della politica estera italiana, 1943-1950." Storia e Politica, 14 (1975): 295-317; Pierre Guillen, "La reinsertion internationale de l'Italie après la chute du fascisme, 1943-1947," Relations Internationales, no. 31 (1982): 333-49.

886. Woller, Hans, ed. Italien und die Grossmächte, 1943-1945. Munich, 1988.

See particularly Jens Petersen, "Sommer 1943," pp. 23-48; James E. Miller, "Der Weg zu einer 'Special Relationship': Italien und die Vereinigten Staaten, 1943-1947," pp. 49-68.

The Salò Republic

887. Annali della Fondazione Luigi Micheletti, vol. 2: La Repubblica Sociale Italiana, 1943-1945, ed. Pier Paolo Poggio. Brescia, 1986.

Papers delivered at a 1985 conference in Brescia include studies of Salò's relationship with Nazi Germany.

888. Bertoldi, Silvio. Salò: Vita e morte della Repubblica Sociale Italiana, 3d ed. Milan, 1978.

Best general account, based in part on primary sources. Another recommended survey is Giorgio Bocca, La repubblica di Mussolini, 2d ed. (Bari, 1977).

889. Caudana, Mino. Processo a Mussolini, 3 vols. Rome, 1964.

Report on the Verona trials, 1944, including that of Ciano.

890. Coceani, Bruno. Mussolini, Hitler, Tito alle porte orientali d'Italia. Bologna, 1948.

Origins of the postwar Trieste problem from the Salò perspective. See also Novak, Valdevit (#850); De Castro (#868); Stuhlpfarrer (#897).

891. Deakin, F. William. The Brutal Friendship: Hitler, Mussolini and the Fall of Fascism. London, 1962.

Magisterial, definitive study of the two final years of the Axis based largely on the files of the Segreteria Particolare del Duce (p. 42). Revised edition of part 1 dealing with Mussolini's fall in 1943 published as The Brutal Friendship (Harmondsworth & New York, 1966); revised editions of part 3 on the Salò years as The Last Days of Mussolini (Harmondsworth, 1966), and The Six Hundred Days of Mussolini (New York, 1966).

892. Kuby, E. Verrat auf Deutsch: Wie das Dritte Reich Italien ruinierte. Hamburg, 1982.

893. Lazzero, Ricciotto. Le SS italiane. Milan, 1982.

Twenty thousand Italians enrolled.

894. Mayda, Giuseppe. Ebrei sotto Salò: La persecuzione antisemitica, 1943-1945. Milan, 1978.

Further on Nazi antisemitism in Italy, Liliana Picciotti Fargion, ed., L'occupazione tedesca e gli ebrei di Roma (Rome, 1979), which includes some documentation. See also De Felice, Zuccotti (#789).

895. Rumi, Giorgio. Il Cardinale Schuster e il suo tempo. Milan, 1979.

On the clerical intermediary amongst German Nazis, Italian Fascists, Allies, and partisans at the close of World War II; appendices of documents.

896. Schröder, Josef. Italiens Kriegsaustritt 1943. Die deutschen gegenmassnahmen in italienischen Raum: Fall 'Alarich' und 'Achse.' Göttingen, 1969.

By the same author, "La caduta di Mussolini e le contromisure tedesche nell'Italia centrale fino alla formazione della Repubblica Sociale Italiana," Storia Contemporanea, 3 (1972): 813-45. See also

Jens Petersen, "Deutschland und der Zusammenbruch des Faschismus in Italien im sommer 1943," Militärgeschichtliche Mitteilungen, no. 37 (1985): 51-69.

897. Stuhlpfarrer, Karl. Die Operationszonen 'Alpenvorland' und 'Adriatisches Küstenland,' 1943-1945. Vienna, 1969. Ital. trans. Le zone d'operazione prealpi e litorale adriatico, 1943-1945, Gorizia, 1979.

Describes the virtual German annexation, 1943-45, of areas gained by Italy in the post-World War I settlement. On the same subject, Mario Toscano, "La controversia tra Salò e Berlino per l'occupazione nazista e per le decisioni annessionistiche di Hitler dell'Alto Adige e del Trentino nei documenti diplomatici della Repubblica Sociale Italiana," Storia e Politica, 6 (1967): 1-59.

7. Colonial Questions

Imperialist Theories and Surveys

898. Goglia, Luigi. "Sulla politica coloniale fascista." Storia Contemporanea, 19 (1988): 35-53.

In the same vein, Marco Palla, "L'imperialisme fasciste," Revue d'Histoire de la Deuxième Guerre Mondiale et des Conflits Contemporaines, no. 139 (1985): 25-46.

899. Preti, Luigi. Impero fascista, africani ed ebrei. Milan, 1968.

Links the expansion of Italy's African empire with the Fascist adoption of racism; has an extensive documentary appendix. See also Luigi Goglia, "Note sul razzismo coloniale fascista," Storia Contemporanea, 19 (1988): 1223-66; Francesco Del Canuto, "I Falascia fra politica antisemita e politica razziale," ibid., 1267-85; Esmonde M. Robertson, "Race as a Factor in Mussolini's Policy in Africa and Europe," Journal of Contemporary History, 23 (1988): 37-58.

900. Rossi, Gianluigi. L'Africa italiana verso l'independenza, 1941-1949. Milan, 1980.

Based on British records.

901. Rumi, Giorgio. " 'Revisionismo' fascista ed espansione coloniale, 1925-1935." Movimento di Liberazione in Italia, no. 80 (1965): 37-73.

See also Francesco Perfetti, "Il mito imperialista ed il nazionalismo italiano," Storia e Politica, 10 (1971): 98-111; Salvatore Sechi, "Imperialismo e politica fascista, 1882-1939," Problemi del Socialismo, 14 (1972): 766-96.

902. Seton Watson, Christopher. "Italy's Imperial Hangover." Journal of Contemporary History, 15 (1980): 169-79.

903. Terracciano, Carlo. La via imperialista del nazionalismo italiano. Saluzzo, 1982.

904. Zaghi, Carlo. La conquista dell'Africa: Studi e ricerche, 2 vols. Naples, 1985.

   Italian colonialism placed in the context of European imperialism at large, but limited discussion of 1918-45 period. See also C. Zaghi, L'Africa nella coscienza europea e l'imperialismo italiano (Naples, 1973).

Colonial Episodes

The diplomatic aspect of the Ethiopian affair is dealt with under Fascist Foreign Policy, and its military dimension under Military Matters. See also Clodomiro (#622); De Felice (#664); Kent (#970); Minerbi (#634); Segrè (#563).

905. Albònico, Aldo. "L'Italia e il mondo iberico nel primo dopoguerra: Velleità coloniali ed economiche, 1919-1923." Nuova Rivista Storica, 66 (1982): 83-132.

906. Borsa, Giorgio. "Tentativi di penetrazione dell'Italia fascista in Cina, 1932-1937." Il Politico, 44 (1979): 381-419.

   See also Roberto Bertinelli, "Note sulla presenza economica italiana in Cina dal 1900 al 1922," Atti dell'Academia Lincea, 39/5-6 (1984): 199-212; Valeria Pastore, "La presenza italiana in Cina nei primi anni Venti," Analisi Storica, 4 (1986): 281-90; Giacomo De Antonellis, "L'Italia in Cina nel secolo XX," Mondo Cinese, 5/3 (1977): 51-58.

907. Ceva, Lucio. Africa settentrionale 1940-1943 negli studi e nella letteratura. Rome, 1982.

   Semi-bibliographical consideration of Italian- and English-language writings on the subject.

908. Clodomiro, Vanni. Libia ed Etiopia nella politica coloniale italiana, 1918-1919. Catanzaro, 1986.

909. Del Boca, Angelo. Gli italiani in Africa orientale, 4 vols. Rome, 1976-84.

   Massive volumes packed with factual information on all aspects of the subject. Complemented by the same author's Gli italiani in Libia, 2 vols. (Bari, 1988).

910. Evans-Pritchard, Edward. Colonialismo e resistenza religiosa nell'Africa settentrionale: I Senussi della Cirenaica. Catania, 1979,

A mix of history and anthropology. See also Cesira Filesi, "Giovanni Amendola, Ministro delle Colonie, e la questione cirenaica, febbraio-ottobre 1922," Rivista di Studi Politici Internazionali, 44 (1977): 77-105, and "La Tripolitania nella politica coloniale di Giovanni Amendola," Africa [Rome], 32 (1977): 517-42; Giorgio Rochat, "La repressione della resistenza araba in Cirenaica nel 1930-1931, nei documenti dell'Archivio Graziani," Movimento di Liberazione in Italia, no. 110 (1973): 3-39;

911. Filesi, Cesira. "Progetti italiani di penetrazione economica nel Congo belga, 1908-1922." Storia Contemporanea, 13 (1982): 251-82.

912. Giglio, Carlo. "La questione del Lago Tana, 1902-1941." Rivista di Studi Politici Internazionali, 19 (1952): 643-86.

See also Giampaolo Calchi Novati, "L'annessione dell'Oltregiuba nella politica coloniale italiana," Africa [Rome], 40 (1985): 400-26.

913. Hess, Robert L. Italian Colonialism in Somalia. Chicago, 1966.

914. Le Houërou, Fabienne. "Des oubliés de l'histoire: Les 'ensablés' en Ethiopie." Revue d'Histoire Moderne et Contemporaine, 36 (1989): 153-65.

915. Negash, Tekeste. Italian Colonialism in Eritrea, 1892-1941: Politics, Praxis and Impact. Uppsala, 1987.

See also Michel Perret, "L'Erythrée, le fascisme et la crise," in Modern Ethiopia from the Accession of Menelik II to the Present, ed. Joseph Tubiana (Rotterdam, 1980), pp. 351-75; Irma Taddia, "Sulla politica della terra nella Colonia Eritrea, 1890-1950," Rivista di Storia Contemporanea, 13 (1984): 42-78.

916. Orlandi, Rosita. "L'occupazione italiane di Rodi e del Dodecanese." Storia e politica, 21 (1982): 1-30.

917. Pizzigallo, Matteo. Alle origini della politica petrolifera italiana, 1920-1925. Milan, 1981.

Continued by M. Pizzigallo, L'AGIP degli anni ruggenti, 1926-1932 (Milan, 1984). The quest for oil lay behind much Italian expansionist policy, especially in Albania and the Middle East. See also Richard A. Webster, "Una speranza rinviata: L'espansione industriale italiane e il problema del petrolio dopo la prima guerra mondiale," Storia Contemporanea, 11 (1980): 219-81.

918. Quartararo, Rosaria. "L'Italia e lo Yemen: Uno studio sulla politica di espansione italiana nel Mar Rosso, 1923-1937." Storia Contemporanea, 10 (1979): 811-72.

919. Rainero, Romain. La rivendicazione fascista sulla Tunisia. Milan, 1978.

On the same topic, Mario Toscano, Appunti sulla questione tunisiana (Florence, 1939), and "La liquididazione della questione tunisiana," Nuova Antologia, 486 (Sept.-Dec. 1962): 3-23, 145-76; Guido Valabrega, "Quelques aspects de la politique italienne en Afrique du Nord," Cahiers de Tunisie, 29/3-4 (1981): 649-55. See too Bessis (#657).

920. ———. "La guerre du Levant français vue à partir d'une source italienne: Le tèmoignage de la Commission italienne d'armistice avec la France." Mondes et Cultures, 45/3 (1985): 473-91.

921. Santarelli, Enzo. "Guerra d'Etiopia, imperialismo e terzo mondo." Movimento di Liberazione in Italia, no. 97 (1969): 35-51.

See also Giuliano Procacci, "Il mondo arabo e l'aggressione italiana all'Etiopia," in Annali dell'Istituto Giangiacomo Feltrinelli, 22 (1982): 229-66; Laila Morsy, "The Effects of Italy's Expansion Policy on Anglo-Egyptian Relations in 1935," Middle Eastern Studies, 20 (1984): 206-31.

922. Sbacchi, Alberto. Ethiopia under Mussolini: Fascism and the Colonial Experience. London, 1985.

Most scholarly account of Fascist Italy's administration of its conquest. See also Michael Palumbo, "The Italian Fascist Suppression of the Ethiopian National Resistance," in Nationalism: Essays in Honor of Louis L. Snyder, ed. M. Palumbo and W.O. Shanahan (Westport, CA, 1981), pp. 193-204; Richard Pankhurst, "The Secret History of the Italian Fascist Occupation of Ethiopia, 1935-1941," Africa Quarterly, 16/4 (1977): 35-86; Giorgio Rochat, "L'attentato a Graziani e la repressione italiana in Etiopia nel 1936-1937," Movimento di Liberazione in Italia, no. 118 (1975): 3-38.

923. Schröder, Josef. "Die Beziehungen der Achsenmächte zur arabischen Welt," in Hitler, Deutschland und die Mächte: Materialien zur Aussenpolitik des Dritten Reiches, ed. Manfred Funke, pp. 365-82. Düsseldorf, 1976.

924. Segrè, Claudio. Fourth Shore: The Italian Colonization of Libya. Chicago, 1974. Ital. trans. Italia in Libya: Dall'età giolittiana a Gheddafi, Milan, 1978.

Excellent scholarly monograph, in contrast to Eric Salerno's sensationalist Genocide in Libia: Le atrocità nascoste dell'avventura coloniale, 1911-1931 (Milan, 1980). See also Italo Persegani, "Per un riesame della politica economica italiana in Libia, 1920-1940," Nuova Rivista Storica, 65 (1981): 572-87.

925. Sofri, Gianni. Gandhi in Italia. Bologna, 1988.

On his visit in 1931 the Indian leader met Mussolini but not the Pope. See also Mario Prayer, "Gandhi e il nazionalismo indiano nella

COLONIAL QUESTIONS

        pubblicista del regime fascista, 1921-1938," Storia Contemporanea, 19 (1988): 55-83.

926.   Strika, Vincenzo. "Il mancato viaggio di re Faysal I in Italia: Rapporti italo-iracheni, 1929-1933." Storia Contemporanea, 15 (1984): 371-98.

        By the same author, "Le relazioni tra l'Italia e il Hijàz, 1916-1925," ibid., 20 (1989): 177-95.

8. Military Matters

General and Miscellaneous Military Studies

Military history is comprehended in some titles under Fascist Diplomacy: Ethiopia and the Spanish Civil War. See also Millett and Murray (#525); Pieri and Rochat (#560); Watt (#529).

927.   Bandini, Franco. Gli italiani in Africa: Storia delle guerre coloniali, 1882-1943. Milan, 1971.

928.   Botti, Feruccio, and Ilari, Virgilio. Il pensiero militare italiano dal primo al secondo dopoguerra. Rome, 1985.

        On the same subject, John Gooch, "Clausewitz Disregarded: Italian Military Thought and Doctrine, 1815-1943," Journal of Strategic Studies, 9 (1986): 303-24.

929.   Buccianti, Giuseppe. Generali della dittatura. Milan, 1987.

930.   Ceva, Lucio. Le forze armate. Turin, 1981.

        A very good politico-cultural treatment.

931.   De Biase, Corrado. L'Aquila d'Oro: Storia dello Stato Maggiore Italiano, 1861-1945. Milan, 1970.

        Also on the general staff, see Lucio Ceva, "Appunti per una storia dello Stato Maggiore generale fino alla vigilia della 'non belligeranza,' giugno 1925 - luglio 1939," Storia Contemporanea, 10 (1979): 207-52; "Aspetti politici e giuridici dell'alto commando militare in Italia, 1848-1941," Il Politico, 49 (1984): 81-120; and #946.

932.   Della Volpe, Nicola. Difesa del territorio e protezione antiarea, 1915-1943: Storia, documenti, immagini. Rome, 1986.

        A publication of the Italian army's historical office. See also Santoro (#960).

933.   Frank, Willard C. "Naval Operations in the Spanish Civil War." Naval War College Review, 37 (Jan.-Feb. 1984): 24-55.

934. Italy, Stato Maggiore dell'Esercito: Ufficio Storico. L'esercito italiano nel primo dopoguerra, 1918-1920, ed. Vincenzo Gallinari. Rome, 1920.

See also Giorgio Rochat, "Alcuni dati sulla occupazione militare adriatiche durante il governo Nitti," Risorgimento [Milan], 18/1 (1966): 29-45.

935. ———. Le truppe italiane in Albania: Anni 1914-1920 e 1939. Rome, 1978.

936. ———. L'esercito italiano tra la prima e la seconda guerra mondiale, 1918-1940. Rome, 1954.

Supplemented by L'esercito italiano alla vigilia della seconda guerra mondiale (Rome, 1957).

937. ———. Un secolo di relazioni militari tra Italia e Svizzera, 1861-1961, ed. A. Rovighi. Rome, 1987.

938. Mockler, Anthony. Haile Selassie's War: The Italian Ethiopian Campaign, 1935-1941. London & New York, 1985.

Best account of continuous fighting in Ethiopia over six years. See also Angelo Del Boca, La guerra d'Abissinia (Milan, 1965); Eng. trans. The Ethiopian War, 1935-1941 (Chicago, 1969). On the naval and aerial aspects of the conquest of Ethiopia, Emilia Chiavarelli, L'opera della marina italiana nella guerra italo-etiopica (Milan, 1969); Guido Matteoli, L'aviazione fascista e la conquista dell'impero (Rome, 1939); Giorgio Rochat, "L'impiego dei gas nella guerra d'Etiopia, 1935-1936," Rivista di Storia Contemporanea 17/1 (1988): 74-109. See also Sbacchi (#922).

939. Rochat, Giorgio, and Massobrio, Giulio. Breve storia dell'esercito italiano dal 1861 al 1943. Turin, 1978.

Reliable survey. Also by G. Rochat, L'esercito italiano da Vittorio Veneto a Mussolini, 1919-1925 (Bari, 1967); "L'esercito e il fascismo," in Fascismo e società italiana, ed. Guido Quazza (Turin, 1973), pp. 89-123.

940. Schreiber, Gerhard. Revisionismus und Weltmachtstreben: Marineführung und deutsch-italienische Beziehungen, 1919-1941. Stuttgart, 1978.

Analogously by the same author, "Italia im Machtpolitischen Kalkül des deutschen Marineführung 1918 bis 1945," Quellen und Forschungen aus italienischen Archiven und Bibliotheken, 62 (1982): 229-69. See also Hans Meier-Welcker, "Zur deutsch-italienischen Militärpolitik und Beurteilung der italienischen Wehrmacht vor dem Zweiten Weltkrieg," Militärgeschichtliche Mitteilungen, 1 (1970): 59-93; Lucio Ceva, "Altre notizie sulle conversazioni italo-tedesche alla vigilia della seconda guerra mondiale, aprile-giugno 1939," Risorgimento [Milan], 30 (1978): 151-82; Mario Toscano, "Le conversazioni militari italo-tedesche alla vigilia della seconda guerra mondiale," Rivista Storica Italiana, 64 (1952): 336-82. On Axis military planning during the Second World War, see Ceva (#945); Schreiber (#963).

941. Sweet, John. Iron Arm: The Mechanization of Mussolini's Army, 1920-1940. Westport, CA, 1980.

Useful technical study. A broader approach is Brian R. Sullivan, A Thirst for Glory: Mussolini and the Italian Military, 1920-1936 (Cambridge & New York, forthcoming). See also U. Barlozetti and A. Pirella, Mezzi dell'esercito italiano, 1935-1945 (Florence, 1986).

Italy's Armed Forces in World War II, 1940-1943

Needless to say, several titles listed above under Fascist Diplomacy and the Second World War include military historical content.

942. Andò, Elio, and Bagnasco, Erminio. Navi e marinari italiani nella seconda guerra mondiale, 2d ed. Parma, 1981.

The inquest on Italy's naval performance in World War II continues. See, for example, Marc'Antonio Bragadin, Il dramma della marina italiana, 1940-1945 (Milan, 1982); Luis De La Sierra, La guerra navale nel Mediterraneo (Milan, 1987); Gianni Rocca, Fucilate gli ammiragli (Milan, 1987); Lamberto Mercuri, "Il processo come testimonianza di storia: L'occupazione tedesca dell'Egeo e il processo e la reabilitazione degli ammiragli italiani," Storia e Civiltà, 3 (Sept.-Dec. 1987): 234-61. See also Sadkovich (#958).

943. Bernardi, Giovanni. La Marina, gli armistizi e il trattato di pace, settembre 1943 - dicembre 1951. Rome, 1979.

Politico-naval study that prints documents from Italian naval archives.

944. Carver, Michael. Dilemmas of the Desert War: A New Look at the Libyan Campaign, 1940-1942. London, 1986; Bloomington, IN, 1987.

Useful one-volume treatment of North African campaigns on which the Ufficio Storico of the Stato Maggiore dell'Esercito has published many volumes (#952).

945. Ceva, Lucio. "L'incontro Keitel-Badoglio del novembre 1940 nelle carte del generale Marras." Risorgimento [Milan], 29 (1977): 1-44.

By the same author, "Vertici politici e militari nel 1940-1943: Interrogativi e temi d'indagine," Il Politico, 46 (1981): 691-700.

946. ———. La condotta italiana della guerra: Cavallero e il comando supremo, 1941-1942. Milan, 1975.

Also on Italy's high command in World War II, see Italy, Stato Maggiore dell'Esercito: Ufficio Storico, Problema dell'alto comando dell'esercito italiano dal Risorgimento al Patto atlantico (Rome, 1985); Howard M. Smyth, "The Command of the Italian Armed Forces in World War II," Military Affairs, 15 (1951): 38-52; Luigi Bertinaria, "Gli armistizi del 1943: Il comando supremo e il Stato maggiore dell'esercito," Rivista Militare, 107/4 (1984): 75-87.

947. Davis, Melton S. Who Defends Rome? The Forty-Five Days, July 25 - September 8, 1943. New York & London, 1972.

Also on Rome in World War II, Raleigh Trevelyan, Rome '44: The Battle for the Eternal City (London, 1981; New York, 1982), Ital. trans. Roma '44 (Milan, 1983).

948. Ellwood, David W. "Al tramonto dell'impero britannico: Italia e balcani nella strategia inglese, 1942-1946." Italia Contemporanea, no. 134 (1979): 73-91.

949. Harvey, Stephen. "The Italian War Effort and the Strategic Bombing of Italy." History, 70 (1975): 32-45.

950. Italy, Marina Militare: Ufficio Storico. La marina italiana nella seconda guerra mondiale, 20 vols. and supplements. Rome, 1950- .

A continuing series of supplementary studies.

951. Italy, Stato Maggiore dell'Esercito: Ufficio Storico. La campagna di Grecia, 3 vols. Rome, 1980.

Official history of a disastrous campaign. Mario Cervi's Storia della guerra in Grecia (Milan, 1965), Eng. trans. The Hollow Legions: Mussolini's Blunder in Greece, 1940-1941 (New York, 1971) is a popular account with documentary appendix; a new ed. (1986) prints fewer documents.

The Greek campaign led on to Operazioni della unità italiane in Jugoslavia, 1941-1943 (Rome, 1978), also published by the army's Ufficio Storico.

952. ———. Guerra in Africa orientale, giugno 1940 - novembre 1941. Rome, 1952.

There are numerous Italian official histories of the campaigns in North Africa; see also Carver (#944).

953. ———. Le operazioni della unità italiana al fronte russo, 1941-1943. Rome, 1977.

Another official military publication on the wartime relationship with Russia is Italia nella relazione ufficiale sovietica sulla seconda guerra mondiale (Rome, 1978). See also Lucio Ceva, "Le operazioni militari italiane al fronte russo, 1941-1943," Risorgimento [Milan], 29 (1977): 171-80; "La campagna di Russia nel quadro strategico della guerra fascista," Il Politico, 44 (1979): 420-46.

954. ———. Unità ausilarie dell'esercito italiano nella guerra di liberazione. Rome, 1977.

Also from the army's historical office, "L'esercito italiano nella lotta per la liberazione," Rivista Militare, 107/6 (1984): 73-82. See too Loris Rizzi, "L'esercito italiano nella guerra di liberazione: Appunti e ipotesi per la ricerca," Italia Contemporanea, no. 135 (1979): 53-81. See also from the Italian army's historical office #875.

955. Pansa, Giampaolo. L'esercito di Salò nei rapporti riservati della Guardia nazionale repubblicana, 1943-44. Milan, 1969.

956. Playfair, I.S.O., et al. The Mediterranean and the Middle East, 6 vols. London, 1954-88.

Volumes in the series of official U.K. military histories of World War II, although they should be supplemented with Ralph Bennett, Ultra and Mediterranean Strategy (New York, 1989). For Italy's official account of naval operations in the Mediterranean, see Italy, Marina Militare (#950).

957. Rochat, Giorgio. "Mussolini, chef de guerre, 1940-1943." Revue d'Histoire de la Deuxième Guerre Mondiale, no. 100 (1975): 43-66.

Other articles on World War II by this prolific military historian include: "Appunti sulla direzione politico-militare della guerra fascista, 1940-1943," Belfagor, 32 (1977): 7-30; "Lo sforzo bellico, 1940-1943: Analisi di un sconfitta," Italia Contemporanea, no. 160 (1985): 7-24; "La crisi delle forze armate italiane nel 1943-1945," Rivista di Storia Contemporanea, 7 (1978): 398-40.

958. Sadkovich, James J. "Understanding Defeat: Reappraising Italy's Role in World War II." Journal of Contemporary History, 24 (1989): 27-61.

By the same author, "Re-evaluating Who Won the Italo-British Naval Conflict, 1940-1942," European History Quarterly, 18 (1988): 455-71.

959. Santoni, Alberto. Il vero traditore. Rome, 1981.

A scheme by anti-Fascist Italian naval officers to sell some of Italy's fleet to the British in 1941. See also Peter Tennant, "How We Failed to Buy the Italian Navy," Intelligence and National Security, 3 (1988): 141-61.

960. Santoro, Giuseppe. L'aeronautica italiana nella seconda guerra mondiale, 2d ed., 2 vols. Rome, 1957.

961. Scala, Edoardo. La riscossa del esercito. Rome, 1948.

   The Italian army's authorized explanation of defeat.

962. Schreiber, Gerhard. Die italienischen Militärinternierten im deutschen Machtbereich, 1943-1945. Munich, 1989.

   See too Lutz Klinkhammer, "Gli interni militari italiani nei lager tedeschi, 1943-1945," Ricerche Storiche, 18 (1988): 297-321; Giorgio Rochat, "La memoria dell'internamento: Militari italiani in Germania, 1943-1945," Italia Contemporanea, no. 163 (1986): 5-30.

963. Schreiber, Gerhard; Stegemann, Bernd; Vogel, Detlev. Der Mittelmeerraum und Südosteuropa von der "Non Belligeranza" italiens bis zum Kriegseintritt der Vereinigten Staaten. Stuttgart, 1984.

   Vol. 3 of Das Deutsche Reich und der Zweite Weltkrieg, for military operations and the politico-economic background of 1939-41. Also on Axis wartime cooperation, G. Schreiber, "Les structures stratégiques de la conduite de la guerre de coalition italo-allemande au cours de la deuxième guerre mondiale," Revue d'Histoire de la Deuxième Guerre Mondiale, no. 120 (1980): 1-32.

964. Strawson, John. The Italian Campaign. London, 1987.

   Authoritative overall account. See also Dominick Graham and Shelford Bidwell, Tug of War: The Battle for Italy, 1943-1949 (New York, 1986).

965. Zilli, Valdo. "Gli italiani prigionieri di guerra in URSS: Vicende, esperienze, testimonianze." Rivista di Storia Contemporanea, 10 (1981): 329-53.

   The same topic is discussed in Morozzo della Rocca (#878). Analogously see Sandra Lotti, "Internati e POW in Gran Bretagna," Rivista di Storia Contemporanea, 17/1 (1988): 110-18; Colette Dubois, "Internés et prisonniers de guerre italiens dans l'Empire français de 1940 à 1945," Guerres Mondiales et Conflits Contemporains, no. 156 (1989): 53-71.

9. Vatican Foreign Policy

Papal Diplomacy in Peacetime

966. Alatri, Paolo. "Un tentativo di mediazione tra Hitler e Pio XI." Ulisse (1953), no. 4, pp. 134-47.

967. Cannistraro, Philip V., and Rosoli, Gianfausto. Emigrazione, Chiesa e Fascismo: Lo scioglimento dell'Opera Bonomelli, 1922-1928. Rome, 1979.

See also Roberto Morozzo della Rocca, "L'emigrazione contesa: Un aspetto della politica ecclesiastica del fascismo," Storia Politica, 20 (1981): 556-65; G. Rosoli, "Santa Sede e propaganda fascista all'estero tra i figli degli emigranti italiani," Storia Contemporanea, 17 (1986): 293-315.

968. Graham, Robert A. Vatican Diplomacy. Princeton, NJ, 1959.

Analytical study by the leading English-language scholar of the Papacy in modern international affairs. By the same author, "La Santa Sede e l'Anschluss austriaco," Civiltà Cattolica, 139/3 (1988): 354-64. See also Graham (#987).

969. Kent, George O. "Pope Pius XII: Some Aspects of German-Vatican Relations, 1933-1943." American Historical Review, 70 (1964): 59-78.

See also William M. Harrigan, "Pius XII's Efforts to Effect a Détente in German-Vatican Relations, 1939-1940," Catholic Historical Review, 49 (July 1963): 173-91.

970. Kent, Peter C. The Pope and the Duce: The International Impact of the Lateran Agreements. New York, 1981.

Surveys the limited diplomatic effect of the church-state rapprochement in Italy from 1930 to 1934. The same author has followed up this monograph with articles on selected aspects of Vatican diplomacy in the 1930's: "Between Rome and London: Pius XI, the Catholic Church and the Abyssinian Crisis," International History Review, 11 (1989): 252-71; "The Catholic Church in the Italian Empire," Canadian Historical Papers (1984), pp. 138-50; "The Vatican and the Spanish Civil War," European History Quarterly, 16 (1986): 441-64; "A Tale of Two Popes: Pius XI, Pius XII, and the Rome-Berlin Axis," Journal of Contemporary History, 23 (1988): 589-608.

971. Minerbi, Sergio. Il Vaticano, la Terra Santa e il sionismo. Milan, 1988.

On the birth of Zionism and inauguration of Britain's Palestinian mandate. See also Minerbi (#634); Ferrari (#985).

972. Rhodes, A.R.E. The Vatican in the Age of the Dictators, 1922-1945. London, 1973. Ital. trans. Il Vaticano e le dittature, 1922-1945, Milan, 1975.

Journalistic but reliable general survey. A brief scholarly account is Frank J. Coppa, "The Vatican and the Dictators between Diplomacy and Morality, 1919-1945," in Catholics, the State, and the European Radical Right, ed. Richard Wolff (New York, 1988), pp. 199-223. See also Angelozzi Gariboldi (#980).

973. Riccardi, Andrea. "Pio XII e la politica internazionale." Il Mulino, 28 (July-Aug. 1978): 614-28.

974. Rumi, Giorgio. "Mondo cattolico e guerra civile spagnola: L'opinione ambrosiana." Rivista di Storia della Chiesa in Italia, 36 (1982): 35-48.

See also Giorgio Campanini, ed., I cattolici italiani e la guerra di Spagna (Brescia, n.d.).

975. Salvemini, Gaetano. "Pio XI e la guerra etiopica," in Opere, III, Scritti di politico estera, vol. 3, ed. Augusto Torre, pp. 741-63. Milan, 1967.

Further on the Papal attitude to the Ethiopian war, Renzo De Felice, "La Santa Sede e il conflitto Italo-Etiopico nel diario di Bernadino Nogara," Storia Contemporanea, 8 (1977): 823-34. See also Kent (#970).

976. Stehle, Hansjakob. Die Ostpolitik des Vatikans, 1917-1975. Munich, 1975. Rev. Eng. trans. Eastern Politics of the Vatican, 1917-1979, Athens, OH, 1981.

Well-documented survey.

977. Stehlin, Stewart A. Weimar and the Vatican, 1919-1933: German-Vatican Relations in the Interwar Years. Princeton, NJ, 1984.

Sound, scholarly monograph.

978. Volk, Ludwig. Das Reichskonkordat vom 20. Juli 1933: Von den Ansätzen in der Weimarer Republik bis zur Ratifizierung am 10. September 1933. Mainz, 1972.

Authoritative work on the famous agreement with Nazi Germany. See also Konrad Repgen, "I Patti Lateranensi e il Reichskonkordat: Pio XI e la politica concordatria con Russia, Italia e Germania," Rivista di Storia della Chiesa in Italia, 33 (1979): 371-419.

979. Wenger, Antoine. Rome et Moscou, 1900-1950. Paris, 1987.

On clerics active in the Soviet Union.

The Vatican in World War II

980. Angelozzi Gariboldi, Giorgio. Pio XII, Hitler e Mussolini: Il Vaticano fra le Dittature. Milan, 1988.

For justification of the oft-criticized Papal conduct during World War II.

981. Caravaglios, Maria Genoino. "La Santa Sede e l'Inghilterra in Etiopia durante il secondo conflitto mondiale." Africa [Rome], 35 (1980): 217-54.

982. Chadwick, W. Owen. Britain and the Vatican during the Second World War. Cambridge, 1986.

Papal diplomacy, 1938-44, as reflected through the British diplomatic mission to the Vatican.

983. Conway, John S. "The Vatican, Great Britain and Relations with Germany, 1938-1940," Historical Journal, 16 (1973): 146-67.

See also the same author's "The Meeting between Pope Pius XII and Ribbentrop," Canadian Historical Papers (1968), pp. 215-27.

984. Delzell, Charles F. "Pius XII, Italy and the Outbreak of War." Journal of Contemporary History, 2/4 (1967): 137-61.

Rests on Actes et documents du Saint Siège (#208). See also Giuseppe Vedovato, "La Santa Sede e la guerra in Europa, 1939-1940," Rivista di Studi Politici Internazionali, 46 (1979): 529-68.

985. Ferrari, Silvio. "La Santa Sede e la questione di Gerusalemme, 1943-1984." Storia Contemporanea, 16 (1985): 139-58.

986. Garzia, Italo. Pio XII e l'Italia nella seconda guerra mondiale. (Brescia, 1988).

Conflict and concurrence between Vatican and Italian diplomacy is also touched on by E. Di Nolfo, "La politica estera del Vaticano e l'Italia dal 1943 al 1948," Storia delle Relazioni Internazionali, 4 (1988): 3-34.

987. Graham, Robert A. Il Vaticano e il nazismo. Rome, 1975.

Collection of essays, many printed earlier in Civiltà Cattolica, on aspects of Papal policy, 1939-45; basic documentation is German. Generally, a riposte to the allegations of Pius XII's failure to oppose Nazism. Graham has written voluminously in Civiltà Cattolica on the Vatican in the Second World War, including: "L'enciclica 'Summi Pontificatus' e i belligeranti nel 1939: La 'strana neutralità' di Pio XII," 135/4 (1984): 441-55; "Il Vaticano nella guerra psicologica inglese, 1939-1945: La storia dei 'sib,' cioé delle 'bugie autorizzate,' " 129/1 (1977): 113-33; "La questione religiosa nella crisi dell'Asse: Il confronto Orestano-Hudal, 1942-1943," 128/1 (1977): 441-55; "Come Von Ribbentrop spiava il Vaticano," 133/4 (1982): 220-32; "Quale pace cercava Pio XII? La Santa Sede negli ultimi anni di guerra," 133/2 (1982): 218-33; "Guerra di gas asfissianti nel

Pacifico? L'intervento della Santa Sede e della Croce Rossa nel 1944," 139/4 (1988): 429-38.

988. ———. The Pope and Poland in World War Two. London, 1968.

989. Hill, Leonidas E. "The Vatican Embassy of Ernst von Weiszäcker, 1943-1945." Journal of Modern History, 34 (1967): 138-59.

On the ambassador's intermediary role between the Papacy and Berlin arising out of the Nazi round-up of Rome's Jews, 16 October 1943, as is W. Owen Chadwick, "Weizsäcker, the Vatican and the Jews of Rome," Journal of Ecclesiastical History, 28 (1977): 138-59. See also Robert Katz, Black Sabbath (London, 1969), and Morley, Papeleux (next extry).

990. Morley, John. Vatican Diplomacy and the Jews during the Holocaust. New York, 1980.

Comprehensive review critical of the Vatican; judgment based on the activity and reports of papal nuncios throughout Europe. See also articles by Léon Papeleux, "Le Vaticane et le problème juif, 1941-1943," Revue d'Histoire de la Deuxième Guerre Mondiale, nos. 107 (1977): 75-84; 115 (1979): 55-67.

991. Morozzo della Rocca, Roberto. "Roncalli diplomatico in Turchia e Grecia, 1935-1944." Cristianesimo nella Storia, 8/2 (1987): 33-72.

Supplemented by Etienne Fouilloux, "Extraordinaire ambassadeur? Mgr. Roncalli à Paris, 1944-1953," Revue Historique, no. 565 (1988): 101-28.

992. Papeleux, Léon. "La diplomatie vaticane et l'Italie après Stalingrad." Revue d'Histoire de la Deuxième Guerre Mondiale, no. 106 (1977): 19-36.

One of a series of articles by L. Papeleux in Revue d'Histoire de la Deuxième Guerre Mondiale (since 1987 Guerres Mondiales et Conflits Contemporaines), based on Actes et documents du Saint Siège (#208). In particular, see "La diplomatie vaticane et Hitler, juin 1940 - octobre 1942," no. 98 (1975): 27-56; "Le Vatican et la crise hispano-américaine de 1941," no. 155 (1989): 43-51; "Le Saint Siège et les belligérants en 1942," no. 150 (1988): 61-75; "Le Vatican, Pétain, De Gaulle, 1944-1945," no. 141 (1986): 77-94; "Le Vatican et l'expansion du communisme, 1944-1945," no. 137 (1985): 63-84. The same author discusses a Papal compromise peace plan in "Les Etats-Unis, Le Saint-Siège et l'URSS en 1942," Cahiers d'Histoire de l'Institut de Recherches Marxistes, no. 30 (1987): 123-37.

993. Rémond, René. "Le Saint Siège et la guerre pendant la Seconde Guerre mondiale," in L'Ecole Française de Rome, Les Internationales et le problème de la guerre au XXè siècle. Rome, 1987.

V. INDEX

This is an index only to publications, including microfilm material in the public domain. In most cases reference is to author or editor (individual or institutional). Where an appropriate author or editor is lacking (e.g., for serial titles and some documentary collections and reference works), a title is listed. Numerals in normal print refer to page numbers, in bold print to the entry numbers in Chapter IV (Bibliography).

Académie Diplomatique Internationale, 72
Acciaiolo, N., **862**
Adám, M., **268**
Adami, V., **157**
Adamthwaite, A., **209**
Adler, W., **656**
Affari Esteri, **105**
Aga Rossi, E., **218**, **863**, **883**
Alatri, P., **375**, **553**, **646**, **966**
Albertini, A., **554**
Albertini, L., **182**
Albònico, A., **864**, **905**
Albrecht, D., **204**
Albrecht-Carrié, R., **55**, **210**, **584**, **617**
Alcock, A.E., **530**
Aldrovandi Marescotti, L., **281**
Alessandrini, A., **319**
Alfieri, D., **349**
Alloatti, F., **84**
Almanach de Gotha, **81**
Aloisi, P., **153**, **282**
Altermatt, U., **838**
Altherr, M., **865**
Altreitalie, **106**
Ambrosini, M.L., 40
Amè, C., **350**
American Committee on the History of the Second World War, 56; **12**

American Historical Association, 56, 67; **1**, **33-34**
American Historical Review, **123**
American History: A Bibliographic Review, 87
Amoretti, G.N., **851**
Analisi Storica, **107**
Anchiere, E., **13**, **211**, **695**, **779**
Andò, E., **942**
Andrew, C., **518**
Andri, A., **531**
Anfuso, F., **156**, **320**, **373**
Angelini, M., **694**
Angelozzi Gariboldi, G., **980**
Annali della Fondazione Luigi Micheletti, **887**
Annuaire internationale des archives, 52
Annual Register, **98**
Annuario di Stampa Italiana, 81
Annuario d'Italia, **90**
Antonescu, I., **470**
Antonicelli, F., **770**
Apolloni, E., 74
Aquarone, A., **519**, **765**, **832**
Ara, A., **532**, **603**
Arbeitsgemeinschaft für die neueste Geschichte Italiens [Gruppo di Studio per la Storia Contemporanea Italiana], 56; **40**

Archivio Storico Italiano, 56
Archivi per la Storia, 56
Archivum, 53, 54
Arcidiacono, B., **865**
Arisi Rota, A., **720**
Armellini, Q., **283**
Armon, T.I., **573**
Arts and Humanities Citations Index, 35
Ascoli, M., **338**
Askew, W.C., **158, 176**
Association for the Study of Modern Italy, 56
Associazione Italiana Editori, **36**
Associazione Italiana per la Società delle Nazioni, **160**
Aster, S., 58; **798**
Attanasio, S., **776**
Auerbach, H., **37**
Avanzi, G., 88
Avon, Earl of, see Eden, A.

Bacini, F., 51
Badoglio, P., **321**
Baer, G.W., 58; **735**
Bagnasco, E., **942**
Baker, R.S., **395**
Balestreri, L., **832**
Bandini, F., **927**
Barbagallo, F., **555**
Barbone, D., **298**
Barbul, G., **470**
Barclay, G.St.J., **585**
Barié, O., **182, 618, 873**
Barker, A.J., **736**
Barrère, C., **433**
Barros, J., **695, 737**
Bartetto, D., **207**
Barzilai, S., **322**
Barzolotti, U., **941**
Bastianini, G., **323, 683**
Battaglia, R., **822**
Baudouin, P., **305, 434**
Bayliss, G.M., 100
Baynes, N.H., **248**
Beck, P.J., **738**
Beck, P.S., **231**
Becker, J., **520**

Bédarida, F., **802**
Beddie, J.S., **245**
Belardinelli, M., **872**
Belgium, Académie Royale, **269**
Bell, P.M.H., **492**
Belloni, M., **351**
Beneš, E., **471**
Benini, Z., **156**
Bennett, R., **956**
Bercel, G., **632**
Bergamini, A., 81
Berio, A., **177, 324**
Bernardi, G., **943**
Bernardini, G., **789**
Bernhard, H., **254**
Berselli, A., **696**
Bertinaria, L., **946**
Bertinelli, R., **906**
Bertoldi, S., **556, 560, 866, 888**
Bertùccioli, R., **174**
Bessis, J., **657**
Besterman, T., 87
Beyens, N.E.L., **472**
Bianchi, G., **159, 334, 387**
Bibliografia Fascista, 23
Bibliographic Index, 87
Bibliographie zur Zeitgeschichte, 37
Bibliothek für Zeitgeschichte, 38
Bidwell, S., **964**
Bigazzi, G., 45
Binion, R., **799**
Biography and Genealogy Master Index, 102
Biography Index, 102
Birchfield, M.E., **265**
Birkenhead, Earl of, **414**
Bissolati, L., **325**
Blatt, J., **586, 619, 670, 695**
Blett, P., **208**
Bloch, C., **721**
Blondel, J-F., **435**
Bloomberg, M., **8**
Blum, L., **236**
Bobev, B., **652**
Bocca, G., **888**
Boehm, E.H., **107**
Bolech Cecchi, D., **800**
Bolla, N., **352**

INDEX

Bonante, L., **867**
Bonelli, F., 45; **545**
Bonnet, G., **436**
Bonomi, I., **191, 284**
Book Review Digest, **102**
Book Review Index, **39**
Borejsza, J., **573, 658**
Borgogni, M., **780**
Borra, E., **353**
Borsa, G., **906**
Bosmans, J., **697**
Bosworth, R.J.B., 31n; **587, 620, 696,** 861
Bottai, G., **285**
Botti, F., **928**
Boulding, E., **9**
Bourdin, J., **802**
Bourne, K., **231**
Bouton, S.M., **530**
Bova Scoppa, R., **326**
Boveri, M., **533**
Bovio, O., **14**
Bowers, C.G., **396**
Boyd, C.E., **1**
Braddick, H.B., **757**
Bragadin, M'A., **942**
Braunthal, J., **188**
Breccia, A., **698, 833**
Brewster, J.W., **39**
Briand, A., **237**
British Humanities Index, **44**
Brogi, A., **650**
Broszat, M., **851**
Brown, B.F., 51; **202, 303**
Browning, C., **834**
Bruccoleri, G., **160**
Brügel, J.W., **722**
Brundu Olla, P., **801**
Brusasca, G., **93**
Bruti Liberati, L., **573, 604**
Buccianti, G., **286, 738-39, 929**
Bulletin of International News, **99**
Burgwyn, H.J., **56, 699, 720, 734, 781**
Butcher, H.C., **306**

Cabella, G.G., **338**
Cadogan, A., **307**

Calabrò, L., **354**
Calchi Novati, G., **912**
Campanini, G., **974**
Candeloro, G., **543**
Canevari, E., **335**
Cannistraro, P.V., 83; **73, 659, 700, 817, 967**
Cantalupo, R. [Legatus], **355, 607, 684**
Caravaglios, M.G., **738, 981**
Carbone, G.A., **528**
Carboni, G., **356**
Carlucci, G., **198**
Carocci, G., **186, 701**
Caroli, G., **621, 699, 740, 835**
Carpi, D., **834, 836**
Carr, E.H., **493**
Carrillo, E., **608**
Carroll, B.A., 87
Carton de Wiart, A., **407**
Carucci, P., 45, 53, 55
Carver, M., **944**
Case, L.M., 53
Casmirri, S., **708**
Cassels, A., **515, 565, 573, 660, 702**
Castellano, G., **357**
Castronovo, V., 83; **545**
Casucci, C., 41; **166, 661**
Catalano, F., **767, 837**
Cattell, D., **768**
Caudana, M., **889**
Cavallero, U., **286**
Cavallo, A., **838**
Cavallo, P., **877**
Caviglia, E., **358**
Cecace, P., **867**
Cecil, R., **408**
Celovsky, B., **782**
Center for Research Libraries, 56, 76, 85
Centomila, 83
Centre National de la Recherche Scientifique, 53; **802**
Ceplair, L., **494**
Cermelj, L., **534**
Cerruti, E., **327**
Certutti, M., **662**
Cervi, M., **543, 951**

INDEX

Cesari, M., 83
Ceva, L., 83; **161, 907, 930, 931, 940, 945-46, 953**
Chabod, F., **566**
Chadwick, W.O., **982, 989**
Chamberlain, A., **704**
Chambrun, Count C.P. de, **437**
Chandler, A.D., **219**
Charles-Roux, F., **438**
Chatfield, A.E., **409**
Chiara, P., **553**
Chiarini, R., **642**
Chiavarelli, E., **938**
Chi E?, 82
Child, R.W., **338, 397**
Childs, J.B., 113
Chiodini, L., **768**
Chukumba, S.U., **741**
Churchill, R.S., **831**
Churchill, W.S., **224, 260, 410**
Cialdea, B., **742**
Ciano, E., **328**
Ciano, G., **192, 287;** Personal Papers of, 47, **183**
Ciccarelli, O., **843**
Ciuffoletti, Z., **162**
Civiltà Cattolica, 82
Clark, M., **544**
Clarke, M., **21**
Clemente, V., **723**
Cliadakis, H., **839**
Cline, M.W., **19**
Clio, **108**
Clodomiro, V., **622, 908**
Clough, S.B., **545**
Coceani, B., **890**
Codignola, A., 83
Cofrancesco, D., **569, 827**
Colapietra, R., **163**
Colarieti, M., **164**
Colarizi, S., **823**
Collotti, E., **243, 609, 656, 724, 824**
Colosimo, G., **359**
Colton, J., **812**
Commène, N.P., **473**
Conference Group for Italian Politics and Society, 57
Conference of Ambassadors, 216

Consiglio Nazionale delle Ricerche per la Toscana, 45
Constantini, F., **360**
Conti, C., **156**
Contini, G., 42, 55
Conway, J.S., **983**
Conzemius, V., **57**
Cook, C.P., 53, 64; **91**
Coppa, F.J., **74, 586, 623, 972**
Coppola, F., **685**
Cora, G., **329, 610**
Cordova, F., **557**
Corradini, E., **193, 686**
Cortada, J.W., **769**
Costa Bona, E., **803**
Council for European Studies, 53, 57
Council on Foreign Relations, **10**
Coverdale, J.F., **770**
Craig, G., **495, 521**
Cremona, P., **597**
Cresciani, G., **573, 663, 861**
Crespi, S., **288**
Cretella, L.A., **638**
Crippa, B., 45
Croce, B., **289**
Crozier, A.J., **748**
Cruger, D.M., **5**
Cunsolo, R.S., **58, 546**
Current Biography, 102
Currey, M.I., **588**
Curtwright, L.H., **839**

Da Baranca, M., see Lanza, M.
D'Amelio, M., **611**
D'Amoja, F., **624, 725, 783**
Dampierre, R. de, **439**
D'Angiolini, P., 55; **186**
D'Annunzio, G., **188, 321, 687**
D'Aroma, N., **290, 556**
Dassovich, M., **804**
Davis, J., **21**
Davis, M., **947**
Dawes, C.G., **308**
Deakin, F.W., **188, 891**
Deambrosis, M., **165**
De Antonellis, G., **906**
De Biase, C., **931**
De Bono, E., **159, 362**

INDEX

Debyser, F., **59**
De Castro, D., **868**
Decleva, E., **589, 671, 680**
De Conde, A., **495, 601**
De Courten, L., **625**
De Felice, L., 42
De Felice, R., 49; **166, 188, 287, 293, 297, 334, 558, 601, 647, 664, 789, 793, 825, 975**
De Gasperi, A., 83
Degli'Innocenti, M., **162**
De Grand, A., **565, 567, 575**
Degras, J., **258-59**
De La Sierra, L., **942**
Del Bo, D., **590**
Del Boca, A., **909, 938**
Del Buono, O., 83
Del Canuto, F., **899**
De Leonardis, M., **869**
Dell, R., **530**
Della Peruta, F., 54
Della Volpe, N., **932**
De Luca, A., **627**
De Lutiis, G., **547**
Delzell, C.F., **11, 212, 568, 984**
Denecke, L., 70
Depoli, A., **363**
De Risio, C., **840, 847**
De Robertis, A.G., **841**
De Rosa, G., **545**
De Rosa, L., **545, 601**
De Stefani, A., **184**
Deutsches Historisches Institut in Rom [Istituto Storico Germanico in Roma], **40**
De Vergottini, T., **626**
De Vincentiis, M., **723**
Dexter, B.V., **10**
D'Hoop, J-M., **13**
Diggins, J.P., **817**
Dilks, D.J., **307, 518, 805, 807**
Dimitrov, I., **784**
Dinale, O., **338**
Di Nola, C., **364**
Di Nolfo, E., **218, 495, 665, 703, 842, 849, 872, 883, 885, 986**
Dipper, C., **778**

Direzione Relazioni Esterne Ansaldo, 45
Di Roberto, R., **726**
Di Scala, S., **637**
<u>Dissertation Abstracts International</u>, **103**
Ditmas, E.M.R., **100**
Dixon, J.P. and P., **411**
<u>Dizionario biografico degli italiani</u>, **84**
Djordjevic, D., **655**
Dobrinescu, V., **792**
Dockrill, M.L., **231**
Doenitz, K., **453**
Dolfin, G., **291**
Dollfuss, E., **188**
Dollmann, E., **454**
Domarus, M., **188, 248**
Donosti, M., see Luciolli, M.
Dore, G., **601**
Dreyfus, M., **16**
Dubois, C., **965**
Dülffer, J., **695**
Dulles, A., **398**
Dumoulin, M., **666**
Dunmore-Leiber, L., **102**
Duroselle, J-B., **591, 806**
Dutton, D., **704**

Eckert, G., **623**
Ecole Française de Rome, **522**
Eden, A. [Avon, Earl of], **412**
Edlmann, B., 88
Edwards, J., **771**
Edwards, P.G., **704, 738**
Ehrmann, H.M., 69
Eisenhower, D.D., **219, 399**
Elie, H., **440**
Ellwood, D.W., **870, 948**
Elze, R., 73
Ensign, M.S., 107
Erdmann, K-D., **246**
Esch, A., 73
<u>European History Quarterly</u>, **124**
<u>European Studies Review</u>, see <u>European History Quarterly</u>
Evans-Pritchard, E., **910**

INDEX

Fabiano, D., **705**
Faldella, E., **772**
Farber, E.I., **2**
Fasano Guarini, E., **696**
Fasce, F., **545**
Federzoni, L., **193**, **331**, **688**
Feiling, K., **807**
Fejto, F., **644**
Fellner, F., **655**, **698**
Feltrinelli, see Fondazione Feltrinelli
Ferrantini Tosi, F., **826**
Ferrari, S., **985**
Ferraris, L.V., **612**
Ferretti, V., **671**, **785**
Filesi, C., **910**, **911**
Filipelli, R.L., **873**
Fillipone Thaulero, G., **871**
Fingeller, H., **530**
Fink, C., **496**
Fink, C.F., **87**
Fiorentino, F., **870**
Fischer, B., **592**
Fischer, F., **2**
Flandin, P-E., **240**, **441**
Flora, F., **80**
Flussio, L., **638**
Fondazione Feltrinelli, **258**
Fonti, G., **84**
<u>Foreign Affairs</u>, **125**
Foreman, J., **771**
Forges Davanzati, R., **689**
Foschini, A., **365**
Foster, J., **61**
Fotič, C., **474**
Fouilloux, E., **991**
Framke, G., **530**
France, Archives Nationales, 67
France, Assemblée Nationale, **238**
France, Bibliothèque Nationale, 78
France, Ministère des Relations Extérieures [Ministère des Affaires Etrangères], 64-65; **239**
Franco, F., **177**
François-Poncet, A., **442**
Frank, W., **775**, **933**
Frassati, A. and L.G., **185**
Freri, O., **75**
Friedlander, S., **205**

Funderbark, D.B., **808**
Funk, A.L., **12**
Funke, M., **743**, **786**, **923**

Gabriele, M., **755**
Gabrieli, F., **47**
Gaeta, F., **83**; **546**
Gafencu, G., **475**
Galasso, G., **823**
Galli, C., **292**
Gallinari, V., **934**
Gallo, B., **672**
Gamelin, M., **443**
Garamvölgyi, J., **838**
Garbari, M., **60**
Garland, N., **872**
Garnier, J-P., **444**
Garosci, A., **680**
Garzia, I., **986**
Gasbarri, C., **48**
Gassler, R.S., **9**
Gat, M., **865**
Gatzke, H., **523**
Gayda, V., **690**
Gehl, J., **788**
Gencarelli, E., **55**
Gentile, E., **667**
<u>Gerarchia</u>, 82
Germany, Auswärtiges Amt, 244-45
Germany, Reichskanzlei, 246
Germino, D., **569**
Gerra, F., **648**
Giambartolomei, A., **840**
Giannini, A., **61**, **143**, **147**, **194**, **332**, **593**, **627**
Gibson, H., **287**
Gifuni, G., **189**, **300**
Gigli, G., **822**
Giglio, C., **38**, **39**; **912**
Gilbert, F., **521**
Gilbert, M., **831**
Gill, D., **73**
Giolitti, G., **186**, **195**, **333**
Giordano, G., **613**, **727**
Gladwyn, Lord [Jebb, H.M.G.], **413**
Gnirss, C., **24**
Goebbels, J., **309**
Goglia, L., **167**, **744**, **764**, **898**, **899**

INDEX

Goldman, A.L., **757**
Goldmann, N., **476**
Gonella, G., 83
Gooch, G.P., **527**
Gooch, J., **525, 928**
Gore-Booth, Lord, **95**
Gothier, F., 113
Graham, D., **964**
Graham, H., **773**
Graham, R.A., **206, 208, 968, 987-88**
Grandi, D., **168, 187, 196, 293, 334**; Papers of, 49
Granier, G., 68
Grassi, F., **85, 167**
Grassi, G., **826**
Gravelli, A., **691**
Graziani, R., **154, 335**
Grazzi, E., 366
Great Britain, British Library, 77, 85, 107
Great Britain, Cabinet, **229**
Great Britain, Foreign Office, 62; **230-32**
Great Britain, Imperial War Museum, 54
Great Britain, Ministry of Economic Warfare, **82**
Great Britain, Parliament, **147, 233, 264**
Great Britain, Public Record Office, 61-62
Great Britain, Royal Commission on Historical Manuscripts, 64
Greece, Ministry of Foreign Affairs, **270-71**
Gregory, W., **25**
Grenville, J.A.S., **213**
Gretton, P., **769**
Grew, J.C., **310**
Grimsted, P.K., 70
Grispo, R., 41, 45
Guariglia, R., **169, 336**
Guarneri, F., **367**
Guercio, M., 45
Guerres Mondiales et Conflits Contemporaines [Revue d'Histoire de la Deuxième Guerre Mondiale], **126, 578, 828**

Guerri, G.B., **170, 285, 559, 563, 614**
Guida, F., **604, 621, 628**
Guide to Microforms in Print, **41**
Guide to Reprints, **42**
Guillen, P., **670, 885**
Gutman, Y., **834**

Hachey, T.E., **230**
Haensch, G., 78
Halifax, Lord [Wood, E.F.L.], **414**
Hamilton, A., **570**
Hankey, M., **216, 415**
Harcourt, F., **3**
Hardie, F.M., **745**
Harper, J.L., **873**
Harrigan, W.M., **969**
Harris, B., **761**
Harris, C.R.S., **874**
Harvard University, Widener Library, 75
Harvey, J. and O., **311**
Harvey, S., **949**
Hassell, U., **312**
Hayner, P.B., 72
Hazlehurst, C., 64
Headlam Morley, J. and A., **416**
Heiber, H., 69; **789**
Heims, H., **248**
Heineman, J.L., **706**
Helde, T.T., 87
Henderson, N., **417**
Henke, J., 68
Herde, P., **843**
Herford, C.H., **530**
Hermon, E., **707**
Herriot, E., **445**
Hess, R.L., **913**
Highley, A.E., **746**
Hildebrand, K., **520**
Hill, L.E., **256, 782, 989**
Hillgruber, A., **247**
Himmler, H., **250**
Hinsley, F.H., 69; **831**
Historian, **127**
Historical Abstracts, **104**
Historical Association [British], **43**
Historical Journal, **128**

Historische Zeitschrifte, **129**
History, **130**
Hitler, A., **177, 188, 247, 248, 455**
Hoare, S. [Viscount Templewood], **418**
Hodgkinson, H., **535**
Hoepke, K-P., **708**
Hoettl, W. [Hagen, W.], **456**
Hooker, N.H., **222**
Hoover Institution, 76, 85
Hore-Belisha, L., **313**
Horthy, M., **272, 477**
Hory, L., **851**
House, E.M., **220, 401**
Howe, G.F., **1**
Hughes, H.S., **521, 548**
Hull, C., **400**
Humanities Index, **44**
Hungary, Ministry of Foreign Affairs, **273**

Iadarola, A., **738**
Iatrides, J.O., **221**
Ilari, V., **928**
Index to Book Reviews in the Humanities, **39**
Informazione Bibliografica, **45**
Institut für Zeitgeschichte, 79; **309**
Intelligence and National Security, **131**
Interlandi, T., **693**
International Affairs [London], **132**
International Commission for the Teaching of History, **13**
International Committee of Historical Sciences, **4, 46**
Internationale Jahresbibliographie der Festscriften, **47**
International History Review, **133, 594**
International Military Tribunal [Nuremberg], 69; **249**
International Who's Who, **86**
Iordan, C., **699**
Isnenghi, M., **832**
Israelien, V.L., **787**
Istituto della Enciclopedia Italiana [Trecanni], **77**

Istituto per gli Studi Politica Internazionale, **168, 298, 591**
Istituto Storico Germanico in Roma, see Deutsches Historisches Institut in Rom
Italia Contemporanea [Il Movimento di Liberazione in Italia], **112**
Italian Armed Forces Records, 39
Italian Quarterly, **134**
Italy, Archivio Centrale dello Stato, 41
Italy, Archivio Storico del Ministero degli Affari Esteri, 37
Italy, Biblioteca della Camera Fascista, **26**
Italy, Centro Nazionale per il Catalogo Unico, 74, 107; **48**
Italy, Consiglio di Stato, **155**
Italy, Council of Ministers Information and Copyright Services, **50**
Italy, Giunta Centrale per gli Studi Storici, **49**
Italy, Governo, **171**
Italy, Istituto Centrale di Statistica, **92**
Italy, Marina Militare, **950**
Italy, Ministero degli Affari Esteri, **87, 93, 144, 146-47, 172-74**; Comitato per la Documentazione delle Attività Italiane in Africa, **149**; Commissione per la Pubblicazione dei Documenti Diplomatici Italiani, **148**
Italy, Ministero della Difesa, **875**
Italy, Ministero dell'Economia Nazionale, **144**
Italy, Ministero delle Finanze [Ministero del Tesoro], **27**
Italy, Ministero dell'Interno, 54; **88**
Italy, Ministero per i Beni Culturali, 54
Italy, Parlamento, **150**
Italy, Partito Nazionale Fascista, **151**
Italy, Stato Maggiore dell'Esercito, **14, 157, 175, 872, 875, 934-37, 946, 951-54**

INDEX

Jackson, G., **776**
Jacobsen, H-A., **214**
Jacobson, J., **497**
Jacomini di San Sevino, F., **156, 368, 727**
Jagschitz, G., **729**
James, H., 58
James, R.J., **809**
Jannelli, P., **294**
Jarausch, K.H., **727**
Jedlicka, L., **274, 656**
Jedrzejewicz, W., **480**
Jochmann, W., **248**
Johnson, D.W., **165, 401**
Johnston, R.H., 58
Journal of Contemporary History, **135**
Journal of Modern History, **136**
Justus, V., see Macchi di Cellare, D. and E.

Kállay, N., **478**
Katz, R., **989**
Keesing's Contemporary Archives, **99**
Keith, A.B., **215**
Kent, B., **498**
Kent, G.O., 67; **989**
Kent, P.C., **970**
Kerekes, L., **275, 728, 788**
Kernek, S.J., **645**
Keserich, C., **696**
Kesselring, A., **457**
Kettenacker, L., **818**
Kile, B., 113
Kimball, W.F., **224**
Kimche, J., **883**
Kimmich, C.M., 58
Kincade, W.H., 72
Kindermann, G-K., **729**
Kirkpatrick, I., **419, 558**
Klibansky, R., **338**
Klinkhammer, L., **962**
Knox, M., **196, 524-25, 571, 844**
Koenig, W.J., 61
Kogan, N., **870**
Kolko, G., **499**
Kordt, E., **458**

Kovaleff, T.P., **817**
Kramm, H., **28**
Krausnick, H., **250**
Kuby, E., **892**
Kuehl, W.F., **5, 89**
Kulischer, E.M., **500**
Kunz, D., 58
Kupper, A., **204**
Kutakov, L.N., **787**
Kuzmanova, A., **740, 750**
Kybal, V., **479**

La Francesca, S., **572**
Lagardelle, H., **446**
La Marca, N., **595, 644**
Lamb, R., **501**
Lanfranchi, F., **369**
Langer, W.L., **20**
Lansbury, G., **420**
Lansing, R., **402**
Lanza, M. [Simoni, L.], **302**, [Da Baranca, M.], **361**
Lanza d'Ajeta, B., **155**
La Palombara, J., **549**
Lasturel, P., **695**
Latour, C., **793**
Laurens, F.D., **747**
Laval, P., **240, 314**
Layton, R.V., **459**
Lazzero, R., **893**
League of Nations, **264-66**. See also United Nations Library
Ledeen, M.A., **558, 573, 646**
Lederer, I., **649**
Lefebvre D'Ovidio, F., **732, 748**
Legnani, M., **749, 826**
Le Houërou, F., **914**
Leistner, O., **47**
Leoncini, F., **595**
Leoni, F., **82**
Lessona, A., **197, 337, 692**
Lestz, M.E., **709**
Lewanski, R.C. and R.J., **53, 72, 74**
Licata, G., **81, 82**
Liddell Hart, B., **253**
Liebitzky, E., **274**
Lindeck-Pozza, I., **629**
Link, A.S., **227**

253

Linsenmayer, W.S., **845**
Lipski, J., **480**
Lisbon Papers, 35
Litvinov, M., **481**
Lloyd George, D., **376, 421**
Lobies, J-P., 102
Lochner, L., **309**
Lodolini, E., 54
Lönne, K-E., **630, 668, 708**
Lötzke, H., 70
Lopez Celly, A., **730-31**
Lotti, S., **965**
Low, A.D., **788**
Lowe, C.J., **596**
Lowell, L.A., **267**
Luciolli, M. [Donosti, M.], **330**
Ludecke, K.G.W., **459**
Ludlow, P., **234**
Ludwig, E., **338**
Lukač, D., **846**
Lukowitz, D., **810**
Lungonelli, M., 45
Lupu, N.Z., **740**
Lussu, E., **876**
Lyttleton, A., **558, 574**

Macartney, M.H.H., **597**
Macchi di Cellare, D. and E. [Justus, V.], **295**
MacDonald, C.A., **811**
Maček, V., **482**
Macfie, A.L., **631**
Mack Smith, D., 81; **544, 550, 558, 669**
Macmillan, H., **315, 422**
MacVeagh, L., **221**
Màdaro, L., **29**
Magistrati, M., **370**
Magris, C., **532**
Maier, C.S., **502**
Maini, R., 107
Malagodi, O., **371**
Malatesta, A., **75, 76**
Malfèr, S., **632, 697**
Manchev, K., **750**
Manheim, R., **455**
Manning, A.F., **710**
Mantoux, P., **216**

Manuel, F.E., **634**
Manzano, S., 45
Marcoaldi, F., **184**
Marder, A.J., **755**
Mariano, E., **188**
Mariano, G., **847**
Marinotti Dorigo, St., 50, 51
Marks, S., **503, 694**
Marrus, M., **834**
Marsico, G., **650**
Martel, G., **515**
Martini, G.S., 88
Marzari, F., **596, 852**
Mason, J.B., 100
Masotti, P.M., **372**
Massagrande, D.L., **711**
Massobrio, G., **939**
Matteini, M., 81
Matteoli, G., **938**
Maugeri, Francesco, 83
Maugeri, Franco, **338**
May, E.R., **524**
Mayda, G., **894**
Mayer, A.J., **504**
Mayer, S.L., 61
Mayor, A., **287**
Mazzetti, M., **176**
Mazzolini, S., **373**
McGuire, C., **598**
McSherry, J.E., **244**
Meckler, A.M., **41**
Medlicott, W.N., **847**
Meier-Welcker, H., **940**
Melchionni, M.G., **633, 639, 650**
Mellini Ponce de Leon, A., **373, 848**
Melograni, P., 83
Mercuri, L., **235, 855, 870, 877, 942**
Messick, F.M., **15**
Meyriat, J., 113
Michaelis, M., **563, 708, 789, 790**
Michel, H., **13, 812**
Migone, G.G., **602, 712, 817**
Miller, D.H., **316**
Miller, J.E., **849, 886**
Millett, A.R., **525**
Milza, P., **16, 601, 670**
Minardi, S., **713, 732, 748, 751**
Minerbi, S., **634, 789, 971**

INDEX

Minney, R.J., **313**
Minniti, F., **175, 837**
Mira, G., **579**
Missori, M., **88**
Mitchell, B.R., **94**
Mockler, A., **938**
Moellhaussen, E.F., **460**
Moffat, J.P., **222**
Mohraz, J.F., **87**
Mola, A.A., **167, 556, 875**
Mommsen, W.A., 70
Mommsen, W.J., **818**
Mondini, L., **374**
Monroe, E., **536**
Montanelli, I., **543**
Montenegro, A., **671**
Monzie, A. de, **447**
Moodie, A.E., **537**
Morelli, A., **672, 730, 834**
Mori, R., **171, 752, 790**
Morley, J., **990**
Morozzo della Rocca, R., **878, 965, 967, 991**
Morsy, L., **921**
Mosca, R., **30, 183, 376, 526**
Moscati, R., **169**
Moulton, H.G., **505**
Movimento di Liberazione in Italia, see Italia Contemporanea
Mowat, C.L., **506**
Muggeridge, M., **183, 287**
Mugnaini, M., **733**
Mulino, Il, **109**
Murialdi, P., **83**
Murphy, R.D., **403**
Murray, W., **507, 525, 813**
Musat, M., **792**
Musso, C., **879**
Mussolini, A., **188**
Mussolini, B., 77, **152, 177, 188, 198, 257, 338, 450, 456**; Personal Papers of, 42
Mussolini, R., **339**
Mussolini, V., **340**

Natali, C., **575**
"National Inventory of Documentary Sources in the United States," 58

Navarra, Q., **341**
Negash, T., **915**
Nelli, H.S., **645**
Nello, P., **196, 615**
Nenni, P., **296**
Neulem, H.W., **827**
Neurath, K., **695**
New York Public Library, 75, 85
New York Review of Books, **141**
Nicolson, H. and N., **423**
Nigro, L.J., **645**
Nitti, F.S., **199, 375**
Nobile Stolp, G., 107
Noel, G., **208**
Noel, L., **448, 640**
Noether, E.P., **1, 584**
Noiret, S., **637**
Nolte, E., **508, 576**
Northedge, F.S., **509**
Novak, B.C., **850**
Nuova Antologia di Lettere, Arti e Scienze, 113
Nuova Rivista Storica, 114
Nuti, L., **62**

Oldenhange, K., 68
Olla Repeto, G., 55
Olton, R., **79**
Orano, P., **693**
Orlandi, R., **916**
Orlando, V.E., **200, 376**
Ormos, M., **698**
Orsi, P.L., **71**
Ortona, E., **297, 377**
Ortu, G.G., **876**
Overy, R.J., **510**

Palic, V.M., 113
Palla, M., **287, 898**
Pallante, P., **841**
Palm, C.D., **76**
Palmer, A., **91**
Palumbo, M., **708, 922**
Palumbo, P.F., **46**
Panhuys Polman Gruys, P. van, **145**
Pankhurst, R., **741, 922**
Pansa, G., **955**
Paoli, G., **651**

Papagos, A., **483**
Papeleux, L., **990, 992**
Papen, F., **461**
Parch, D., 84
Parilli, L., **369**
Parker, R.A.C., **753, 822**
Parlati, G., **567**
Parri, F., **378**
Passato e Presente, **115**
Passmore, R.J., **9**
Pastore, V., **906**
Pastorelli, P., 48; **63, 190, 303, 635, 652**
Pasvolsky, L., **505**
Paul-Boncour, J., **449**
Pavlowitch, S.K., **734, 851-52**
Pavone, C., 54; **186**
Paxton, J., **91**
Paxton, R., **834**
Payne, S., **774**
Perfetti, F., **739, 901**
Perich, G., **852**
Perona, G., **64**
Perret, M., **915**
Persegnani, I., **924**
Petacco, A., 55
Peter II, King, **484**
Petersen, J., 54, 73; **65, 520, 558, 573, 673, 790, 886, 896**
Peterson, A.F., 76
Peterson, M., **424**
Petracchi, G., **613, 636, 878**
Petricioli, M., **526, 637-38**
Petrie, C., **704**
Petsales-Diomedes, N., **639**
Phillips, W., **404**
Picciotti Fargion, L., **894**
Picker, H., 248
Pieri, P., **560**
Pietromarchi, L., **379**
Pillon, G., **547**
Pini, G., **342, 558**
Pink, G.P., **511**
Pinzani, C., **869, 872**
Pirella, A., **941**
Pirelli, A., **298**
Pius XI, Pope, **207**
Pius XII, Pope, **207, 224**

Pizzigallo, M., **619, 638, 714, 917**
Plaisant, L.M., **876**
Plano, J.C., **79**
Playfair, I.S.O., **956**
Plehwe, F-K., **462**
Poggio, P.P., **887**
Poletti, C., **223**
Poliakov, L., **251**
Polimadei, P., **721**
Politico, Il, **110**
Pommerin, R., **789**
Ponte, Il, **111**
Pope, B.H., 107
Popisteaunu, C., **792**
Potemkin, V., **512**
Potra, G.C., **740**
Pottecher, F., **812**
Poulain, M., **715, 719**
Poulantzas, N., **577**
Poulton, H.J., 100
Pratt, L.R., **813**
Prayer, M., **925**
Preston, P., **773**
Preti, L., **899**
Preziosi, G., **693**
Pricolo, F., **380**
Prittwitz und Gaffron, F., **463**
Procacci, G., **754, 921**
Public Affairs Information Service (PAIS), **51**
Pugh, M., **764**
Puntoni, P., **299**
Pupo, R., **880**
Puzzo, D.A., **775**

Quaroni, P., **343, 727**
Quartararo, R., **755, 814, 873, 918**
Quartaro, R., **558**
Quazza, G., **939**
Quellen und Forschungen aus italienischen Archiven und Bibliotheken, **137**

Rabel, R., **868**
Ragatz, L.J., **31**
Ragionieri, E., **543**
Rahn, R., **464**
Rainer, J., **632**

INDEX

Rainero, R., 674, 815, 842, 919-20
Randall, A., 425
Ránki, G., 538, 728
Rapone, L., 816
Raspin, A., 837
Rassegna degli Archivio di Stato, 45, 54, 56
Rath, R.J., 698
Rauti, P., 198
Reed, D., 76
Relations Internationales, 138
Relazioni Internazionali, 116
Rémond, R., 802, 993
Renda, A., 188
Reno, E.A., 265
Renouvin, P., 802
Renzi, W.A., 643
Repgen, K., 246, 978
Réti, G., 698, 792
Reut-Nicolussi, E., 530
Review of Politics, 139
Revue d'Histoire de la Deuxième Guerre Mondiale, see Guerres Mondiales et Conflits Contemporaines
Revue d'Histoire Diplomatique, 140
Reynaud, P., 450
Reynolds, M.M., 87
Reynoso, F. de, 485
Rhodes, A.R.E., 553, 972
Ribbentrop, J. and A., 465
Ribuolli, P., 223
Riccardi, A., 973
Riccardi, L., 699
Ricci, L., 81
Rich, N., 517
Richardson, C.O., 748
Ridòmi, C., 381
Rintelen, A., 486
Rintelen, E., 466
Riosa, A., 653
Ritschel, K.H., 530
Rivista di Storia Contemporanea, 117
Rivista di Studi Politici Internazionali, 118, 177
Rivista Storica Italiana, 119
Rizzatti, M.L., 91
Rizzi, L., 954

Roach, J.P.C., 6
Roatta, M., 156, 382
Roberts, S., 77
Robertson, E.M., 252, 743, 756, 899
Robertson, J.C., 757, 764
Robinson, F., 3
Rocca, G., 942
Rochat, G., 167, 178, 560, 563, 738, 910, 922, 934, 938, 939, 957, 962
Roche, E., 727
Rodd, J.R., 426
Röder, W., 79
Romano, C., 84
Romano, S., 561, 587, 675
Romano Avezzana, C., 791
Romeo, R., 545
Rommel, E., 253
Roosevelt, F.D. and E., 224, 260
Rose, N., 757, 809
Rose Garden Papers, 47
Rosen, E.R., 623, 838, 853
Rosen, V., 338
Rosenman, S.I., 224
Roskill, S., 415
Rosoli, G., 700, 967
Ross, D., 729
Rosselli, A., 676
Rosselli, C., 661
Rossi, C., 338
Rossi, F., 383
Rossi, G., 900
Rossini, G., 599
Rosso, A., 384
Rota, E., 20
Rothstein, A., 260
Rouad, A., 744, 758
Rovighi, A., 937
Royal Historical Society, 1
Royal Institute of International Affairs [Chatham House], 77, 85; 100, 217, 348, 661
Rubatscher, V.M., 793
Rugafiori, P., 546
Rumi, G., 66, 698, 716, 895, 901, 974
Rusinow, D., 539

Sabille, J., **251**
Sabine, C.M., **179**
Sadkovich, J.J., **717, 837, 958**
Sailer, K., **188**
Sakmyster, T.L., **792**
Sala, T., **824, 854**
Saladino, A., 55
Salamone, A.W., **586**
Salandra, A., **189, 300, 344**
Salata, F., **727**
Salerno, E., **924**
Salierno, V., **553**
Salotti, G., **648, 880**
Salvatore, L., **875**
Salvatorelli, L., **579, 677**
Salvemini, G., **321, 580, 678, 975**
Santarelli, E., **562, 581, 921**
Santomassimo, G., **558**
Santoni, A., **840, 959**
Santoro, G., **960**
Sapelli, G., **545**
Sarkissian, A.O., **527**
Sarraz-Bournet, M., **451**
Sarti, R., **11**
Satow, E.M., **95**
Sbacchi, A., **759, 922**
Scala, E., **961**
Scarcia Amoretti, B., **167**
Schaf, F.L., **19**
Scheuch, H., 34
Schieder, W., **778**
Schiffrer, C., **534**
Schmidt, P., **467**
Schmitz, D.F., **817**
Schneider, B., **208**
Schreiber, G., **940, 962-63**
Schröder, J., **17, 896, 923**
Schüdekopf, O.-E., **623**
Schulla, R., **632**
Schuschnigg, K., **487**
Schuster, I., **180**
Schwandt, E., 67
Scialoja, V., **194, 201**
Sebastian, P., **855**
Secchi, S., **582, 878, 901**
Segrè, C., **563, 924**
Segreto, L., 45; **545**
Selby, W., **427**

Senesi, L., **67**
Senise, C., **385**
Serra, E., 34, 44, 56; **96, 97, 190, 304, 591, 640-41, 727, 757, 760, 881-82**
Serrano Suñer, R., **488**
Sestan, E., **75**
Seth, R., **80**
Seton Watson, C., **231, 551, 818, 902**
Seton Watson, H., **540**
Seymour, C.M., **220, 401**
Sforza, C., **301, 345, 513, 540, 552**
Shanahan, W.O., **922**
Sheehy, E.P., **100**
Sheppard, J., **61**
Shorrock, W.I., **657, 819**
Siebert, F., **856**
Sierpowski, S., **600, 857**
Signoretti, A., **82**
Signori, E., **879**
Silva Seitenfus, R., **733**
Silvestri, C., **386**
Simon, Lord J., **428**
Simoni, L., see Lanza, M.
Skorzeny, O., **468**
Slipchenko, S., 70
Slocum, R.B., 102
Smith, A.L., **214**
Smith, B.F., **883**
Smith, M.J., **18-19**
Smyth, D., **68**
Smyth, H.M., 55; **872, 946**
Snyder, L.L., **922**
<u>Social Sciences Citation Index</u>, 35
Society for Italian Historical Studies, 57
Sofri, G., **925**
Soleri, M., **346**
Sonnino, S., **190, 202, 303**; Papers of, 51
Sontag, R.J., **245, 514**
Soprintendenza Archivistica per il Lazio, 45
Sori, E., **601**
Spain, Ministry of Foreign Affairs, **276**
Speranza, G., **317**

INDEX

Spindler, K., **718**
Spini, G., **602**
Spriano, G., **636**
Staderini, A., **642**
Stafford, P.R., **820**
Starhemberg, Prince E.R., **489**
Starrett, K., **181**
Statesman's Year Book, **101**
Steed, H.W., **429**
Steed, R.H.C., **467**
Stefani, F., **537**
Steffanson, B.G., **181**
Stegemann, B., **963**
Stehle, H., **976**
Stehlin, S.A., **977**
Steiner, Z., **97**
Steurer, L., **530**
Storaci, M., 51
Storia Contemporanea, **120, 664, 829**
Storia delle Relazioni Internazionali, **121**
Storia e Politica, **603**
Strawson, J., **964**
Stresemann, G., **254**
Strika, V., **926**
Strong, K., **430**
Stuart, G.H., **541**
Studi Albanica, **652**
Studi Storici, **122**
Stuhlpfarrer, K., **793, 897**
Suarez, G., **237**
Sullivan, B.R., **278, 525, 761, 941**
Summonte, C., **164**
Susmel, E. and D., **152, 188, 558, 614**
Sutton, E., **254**
Suvich, F., **156, 387**
Sweet, J., **941**
Sweet, P.R., **188**
Switzerland, Commission Nationale pour la Publication des Documents Diplomatiques, **277**
Szabo, L., **278**
Szembek, J., **318**
Szinai, M., **272**
Szücs, L., **272**

Taddia, I., **915**
Talami, G., 81
Tambach Archives, 69
Tamburrano, G., **562**
Tannenbaum, E.R., **584**
Tarbert, G.C., **38**
Tarchiani, A., **388**
Tassoni Estense, A., **389**
Tattara, G., **545**
Taylor, A., 113
Taylor, A.J.P., **515**
Taylor, M.C., **218, 224**
Taylor, T., **455, 782**
Temperley, H.V., **100**
Templewood, Viscount, see Hoare, S.
Tennant, P., **959**
Tentori Califano, M., 107
Teodori, M., **602**
Terracciano, C., **903**
Thayer, A.J., **185**
Thomas, D.H., 53
Thomas, H., **776**
Thompson, G., **431**
Tillett, L.R., **762**
Times Literary Supplement, **141**
Tittoni, T., **194**
Todorovski, G., **858**
Togliatti, P., **679**
Tolomei, E., **347**
Tomasi della Torretta, P., **390**
Tombaccini, S., **680**
Toomey, A.F., **87**
Torre, A., **678, 975**
Torunsky, V., **695**
Toscano, Mario [1], 55; **20, 93, 188, 282, 475, 528, 530, 643, 763, 793-94, 830, 859, 872, 878, 881, 897, 919, 940**
Toscano, Mario [2], 69
Toynbee, A., **100**
Tranfaglia, N., 83
Trevelyan, R., **947**
Trevor Roper, H., **248, 309**
Troebst, S., **717**
Tsakalakis, A., **542**
Tsirpanlis, Z.N., **70**
Tubiana, J., **915**
Tuminetti, D.M., **391**

Udina, M., **534**
Ulrich's Periodicals Directory, 107
Umiltà, C., **392**
U.N.E.S.C.O., 113; **52**
Unione Internazionale degli Istituti di Archeologia, Storia e Storia dell'Arte in Roma, 74
United Nations Library, 71
United States, Department of State, 53; **216, 225-26**
United States, Library of Congress, 61, 75, 84
United States, National Archives, 39-40, 42, 59-60, 67-70
United States, National Historical Publications and Records Commission, 58
United States, National Union Catalog, 75
United States, National Union Catalog of Manuscript Collections, 61
United States, National Union New Serial Titles, 107
Urban, J.B., **636**
U.S.S.R., Ministry of Foreign Affairs, **245, 260-63**

Vaccarino, G., **824**
Vaccaro, G., **83**
Vaïsse, M., 66
Valabrega, G., **919**
Valdevit, G., **850**
Valente, B., 45
Valeri, N., **564**
Valiani, L., **241, 644, 654, 770**
Valsecchi, F., **604**
Van der Esch, P., **775**
Vansittart, Lord R., **432**
Varè, D., **348**
Varsori, A., **613, 845, 860, 875**
Vatican, Secrétairerie d'Etat, **87, 208**
Vaudagna, M., **817**
Vaussard, M., **71, 282**
Veaner, A.B., **41**
Vedovato, G., **605, 616, 738, 777, 984**
Venturi, A., **636**

Vernazza, M., **519**
Vesenyi, P.E., 106-7
Viault, B.S., **839**
Victor Emmanuel III, King, 299
Vierteljahrshefte für Zeitgeschichte, **142**
Vigezzi, B., 84; **371, 606, 842**
Villari, L., **681**
Visconti Prasca, S., **393**
Visconti Venosta, G., **884**
Vitetti, L., **304**
Vivante, C., **696**
Vivarelli, R., **583**
Vogel, D., **963**
Vogel, R., **233**
Vogelsang, T., **38**
Voigt, K., **795**
Volk, L., **978**
Volpi di Misurata, G., **203**
Vujosevič, J., **854**

Wagnière, G., **490**
Waley, D.P., **764**
Walford, A.J., 100
Walters, F.P., **509**
Walworth, A., **645**
Wank, S., **698**
Warner, G., **812, 885**
Waterfield, G., **821**
Watt, D.C., **231, 242, 255, 516, 529, 796, 802**
Webber, R., 85
Weber, H.H., **8**
Webster, R.A., **917**
Weinberg, G.L., **455, 517**
Weiss, K., **656**
Weizsäcker, E., **256, 469**
Welles, S., **405**
Welsch, E.K., 64, 67, 78, 79
Weltkriegsbücherei, 32
Wenger, A., **979**
Weygand, M., **452**
Whealey, R.H., **257, 778**
Wheatcroft, A., **510**
White, S., **496**
Wile, A.N., **7**
Willequest, J., **666**
Williams, S.P., 85

INDEX

Wilson, H.R., **406**
Wilson, W., **227**
Wise, G.S., **834**
Wiskemann, E., **797**
Wolff, R., **972**
Woller, H., **886**
Woodland, C., 64
Woodward, E.L., **831**
Woolf, S.J., **861**, **885**
<u>World of Learning</u>, 72
World Peace Foundation, **267**
Wright, G., **514**
Wright, M., **21**
Wrigley, D.W., **228**
Wynot, E.D., **659**

Yearwood, P., **695**
Young, M.L. and H.C., 75
Young, R.J., 58; **75**

Zachariae, G., **338**
Zaghi, C., **904**
Zamboni, G., **719**
Zani, L., **682**
Zanussi, G., **394**
Zarca, A., **328**, **339**
Zeller, O., **53-54**
Zeno Zencovich, L., **613**
Zermeli, S., **279**
Zernatto, G., **491**
Zervos, S.G., **280**
Ziegler, J., **22**
Zilli, V., **965**
Zincone, V., **188**
Zinojinovič, D., **655**
Zucaro, D., **296**
Zuccotti, S., **789**
Zuroff, E., **834**

6 2 75

SW
581.63   Hicks
HIC   Desert plants and people

c. 3 - Imperial
5 95

TRANS PECOS LIBRARY SYSTEM
EL PASO MAJOR RESOURCE CENTER

Imperial Public Library
Imperial, Texas